My
Green Age

Sara and I at Crane's Beach, Ipswich

My Green Age

EDWARD WEEKS

An Atlantic Monthly Press Book
Little, Brown and Company — Boston — Toronto

FIRST EDITION

T 02/74

Library of Congress Cataloging in Publication Data

Weeks, Edward, 1898–
  My green age.

  "An Atlantic Monthly Press book."
  1. Weeks, Edward, 1898–   I. Title.
PN4874.W369A29   070.4'092'4 [B]   73-13627
ISBN 0-316-92790-2

ATLANTIC–LITTLE, BROWN BOOKS
ARE PUBLISHED BY
LITTLE, BROWN AND COMPANY
IN ASSOCIATION WITH
THE ATLANTIC MONTHLY PRESS

Acknowledgments

Lines from "The Soldier" in *The Collected Poems of Rupert Brooke* are reprinted by permission of Dodd, Mead & Company; Sidgwick & Jackson Ltd.; and Mc-Clelland and Stewart Limited.

Lines from "A Letter to Charles Townsend Copeland: Le Baron Russell Briggs," in *Collected Poems* by Robert Hillyer, © 1961 by Robert Hillyer, are reprinted by permission of Alfred A. Knopf, Inc.

Lines from "Futility" are from *Collected Poems* by Wilfred Owen. Copyright Chatto & Windus, Ltd., 1946; © 1963. Reprinted by permission of New Directions Publishing Corporation, the Executors of the Estate of Harold Owen and Chatto & Windus, Ltd.

The letter from Felix Frankfurter to M. A. De Wolfe Howe is reprinted by permission of the Harvard College Library.

Letter from Thornton Wilder to Edward Weeks is reprinted by permission of Mr. Wilder.

Letter from Carl Sandburg to Edward Weeks is reprinted by permission of Carl Sandburg Marital/Family Trust U/A 4/29/63.

The lines from "Give My Regards to Broadway" are reprinted by permission of Edward B. Marks Music Corporation. Copyright GEORGE M. COHAN MUSIC PUBLISHING CO., INC.

Lines from "I've Got a Shooting Box in Scotland" by Cole Porter. Copyright 1916, 1944 by G. Schirmer, Inc. Used by permission.

Lines from "The Crew Song" by Cole Porter are used by permission of The Cole Porter Musical and Literary Property Trusts.

Published simultaneously in Canada
by Little, Brown & Company (Canada) Limited

PRINTED IN THE UNITED STATES OF AMERICA

FOR PHOEBE

Preface

IN THIS BOOK I have tried to recapture the wonder and bewilderment of one who was struggling to find where he belonged during the first forty years of this fantastically changing century. To borrow a threat from Mark Twain: "Anyone who accuses me of name dropping will be shot!" My memoir, like my life, is full of people; my success as an editor depended on how we worked together, and I consider it a privilege as well as a pleasure to remember them.

Some episodes have appeared in my earlier writing, though not in continuity nor with such personal involvement as I hope now gives them fuller meaning. Memory is beguiling and to keep me accurate I have turned to friends and contemporaries who were with me at various stages. For help with my New Jersey chapter I wish to thank Mrs. Carroll Badeau, Mrs. Fred C. Seely, Mrs. Franklin Morrell, Mrs. James P. Whitlock, John C. Weeks, Samuel Bonnell, Judge Frederic R. Colie and his wife, Roxanne, and William C. Stryker of Princeton University. For help with the chapter on France: Stuart B. Kaiser, Kenneth B. Norton, Robert A. Reaser, Charles C. Leonard, and George Richmond Fearing, Jr. For the Harvard years: Mrs. Ruth Whitman Pennypacker, James N. White, David McCord, and Mrs. Henry James. To remind me of England I turned to H. R. Creswick, R. Keith Kane, Denning Miller, A. M. Dobson, and Everett C. Case. To remind me of Greenwich Village and Horace Liveright: Manuel Komroff, G. Berry Fleming, and Mrs. Gordon Rentschler. For an objective view of the Lincoln Letters, I needed the help of the historian Paul Angle; and for an impersonal view of Harry Crosby, I consulted Geoffrey Wolff. In recalling my early days at the *Atlantic*, I welcomed the advice of Donald B. Snyder, Stewart Beach, Mrs. Richard E. Danielson, and Mrs. Madelin Gilpatric; and the corrections of Louise Desaulniers,

Jean Whitnack, Peter Davison, Upton Brady, Natalie Greenberg, and J. Randall Williams, and of those three indispensables, my secretary, Virginia Albee; that clear-headed critic, Phoebe-Lou Adams; and my encouraging editor, William Abrahams. But for any errors that survive I am solely responsible.

William C. Schoettle kindly gave me access to the pictures of Bay Head. The clarification and reproduction of the photographs and family snapshots were handled with patience and skill by Robert Mason and Robert L. Scott.

EDWARD WEEKS

My
Green Age

I

WHEN MY MOTHER was in the dreary process of moving out of our old home in Elizabeth, New Jersey, she sent off to me, the eldest of her six children, a square brown cardboard box. It arrived in Boston with no explanation and I did not bother to open it for some time; when I did, it was with the surprise of finding forgotten vestiges of my youth. Had she kept such mementoes for each of us, I wondered, as I explored the open carton? On the top was an official-looking letter addressed to me from Princeton University and postmarked July 1913. I unfolded the crisp paper and read:

Dear Mr. Weeks:

We have the honor to inform you that in the Princeton Entrance Examinations taken at Newark Academy, June 5–9, you received the following grades:

Latin I	E
English A	E
Algebra I	D
Plane geometry	F
German I	E

At the bottom of the form was the rating:

A	Excellent
B	Good
C	Fair
D	Passing
E	Failure
F	Bad failure

I was fifteen when I suffered that first confrontation with college examinations and it blew my hopes for Princeton sky-high. Humiliations

3

like that hang in one's attic: I recalled the dread with which I seated myself at a desk in that unfamiliar school where the exams were given, the feeling of frustration which deepened as I tried to cope with the severe, unexpected questions, my panic when the proctor announced, "You have thirty minutes to go." A slow worker even under encouraging circumstances I did not finish any of those examinations, the like of which I had never seen before.

Beneath some other papers in the box, wrapped in tissue paper, was a small cheap brier pipe with prongs at the base to keep the bowl upright. With it and a package of Barking Dog Tobacco — "It Never Bites" — I first proclaimed to the summer colony of Bay Head that I was a smoker. The occasion was the finals of a mixed doubles tournament, played in the center court at the Yacht Club with a gallery of onlookers and I in the referee's chair. As the players were changing courts at the end of the first set, I produced my pipe and filled it, struck a match, cupped the flame, and sucked in a long breath of Barking Dog, casually, as if I had done so for years.

It was a hot morning, the play was very even, and as I called the serve, followed the returns from side to side, and continued to stoke my pipe, I gradually became aware of my dank forehead and a queasiness in my midriff. When the ball began to dance in the heat waves, I climbed down from my high seat and with an airy wave to the players hurried off the court, making for the men's dressing room. But I didn't quite reach the swinging doors in time and the humiliation of vomiting in full view stayed with me for what was left of the summer. I thought I had thrown the pipe away, but Mother had a way of retrieving things.

Below the pipe was a collection of programs, the Prize-Speaking in which I recited a cut version of Kipling's "Wee Willie Winkie," the senior play in which I acted the part of the wizened, hypochondriac grandfather, and among them, a photograph of an eight-oared gig leading in a close race, with me in the stern, a hunched-up, shouting little coxswain. The race was rowed in the Inlet, leading into Lake Cayuga, where the Cornell crews practiced until the ice froze it over. I had never handled a boat until that autumn of 1915 and in the picture I was tasting one of my brief moments of triumph under Charles Courtney, then the most successful and caustic crew coach in America. As the lightest man in the freshman class — I weighed 94 pounds — I was an obvious candidate for that stern seat and I learned the rudiments quickly enough: how to call the stroke, how to spot a man who was "shooting his tail" (kicking his seat back instead of pulling it back), how to detect the awkwardness in hands and shoulders that set a boat to rolling instead of running evenly between strokes — the leap and

4

run of a balanced, powerful crew no coxswain will ever forget. I learned how to step in and out of my seat without putting weight on the thin cedar skin, and at dusk when the crew was in the showers and the shell was on its rack I would rub down the long, glistening hull with affection.

One of the onerous duties of the freshman coxswain as spring came on was to navigate the coeds of Sage and Risley in four-oared gigs over the curving, half-mile course on Risley Lake. It was onerous because we had to do it in the early afternoon before we went down to the Inlet for our regular practice, and even more so because in those days the coeds were such objects of ridicule. I drew the junior crew, stroked by Gertie Fisher who, rumor had it, possessed the best dimensions of any girl in Cornell, and as far as I could see, the rumor was correct. She not only had good breasts and legs, she had power, and my boat won the class championship going away. As a reward the two finalists, the junior and the senior fours, were permitted to take over the varsity crew quarters for one afternoon and to launch an eight-oared shell on Cayuga under the watchful eyes of Coach Courtney. That they had never rowed together in an eight seemed not to figure.

With Gertie and her winning crew in the four stern seats and the seniors in the bow, Courtney in his familiar launch and Mrs. Courtney knitting as a chaperon should, we set forth. It was soon apparent that one of the front four, call her Margaret, was kicking her seat back with regularity, causing the boat to roll. Courtney drew up beside us. "Number Three, you're sh——, you're kicking your seat back," he cried in his high, penetrating voice. "Number Three, don't shoot your tail that way! *Don't shoot-your-tail!*" On we labored with Margaret swaying and in tears; then Mrs. Courtney tugged her mentor's coat, he pulled down the throttle, the launch shot ahead and I was left, to slow the stroke down and console.

I was knocked out of contention for the freshman crew in spring vacation when we were rowing morning and afternoon on the lake in cold choppy weather. Courtney had laid down the rule that on leaving the Inlet the cox should take a right-angle turn into Cayuga and when one afternoon, eager to catch up with the four boats ahead, I curved a short cut, he stopped his launch, lifted his megaphone, and screamed at me. "You little fool. You've just taken your shell over sunken piles! Do you want to sink your crew in water like this?" Silence, with everyone listening. That error was compounded when, later, in a time-trial my No. 6 got a cramp in his right arm and was having the devil of a time getting his oar out of the water; I did not have the sense to lower the stroke and bring us in a decent, instead of a floundering, second. From then on I was no longer in the first boat. What I lacked was mature judgment and that command of exhortation and profanity with which an inspired cox like Carson of Yale brought in a winning crew.

That I should go to Cornell was my father's idea, not mine. After the disastrous beginning I did better in the examinations and could have squeaked my way into Princeton "on condition," meaning that I might work off my weaker subjects in my first year. "You'll just fritter away your time down there," said Dad. "You're pretty good at math and that's the basis for engineering." But it was not my basis. I lacked the imagination to find my way in physics and calculus; I dropped behind in the courses that really counted, getting good marks only in mechanical drawing, astronomy, and shop, and my incomprehension warned me long before the Dean's office did that I would be on probation or "busted out" by the end of my freshman year in 1916.

2

I wonder if there is any ignominy harder to outgrow than that of being a runt. I have known very small men who in mid-life could not bear to be handled, not even by an affectionate pat on the shoulder. But one cannot stand on dignity when a shrimp. To have one's hair continually rumpled and one's necktie jerked into a hard knot, to be called "Beakstein" or "Rabbit" because one's nose and ears were the conspicuous features, to be precluded from athletics, — all this adds up to a humiliation for which one must find compensation. I was too slow a reader, too unsure of myself in examinations to lead in scholarship, but where I could win was in public speaking and in acting, for I memorized quickly and had a touch for comedy. In such performances my mother encouraged me to do the different rather than the traditional.

During the interim of nearly two decades while I was waiting for the miracle of growth and understanding, I knew that I was a disappointment to my father. He was a big man physically, over six feet, with a splendid torso, much admired in his bathing suit; he had the prominent Weeks nose and his eyes were gray and confident, for he had supported himself with more than average success since the age of eighteen. A designer of cotton fabrics and a compelling salesman, he would dream up a new series of patterns suitable for dresses, shirtwaists, pajamas, take them south to his favorite mills at midyear, and then tour the country selling the more attractive samples in thousands of yards. From these long absences he would return, hungry for Mother (when their bedroom door was closed, I was discreet enough to stay away), eager to resume his church work at St. John's where he was a vestryman, polish his part as end man in the blackface minstrel shows, play the tennis and bridge whist at which he loved to gamble. In his absorption he had little time for us children and trusted Mother to bring us up until we were old enough to be companionable.

Our branch of the Weeks family had been identified with New York ever since the first Jonathan settled in Oyster Bay, Long Island, in 1670, and although my grandfather Weeks, an improvident, gentle man, had moved out to New Jersey for the sake of economy, Dad regarded himself as a native New Yorker — he liked to point out the house on West Fourteenth Street where he had been born — and he returned to his place of business in lower Manhattan each morning with zest. There was a ritual about his send-off. From his bathroom we would hear him singing as he shaved with one of his freshly stropped straight razors,

> *In old New York,*
> *In old New York,*
> *The peach crop's always fine.*
> *They're fine and fair and on the square*
> *The maids of Manhattan for mine . . .*

or George M. Cohan's latest hit:

> *Give my regards to Broadway,*
> *Remember me to Herald Square,*
> *Tell all the gang at 42nd Street*
> *That I will soon be there . . .*

Then, a shout to my mother, who with the children was already at the breakfast table: "Rica, tell Helma to put my egg on!" And a moment later, down he would come. The egg was invariably poached; with four decisive swipes of knife and fork, egg, toast and bacon would be quartered and washed down with black coffee. "Ned," Mother would venture, "something really needs to be done about the asparagus bed . . ." "Yes, dear," Dad would reply, wiping his moustache as he stood up. "I've told you before — get a man. Get a man!" And the front door would slam as he hurried to join the other commuters at the North Elizabeth station.

Our asparagus bed produced the most tender shoots in our part of town for about ten years and then suddenly ceased to yield. Dad paid for a replanting but claimed that Pat Golden had put them in upside down as few stalks ever broke the surface thereafter. The bed was one of several evidences of the taste of Clinton Mackenzie, the architect who built our house for himself, in addition to several of its neighbors, at the turn of the century and christened the new street Clinton Place. He liked to play pool, so our front room held a Brunswick pool table with a cue rack, wire markers overhead and a long leather-cushioned bench for spectators. Dad had his cellarette in one corner, and from his travels had brought back some crude, funny cartoons which hung on either side of the fireplace. This was where he served cocktails and where, because of my home practice, I managed to extract dimes from my friends Hump Jones and Bud Davidson when we played bottle pool for keeps. At the entrance of the poolroom hung a large moose head which Dad claimed to have shot in New Orleans with three cocktails.

Mr. Mackenzie had liked flowering plants and had built himself a glass-enclosed conservatory opening off the dining room, so we ate with the fragrance of warm moist earth, and, at Easter, of lilies. He also liked fruit, and in our cutting garden were a quince tree whose rock-hard crop Mother converted into delicious jelly and crunchy preserves, a pear tree which produced sweet Seckels when it wanted to, and a cherry tree that was always a disappointment because the birds got there first. There was a stable for Mr. Mackenzie's riding horses, and a playhouse far enough away for the elders not to know what was going on.

Clinton Mackenzie must have been a very large man, for in his bathroom he installed on a tile dais what was certainly the largest and highest bathtub in Elizabeth. Only an adult could climb into it. Mr. Hoge, who bought the house after we dispersed, was a do-it-yourself bug. When he decided to get rid of the monster he pried it off, tilted it through the doorway, and started it down the front stairs, using the cellar door as a ramp. But once in the front hall the monster was immovable; guests had to use the back way for three weeks. Mrs. Hoge wrote this up amusingly and I bought the sketch for the *Atlantic*. Mother was indignant: "Son, how could you let her make fun of our dear old house!"

Like all architects, Mr. Mackenzie made one mistake: the east wing of the house — conservatory, dining room, pantry, kitchen, and laundry with its huge brown icebox, loaded from the top — had a cellar beneath and was always warm. The west wing with the showrooms — the parlor leading through an arched doorway into the library — was perennially chilly, which was natural enough as it had neither cellar nor adequate heating. The architect must have assumed that the body warmth of many guests would provide the difference and this it did once a year, on Christmas afternoon.

Commuting, even in the much more leisurely days of 1910 when trains were so frequent, was a strain. Grandfather Weeks had died on the train and it sometimes seemed to me a wonder that Father didn't —

My maternal grandparents: Eliza Gracie Suydam and Colonel Charles Crooke Suydam

The Colonel fifty years later

My great-great-grandfather, Charles King, and Eliza Gracie Suydam (Aunt Liz)

that buoyant, handsome, irascible man, always in a hurry, who I felt would have liked his eldest to be a plunging fullback and was puzzled by what he got.

Father always made it a point to be back in New York when the Giants played in the World Series and this was one spree he shared with me and my brother Rufus, five years my junior. We looked forward to it from the day we knew he had reserved the seats and I can remember every detail: the ride in to that vast iron cage of the Pennsylvania Station, where the steam engines stood panting like racehorses, our scurry over the wooden planks, dodging the dray horses, and then the ferry trip across the windy Hudson, the Flatiron Building looming up against the October sky and the wooden piers groaning as we nosed into Cortland Street. We lunched early at the Merchants' Club, where Dad presented us to his friends nearby and where our lamb chops and Delmonico potatoes were topped off by a dessert we could never have at home, meringue Chantilly. Then the long trip on the Elevated uptown to the Polo Grounds, every car crowded with fans, and the good-natured pileup at the turnstiles. We were always a little late. "Hold on to my hand, Rufus!" Dad would say to my brother as we ran down the concrete, entering as the stubby Muggsy McGraw, the Giants' manager, and the lank, dark-suited Connie Mack were conferring with the umpires. When we were seated at last, in the grandstand back of first base, Dad checked the scorecard while we spotted the players we knew by heart: the great Christy Mathewson, who was warming up; and Rube Marquard, the fireballer in his blue jacket, who would pitch tomorrow; Chief Myers, the catcher and an Indian, who was always greeted with war whoops when he came to bat; and Art Fletcher, the shortstop, who after a crucial hit forgot to touch first base and cost us the victory. As the afternoon shadow fell on our seats, we grew cold from excitement. "Here, boys," said Dad, "stuff this newspaper under your sweaters. It'll warm you up and maybe bring us luck." The Giants could beat anybody but Connie Mack's Athletics with that killer, Home Run Baker, at third.

3

When I was an Overseer of Harvard I once tried to argue with President James Bryant Conant about the injustice which the I.Q. tests inflicted on slow starters such as I had been. But he was skeptical: the percentage of those who have a delayed intellectual awakening was, he thought, too small to bother with. My experience tells me otherwise and of this I am sure: that the small boy and the slow boy instinctively turn to women for the encouragement they need.

My mother, Frederika Suydam, was next to the youngest of "the

11

Suydam girls," the six daughters of Charles Crooke Suydam, late lieutenant colonel of the 3d New Jersey Cavalry. When Fort Sumter was
fired on, he closed up his law office, got a captain's commission, and in
a tent on Battery Park signed up the volunteers for the regiment he
was eventually to command. Like many veterans then and since, his
five years in uniform unfitted him for the peace that followed.

Because I was for five years her only child I could not fail to be
imbued with my mother's aspiration, with her respect for economy,
drilled into her from girlhood, with her fastidiousness. "Your Ted," a
sister-in-law once remarked within my hearing, "will never be good-
looking, Rica. But he is a *neat* boy." Mother taught me order, to care
for my clothes, and to pick up for the younger. Love for the flag and
religious faith were implicit in her loyalty. I never doubted that she
was good-looking and I learned to read her eyes, the light in them at
Dad's approach, the merriment or sternness when she spoke to me. Before her marriage, Mother, like her sisters, had to support herself, and
this she did with her lovely high soprano. She studied under Walter
Damrosch, whom she revered, and she sang in the oratorios he conducted. By the time I appeared, her professional concert work lay behind her and I listened to her as the soloist in the choir loft of St. John's
or singing to my father in the library after dinner or in the summer
twilight when we were becalmed on Barnegat Bay. Head thrown back,
she would lift "Mandalay" or "The Land of the Sky Blue Water" or
"Pippa Passes" to the stars. Listening to her throughout my boyhood,
again and again I would have to duck my head: her feeling shone
through the words and reduced me to tears. She was deeply in love with
my father and as long as that love held firm she was undaunted. So
she wanted us to be.

Elizabeth was the first permanent English settlement in the Province
of New Jersey, founded in 1664 by settlers from Long Island and Connecticut. As a friend of Ed Bonnell I had lunched with his aunts in
its oldest dwelling, the Bonnell House (1680), and as a boy scout I had
patrolled the woods of Liberty Hall (1773), built by William Livingston,
Washington's friend and New Jersey's first governor, and for seven
generations thereafter the home of the Kean family. By some miracle
both have survived.

In our republic, where rank is not inherited, we celebrate the achievement of our ancestors by passing on their names to the younger generation. My great-grandmother on the maternal side was Eliza Gracie, the
eldest daughter of Eliza Gracie and Charles King, who before his presidency of Columbia College maintained a stylish country house, Cherry

My mother, Frederika Suydam Weeks, with my sister Eliza's arm around her neck. Frederika, my other sister, is looking at my brother Rufus, whom she adored

Lawn, on the outskirts of Elizabeth. Charles inherited his ability from his father, Rufus King, who moved up to Boston from Essex County, Massachusetts, to become a prominent Federalist, a leading spirit of the Constitutional Convention, and later Minister to the Court of St. James's. It was a Weeks tradition that the eldest son should be christened either Edward Augustus (a middle name I detested) or Edward Francis, and my first sister, Frederika, was given Mother's name, but for the others, family pride was responsible: my next brother, with whom I shared a double bed on our top floor, was the ebullient, lovable Rufus King; Jackie, the brother next below him and the family comedian, was named for John Carnes, colonel of the Ancient and Honorable Order of Artillery; my younger sister is Eliza Gracie (as are her eldest daughter and her granddaughter); and my youngest brother, twenty-one years my junior, was Hendryk Suydam Weeks, to celebrate our Dutch inheritance. There is an innocent vitality in all this, in a country so young that although wealth may have vanished, the heirlooms and the luster of the old names are still cherished.

One of our most precious heirlooms was the tricolor sash which General Lafayette wore when he stepped ashore at Castle Garden in New York in 1824. Charles King was a personal friend of the Marquis, and he attended the reception accompanied by his daughter Eliza Gracie, who in her fluent French delivered the address of welcome. She was thirteen, clad in deep mourning for some relative; the General remarked that she was too young and fair to be so somberly garbed, and thereupon took off his tricolor sash and tied it about her. . . . Long before my time the sash had been subdivided by the family shears for the different descendants and a small cutting of Mother's portion was sewn into my uniform when I sailed for France in 1917.

"It is required of a man," said Justice Oliver Wendell Holmes, "that he should share the passion and action of his time at peril of being judged not to have lived." Of my elders it was my maternal grandfather, Colonel Charles Crooke Suydam, who embodied this truth. What I saw on a Sunday morning in 1908 was an erect gray-head, with the air of command, broad shoulders, a wide brow and a dominant nose. In fair weather I was permitted to leave the family pew in St. John's just before the sermon, and crossing Broad Street, call for Grandfather at the Mattano Club where he lived. That club was always a disappointment — it never had anything sweet to offer a ten-year-old. Perched on a slippery, black-leather chair I would be served a scoop of strong cheese, two dry biscuits, and ginger ale so sharp that it made me sneeze. Then when he had finished his whiskey and soda we would make our way slowly up

14

North Broad Street toward our house on Clinton Place. In his Prince Albert and starched linen, with the Loyal Legion on his lapel, his cane and silk hat he was out of the past; people would bow, and if we passed a veteran he might salute with a "Fine day, Colonel!" It was a stately procession of two and I was proud to be part of it.

Perhaps it was my small size which appealed to him, or perhaps it was my curiosity about books. He had the habit even when he could not afford it of buying books in sets — Breasted on Egypt, Thackeray's complete works — and our edition of Kipling, in the brown linen binding with the cartouche of an elephant on the cover, the first author of whom I read every word, was originally his. He took me on my initial visit to Washington, where we shared a vast double bed at the old Willard Hotel, and I remember the fragrance of the "4711" he used on his handkerchiefs — and his insistence, after our first night, that I cut my toenails! We visited the Capitol, the Library of Congress, and the Smithsonian Institution, where we paused for what seemed to me hours before the portraits of the Indian chiefs against whom General Miles and Grandfather's fellow officers had campaigned. In words more impressive for being terse he told me of the march-past up Pennsylvania Avenue, all one day and half the night, of the returning Union armies at the war's end.

Every grandson knew the stories about the Colonel and liked to have them repeated by his daughters: how he had had three horses killed under him, bullets through trouser legs and hat but never wounded; of the night when his horse stepped into a hole in the ground, fell, and rolled on him. A brother officer came to his aid and kept him walking, walking lest his back stiffen, though the pain was severe; when at last they reached Grandfather's quarters and Grandma opened the door, he fell across the threshold in a faint. The mark of the saddle was on his bruised back for weeks but no bones were broken. His narrowest escape was when he and his orderly were captured by Mosby's guerrillas, who fought and plundered on their own. They took from him his watch and money, cracked his ivory miniature of Grandmother with the butt of a revolver, and were about to string him up when an Indiana regiment happened along and the guerrillas fled. We knew that at twenty-seven he was in command of the 3rd New Jersey Cavalry, was promoted to be chief of staff for General Keyes, and had seen action at Gettysburg and Chickamauga and in the Peninsula campaign, but very little of this did we get from the Colonel himself. He would never attend the annual Encampments of the Grand Army of the Republic, as the reunions were called, and although he encouraged me to study the woodcuts of the battles in *Harper's Illustrated Weekly,* he refused to take any interest in Mathew Brady's photographs of the war. He had seen it.

What I did not realize until later was that he could not rekindle much of an incentive in civilian business after those glamorous and challenging years of action. He thought to make a fresh start and with his inheritance he bought a seat on the New York Stock Exchange and for a time prospered. Then he had an attack of brain fever shortly before Black Friday, the crash in 1875 that wiped him out, and after recovering he went back to his early profession as an estate and corporation lawyer. One of his clients was Hetty Green, the wealthiest woman of her time, until her temper and the old Dutch in him brought their association to an abrupt close. In spite of a dwindling income and his wife's invalidism he held the fort, but by then the enterprise in his household came from his six girls, and in a grandson like me perhaps he saw the faint image of the infant son he had lost.

I have his commission signed by President Lincoln and, in addition to his big hooked nose (I naturally admire long noses) I inherited his tendency to transpose words. I can lapse into spoonerisms as easily as he did. His nephew Howard, unfortunately for the Colonel, had married a girl called Kate and nothing could prevent Grandfather from referring to them as "Koward and Hate." One of his daughters had a beau named Ed Runyon, whom the old gentleman teasingly referred to as "the Red Onion" and could not help addressing as "Mr. Onion" when the young man came to call. At Grandmother Suydam's grace was always spoken before meals, as it was in my home, and at one Sunday supper with all daughters present the Colonel began the familiar blessing ("Sanctify, O Lord, this food to our use . . .") "Lanctify O Sord," stopped, cleared his throat, and began again, "Lanctify, O Sord," stopped, and tried for the third time with the same result. The girls were bursting when gravely he turned and said, "Mother, will you please ask the blessing," which she did, a different one: "For what we are about to receive, the Lord make us truly thankful . . ." and the gale of laughter which obliterated the "Amen" must have carried to Heaven's gate. This trait, which I have passed on to my son and grandson, is now regarded as a symptom of a "Left Reader," a slowness in adjustment both in reading and writing that is not a laughing matter, much more prevalent among boys than girls, but one which can be corrected by patient teaching.

Grandfathers, age permitting, hand down the imperishable standards and I like to think that from the Colonel, in addition to his style, I acquired the liberalism which set him implacably against capital punishment a century ago, so that he would not practice law in New Jersey, where a thief could be sentenced to death. The critical faculty on which my future would depend may have come in part from his Dutch cussedness.

What I unquestionably inherited from him was my admiration for President Lincoln. In 1861 Grandmother Suydam, then in her mid-twenties, had moved down to Washington to be closer to the Colonel, and she and my grandfather were among the attractive young couples who caught Mr. Lincoln's eye at the White House receptions. There was a story treasured by my aunts that in mid-evening when Grandma was on the President's arm, the gaunt, tall figure stooped down and whispered, "And now, my dear, if you will excuse me I think I shall retire. My corns are hurting." Apocryphal or not, that story served as a bridge from their Mr. Lincoln to my Theodore Roosevelt.

I knew T.R.'s accomplishments by heart. How he had entered Harvard, scrawny and wearing glasses, and had persistently built himself up, with dumbbells and boxing lessons, to become the champion lightweight. How, after graduation the hunting and ranching he did in the Dakota Badlands made him an expert horseman, and how at the outbreak of the Spanish-American War the cowboys followed his lead into the Rough Riders, cavalry whose charge up San Juan Hill was our most glamorous victory and gave T.R. his national reputation. He took all his gusto with him to the White House, "busting the trusts," "speaking softly and carrying a Big Stick," as the cartoonists reminded us, exclaiming "Bully!" at what he liked, flashing his white teeth and pounding his fist as he told the country what was good for it.

When it was known that T.R. was coming to Elizabeth in his campaign as a Bull Moose to speak and afterwards dine with Edgar A. Knapp, who had served under him in the Rough Riders, I longed to shake his hand. The Knapps were our neighbors, their handsome new brick house on North Broad Street was only a block away, but there would be too many elders for me to have any chance of seeing him there. Early in his campaign speech at the armory, he made an impromptu aside, "My platform is not as shaky as this one," which was much quoted in town after his departure. That he had gone back on his pledge not to seek a third term I did not appreciate; I thought only of what a leader he had been. When dinner was over, I slipped out and stood opposite the Knapps' house, staring at the lighted windows and imagining the vital presence of T.R. within.

My introduction to Woodrow Wilson in the flesh occurred when as Governor of New Jersey he and his family spent the summers in the "Little White House," at Sea Girt. The National Guard had their encampment there and on Saturday afternoons my Aunt Margaret Brewster, a good friend of Mrs. Wilson's, had a standing invitation to watch the Governor review the troops. On more than one occasion she took her son Sidney and me with her. In our long white ducks, stiff collars and blue serge coats, we applauded the dusty performance, after which we entered the shaded mansion to be rewarded with the coldest, most delicious lemonade I can remember. Then with sticky fingers we shook hands with the Governor. Lincoln, T.R. and Woodrow Wilson were the three Presidents in my pantheon and I have never lost my pride in any of them.

4

Fears lurk in every childhood, some that seem instinctive and inexplicable, others whose cause we know. I lived with a horror of high places which I have never outgrown. When I was seven an outbreak of polio on the Jersey coast persuaded my parents to spend the hot months in the Blue Ridge Mountains above Baltimore. There the favorite excursion for weekends was for five or six couples to hire the two-team carryall to tug them and their picnic supper to the peak of Buena Vista, from whose observatory on a clear evening one could see three states. On the promise of being quiet I usually went along. The winding drive up the mountain was fun but I dreaded the ordeal to follow. Arrived at the clearing the hostess for the occasion would lay out the supper on the picnic table while the rest of the party climbed up the stairs of the observatory for the view at the top. I don't know how many steps there were, a hundred perhaps, but I do know that from my diminutive height the view I had of Lover's Leap in the opening between the steps, the sheer drop down the rocky flank with the tips of the pines far below, was terrifying. When at last we reached the platform I had lost any desire to see those three states; all I wanted was to stand in the center away from the rail, lest I throw myself over as the Indian lover was said to have done. I resisted Dad, who wanted to lift me for a better view, though I could not explain why.

Some months after this my navy cousins set sail for Guam, where Uncle Raymond Stone had been appointed aide to the governor and from Hong Kong they sent me a postcard of the harbor showing the ships and in the background the broad strand that zigzagged up to the top of the mount. That did it. What I had seen at Buena Vista fused with what I imagined must be a sheer drop at the backside of Hong Kong. In dreams that would recur for years I was taken up that implacable zigzag, made to face the appalling abyss with people like ants at the bottom, and just as I sucked in my breath to fling myself over — fright would awaken me.

It took me forty years to piece this together and by then the reaction was automatic: when Robert Moses guided me, in the elevator with the hard hats, to the top of the skeleton United Nations building, then open to the skies, and urged me to the edge for a better view of lower Manhattan, I said, holding fast to the elevator shaft, that I could see plenty from where I was. The picture or film of a Mohawk steelworker riding a girder seventy stories high makes my stomach turn over. Yet, oddly, once encased in a plane I am untroubled — save, as I suspect we all are, when stacking through fog or snow for a landing. We acquire a fatalism about flying.

More predictable was the danger I was likely to encounter when I went on an errand to Grandmother Weeks's. It was a long walk and when I passed under the Pennsylvania tracks at Fairmount Avenue I knew I was entering enemy country. It was not that the gang there held anything against me but I was small and neat, a stranger from the north end and therefore fair game. Saturdays were the worst because they'd all be together and having spotted me might be on the lookout for my return. The pack came after me one June morning, jeering and hurling taunts. I was too scared to look back and there was no use trying to run; they were bigger. I simply walked just as fast as I could. They slowed down to a walk, too, but their legs were longer, and when the stalking brought them within fifteen yards I had to make my move or be skinned alive. Not looking back, I turned up the flagstones leading to a strange house whose door, I noticed, was mercifully open. There was no one about as I entered; the hall led me back to the kitchen — no one there either — so I tiptoed down the back steps and, keeping in the shadow of the house, skimmed over the wooden fence — and was home free.

But more insistent than dreams or intimidation, rather like a sensitive tooth, was the dread that I could not excel. Not even at tennis, the only game at which I was better than average. I played my way into five finals before I won my first silver cup.

Help came from above, from my mother's eldest sister, Eliza Gracie Suydam. Aunt Liz all her life was the utility man in households where there was too much work and too little money. When her mother became an invalid she put aside marriage to dress and bring up her five younger sisters; she held the family together, keeping house for the Colonel after Grandmother's death, and to make up for the children she might have had she picked her favorite nephews — first, Nick Brewster; then me; then my navy cousin, John Stone — to be her special wards. She imbued us with her spirit, she was a superb teacher, and she brought each of us closer to the adult world. She was my godmother, and she worked at it.

My father, Edward A. Weeks, spruced up
for a trip to Europe

Eliza Gracie Suydam, my Aunt Liz, the oldest of the aunts

When I came down with whooping cough, I was shipped off to stay with the Colonel and Aunt Liz, and during my three months' quarantine we began reading the Bible together at bedtime, with her interpolation and omitting only "the begats," a reading which we continued for years. As my whoops began to subside and I could go out, Grandfather put a dollar in an old billfold and Aunt Liz "planted" it where it couldn't be missed — the first cash I have ever found. She did things for fun, wading with me at Bay Head before breakfast as we searched for moonstones at low tide; she remembered my fondness for Huyler's butterscotch kisses and I could talk to her about girls as I never could to my mother. In answer to one of my effusions she wrote, "You misspelled 'together.' Think of it as 'to-get-her' and you won't do so again." When I published my first short story in the school paper, she sent me a dozen Eberhard Faber pencils. And when I was courting in earnest and told her I hoped to be engaged, she wrote, "My grandmother used to say, 'Marriage is two wild animals — Bear and Forbear' " — quaint words whose truth I would later appreciate.

To my generation her looks never changed: she was spare and erect; her hair, once fair, was now as gray as her eyes — her eyes were what you remembered and her cheery laugh. The family used to tease her about Admiral Ross, a suitor who seems not to have forgotten her, but she had no time for romance. Working at a dozen meager-paying jobs — companion, secretary, branch librarian — nursing her parents, filling in when the married sisters needed her, she seemed selfless and impervious to age.

She instilled in all of us a pride in our heritage. Born in 1861, she had gone with her mother and her white nurse, when they followed Grandfather in his campaigns — to Washington, Yorktown, and Williamsburg. President Lincoln had lifted her up in his arms; in Washington, Dr. Gerry, the head medico, used to take her on his morning visits to the hospitals, to cheer up the wounded ("It may have helped them," she wrote, years later, "but no one thought of the impression it made on a sensitive child. I grew up with a horror of hospitals") and in the elation at the war's end Grandmother sent her to say good-by to her soldier friends, clad in a white frock, blue sash, white shoes and socks. She returned minus shoes, sash and socks, frock rumpled and with one golden curl missing.

As a young girl she often visited the King Mansion in Jamaica, Long Island, which Rufus King had built for his retirement, and long after his death she was made to recite "The Lady of Shalott" standing before his desk flanked by the busts of George Washington and Alexander Hamilton. She was a friend of Mary King, who married a French diplomat and became the distinguished Mme Waddington of Paris, and her hero among the other cousins was Captain Billy Halsey, whose son, an admiral, became the famous "Bull" Halsey of World War II.

Elizabeth, at the time I am writing of, had little cash for the preservation of its historic dwellings: the pre-Revolutionary Carteret Mansion, whose lawn sloped down to what had once been a navigable river, was replaced by a firehouse, and when the time came for Cherry Lawn, where my grandmother had been born, to be torn down, the Suydam girls, led by Aunt Liz, planned a farewell party to be held in the desolate reception room. A colonial doorway with side lights led to it, the walls were paneled with garlands of flowers in relief, and opposite the door was a wide fireplace. With their beaux helping, the place was cleaned, the floor hand-waxed, and the fire laid, and on the Tuesday evening after Easter the guests arrived, in costume, each with candles, the girls bringing cake and sandwiches, while their escorts chipped in to pay the musicians — a violinist and a harpist. Thus the big room came back to life in candlelight with waltzing couples and the fire blazing. As the candles dwindled toward midnight a march was formed, led by one of the sisters carrying an American flag, and her escort balancing a large cake for Grandmother, whose birthday it was. As she cut the cake and the shadows lengthened, Cherry Lawn had its reprieve.

When I moved to New England and my editing improved, I coaxed Aunt Liz to write me about her girlhood, and her remembrances I threaded together from her letters in a memoir, *A Descendant of Kings,* which I had privately printed for her eightieth birthday. Two years later in her tiny apartment, her arthritis almost unbearable, she broke down and told me she did not want to go on living. She could no longer do for herself, and she would not be a drag. And for the only time in her life she gave in.

I cannot speak for girls, but I know that aunts (I had eight — three on my father's side, five on my mother's) have a beneficial effect on their nephews. They praise, they criticize kindly, they look for early evidences of character which are overlooked in the traffic of home. Each of Mother's married sisters "adopted" me when it was convenient. To Aunt Margaret, the handsomest of "the Suydam girls," the one most like the Colonel, I owe my familiarity with small boats. Her husband, Uncle Jamie Brewster, was one of the ablest yachtsmen on Barnegat Bay and he taught me, as he taught his sons, how to handle a sneak box and a sloop like their Gloucester One-Design. I was in and out of their cottage every summer, and their attractive daughter, Alice, their older son, Nick, a semi-invalid and compassionate, and Charlie, the contentious redhead, kept me from being too fresh. My pretty Aunt Alice Bigley, with her short pert nose and provocative mouth, trained as a nurse at Johns Hopkins Hospital, and when I visited her and Uncle Joe we spent hours poring over the blueprints of her hospital experience, I being fascinated by the pictures of what the doctors extracted periodically from the stomach of a sword swallower: there they lay on a cloth, the chains, the bullets, the hardware which he swallowed for his living. To be with Aunt Esther, high-spirited and the youngest, and Uncle Raymond Stone, whom she called Mate, was to be imbued with their devotion to our navy. He was a conspicuously able navigator, especially in the South Pacific, and when he was on sea duty the family lived in Annapolis. Their eldest son, Ray, Jr., was my contemporary, and on my visits we explored together the gallery of ship models, the tomb of John Paul Jones, the miniature submarine operated by a crew of three — all the enticements available to a twelve-year-old at the Naval Academy. Aunt Emily, like Aunt Liz, a spinster, lived with us for several years while she was supporting herself as a field worker in the campaign against tuberculosis; dear "N.A.," lonely, practical, sentimental, her walls papered with family snapshots, she was effusive over each of us, but especially the nephews. With me she shared her love for Mark Twain, reading aloud *A Connecticut Yankee in King Arthur's Court* and *The Innocents Abroad,* and she took a personal pride in our small doings that made them seem larger.

5

I cannot recall any American autobiographer who professed to be happy about his schooling, certainly not Henry Adams, whose *Education* is as full of self-deprecation as a porcupine of quills. Of his years at Groton Dean Acheson thought so little that he never alludes to them in his reminiscences. Suffice it to say that at Pingry, the country day school for boys, which I attended for eleven of my twelve grades, the teaching was superior to my capacity to assimilate.

There were three teachers at Pingry to whom I continue to be grateful: first, Miss Harriet Budd, who saw us through the transition from the lower to the upper forms. A tall, broad-shouldered woman with kindly features and high-piled gray hair into which she would thrust her yellow Mongol pencils, she held her class of adolescents with a firm grip. Her deep voice had an undertone of conviction. "Ted," she would say, "you can do better than that," and I believed I could. There was a manliness about her, and if she was the best-loved of the faculty it was not only because of her clear-mindedness and fair discipline but because her spirit touched our egos. "Bill," she said to Bill McPherson, who was the strongest boy in my class, "you shouldn't rough up Ted.

You should stand up for him. He's not your size." And then, turning to me, "Pete" (Pete was the nickname she used for any of us when she wanted something to be remembered), "now, don't you provoke him!" (She well knew that the only retaliation for a shrimp was to jeer, and run.) On days when we came prepared and the lesson went briskly she would cut short the classwork and read aloud. She picked the books, narratives mostly, with an occasional bright passage of biography, and the vivid prose, so much more alive than our textbooks, was a reward out of all proportion to the ten minutes it took.

The very young delight in melodious words whose meaning they guess at, as Kipling well knew when he wrote the *Just So Stories;* they accept fantasy as the real thing, as in *Alice in Wonderland* or *The Wizard of Oz,* and they weep over animal stories in which they sense that death is inevitable, as it is in *Lobo the Wolf* by Ernest Thompson Seton, or in that Scottish classic *Bob, Son of Battle*. When Miss Budd read aloud to us "The Winged Hats," Kipling's glorious, evocative story of Roman Britain from *Puck of Pook's Hill,* it was we who were in the legion, trudging up to Hadrian's Wall, we who fought off the Picts, despairing of reinforcements now that Rome was besieged. The dogged courage of Parnesius, the young centurion, in the face of hopeless odds was what she wanted us to remember.

Such magic with words seemed unrelated to my struggle with English grammar until Dr. McMahon let a little light into my skull. The "Doc" was our Latin teacher, a stern rugged Scot whose high coloring and shining bald pate was in sharp contrast to his dark clothes. He drilled us in Latin syntax — subject, verb, object, relative clauses; he made us understand that in Caesar's terse marching prose each word had its place like a soldier in the ranks and that its meaning could be determined by the ending, by the case — the genitive, the dative, the ablative. Slowly with recognition came understanding to a boy not always given to finishing his paragraphs.

Had the Eleven Plus Examinations, which now determine the academic future of eleven-year-olds in Britain, been in force eighty-five years ago, one wonders whether Winston Churchill would have been permitted to enter Sandhurst. In the Latin test he took on entering Harrow, he wrote "Winston Spencer Churchill" at the top of the sheet and that otherwise unmarked paper was what he handed in when the time was up. As the son of the brilliant Chancellor of the Exchequer he was admitted, but he was forbidden to study Latin and instead spent three years under Mr. Somervell, studying English. What he learned from that patient teacher he has expressed in his autobiography, *My Early Life:*

Mr. Somervell — a most delightful man, to whom my debt is great — was charged with the duty of teaching the stupidest boys the most disregarded thing — namely, to write mere English. . . . He had a system of his own. He took a fairly long sentence and broke it up into its components by means of black, red, blue, and green inks. Subject, verb, object: Relative Clauses, Conditional Clauses, Conjunctive and Disjunctive Clauses! Each had its colour and its bracket. It was a kind of drill. We did it almost daily. As I remained in the Third Fourth (B) three times as long as anyone else, I had three times as much of it. I learned it thoroughly.

Thus I got into my bones the essential structure of the ordinary British sentence — which is a noble thing. And when in after years my schoolfellows who had won prizes and distinction for writing such beautiful Latin poetry and pithy Greek epigrams had to come down again to common English, to earn their living or make their way, I did not feel myself at any disadvantage.

The wonderful understatement of that word "disadvantage"! In a humbler vein I can say the same for Doc McMahon: when Caesar's Bridge was built and the parsing and translating at an end, I had a grounding in Latin which imperceptibly strengthened my writing of English.

For the Prize-Speaking, which was contested each June on the platform (covering the baptismal tank) of the Central Baptist Church, we were coached by a little thrush of a woman who opened each practice session by making us fill our lungs and then on tiptoe give forth from the diaphragm: "A-a-a," "E-e-e," "I-i-i," "O-o-o," "U-u-u . . ." She demanded that we be able to sustain a long passage, that we enunciate clearly and not let our voices drop at the end of a stanza or paragraph. I don't know why it should be so but it was always a sweltering evening when we finally performed. The nervous speakers foregathered in an anteroom at the rear of the church, and when their turn came, passed through a door, and with eyes on the steps, ascended the platform to the delivery point, faced the audience — and declaimed. A single prompting could kill your chance for the gold piece and to get really stuck in mid-flight was appalling; also, since our Thrush lacked a sense of humor, there was always the chance that a double-entendre would hit the funny bones of the parents, schoolmates, and the sprinkling of girls, perspiring in sympathy in the pews, as it did after the intermission on one occasion, when the speaker, all set for a dramatization of "The Black Hole of Calcutta," began with the piteous words, "My God, I want fresh air!" So did everyone else, and the fathers could not restrain their chuckles. But it was fun to win, as I did twice, the second time in the upper division, reciting Kipling's story "Wee Willie Winkie," which with Mother's help I had cut to the prescribed twelve minutes. I relished the applause as I went up to receive the precious envelope; what remained when the cash was gone was the confidence in one's memory and the quelling of butterflies before one spoke.

6

Every boy has heroes and I found mine at Princeton. On fair Saturdays, spring and fall, when I had saved my allowance, I took the 9:01 to Princeton Junction, then the shuttle, and walked up under Blair Arch and into the campus, among the early birds. Mother would pack some sandwiches for me in a shoebox and this I stowed under my seat in the Pennsy and let it ride. There was a college office run by Harry Buxton, an old beau of Mother's, which issued free passes to prep school boys for all but the most important games, so I checked in there first to see what was on the card. Then to Old North where Ray Koehler, '12, roomed. Ray, my most accessible hero, was the best two-miler in college and a man of infinite kindness to an adolescent; he would make sure that I had at least one square meal at his club on Prospect, and I always watched him run. The freshman games were usually played in the morning — in the autumn of 1911 I watched Charles Brickley, a Harvard freshman, kick five dropkicks against Princeton, and in the afternoons I cheered two heroes I did not know. The first was Sanford White, the big end who became immortal when he picked up a loose ball and scored the winning touchdown against Harvard (my parents took me to that one) and a week later when he did the same thing to Yale in the pouring rain. The other was the incomparable Hobey Baker. You could follow his golden head on the gridiron, for he played without a headguard, and on ice, at St. Nicholas rink in New York where I saw him, he was the fastest, most graceful player ever to wear the orange and the black.

In the autumn of 1913, Hobey's last year, the Yale game was played at Princeton. I went down with my parents, and all through the buffet luncheon at the Bill MacLarens' — he was the team doctor and left early to be with the men as they dressed — the excitement built up, rising higher on the slow walk to the game. Mother and I were still on the sidelines and were held back by a cheerleader as the Princeton team trotted out of the field house and halted right by us. "Watch it. There's a woman here!" said a voice. They checked for a moment and I noticed how big and pale and tense they were before they broke out into the bedlam of cheering. The game was a tossup with Hobey's end runs making the difference and twice he carried close enough to the Yale goal line to kick the two placements that put Princeton ahead. Yale recovered a fumble and a gent called Flynn kicked their 3 points. Princeton hung on to its 6 to 3 lead until the dying minutes, with Yale on Princeton's 43-yard line and fourth down coming up. I saw a figure leap up from the Yale bench across the way, strip the heavy sweater over his head and sprint onto the field, holding his hand up. Somebody said, "Pumpelly. He's their dropkicker." We were hushed as he went back to the 50-yard line, leaned forward and stretched his hands out for the snap. (God, don't let it happen!) The ball rose high, end over end, and then rode the wind in its slow descent; it hit the crossbar, dead center, bounced up, hit the bar again and toppled over into the Princeton zone. Tie game. Hobey had followed its flight all the way back to the goalposts, and as he saw the fateful bounce, for a split second he buried his head in his arms. When I recounted every detail of this to Dad, "You've got sharp eyes," he said.

In the spring, if Ray Koehler had no girl with him, we would take sofa cushions from his couch and lean back against one of the old trees in front of Nassau Hall, listening to the seniors sing at nightfall and watching their cigarettes like fireflies in the dark:

> *Doan' you hear dem bells?*
> *Doan' you hear dem bells?*
> *Dey are ringin' out de glory ob de land,*
> *Ob de land.*
> *Doan' you hear dem bells?*
> *Doan' you hear dem bells?*
> *Dey are ringin' out de glory ob de land.*

This song would follow immediately after the bell at Nassau Hall had tolled the hour. Then came:

> *Australian girls are very fine girls,*
> *Heave away, heave away!*
> *With codfish balls they comb their curls,*
> *Heave away, heave away!*
> *Heave away, my bonny, bonny boys.*
> *Heave away, heave away!*
> *Heave away, my bonny, bonny boys.*
> *For we're off for far Australia.*

And after it:

> *Where, oh where, are the verdant Freshmen?*
> *Where, oh where, are the verdant Freshmen?*
> *Where, oh where, are the verdant Freshmen?*
> *Safe now in the Sophomore Class.*

The verses went on through the classes and ended on the pensive refrain:

> *Where, oh where, are the grave old Seniors?*
> *Where, oh where, are the grave old Seniors?*
> *Where, oh where, are the grave old Seniors?*
> *Safe now in the wide, wide world.*

With the tenor or baritone carrying the verse and those on the benches lifting the chorus, the voices held a sentimental affection that made me yearn for the years ahead when I might be here. Drowsy, my mind dwelling on what I had seen, I would drift off to sleep on the train home having first told the conductor to be sure to shake me when we reached Elizabeth.

Hero worship was exalting and so on occasions like Confirmation was the more solemn worship at St. John's. Both sides of the family were Episcopalian and our attendance was regular and unquestioning. The church was brownstone Gothic, a tall edifice on an ancient site where its two predecessors of wood had burned to the ground, the original having been used by the British in the Revolution as a stable for their horses. Why? I wondered — spite? My earliest impressions were formed by our rector, Dr. Otis Glazebrook, a chaplain in the Civil War, now white-haired, his vestments shining as he poured such feeling into the old words, "We have erred, and strayed from thy ways like lost sheep. . . . And there is no health in us. But Thou, O Lord, have mercy upon us. . . ." Here before the chancel we were christened and confirmed, recited the Creed and the prayers we knew by heart, made sacrifices — one of our new gifts for the Missionary Box on the Sunday after Christmas, no candy during Lent — and were bound together by Communion. The memories are sensuous: the odor of flour paste used to stick our cutouts to the linen pages of the books sent to the heathen, and the fragrance of the greens in the church on Christmas Eve when in the candle-lit twilight the arches and vaulting seemed those of a great cathedral. In that wintry afternoon the chancel had a soft, gold radiance as Dr. Glazebrook led and we repeated those magnificent words:

For unto us a child is born, unto us a son is given: and the government shall be upon his shoulder: and his name shall be called Wonderful, Counsellor, The mighty God, The everlasting Father, The Prince of Peace.

A spirit like an electric current ran through me, and when later we rose to sing, "O Little Town of Bethlehem," and the church was filled by the high young voices, I felt that this was our moment of dedication and hearing Mother's voice soaring from the choir my eyes were wet.

28

7

In Pingry there was a chapter of Pi Phi, a national schoolboy fraternity, and thòse elected to it in the second week of junior year came to assembly wearing a black shoelace in place of a necktie. This marked the beginning of a grueling fortnight of initiation, some of which could be evaded if one went out for football. When I appeared in the oval, all eighty pounds, with my horse collar of shoulder pads and my spindly legs, I was not a convincing candidate. Our coach, "Major" Bonnet, a fleet halfback from Williams, played on the scrubs and there were few who dared tackle him once he got up speed. When we lined up for scrimmage with the varsity, I was at center opposite Bob Potts, who outweighed me by 100 pounds. "Pass the ball and lie down," the Major had cautioned me and that was precisely what I did for a fortnight, until the initiation was over and I had my pin. Then I stayed on the field to retrieve footballs and make myself useful as assistant manager; the team accepted me and at the season's end when the new captain and manager were elected behind the closed doors of the library, I heard myself cheered for the first time. In my mind's eye I was already sporting the dark-blue sweater with the white varsity *P*.

Then the blow fell. Father's business slumped — the first of several setbacks — and after Christmas he told me candidly that he could no longer afford my tuition and that I should have to transfer to the high school. A blow to one who was just beginning to gain confidence. It was not that Pingry had made me a snob, it was that I had lost what I had worked for; it was the fact that the Battin High School was at the opposite end of town, five times larger, and our bitter rival. How could I ever find a place in the midst of all those strangers? Curiously, this reversal brought me closer to my old man than I had ever been before: he had confided in me! And educationally, it was a stimulant, forcing me to take the first of many plunges into the deepening pools of experience. At Battin the teachers were all women and able, especially Miss Emory in German and Miss Warner in English, who certified my admission to Cornell. At the outset I felt lost in the large classes and the thronging corridors, so full of girls, some scented, but gradually I found a place: on the tennis team, as a hit in the school play, with my short story in the senior yearbook ("On Being a Runt, with Apologies to George Ade"), and most surprising, when with the help of my friend Dick Berry, I was elected to preside over the school assemblies. What Battin shook out of me was my tendency to conform.

8

In a tribe as large as ours, the ups and downs were common knowledge, freely discussed in the maternal grapevine. I counted twenty-eight first cousins, eighteen of whom lived within walking distance of each other in the pleasant, unpretentious confines of Elizabeth. We attended the same schools, worshipped at St. John's, were taught to dance on Friday afternoons by Miss Emma and Miss Peggy Florence (the waltz, the polka, the Lancers, and "heel-toe and a one-two-three"), and in the summers most of us moved down the Jersey coast to Bay Head on the Barnegat, a colony of some two hundred cottages, board-inghouses girdled with porches, two hotels, Chadwick's general store, and Priest's, for drugs, jiggers and candy — all built on a sandy, treeless strip between the bay and the ocean, with a fish pound at one extremity and the Coast Guard station at the other.

On that anticipated day in mid-June, when we were shepherded by Mother aboard the train for Bay Head (Dad would never travel with us — it was woman's work), with our two bull pups, Tiger and Nassau, in the baggage car, and the canary bird, its cage wrapped in brown paper, on the seat beside me, we entered our summer world. The day coach smelled of red plush, varnish and cinders, and as we trundled our way past Spring Lake, Sea Girt and Point Pleasant, the tracks drew closer to the dunes and in the gaps we saw the sunlight dancing on the sea. Arrived at last, we climbed down into a bedlam, the drivers of the horse-drawn stages from the Bluffs and the Grenville Arms shouting for their passengers, and Mother looking for young Chadwick — the Chadwicks ran everything from the general store to real estate — who would drive us to our cottage.

At Bay Head we were children of the sun and lived through our senses. If one came out early before breakfast the glare of the sunrise on the slick beach at low tide was so dazzling one had to squint. The salty air, the wash of the waves, the sight of the black jetties stretching out to sea, sent one back ravenous for pancakes. The breath of the ocean was altogether different from the breath of the bay as we took our way to the Yacht Club for tennis or the morning's race in our sneak boxes. We noticed the nasturtiums, the morning glories and sweet peas, the scarlet ramblers that set off our favorite cottages, like the Nimicks'. Then walking or bicycling on the boardwalk across the marshes, we smelled the moist dark soil, the sweetish odor of the marsh mallows and wild roses, and saw the tall stands of cattails which when cut and dried would serve us as torches. The breeze from the bay was warmer and less tingling than the east wind, just as the bay itself, when we capsized

The beach at Bay Head on a Sunday

or were pushed into it, was warm and brackish. What I loved about our racing was the slap-slap-slap of the water against the hull as we rounded the buoy and heeled over for a long tack, the scent of paint, hemp and sun-warmed wood emanating from the cockpit as we braced ourselves against the downthrust of the wind. Most of my racing was done with my Brewster cousins as I had no boat of my own, and I learned my tennis on those clay courts. Water never tasted as good as it did from that sweating cooler in the Yacht Club; after four or five sets we drank until the pain appeared between our eyes.

As I tied the strings of my bathing trunks for the swim before lunch I was unconsciously bracing myself for the plunge to come. If the thermometer was over 90 degrees one would dash through the hot loose sand to the firm cool shingle and poise there, wringing one's wrists at the first touch of the sea, then, just as a big breaker began to rear up, one sprinted and dove and one's whole body was shocked by the cold exhilaration. The buoyancy of the salt water conquered any fear of the undertow or of getting out over one's head; I would submerge, float, and then launch myself on a cresting comber to be pummeled and washed up, spitting sand, with my shirttail out. When I toweled off afterwards, my skin felt encased in salt and I was hungry, hoping there would be blueberry pie or fresh peach ice cream for dessert.

The speed of a cup-winning sneak box like the *Miss Cat,* with Commodore Cattus (all his boats had feline names) at the tiller and big Charlie Cattus handling the sheet, I had experienced as one of the crew, but it was not until I was fourteen and the road connecting Bay Head with Mantoloking, the proud little resort to the south of us, was in use, that I had my first thrill of speeding. My dearest pal, Ed Bonnell, had been given an Indian motorcycle, and riding on the rear saddle, my arms clamped around him, I felt the wind in my face as we edged up to 35 miles per hour. The new road was built of Ocean County gravel and clay, raised perhaps two feet above the sand and bayberry, just wide enough for two cars to pass, with soft shoulders that soon eroded. On week days it was little frequented, an ideal stretch for a challenge that involved four of my contemporaries, all in their teens.

Randy Runyon, at the wheel of the family Buick, had started for Bay Head, with his cousin Fred Colie (later to be a judge on the New Jersey Supreme Court) on the front seat beside him, when he saw that he was being overtaken by Ribbs McAdoo, son of the tunnel builder, also in the family Buick, his mechanic, so to speak, being the near-sighted Billy Studdiford. Both drivers put on speed but the McAdoo Buick was the faster, and just as Ribbs tried to pass, his left front wheel hit a sand hole and the car turned a complete somersault, landing back on its tires with the two boys thrown clear. The only casualty was Billy's spectacles, which were never found. The race had the two communities buzzing, and once was enough.

At nightfall on the broad veranda of the Grenville Arms, we were treated to our first motion picture, in which the actors gesticulated and darted with jerky speed. This was a Pathé picture, taken in Paris, which opened in the bedroom of a boardinghouse with a young man in his nightshirt climbing out of bed to begin his morning ablutions. He is about to dress when he discovers a rip in the seat of his trousers; shouts for the landlady who understands the problem and departs with pants, while our hero gets back under the covers. But something has distracted the landlady from her mending. He calls and fidgets but she has disappeared and finally in exasperation he pulls up the strip of linoleum from underneath his washstand, wraps it around him securely, and sets out to find her. This is a mistake. At the head of the stairs he loses his balance and rolls down the flight, out the open door, and, the house being on a hill, down the street he goes, bowling over everything in his way: an apple vendor, a farmer with a barrow of chickens and eggs, a lady and her beau on a tandem bicycle. The faster he rolls the more damage he does and the larger the army of pursuers, yelling and waving their arms. On he goes, rolling over one of the bridges across the Seine and past Notre-Dame. The film needed no captions and our eyes were streaming with laughter when it ended.

In those summers before the outbreak of the First World War, collegians enjoyed themselves, playing in tournaments, showing off in their varsity sweaters, club hatbands or fraternity pins for the benefit of any girls that might be looking. Some of them did it beautifully. Watching Buzz Law of Princeton dance with Ruth Mann or Buck Bayne of Yale dance with Virginia Ransom would make a young squirt like myself green with envy. We emulated them with just a touch of irreverence: we called ourselves "The Booze Beers" (though we never touched the stuff), we initiated a newcomer with a mock ceremony, and in lieu of fraternity pins we wore safety pins on our bathing suits over our hearts. We had heard that members of St. Anthony's held their pins in their teeth when they stripped for bathing but we didn't go that far. And once a summer we held an overnight encampment up the Metedeconk River. (One night was all we could stand — the hard, fried potatoes, stewed tomatoes, and blackened bacon gave us heartburn.) We bunked in two tents, in one the sensualists who talked of sex and smut, in the other those trying to sleep. Ford, ringleader of the sexy tent, would name those older girls who had lost their virginity — said you could always tell from the way they walked with their toes turned out. We

33

The Booze Beers. I am probably the skinny one at the left

didn't believe him. It never occurred to us that girls had to turn their
toes out when they put on longer dresses.

Labor Day weekend, followed by the appearance of hunters, foretold the end of summer. Great flocks of snipe, white wedges of the
little longbills, would skim by close to shore and on the desolate dunes
to the south it was short work to build a blind of sand, bayberry and eel
grass. A platoon of clamshells, mounted close to the water on thin sticks,
would serve as decoys. Sam Bonnell, Ed's older brother, and the
Burgwins came back with bags of seventy or more, and when my
Brewster cousins asked me to go along with them and watch the sport
I did. I spent the night at their cottage, for we were to be up at 3:30
A.M.; we gulped down a hot breakfast and after an hour's drive to the
blind, Sidney and I set up the decoys at the water's edge as the sun
rose. We could see the snipe from afar: Nick and Charlie would
whistle them in and give them both barrels; one or two would plummet
into the trough while the survivors veered out to sea. Sid and I were
the collectors and we chased the cripples, stoning them with driftwood.
In the chase I retrieved the first three, then a very small snipe with a
broken wing who could go no further turned to face me and I was
overwhelmed with the feeling that he was defenseless and that I was
ashamed. I never went again.

I do not think my father hankered for Bay Head as I did. He was a
good swimmer and enjoyed the salt water and the bridge games in the
evening, but sailing, even on Harry Buxton's big catboat, *The Romp*,
made him restless, and if a northeaster drenched the tennis courts and
denied him the chance to play men's doubles, he was disconsolate. I
used to meet his train late Friday afternoons and accompany him to the
beach for his dip before supper. One evening as I sat watching him
beyond the breakers it seemed that despite his strokes he was being
swept away from shore; I feared he was in a sea puss and ran down to
the water's edge. "Ted, you'd better get help," he shouted. "I can't get
out of this!" I looked back toward the boardwalk — no one! I raced
through the loose sand, took a quick agonizing glance back and he
waved. Thank the Lord, he was clear of the undertow and heading in.
He shook himself as he came up the firm sand and I seized his wet hand.
"Don't tell your mother," he said.

When my friend from home, Paul Mravlag, came down to our cottage
for a week's visit, Dad proposed to take us camping overnight up the
Beaver Dam Creek where there was said to be good fishing for small-
mouth bass. This was most unusual; I had never known him to hunt or
fish, but the expedition assumed reality when Charlie Brewster agreed
to sail us, with a rowboat in tow, to a campsite Friday afternoon, and

35

pick us up with our catch on Saturday morning. Rods we also borrowed from the Brewsters, Mother prepared the commissary, and before Dad's arrival Paul and I purchased a bucket of minnows and found a manure pile for our worms. The weather could not have been more auspicious, with a warm southwesterly breeze. We tacked to the mouth of the Beaver Dam, and as the stream narrowed, we came to a sandy point with a backdrop of scrub pine and a rock grill others had used. We rowed ashore with our blankets, frying pan, food, gear and the minnows, beached the boat and waved our thanks to Charlie.

Dad helped us cut pine boughs which would serve as a mattress and these we placed in the soft grass on the knoll above the beach, first smoothing away the dead branches; them as the sun was setting we went out to try our luck. Probably we were too early, for the rings did not begin to show until much later. With our worms all we caught were perch and pickerel, too small to keep. Dad said the bass should bite before sunrise and with that anticipation we came in for supper: fried bacon, baked beans and canned tomatoes. Paul had a second helping but the tomatoes made me burp — "Can't you stop that?" "No." — and on this sour note, after brushing my teeth, I stretched out on my pine-needle bed. The wind had dropped as dark fell and fireflies appeared. So did the mosquitoes, New Jersey's finest, myriads of them. I slapped and squirmed and when I pulled up the blanket I was too hot. "Try covering your face with this newspaper," Father suggested — he'd brought it along to start the fire for breakfast — but once a bug got under that shield the slapping resounded. About midnight Dad exploded. "God damn it!" he said. "We'll have to row home. This is unbearable." In silence we loaded everything into the rowboat and shoved off, Dad at the oars. It was slow going, and when Paul and I took turns with one oar the course was corkscrew. At last we passed between the silent boats at their mooring and sidled up to the Yacht Club dock. Dad made fast, climbed up and stretched, and I started passing the freight; he hefted the bucket of minnows, some of them alive, set it down, and "Oh for God's sake!" he said and kicked it into the bay.

We took the long, dark trudge back to the cottage in silence but our entry awoke Mother. "Ned," she called, "is that you?"

"Yes," said Dad, "who the hell did you expect!"

On the slowly moving escalator of the teens, it is surprising to discover that one is getting older. At Bay Head, where the pattern of summer varied so little before the First World War, there were two incidents that told me I was. The first was when, at sixteen, I brashly asked Claire, a very attractive girl, quite my senior, if I could take her to a Wednesday evening hop. I had seen how rapturously she danced with a dressy young lawyer named Van Vechten who came down on weekends to monopolize her. But there was no reason why I couldn't beau her in between and it should be fun. As I led her on the floor, past the stag line, and took her in my arms I heard my cousin Charlie Brewster exclaim, "Well, will you look at this!" It was a renewable date, and as we walked and talked on the boardwalk between dances I felt mature.

The second incident was more spectacular. Each year on the Saturday before Labor Day the Water Sports were held in a cove on the north shore of the Metedeconk River. Rafts were moored one hundred and fifty yards apart and the wide waterway between them, lined on either side by sneak boxes, catboats and houseboats anchored gunwale to gunwale, became the staging ground for tub races, canoe races, swimming races and tilting contests. The boats were crowded with picnic baskets, bottles and spectators, the elders shielding themselves from the sun with parasols or black umbrellas. Commodore Cattus's yawl was the reviewing stand, where the winners were announced by megaphone and the silver cups awarded. The tilting, which could be savage, was the climax and after that everyone up-anchored and sailed or was towed back to the Yacht Club, while across the water drifted the "Whiffenpoof Song" or "Moonlight Bay."

The tub race, the opening event, was for the shrimps — the lighter the better. I sat in a round wooden washtub, facing backwards at a dangerous angle and, using my hands as paddles, splashed ahead. The trick was to steer a straight course, keep my balance, and ship as little water as possible. Of the nine tubs to start three would be lucky to finish the thirty yards and the race usually went to the tortoise — someone as skinny as I.

The tilting, which took place at sunset, was for the big guys, fought in canoes, the warrior upright in the bow and armed with a nine-foot bamboo pole, a cloth-covered swab at its tip. The objective was to knock an opponent off his feet and triumphantly overturn his canoe. The tilting between evenly matched teams might go on for a long time, especially if there was a grudge carried over from the previous year.

The summer I danced with Claire, my friend Ed Bonnell and I paired up for the tilting and to our surprise survived the elimination bouts in the morning in which we first sank a canoe of our contemporaries and then after a long skirmish knocked out two young bachelors who must have had a hang-over. So we made it to the finals. Ed, who was going to Exeter, was all that I was not: solidly built with powerful arms and the sunniest temper in the world. In the canoe he braced himself like a rock, while in the stern, paddling on my knees, I offered a minimum target. We were the underdogs as we slid out in the lowering sunlight and were cheered; held our own in the early feinting and Ed got in one lunge that had his opponent off balance and grabbing for the gunwale. I thought we had them and poured in; their stern paddle backing so skillfully that suddenly he had the angle on us. It was death if they caught you broadside, and now instead of winning we were in trouble, with Ed swiping and ducking as I tried desperately to get us in line. We nearly were when the enemy's swab caught Ed in the flank and projected him right out of the boat. It was my fault and I knew it.

We of the Jazz Age, as it came to be called, were discovering the intoxication of dancing: we took the beat from the "St. Louis Blues" and "Alexander's Ragtime Band" and found our model in Irene and Vernon Castle. The Castles were a slender, beautifully matched couple and in their innovations such as the Castle Walk, they abandoned the open embrace of the waltz for a head-to-head intimacy that was graceful and close. As I watched them stop the show in *The Sunshine Girl,* the top musical of 1913, I was trying to memorize, not only the style, but how he held her, the right arm pressed to the small of her back, the left, his guiding arm, not curving out at right angles from the body but crooked at the elbow, the hand pointing straight up, with her arm locked within. In such a close embrace Vernon's right knee gave the signals and when they turned his right leg became the pivot about which she spun.

The Castle Walk was a long, stiff-legged stride ornamented with pirouettes — "the Castle Walk, the Castle Walk" (two long steps), "the Castle Walk, the Castle Walk" (two more), then came the fancy work with Irene twirling around him light as thistledown. It needed space but they had the full stage and they danced as one.

It was not easy to imitate them, but if I had a girl my size who could dance, it was fun to try. School proms were staid affairs: each dance was numbered and one was stuck with the partner whose name was written on your card until the music halted — never soon enough if she was shy or a pill. But during the winter holidays, at tea dances, or *thés dansants* as the more stylish hostesses called them, I could chase the girl I wanted, steer her out of the crush into an open corner, and there — until she was cut in on — we'd improvise and show off to the violins of Meyer Davis, or the Van Epps with their banjos and saxophones. As our favorite tunes, "Avalon" and "Poor Butterfly," were played and replayed, our rhythm generated a warmth in which I was aware of the soft pressure of her breast and, if she was daring, of the responsiveness of her legs that was more than a little exciting. We were too absorbed in what we were doing to draw comparisons, but this was very different from the dancing school gallop of the polka; in the fox trot, maxixe and tango we discovered an intimate pleasure the chaperons never guessed.

My mentor in dancing, as in so many things, was a girl named Ellen Dudley. An only child, rather mannish in her clothes and decisive where I might be hesitant, she brought zest to everything she did and, oddly, liked having me along. Sturdy and strong, with skin like alabaster and merry brown eyes, she was the natural leader in school and at any party. She lived with her parents in a comfortable Victorian house in the western part of town, a good two miles from my home, but luckily for me her cousins, the Dimocks, had one of the show places in our neighborhood and she frequently drove up to see them in her basket phaeton with a fringe on top and her Irish shepherd, Captain, trotting underneath. That was a sight to see, and sometimes I could flag her down; she was the person I consciously dressed for, happy when she liked my new striped tie or wing-tipped shoes. There was never any spooning (the word before Scott Fitzgerald), not with me, and when once in the swirl of the maxixe my hand brushed her breast I shivered, but she merely smiled. We had seen the Vernon Castles perform in New York and with rugs rolled back and her Victrola playing we tried to copy their every step and mannerism.

At Vassar Ellen ran pretty much everything. When I went to Cornell she said she hoped I would join the Zeta Psi Fraternity (to which her cousin, Ned Dimock, had been elected at Yale), and when I did she seemed pleased. When I wrote her early in 1917 that I intended to leave college and volunteer in the American Field Service, she said, "Come on up to Poughkeepsie and talk things over." The first morning before the whole college she mischievously led me down to one of the front pews in chapel, and at no time tempted me to express the devotion I felt. A doctor, I believe, had warned Ellen that she would probably never have any children and perhaps this was why she laughed at sex. Without half trying she cultivated in me adoration and chastity, and when Barney, the Byron of our class, remarked in my hearing that a fire escape was a handy place for a girl, " 'cause you could get such a good grip with your toes," he was speaking of a world I never knew.

Aggressiveness is acquired by men all too readily in America: the tender, responsive side of our nature is determined in our first fifteen years, and it is determined by women.

II

E B. WHITE, who is so delightfully correct in what he says, when interviewed on his seventieth birthday, remarked to the reporter from the New York *Times*, "Old age is a special problem for me because I've never been able to shed the mental image I have of myself — a lad of about nineteen." I see myself on my nineteenth birthday, February 19, 1917, as a bewildered little guy who had tasted failure and knew he would taste more of it if he remained in Ithaca, a town on its ear with war fever, to take the spring examinations. In the preceding Christmas holidays I had convinced my parents that I was a misfit in engineering and that the most useful thing I could do was to volunteer as an ambulance driver in the American Field Service with the French army. Sam Paul of Philadelphia, a friend in my fraternity, had fired me with the idea: he had driven an ambulance at the front for six months before coming to college and was sure that an ex-coxswain could do the job.

There was one drawback: I did not know how to drive, a fact I tried to disguise in my application. We did not yet own a car, and while father believed, in his words, that he could "operate the machine," the operation of those he occasionally hired on a Sunday to drive us and our cousins, the Churches, to a celebrated restaurant in Lakewood some thirty miles away, was so erratic that what with stalling, punctures, and breakdowns, we rarely reached our destination. Instead of enjoying a slick meal, we would have to spend the money on a new tire and tube or on a team to tow us to the nearest garage.

The letter of acceptance from the AFS headquarters, after a few words of welcome, stated the amount I would have to pay for my passage to France and warned that there would be a delay of several weeks before a berth was available; in the interval it recommended that I get as much experience as possible as a driver and mechanic, and then went on to itemize the uniform I should need — the regulation U.S. Army tunic, baggy pants, rolled puttees — wool shirts, socks and heavy underwear. So I went to work as a grease monkey, unpaid, in a service station for White Trucks in lower Manhattan, watching and passing tools to defter hands as they stripped down a motor or repaired a body. The only job I could be trusted to do alone was with a grease gun; what I looked forward to were the test runs when with the inspector I jolted over the cobblestones, seated beside him on a board strapped to the bare chassis; the test over, we swapped places and I steered us home in low gear.

Dad and I were commuting together. I who had disappointed him in many ways was about to do a job he envied, and he showed his affection by taking me to his shirtmaker to be measured for four of heavy khaki flannel. We visited the old tailor after hours and his breath told us that he'd been at the bottle. Evidently he lost sight of my dimensions, for after an interminable delay, when the shirts were delivered they had been cut to Dad's big torso, with a 15¾-inch collar and 35-inch sleeve. I was vain about my clothes, and as I tried on this outsize garment with the gaping collar and cuffs that reached below my hands my heart sank.

When one is going to war — or on a honeymoon — every incident sticks in mind. The clerk in Newark to whom I applied for a passport began filling out the questionnaire:

"Hair?"

"Brown."

"Eyes?"

"Gray."

"Nose?" I hesitated. "Roman," he said, scrutinizing it. (Roman! Well, what do you know!)

"Height?"

"Five feet, seven," I said, adding a little.

"You don't look it . . ."

I took my typhoid shots, after which I went to the family dentist, Dr. Woolsey, to have my teeth filled. There seemed to be a good many cavities, and on the last appointment, as he reached in with the buzzer, he remarked in his dry way, "I don't see why we bother with all this when you'll probably be torpedoed on the way across . . ."

The weeks passed and I chafed at the delay, for like everyone destined for France I longed to get into the action before it was over. At White Trucks I became more proficient with wrench and grease gun and had been accepted as a harmless innocent by the older mechanics; we had our sandwiches and draft beer at noon in a nearby café and they questioned me about what I'd be doing on the other side. At last came the

41

notification that we would sail on July 9. I spent the final weekend with Ellen at her uncle's fishing camp, Peekamoose, in the Catskills, where she let me drive the family Buick and coached me in turning around at the crossroads and in backing on those narrow dusty lanes. Trout for supper, and then, take care of yourself and good luck!

2

To one who had never been at sea, the French liner *Espagne* seemed as gay and crowded as a party in fancy dress. There were French officers in horizon blue with gold-braided scarlet kepis; Italian *bersaglieri* in olive green; an American medical unit, the nurses in their dark-blue cloaks; some quite pretty Red Cross girls; and about two hundred of us ambulance drivers.

We had been paired off alphabetically, and when I entered my tiny stateroom, well down over the propeller, it was to find that my room-mate, a man named Wiggin, had already preempted the lower bunk. The mirror above the washbowl reflected that in my high-collared khaki tunic, devoid of insignia, with the cuffs of that preposterous shirt protruding inches below the sleeves, I was not a prepossessing sight, but this was forgotten in the clamor of departure. In the late afternoon I stood at the rail waving at my parents on the dock below. Beside me was a tall figure in a well-fitting English officer's tunic on which I spotted the Croix de guerre ribbon and the shoulder tab of the American Field Service. He introduced himself as Whitney Warren, Jr., going back for a second enlistment, and asked casually if I had my steamer chair. On hearing that I didn't, "Good God," he said. "Give me twenty-five francs quick!" and with it he fled. "Here," he said on his return, offering me a numbered card. "You're lucky. The purser said it's the last chair available." We were out in the channel by now and the bar seemed the best place in which to thank him. He ordered a martini, I an orange blossom.

At dinner I had my first taste of French cooking with its rich sauces and whipped-cream desserts. The sway of the saloon made my stomach queasy and watching the horizon rise and fall through the porthole did not stabilize matters. Draw the curtain on what followed: it must have been just as unpleasant for the man in the lower berth as for me above. I did catch some sleep at dawn and the poor devil had shaved and departed before I awoke. Breakfast was unthinkable and I had resigned myself to retching misery when the door opened and in came a square solid man in a Harvard varsity sweater bearing a quart of champagne and two thin-stemmed glasses. "I'm Greg Wiggin," he said. "There's only one sure cure for seasickness — champagne. Get this first glass down

42

and you'll feel better." After some gagging I got it down and as we emptied the bottle my condition improved. He steadied me as I shaved and then led me up to the promenade, where we did lap after lap around the deck. I felt too insecure to go down for lunch, so we found my steamer chair and persuaded the steward to bring me some consommé and toast.

When my neighbors returned from their meal, I found myself in the midst of Bostonians: on my right a tall, lean guy with a charming smile, who introduced himself as Harry Crosby, and on my other side, Betty Beal, his cousin, and her mother. The latter were on their way to join Mr. Beal, who had been working in the American Embassy in London since the outbreak of war. Crosby's uniform was as misshapen as mine, and I saw he was having the same trouble keeping his puttees tightly rolled about his thin shanks. My ear caught the cultivated Boston accent and I began noticing the difference. In the family circle I perked up. When tea was served I wolfed down three cups and innumerable *petits-beurre,* which I thought the tastiest biscuit in the world. Thanks to the Wiggin Cure I was ready to brave the restaurant for dinner and accepted Crosby's invitation to join him for a drink.

In those forty minutes we took to each other. His skullcap of soft brown hair, crew-cut, his dark eyes and sensitive mouth were of a boy turning man; he was brimming with life and when he laughed his lips had a mischievous curl. We were of the same age. He had been at Plattsburg in the summer of 1916 and was eager to break away from St. Mark's before graduation but his mother persuaded him to stay until he had passed his entrance examinations for Harvard. Yes, he'd been in Europe before — to the Lido, to Venice and Paris. The French he spoke to the waiter came easily, and he said he'd done quite a lot of driving in the family Studebaker, and when the old man would let him have it, in his Pa's Lancia. Listening, I felt countrified.

Through Harry I met three of his Boston friends: George Richmond Fearing III, called "Tote," tall, ruddy, with really eloquent French and an eye on the girls; sturdy, blond "Tugger" Fay, a football star at St. Mark's; and Stuart Kaiser, a Harvard senior who had been with Harry at Plattsburg. Kaiser, dark-complexioned with gray-green eyes, was reserved, but when something struck him as funny he would dissolve in silent mirth, his shoulders shaking. We got on well; he liked cards as much as I did, and after dinner we would hunt opponents for a couple of rubbers of bridge.

Two nights after our sailing, the *Espagne* was blacked out, all portholes covered. That we had entered the U-boat zone was signalized by our French gun crew, who in broad daylight scored several near-misses on some wooden crates that had been dropped astern. There-after we went through lifeboat drill and solemnly patrolled the deck by night on two-hour shifts. Harry wore a wristwatch with an incandescent face. "You'd better not wear that," said his relief at midnight. "No telling if a periscope could pick it up!" But we saw no submarine and our lightheartednes returned when we were joined by a destroyer escort in the Bay of Biscay.

Cole Porter, a Yale man, with jet-black hair parted in the middle, was our musician and on a zither with a piano keyboard, which he strapped about his neck, he would accompany a quartet or play his own songs. I remember one about Yale:

> *I want to row on the crew, mama.*
> *That's the thing I want to do, mama.*
> *To be known throughout Yale when I walk about it,*
> *Get a boil on my tail and then talk about it. . . .*

And his best and latest lyric:

> *I've a shooting-box in Scotland,*
> *I've a château in Touraine,*
> *I've a silly little chalet*
> *In the Interlaken Valley,*
> *I've a hacienda in Spain,*
> *I've a private fjord in Norway,*
> *I've a villa close to Rome,*
> *And in traveling*
> *It's really quite a comfort to know*
> *That you're never far from home!*

That became the *Espagne*'s theme song, hummed by the night watch who trod softly in the moonlight. With us were two beautiful divorcées who wanted more than strenuous petting, and a sprinkling of nurses who enjoyed the view of the stars, seen horizontally in the lifeboats after dark. Plenty of temptation for those who a week before had privately vowed not to lose their cherry. Certainly we were all getting to know each other better when our ship entered the Garonne River, gliding by those toy villages, so peaceful in the afternoon sunlight, to deliver us to Bordeaux. As we drivers marched over the cobbles to the railway station pedestrians exclaimed, "*Ah, les Américains!*" and bottles of wine and flowers were thrust into our hands. No sleep that night as we rode the wooden benches in third class with our little engine whistling at each dimly lit village crossing, but the confusion and color of the Gare d'Aus-terlitz in the July dawn, the French blue uniforms everywhere, the

widows in mourning, the couples parting, the banging of the compartment doors and the warning screech of the locomotives were my first
impression of Paris at war.

Our headquarters, 21 rue Raynouard, which we were never to forget,
had been loaned to the American Field Service by the Comtesse de la
Villestreux and members of the Hottinguer family. In its park of five
acres, certainly the most beautiful within the fortifications of Paris, on
the lower level by the bank of the Seine, was the assembly ground for
threescore ambulances, Model T Fords with a blue wooden compartment mounted on the rear chassis, just large enough to hold three
stretcher cases; the cars in various stages of readiness were parked
under the enormous old trees. Thence a winding drive led up the
sloping terraces, past the formal gardens and a magnificent grove of
chestnuts, to the front of the château, which topped the hill of Passy.
To either side were temporary barracks and from the château terrace
through the foliage one could see the glint of the Seine, and rising above
the ancient chestnuts, the slender, lacy Eiffel Tower. "21" was where
we formed up, where we listened to the veterans and where we
always returned on leave.

The first day, squatting or reclining on the shadowed terrace, we were
given a welcome by Colonel A. Piatt Andrew. He may have spoken it
many times, but in his handsome, casual way the words touched us:
how pleased he was to have us aboard; a reasonable caution about our
behavior in Paris; how war-weary but tenacious we would find the
French; the incredible number of *blessés* our sections had carried since
1915; and, finally, the definition of our rank — in the French army we
would be treated as *aspirants,* a grade between the enlisted man and
the *sous-lieutenant;* our pay would be about $1.50 a month (laughter);
in addition we would receive a daily canteen of *pinard,* and each week
a sliver of soap and a ration of tobacco that would blow our hats off
(more laughter). Whether we drove an ambulance or a truck we
would be doing a man's job. . . . On the third day the *Espagne*
contingent was lined up by Stephen Galatti, Andrew's second-in-
command, who read off the names of those destined for ambulances
and those who would be driving ammunition trucks in the camion
service. As far as I could judge, the younger and slighter men went to
ambulances, those sturdier and with any experience in heavy equipment — Greg Wiggin among them — into the TMU.

Paris was alluring — but not in my clumsy, hot clothes. At the first
opportunity, I taxied down to Lloyd's, the tailor Galatti recommended,
to be fitted for a whipcord uniform: English tunic with deep pockets,
Field Service buttons and insignia, *also* shirts of light cambric, a gray

silk knitted necktie, wide leather belt, and a cap with visor and the AFS eagle. Afterward with Harry and Tote I had a gorgeous dinner at the Café de Paris. The new uniform was ready in forty-eight hours and made me feel debonair; in it I checked my misfits at the University Club, together with the Slazenger tennis racket I had brought over with me, then went to feast on the delectable cream-filled pâtisserie at Rumpelmayer's. Later that afternoon, I wondered about the remark an older driver from Pittsburgh made as we strolled the path at "21": "This is a funny outfit, men like myself glad to get away from the past, not much caring what happens, and young guys like you so eager for experience . . . Well, let's hope we meet again on leave."

On the last night before training camp, Stu Kaiser, Harry and I went to the Folies-Bergère, where I learned that brandy and I disagree. I was never to lose my fascination for that smoke-hazy spectacle, half in spotlight, half in shadow, where the Aussies with their big turned-up hats, the elegant Britishers in their burnished boots, and the French aces wearing their Croix de guerre with palms beyond counting, one for each victory, made me feel very incidental, and where what was happening onstage, in a swift argot of which I understood only a little, was no less entertaining than the play between the cocottes and the soldiers at the bar in the foyer, of which I understood more. We grinned at the girls and Harry had some banter with them, but they did not appeal. They looked so used.

At our training camp in the Marne we folded away our finery in our small trunks and got down to business. At May-en-Multien we were quartered in a stone gristmill, said to be three hundred and fifty years old; the Boche had occupied it for a week in September, 1914, now it was our barracks. When the miller turned on the mill wheel, we heard the creak of the pulleys and the huffing of the ancient organism.

Our commandant, our *Chef*, was the stocky, amiable John R. Fisher of Vermont, whose job it was to size us up. We were awakened at six in the morning by the jangling of the old bell in the courtyard. At roll call a third were detailed to kitchen fatigue, peeling potatoes, and to cleaning up the latrine, and after breakfast the rest went out to be drilled by a French sergeant. His commands: "*Attention! En ligne! Face à gauche!*" — he repeated for those still dopey, "*A gauche!*" ("Turn left, you idiot," someone would whisper). "*A droite par quatres!*" All this we would obey in double time with short jumpy steps so unlike the "hup-two, three, four" at home. Eventually his shout, "*Rompez vos rangs!*" dismissed us from this charade, and we then applied ourselves to the *voitures*, the old cars on which we practiced.

It was now that Tote Fearing, from having driven his father's fancy,

The limber, dogged, indispensable Ford and its driver, New Yorker Malcolm Schloss, November 1917

gear-shift cars much too fast in Boston, was promoted to instructor, for better than any of us he could get life out of these antiques. His pet was an ancient Morris which had only second and high gear; with repeated hand-cranking he would wake it up and then a novice like myself would take the wheel and stall it dead. I had a harder time mastering the three foot-pedals of the Model T Fords: the brake on the right; reverse in the center, and the pedal on the left for low and high speed. You started in low with the pedal depressed, fed her gas with the hand throttle below the steering wheel, and as you gained momentum you fed her more gas and eased the pedal up through neutral and into high. In this transition the Ford was balky, and if you went light on the throttle or spark the car would stall or shudder and buck (guaranteed to open wounds if there were wounded within). She could be just as ornery when you were cranking up the motor. There was an emergency brake which if you remembered to pull it back kept the car in neutral; if you didn't you suddenly found yourself pushing desperately against the radiator, trying not to be run down by an ambulance in high gear.

The Fords were the telltales for those without experience, especially in reverse. We had, of course, no rear mirrors, and in backing, the driver had to lean far out to see around the body, always doing the right thing with that touchy middle pedal. Harry and Stu Kaiser breezed through their tryouts and were then exempt but I was one of the group who needed practice. The *Chef* had laid out a twisting course down which we backed between wooden obstacles, like a steeplechase in reverse, and those waiting to drive would jeer when we hit one, as I usually did. In repairing punctures, we mounted the jack on wooden blocks to steady it in the mud and we attacked the flat with two thin-tongued tire irons, pried it off the rim, searched for hobnails or an embedded rock, replaced the tube, cursed the tire back on the rim, and finally inflated the new tube with a hand pump. In 1909 when he won the Vanderbilt Cup race on Long Island, Harry Grant and his mechanic changed a tire in a minute and a half. On a flat dry road I could do the job in about twenty-five.

The wife of our *Chef* was Dorothy Canfield Fisher, the novelist, who did her best to make the army rations more palatable for us. Americans never appreciate what creatures of habit we are in our eating until we are thrust in a milieu where almost everything about the cooking is different and there is no escape. In the mill on the Marne, since we were far to the rear, our meat ration was horse, gray and tough-fibered if served as steak, brown and tough-fibered if it came in a stew. I did not like the taste or the chewing, so I cut it thin and ate as little as

At the St.-Quentin Front, September 1917

whose left leg had been horribly shattered. The blood was soaking
through the bandages and it was my job to keep his limb from touching
the wooden frame of the stretcher or the iron hinge beneath the
canvas. It was my first sight of the torture inflicted by the swaying of
the car and the jiggling of the *brancard.*

3

At last in the downpour of a Sunday our division moved back into
the lines and we drove up in convoy to relieve the French section we
were replacing. Now we heard the guns and watched the antiaircraft
bursts vainly pursue the planes overhead; now we could head our
letters, "At the Front," and we were, I am sure, the only tiny fraction of
that body of men who looked forward to being under shellfire. At home
the English books *The First Hundred Thousand* by Ian Hay and Guy
Empey's *Over the Top,* novels like *Mr. Britling Sees It Through* by
H. G. Wells, and *Sonia* by Stephen McKenna, the poems of Rupert
Brooke and Alan Seeger ("I have a rendezvous with Death / At some
disputed barricade . . .") had conditioned us to expect a kind of purify-
ing heroism at the Front, and we would share in it.

What we found was the French *poilu* in faded blue, older than ourselves, war-weary, disillusioned but dogged, who had learned by experience how to survive. He survived the cold by wearing a flannel
bellyband and a scruffy woolen uniform and by chafing his icy feet
after standing for hours in the liquid French mud; he survived the
German shelling by noting how methodically the salvos came in — five
shells, nine shells, so often a set number and at a prescribed time over
trench or crossroads; and he survived gastronomically by always having
a pot of coffee and a dark brown stew, into which he put onions, carrots,
a rabbit, a pigeon — whatever he could shoot or find in the gardens
behind the demolished houses — slowly simmering for his *popote.*
Those from the outset were the lessons we learned from the *brancardiers,* the stretcher-bearers, men old enough to be our fathers,
grizzled, some of them previously wounded, who had been phased out
of the infantry to give first aid in the forward line, and to bring the
wounded in a two-wheeled *brouette* or a *pousse-pousse* to our *poste de
secours,* the *abri* twenty-five feet underground where we and the doctors
waited. They taught us idiomatic French without ever evincing the
faintest desire to learn English; they were curious as to why we were in
the war and what we hoped to get out of it; after a harrowing night
drive they braced us with coffee laced with brandy; and as time deepened our affection for each other, they gave us letters to their wives and
daughters when we went on leave. They, not the doctors, were our
teachers.

The *abri* was an underground emergency ward, beam-supported and so well protected that it was vulnerable only to a direct hit. One descended a long, inclined stairs, wide enough to admit the stretcher-bearers, to a room big enough for an operating table and medical equipment, and along the walls, the bunks or stretchers on which we all slept. In charge was a *médecin*, a young doctor, whose job it was to bandage and brace the mutilated for the jolting ride to the field hospital.

The sector we took over was east of St.-Quentin, which was in German hands, at the hinge between the British and the French. The Boche had recently staged a short withdrawal to eliminate a salient: villages in the path had been pounded into rubble with hardly a roof standing; the *abris* still had German signs and their discarded equipment was lying about. Our camp at Lanchy was on a plain, treeless and so level we could see the spires of the St.-Quentin Cathedral and the Germans' observation balloons five miles distant. The road close to the Front, on each side, was camouflaged with long strips of gray-green fabric and up this corridor at dusk, when there was less chance of our dust being spotted, four ambulances would go, one for each of the two forward *postes de secours* at Holnon and Maissémy, and two for a relay station under a hill midway between. From the Front to the field hospital was a distance of fifteen miles and additional ambulances, operating a day shift, took the serious cases still further back to surgical centers in Ham or even to Noyon, where there were Red Cross girls to flirt with, and omelets and ice cream for the loiterer.

We drove without lights or windshields and the red crosses painted on the roofs and walls of the ambulances were more for decoration than defense; if we got caught in heavy shelling, it was either bad timing on our part or bad luck. We learned to listen instinctively. In the evening quiet we could hear the far-off but distinct thump of the German 105's, then in a split second the approaching scream followed by the crump! which told us how safe or near we were; if the scream became a crescendo and we saw the geyser of earth, we got the hell out — if we could. Crossroads were always a hazard, especially if one was caught in a line of camions and horsedrawn 75's, that superb French fieldpiece. The Boche had been here recently; he had pinpointed the roads, and he sent his big stuff in, usually at set intervals, but not always.

Harry was nearsighted, so in heavy rain or the predawn fog when his glasses misted over I would drive. I was gaining confidence, though not without mishap. One misty night with me at the wheel we paused to pick up two French officers going back into the lines; they sat beside me with Harry perched on the left mudguard. We made our first contact with a looming, lumbering water wagon. Fortunately I had room to turn out, the collision was glancing, the horse unhurt, but

Harry was dislodged with some American profanity which amused the company. Our second was more threatening: an ammunition caisson drawn by six horses came on the gallop out of the dark; I was boxed in by a stone cliff and it was up to the rider on the lead team to swerve, which he did, crumpling my mudguard and sending Harry sprawling over the hood with a stream of insults beginning, "*Merde, alors, cochon!* . . . *!*" beautiful to hear. So was the rebuttal.

We had no way of knowing that this was the most tranquil sector on the French Front; most of our calls were for *malades,* the sick; Stu Kaiser went twenty days before he carried his first wounded *poilu.* With so much time on our hands we explored. Everyone collected trophies, beginning with *briquets,* the cigarette lighters the *poilu* made out of empty shellcases. We sought anything German — belt buckles, bayonets, epaulettes — with a Luger pistol, an Iron Cross, and the spiked dress helmet of the Prussian Guards the big prizes. My diary reminds me that "Harry ate dinner with a knife that had killed two Germans" — evidently that was the story that went with it. In the twilight after supper those off duty would traverse the plain to the nearest landing field, where mechanics would be tuning up the two-seated bombers and where Harry with his wheedling French was the first to go aloft. We visited the battery of French 75's, where for a package of American cigarettes the crew permitted me to lob a shell at the Boche. We were invited to have coffee in a telephone *abri* where the nest of wires made connection with the artillery posts, the front lines, and the observer high up in his French "sausage," and with the English on our left flank ("Wouldn't it be great to put through a call to Manchester, Massachusetts!" said Harry). Some got special permission from Lieutenant Speers to visit the listening posts only fifty yards from the German trenches, and at night in our tents by the light of candles stuck in wine bottles we read — I, Lockhart's *Napoleon;* Harry, the Bible or *The Rubáiyát* — or we gambled at *vingt-et-un* or poker, at which (but not at dice) I was lucky. The games took place in a stout little tent of French waterproofs, neatly entrenched to keep the rain out, which Kaiser and I had purchased for 50 francs from the French drivers we relieved.

In all this tranquillity we were occasionally shocked by the appalling wounds. Harry was in the pit of the *abri* one morning when a *poilu* our age was carried down streaming blood. His whole right cheek had been shot away, nose smashed in, no jaws or teeth left, under his eyes the torn skin a dead blue. It was a question whether he would live to reach the field hospital, but he did survive that dreadful hour on the road, and then in the reception tent, the stretcher was lowered, there was hesitation and questioning — Had he been brought to the right place? No, he'd have to go on . . . Where were his papers? — and Harry was furious. God damn it, he muttered, in an American hospital this man would be on the operating table in a minute!

Such impressions and the sight of the dogfights in the sky above us, when at sunset the German pilots came out of the sun looking for trouble, made us wonder — were we really doing a man's job, were we in any sense *embusqués,* that French word for slackers that made us sensitive? We felt that our exposure was minimal compared to that of the pilot, the *poilu,* or the *brancardier,* and from what we had heard at rue Raynouard we knew that many drivers before us had eventually transferred into the Lafayette Flying Corps or been commissioned in the French artillery. But it was not the question of transfer which confronted us when a staff car with three American officers, one a very young medico, drove into camp on August 31; they came to enlist us in the United States Army Ambulance Service with the rank of private, and the choice was whether to sign on for the duration, be demobilized in Paris, or return to the States. Some were rejected for physical reasons; Harry, who had been crabbing at the food, the French, and the weather, said he'd be goddamned if he'd join, and Fearing and Fay sided with him; but the majority of us who were still imbued, signed up. It meant that in time we would exchange our AFS uniforms for GI issue, that we would be paid $33 a month, *but* that we would continue to serve with the French infantry and subsist on their rations.

With the arrival of Phil Shepley, Harry's old friend and classmate, a tall, good-looking Yankee who could do anything with his hands, they drove together as planned and I formed a new partnership with Richard Salinger of Brookline, whom we had acquired at the Mill. Dick, short and chubby with twinkling blue eyes, was as wry as he was dear. He was a congenital pessimist whose short bark of laughter warned you not to take him too seriously. A student of the theater, with skill in versification, he had been tempted to write, and his work as a special student at Harvard in Professor George Pierce Baker's course in playwriting and production had left him, like myself, uncertain of the next step. More tense than he appeared, he was plagued by a nervous indigestion which army fare intensified. I have a picture of him in any one of a dozen cantonments, reclining in his blankets, passing his hand over his stomach and belching softly as he murmured, "Jesus, lover of my soul!"

As a driver I was the more aggressive and he the more contemptuous of mechanical detail. When the time came to lubricate our brute of a Fiat, we tossed a coin: I won the front end, he the rear end and differential. The car had already been jacked up on wooden blocks and our mechanic had removed the left rear wheel, which needed repair. This gave Dick more elbow room. Lying flat on his back he unscrewed the plug from the differential and proceeded to pump in grease from the grease gun. The grease was cold and came slowly; to get a better purchase he slued around, braced his left foot against the blocks and, grunting, managed to push the jack out from under. The axle, unsupported, plunged into the ground pinioning Dick across the breast with about an inch to spare. We came running, and when it was clear he was not injured, we paid no attention to his plea, "Come on, you guys, get me out of this!" Weak with laughter, we asked each other, "How the hell could he do it?"

The autumnal rains were early, turning our camp, the roads and the approach to our *poste de secours* into liquid mud, inches deep. We greased our hobnailed shoes but our feet were numb, warm only when we were in our blankets. In the forward *abris* the clay walls dripped and we saw our breath before we snuffed out the candle. The rain and inactivity added to our gripe and as the third month in this somnolent sector petered out, we grew restless to be a part of the real war.

Dick's proficiency as a mechanic may have been questionable but he had a cool head, as he proved in late October when he went up to Paris to take his preliminary tests as a pilot in the American Army Air Force — and passed. "Strapped me in a damn little seat and spun me up and over at every crazy angle. If you get sick you're out," he told me on his return. He was the first of us to opt for a transfer, but he was not yet in; they told him that the army already had more fliers on their way to France than there were planes for, and he'd be notified later. Well, if Dick could make it, I could, and with the lieutenant's permission I applied for transfer to aviation. (There is no telling what kind of pilots we might have made for we never heard from them again.)

Crosby and Fearing changed their minds and enlisted for the duration; it seemed inevitable that we with our surplus of drivers would be broken up for replacements. At daybreak on October 31 we departed from Lanchy with no regret: we were to return our gutless Fiats to their base in Noyon, and after a night in Paris proceed to Bar-le-Duc to take over the twenty Ford ambulances of old Section 29, then at Verdun. At first we drove in order, two lengths between each Fiat, but once we had reached the straight, poplar-lined road, Fearing who was driving the staff car gave it the gas and our convoy turned into a chariot race as drivers shoved by each other derisively — a few got up to 35 mph — and gendarmes at the crossroads gaped.

That was our last fling of coltishness. The trucks that were waiting for us at Bar-le-Duc drove us into a more formidable world: the roads

56

were jammed with camion trains, heavy artillery, dispatch riders on motorcycles, troop replacements moving up. Everything was camouflaged, even the narrow-gauge railway. There was a grimness here which fitted the rumors we had picked up at St.-Quentin. The forts at Verdun were France's stronghold and they had been critically threatened by the assaults of the Crown Prince's army corps. The German casualties were estimated at 300,000 and in the struggle for Mort Homme, a key point, mutiny broke out in certain French regiments which General Pétain put down with executions. The forts held and the slogan *"Ils ne passeront pas"* ("They shall not pass") echoed throughout France in 1917. Now we were in the act and we were awed.

Three miles from Verdun in the stone barracks at Belrupt the veterans of Section 29 were waiting to be relieved, and from Dick English, their quiet-voiced spokesman, we got the word. They were attached to an attacking division, now in reserve. Verdun, he said, was hell on wheels, the toughest sector on the French Front; eight of their drivers had been decorated, one killed, one wounded. . . . We could have listened to more but Lieutenant Speers sent for Dick and me. We were, he explained kindly, two of the six drivers he was obliged to transfer to Section 32, which had just come out of the lines after thirty-five days working *postes* at Fort Douaumont and Vaux. They were *en repos* only fifteen miles away; their discards had gone home and they needed men. He saw we were downcast and added, "I'd probably have lost you both to the Air Force anyway" as he patted Dick's shoulder. We knew he was right to stick with the more experienced, but it was sad to part from friends to whom we had come so close. With Arthur Brickley, a younger cousin of the famous Harvard dropkicker; Lockhart Baum, an efficient, diffident engineer from the Massachusetts Institute of Technology; Bob Wallace, who I think was our baby; and Charlie Leonard, in days to come a fine driver and photographer and our favorite cook, we bundled our duffle back into the truck that had brought us and were waved off affectionately to a new future.

4

Section 32 was originally recruited from the City Club of New York; only one was over thirty but most of them were older and more sophisticated than we were. I remembered some of them from the training camp in the Marne. We were first in the field but instead of Fiats they had drawn brand-new Fords and from the outset had been attached to the Algerian Division, the 37th. We were welcomed by their veteran *Chef*, Lieutenant Keith Vosburg, a blond Californian in his mid-thirties, and taken in hand by his two sergeants, gray-haired Jim Ives, charming and casual, and brisk Gurnee Barrett, Columbia 1910,

The Algerians, with five ambulance drivers. The most decorated sergeant in the French army sits next to the captain in the white goatskin. The ambulance drivers in the back row are: Plass, de Vore, Reaser, and myself next to the end. O'Brien is to the left of the second row and the only married man among us (both of them would eventually command sections of their own). As the day wore on, I began to place nicknames with faces; they seemed a rangy, competent lot. That evening at supper Vosburg introduced each of us informally as we stood up to be identified and in the aftermath I noted three individuals: Joe Lyons, obviously competent, said to be in line for a decoration; Don Call, very tall, very debonair with his trim moustache, who had acted on Broadway; and dark-haired, dark-eyed Johnny Mungan, clowning and wisecracking, with his take-off of Charlie Chaplin. There is a comedian in every unit and Johnny was ours.

Part of their *esprit* came from their pride in being with the Algerian Division. It was made up of the 1st and 3d regiments of Zouaves, the 2d and 3d Tirailleurs, and the Spahis cavalry, dismounted. A composite of Frenchmen, half-castes, and tribesmen from Algiers, officered by the pick of St.-Cyr, khaki-clad, wearing the red fez, hard-looking, professional, deadly in night patrols, on which they collected the earlobes of their victims, they marched when on show to the stirring strains of "Sambre et Meuse," and in crises were called on, with the Foreign Legion and the Chasseurs Alpins, to do the impossible.

Their ambulances, so spotless at the rue Raynouard three months earlier, were in serious need of repair: fourteen had been hit by *éclats* (shell fragments), and on one night within an hour four cars had been put out of commission, one turning turtle in the mouth of a huge shell hole (no *blessés* aboard fortunately, and the driver was unhurt). As we helped put on new radiators and change bands, axles, and tires, we were inoculated with tales of the division and of what it was like at Carrière Sud, the most exposed of their three *postes,* which was in clear sight of the Germans and which they frequently could not reach until the shelling had moderated. An old quarry burrowing thirty feet down in the limestone, the *abri,* what with the fumes of the acetylene gas (for light), the chloride of lime (for disinfectant), and the odor given off by dirty wet clothes, blood-stained blankets and bandages, produced, in Gurnee Barrett's words "a very special atmosphere." The round trip from Carrière Sud to the evacuation hospital and return took four hours. Even so, from their three *postes* they had pulled out three thousand wounded in little over a month. The night driving, the desolation, and the rats were what they talked about.

In the humdrum of refitting and while recruits from Algiers filled out the regiments, we new hands were given the chance to drive on sporadic calls, carrying pneumonia cases mostly, for it was now November, to the rear. My turn came with Robert Reaser, a slender, likable guy from Yonkers, whose car ran like clockwork, and when the *malades* were off

59

our hands, we paused in Bar-le-Duc for an omelet, jam and toast and to compare notes. He was a painter who had studied for six months at the Art Students League and had his sketchbooks with him. As I came to know him better, those long fingers of his could do anything: repair a wristwatch, cut hair, draw a portrait, find what was wrong in a motor — anything but play checkers, at which I beat him consistently. I questioned him about our lieutenant. Vosburg, he said, was an attractive Californian, a veteran of one of the earlier sections, intellectual, fair-minded, but adamant on two points: he would not tolerate a driver's being liquored up when on duty or liable for call, nor excuse one who let the oil in the crankcase get so low that the bearings burned out. A driver would be removed from his car on either count.

Then from Vosburg himself came the happy announcement that Dick and I were granted a ten-day *permission* (leave) along with a handful of their more deserving men. We were dispensable in the quiet interval and technically we did have a narrow margin of seniority. I suspected that Dick had set up tentative arrangements while in Paris for those tests. Wealthy Parisians, friends of his family, had offered us their villa on the Riviera, at Villefranche on the outskirts of Nice, fully staffed and all to ourselves. On our way through Paris, we spruced up and taxied out to the Faubourg St. Germain to dine with our benefactors, and after two martinis I was tongue-tied in a pleasant daze. I was still not sure of myself with alcohol, much preferred champagne to hard liquor, and was just developing a palate for the vintage Bordeaux and Burgundy which made that dinner party so festive and so fantastically different from supper the night before.

Our trip to Nice took thirty-six hours, for the Italians had given way on the Piave and we were repeatedly sidetracked to let French troop trains go through, carrying divisions that would shore up the retreat. With our bags and my tennis racket we were delivered to the villa at sunset and fell in love with the place. The house at the very tip of Villefranche Harbor was exquisitely furnished, the butler considerate, the Italian maid curvaceous and pretty. The French windows of the library gave onto the terrace and from the terrace where we sipped our vermouth we watched a convoy, shepherded by destroyers, settle at anchor, lights blinking, bells sounding across the water. Follow this with *homard* and for dessert a delectable mystery known only to the chef, a demitasse under the stars, two chapters of a biography of Marie Antoinette, a hot tub and linen sheets, and where were you? Sound asleep.

After a lazy breakfast on the terrace — huge purple grapes, huge bowls of café au lait, fried eggs and apricot preserves — we boarded

Suzanne Lenglen belting the ball, Nice, November 1917

the tram and found our way to the Nice Lawn Tennis Club, where we were welcomed by a Monsieur Lenglen, the secretary. I showed him my racket and white socks, and said *"J'aime beaucoup le tennis";* he wrote out a guest card, rustled up white flannels, shirt and shoes, and forty minutes later I was rallying with his daughter Suzanne, the champion of Europe. We played together each morning thereafter except Sunday, when with three men she put on a doubles exhibition for the Red Cross. In the spring of 1914, R. Norris Williams of our Davis Cup team had promised her a welcome in the United States and I thought it a pity that the war had dashed her hope of being acclaimed the best in the world. She was not pretty but on the court she was soignée in her short, pleated white skirt and white bandeau about her black hair, fast and devastating for she stroked from either side with more length and power than I had ever seen a woman do. Her serve had neither the spin nor speed that Helen Wills would bring on from California and as my serve came back I could take a couple of games a set from her but never the set. She coaxed me into a handicap singles tournament in which I was on my way to winning the semifinals when momentarily my eye was dazzled by the white buildings above the plane trees and my wild shot knocked the flowered hat off the head of an elderly spectator. This upset her as it did me, but not Dick, who choked with laughter. In the haste of my last day I left my billfold in my borrowed pants; Suzanne retrieved it and sent it to me, and the note she enclosed convinced the Doubting Thomases in the section.

All the tennis I wanted, sometimes twice a day on those beautiful clay courts, followed by a shower and a light lunch on the Promenade — broiled turbot with an endive salad, and once snails, which disagreed with Dick; an afternoon at Monte Carlo where, being in uniform, we were not permitted inside the casino; another with Dr. Gros, one of the founders of the Lafayette Escadrille, who related the exploits of young pilots like Tommy Hitchcock, Norman Prince, and Raoul Luftberry. As Nice lit up, one of us would remark, "Let's go back," back to Villefranche, where a better cuisine and wine awaited us than we knew how to find in town. There was a dream-like luxury about that villa that made us feel relaxed and satiated. I admit to desultory speculation about that Italian maid, but by nine o'clock I was always too sleepy, and now shall never know.

5

It seemed symbolic to pass out of the bright sunlight into the dark tunnels that brought us to Paris. At "21" we were told that our new section had just gone back into the lines at Glorieux and that the quickest way to reach them would be via our old outfit, who were still operating from their cantonment on the outskirts of Verdun. Tanned and flossy from our *permission* we were dropped off by a friendly camion driver who had given us a lift out from Bar-le-Duc, and the first to greet us was Harry Crosby, in wooden sabots, heavy socks and a sheepskin coat over his layers of sweaters. When he heard where we had been he said we were lucky bastards and proceeded to tell us what we had missed. I had never known him so nervous and realized why as he led us to the remains of his car, the top and one whole side of it blown in two nights before by a shell that had wounded Spud Spaulding and by some miracle had never so much as scratched Harry. He held up the shrapnel-pierced backboard against which he might have been leaning. "Jee-sus!" said Dick.

There had been heavy shelling of the roads in the predawn, when Ben Weeden and Harry drove their ambulances up to the *poste* at Houdromont, where Spud Spaulding was on duty. As they reached the narrow parking space, Harry, in backing around, stalled in front of Spaulding's car with Spud, in the doorway of the *abri,* jeering at him, when a shell burst not ten yards away on the top of a stone ridge. Harry had instinctively dropped to the floor of his car, which, he says, "saved my young life," while *éclats*, rocks, mud shot past and over him. Shell fragments struck Spud in the chest knocking him back into the *abri* and both cars in the line of fire were demolished, but not Weeden's. After a pause while Spud was given morphine and his wound was dressed they shoved him and two other stretcher cases into Ben's car, and Ben with Harry beside him coolly started back. They were caught in another salvo behind a truck which was stuck in the middle of the road and Spud was hit a second time by *éclat* which passed through the brass nameplate (of the donor) on the wall of the car.

Harry, again in one of his pious moods, had been reading the Bible the day before and had paused over the passage in Romans 10:13: "For whosoever shall call upon the name of the Lord shall be saved," and he says in his journal that during the ordeal he "prayed as never before," which he believes saved him. He had been taken off duty for a week. They don't give Purple Hearts for near misses, but I wondered how long a shock like that lasts.

We got more of the story from Lieutenant Speers before being relayed to our camp at Glorieux, on the west side of Fort Douaumont. Spaulding, he said, was recovering and would surely be decorated. The division was pleased with their work but the cars were in bad shape, all but two had been hit, though none as badly as Harry's. Everyone was dog-tired, they'd be damn glad to go *en repos*. His regards to Vosburg, and good luck!

I think of Verdun always under leaden skies, misty when it was not

Harry G. Crosby, two years after Verdun

raining, with that deep liquid mud that froze the feet. Nothing would keep the chill out; I remember waking in my blankets, grateful that at last my feet were warm. At St.-Quentin one could safely prowl through a deserted village, photographing the Crucifix still hanging unharmed in the chancel of the roofless church. At Verdun there was not pathos but desolation: in this rolling country the villages were reduced to flat rubble, the woods to black severed stumps, the fought-over Front to a moon surface of undulating shell craters, infested with rats. Verdun was the pivot of the French army, and the organization that held it: the big naval guns on the railway sidings, the airfields and masked batteries, the ceaseless replenishment of men and food and ammunition on the unprotected roads gave us a new appreciation of French valor. Our job was to pick up the pieces.

The Algerians had been sent back in to recapture Hill 344, which they did. Dick and I arrived on the eve of the assault and were immediately assigned as aides. On starless nights the road had a dull gleam, like a stream, and that we were nearing the trenches we could tell from the *arrivés* (the incoming shells), the star shells, and the piles of partially cracked rocks (their sharp edges hell on tires) with which squat little Annamites were filling in the worst of the pits. On the pitted stretches I would walk in front of the radiator, a white handkerchief on my shoulder, feeling the way, while the driver ground along in low gear, trying not to lurch or stall; at his back the *couchés*, the stretcher cases kept crying, "*Doucement! Doucement!*" ("Slowly! Slowly!") or, if Algerian, "*Ai! Ai!*" as they beat with their fists on the walls of the ambulance. The limber little Fords made it where heavier cars would have mired, but after 16 kilometers it was not uncommon for only one of the three stretcher cases to be living when we reached the hospital. The spike of *la gnôle* (white mule) in our coffee, which the *brancardiers* gave us before we started back for the next load, was momentarily relaxing, but I was learning that during an attack when everyone was on call, the drivers might get a bit of a respite but the mechanics none. Collisions with trucks and artillery caissons were inevitable and what with stove-in radiators, broken axles and burned-out brake bands, a third of the twenty cars might be grounded. During our ten days at Glorieux we transported 2,400 wounded and toward the end, as the shell wounds decreased, the cases of frozen feet (*pieds gelés*) were mounting. This was the Algerians' only weakness: they could not cope with the cold; they kept wrapping their numb toes in more damp cloths until they had club feet with little circulation. "*Ai! Ai! Ai!*"

The experience at Verdun, partly vicarious, partly my own, set a pattern for the worst of the days to come: they were either as bad or not.

Now the French put a premium on their decorations. There were only two for which the enlisted man was eligible: the Croix de guerre, and the Médaille militaire, which carried a pension; had Spaulding been mortally wounded or crippled he would have received the Médaille, but since he recovered, he was given the Croix. We all had hopes of sometime winning that bronze cross with its green and red ribbon, and it was a matter of pride that after their first month in action at Carrière Sud, five drivers of our new section had been decorated with the Croix, three with the silver star of the division, two with the bronze star of regimental citations, and that the section itself had been officially cited by our general in these words: "Some months ago, you came to us as strangers, but now the men of my division regard you as brothers and I look upon you as my children. You have recently been called upon to perform a difficult and dangerous task. Your performance has been above criticism. In a word, you have shown yourselves to be as brave as the men who fight in the trenches. I therefore take great pleasure in presenting you with the highest honor that is within my power to bestow."

6

In war the sequel to violent action is a period of boredom in which one drills, gambles, reads, and rests the carcass. Early in December the division was relieved and ordered into winter quarters in the Vosges Mountains. In preparation for the long drive, Dick and I — one driver having gone on an alcoholic binge and another being ill — were entrusted with ambulances of our own. This was my first promotion, and haunted by the uncertainty of whether there was enough oil in the crankcase, I scuffled underneath in the packed snow to see if, before our departure, the petcock when opened would drip. It did, so I scuffled out — leaving it open. Fortunately as the convoy was lining up, the driver behind noticed the fresh black streak and I scuttled down again and closed the damn thing before there was trouble. By such small margins are reputations preserved.

Winter quarters have a warm, romantic sound and ours this Christmas of 1917 certainly had its points. The cars were lined up in deep snow on either side of the avenue leading to the modest château at Darnay. The officers were billeted in the château; most of the drivers dawdled or slept on their stretchers in the conservatory, whose brick walls and snow-blanketed glass roof provided a long ward lit by candles and made tropical by a wood stove. The only daylight came through the door when opened, which wasn't often. Dick and I with four others drew the gatehouse, a cozy room with a window and open fireplace.

Once again we had outdistanced the mail truck and it was depressing to have no word from home. Vosburg cheered us up by bringing back from the village in a cigar box a tiny black puppy. Bobby, as we named him, was a wire-haired pointing griffon and a smart one; he gravitated to the foot of Reaser's bed — Bob became his master at the war's end — and as our mascot his gambols and affection were a constant delight. For baths our camion took us in groups to a wooden shed where we soaped beneath hot showers — but not until we first scoured our heavy underwear for cooties. You turned the garment inside out and held each seam close to a candle: when the cooties felt the flame they popped. Incidentally those cursed flannel shirts of mine came in handy, the cuffs seemed to have shrunk. It never occurred to me that I was growing.

It was only a short walk to the picture-postcard village. There I found "Madame N" and persuaded her to serve us a delicious supper of veal or an omelet, *pommes frites,* and salad, with a bottle of her cellar-cool Moselle; on the spot Dick, Bob Reaser, O'Brien, a most genial Irishman, and I formed a *popote,* to which we invited friends. Madame's husband was at the Front and we brought laughter and francs into her life, but when we appeared for our promised feast on Christmas Eve, the door was bolted, the table set, the bottle empty, and she passed out on the floor. The lonely heart.

With the snow over a foot deep, still falling, and only two cars on call for the *malades,* we had time to laze — too much, thought Sergeant Barrett, who to break up our lethargy, ordered all drivers to fill up their rear lamps with kerosene. True, we were in an area where a light could be used after dark, but still to have to leave our hot room and plunge out in that blizzard — cursing and threatening the dark fate of all sergeants after the war Dick pulled on his boots and sheepskin and joined us. Before filling, the lamp had to be unscrewed from its bracket and this was something not to be managed with gloves on.

Midmorning on my way to post a letter I passed Gurnee, who had evidently finished his inspection. "I wish you'd tell that friend of yours Salinger to step out and take another look at his lamp," he said. I delivered the message and enjoyed with the others Dick's reaction: "Jesus Christ. Now what's troubling the bastard! If I ever meet that guy back in New York . . ." He was gone quite a while, and returned somewhat sheepish. "Anything wrong?" I asked. "Ah, nuts," he said. "I put the damn thing back upside down," and he gave that bark I loved to hear.

Our Christmas mail and packages finally caught up with us after New Year's when a camion stuffed with sacks pulled in before the château. The lieutenant laid on a champagne dinner that night in the village and meantime the conservatory and gatehouse were filled with gay

Christmas Eve in the Vosges, 1917. Bottow row, left to right: Dick Salinger, Charles Kniseley, Ken Norton, Bob Mungan, the French lieutenant, Alec Standing, *Chef* Keith Vosburg, Jim Ives, and Berry Holbrook. On the steps, behind Norton, are: Witherow, Bob Reaser, Schloss, Ed Paynter, de Vore, Tom Dolan, Dave Henderson, Baum, and Bob Wallace wrappings and ribbons, and "Hey, guys, listen to this." At the dinner we set up a pool of 200 francs ($40), half to be awarded to the receiver of the most incongruous gift, half for the most implausible letter. As the first nephew overseas I was heaped in knitting from my loyal aunts and I won the money with a khaki "cootie-string" of angora wool with tapes and this endearing instruction from Aunt Liz, which I read aloud:

My dear Ted:

I am sending you a cootie-string. We are told that you must tie it around your waist, and that then the little insects will be attracted to the body warmth of the worsted. After that has happened, you go off by yourself and hang it on a tree. I hope it works.

Much love — Aunt Liz

Aunt Emily, knowing my fondness for gingersnaps, had sent me a large round cardboard box full of them; on the trip across it had been squashed by something heavy and damp with the result that all the little snaps were compressed into one flat, brown wheel to which, fortunately, the address and part of the wrapping adhered. When the soiled crust was cut away, it was delicious. I had thought there might be a Christmas letter from Ellen, but none came.

The taste and the emotions of home made us grouse. When *would* this damn war be over? we asked, and got a muddy answer when the division was ordered into the lines on the outskirts of Nancy. We were housed in a cold stone caserne in the town of Custines with latrines out in the raw snowy courtyard. The lieutenant was away and in his place we had a substitute, a mean little shavetail who did not know an automobile from a wheelbarrow and who did not know us. Three of the drivers were down with heavy colds and dysentery, the sickest being the conscientious Newberry Holbrook. The "sub" thought Berry was gold-bricking and kept him on his feet. I looked at him with pity as we squatted together at that freezing latrine. Our corporal, Alec Standing, a Scot with a high temper, could not stand it: he went over the sub's head to our *médecin divisionnaire,* a French colonel, and pled with him to see Holbrook. One look was enough and Berry was whisked to the hospital, where in two days he died from pneumonia and peritonitis. We mourned him as our first loss and were angered at the thought that it might have been prevented. If the sub felt any remorse, he did not show it at the funeral service.

In such cold weather the Algerians would be good only for a short thrust; trouble was, the Germans got wind of it and pulled back; our drum barrage fell on deserted trenches and what we gained were a few hundred yards of mud and the capture of the dazed inmates of the pill-boxes. They looked so young and innocent as they shuffled by, following their sullen, stiff-backed officers — much younger than I felt. We none of us realized till later that their capture was the point of the raid: the interrogation of them might throw light on the timing of the German spring offensive, and the place. Again we were *en repos* in those gloomy barracks at Custines, our only reprieve a few hours in Nancy, that lovely, unscarred capital of Lorraine.

The illusion that we were winning, and it was only a matter of time, was swept away by the German break-through of March 21, 1918. It was rumored that Ludendorff was attacking with fresh divisions released from the Russian Front. He had struck at the weakest link, the hinge of the two armies at St.-Quentin, that tranquillity where we had been last summer; the British Fourth Army had been overrun, the breach became miles wide and through it on the Amiens–St.-Quentin highway, with packs on their backs, the German infantry were driving for Amiens. If they captured the Channel ports Germany could demand a settlement. From what we read in the censored press and in the ominous daily communiqués, and from the despair we saw in the faces of our French friends, we sensed that this was the crisis. At Verdun Pétain had been the man of the hour; now it was Marshal Foch, the supreme commander of the Allies, who had to decide when to close the door and where.

It was certain the Algerians would be needed on the Somme, and we changed our tires, brake bands and spark plugs, anticipating the long run that would take us half the length of France. Vosburg, alas, had been ordered elsewhere, and his unloved substitute had been relieved by the tubby, good-natured Lieutenant William Gwynn, so we were again under a command we respected. We pulled out on April 2 and in the rush Bobby was forgotten. His loss was discovered at our first roadside lunch and the lieutenant loaned Reaser his staff car to make a quick rescue. Bobby was still there, sniffing around, and happy to climb aboard. For twenty-one days we drove in convoy, sleeping on the stretchers in our cars in whatever field was handy, from Lorraine to the Marne, to the Somme, from the snowy mountains to the coastal plains of Picardy, from winter to spring, each driver carrying iron rations in case he had to drop out. Poor Dick, at the tail of the convoy, had somehow acquired a cutting edge on the rim of one of his front wheels; it went undetected and caused him puncture after puncture. The mechanics finally went far back for him, found the trouble, filed it down, put on a new tire, and then drove like mad to catch up. I remember their entry as we were finishing a cold supper of potato salad, *singe* (canned "monkey") and jam; Dick was streaked with mud and draped around

Moving up to the Front, avoiding the shellholes, the Somme, spring, 1918

German prisoners helping to load an ambulance at Petit Blanchy, Somme.
Directed by Corporal Alec Standing

the collar of his sheepskin were four deflated tubes. "Goddamn it . . ." he began.

Some twenty-five miles to the north of Amiens is a village on a ridge known as Villars-Bretoneux and, close by, the Hangard woods. This was where Foch ordered the door to be closed, and he had his shock troops ready. The Foreign Legion had entrenched themselves to the right of the highway, and now our Algerians were coming in to their support; across the road on our left were the 1st and 3d Australian divisions. We relieved the Legion on May 2 and here we held the line for ninety-two days.

The Legion and the Aussies had dug their trenches hurriedly — the French never ceased digging those they might have to fall back to — and at the outset the exposure for everyone was more chancy than at Verdun. There had been no time for deep-timbered *abris;* command posts and our *poste de secours* were stone farmhouses or cellars fortified as swiftly as possible. Our G.B.D. or clearing station was in a walled stone farmhouse at the crossroads of La Petite Blangy. We made camp across the road a couple of hundred yards away, were soon spotted by German observers and shelled. We then moved the big tents and kitchen back two kilometers and laboriously cut out a green cross on the chalky ground; this time we were both shelled and bombed. The Boche controlled the air and would occasionally fly low, strafing or bombing the roads. Finally we took refuge in some woods enclosing a ruined château.

What favored the Allies, although we were not to know it from German sources till after the war, was that the two prongs of the advancing German infantry came to a sudden halt at Albert and Moreuil on March 28. By then the Boche had been fighting and marching without letup; for eight days they had not had their clothes or boots off, and as the resistance dwindled and they came at last to supply dumps and to towns well stocked with food and wine, the two points broke ranks. They looted and they feasted and for hours no command was restored. Regiments that should have marched through lay about in rooms and cellars unfit to fight, and when they resumed the next day, cheered with wine and tasting victory, they ran into machine-gun fire from the railroad embankments and to stiffening resistance further back where the French and British field guns had just had time to move in. Amiens was saved by such a narrow margin.

The Germans would not believe that the door was closed, and as their assault intensified they threw in more gas shells than we had ever run into. These landed not with a "wham!" but a "pfft," and the mustard gas hovered close to the earth, clinging to leaves, bushes, and *blessé* blankets, causing burns in any damp spot, in armpits, crotch, under the knee, and temporary blindness if one had no mask. The Australians, who had cut the isinglass eyes out of their masks in the belief that the nose bag was sufficient protection, took a severe beating. Holding wet bandages to their streaming eyes they were evacuated in two-decker bus loads to Amiens. But the gas was tricky stuff: if the wind changed, the attacker was in as much danger as those he was shooting at. The Aussies despite their losses gave no ground, the Algerians were equally tenacious — and kept digging. We were here to stay.

During the gas attacks all drivers got nicked, but we did wear our masks and except for Jack Clap, who was sent to the hospital, our blisters and coughing were superficial. Dick and I took our regular turns, and there was one run I was not soon to forget. Among the younger French officers was a captain of Zouaves, a gay handsome blond who caught my eye. My French was now good enough for a nodding acquaintance; when *en repos,* strolling in his coat of white goatskin and his blue and scarlet kepi with the gold braid, he reminded me of Hobey Baker. Well, it was my bad luck to be first on call when he was brought in to the *poste,* pale as chalk but conscious, with a terrible wound in the groin. The *médecin* applied fresh bandages and ordered the stretcher into the ambulance immediately, with a priest to sit with him in the back. The captain smiled at me faintly, as he was being loaded and I did not have to be told *"Doucement!"* We crept along in low until the worst was past and I called back to say so as we picked up speed in high. Then we came to a small hill and as we slowed I saw that I would have to shift back into low and did so, with that momentary shudder the Model T would make as the band gripped. I tried to ease it in but the car jerked forward, there was a groan behind me and then silence. He was dead when we reached the hospital. "Was it on the hill?" I asked the *aumônier* and he nodded. Had I killed him? Could that last fateful hemorrhage — if that was what it was — have been avoided? I have redriven that piece of road many times in my dreams and there is no answer.

As the hot weather came on, the Germans accepted our roadblock and turned their attention to the Ypres salient. We had more time to ourselves to think of home and animal comfort. To quench my thirst, which the *pinard* did not do, I brewed some tea, corked it in an empty wine bottle, and hid it to cool in the château cellar. At the back of the château the lawn sloped down to a pond with a sandy bottom. The Aussies, when off duty — big, muscular, carefree men, with a minimum respect for rank — would stroll into camp with a "Hi, digger!", strip and join us in the warm water. One independent type brought a couple of hand grenades with him and after his swim he shouted, "Everybody ashore. Fish for supper!", pulled the pin and tossed the grenade in. There was a geyser and the stunned carp that floated to the surface he scooped ashore with his big hat. He gave us three and they tasted muddy. On another warm night, as we drowsed with the tent flaps up, someone for no good reason took a poll of how many of us were still virgins. I acknowledged that I was, so did Dick and Bob, perhaps a dozen.

There was talk of promotions and citations. Gurnee Barrett, twice decorated, left us for the OTC and a section of his own; Alec Standing became top sergeant; the tall, elegant Don Call and his sidekick, Jim Spaulding, transferred to the Tank Corps. Our new noncoms were two close friends from Ohio State University: Sergeant Jim Fullington with his bushy brows and deep voice, who could make any nasty job acceptable, and his deputy, Corporal Kenneth Norton, who had taken over the paper work after Holbrook's death. Ken had a nose as prominent as mine, and his flat, Ohio drawl was a welcome source of humor. We were now veterans of nearly a year, we had our pecking order, we knew what competent mechanics we had, and we kept Charlie Leonard cooking three weeks out of four because he did it so well.

In midsummer the Algerians launched a counterattack which was not to abate until the Armistice. Back we went, past the German signs and equipment, pinching off a trainload of their rations — potatoes and cabbage, jam that tasted like axle grease, no meat, bread with unbaked sawdust in the center — back across the desolate no man's land of 1916, back to an embankment across the canal from Noyon, where the Boche could tell the color of our eyes and the only protection was what you got lying down. This was the spot I associate with the Croix which eventually came to me. Ken Norton got one, too, for he was in command of that nasty spot, and deserved it more than I: he had to stay there, exposed and under fire, directing traffic, while, once loaded, I could get out of range. The *brancardiers* would shove in the stretcher cases, shout, "*Allez vite!*" and scamper back to their holes in the canal bank. On one run the walking wounded crowded into my front seat and sat on the fenders — I once counted eight aboard, three forward, five in the rear.

One new hazard of the German retreat was that we could no longer count on the regularity of their shelling. As the Boche field guns were forced to take up fresh positions, their salvos became sporadic and unexpected, creating roadblocks at the crossroads. On one trip, my car empty, I got wedged in a line of trucks; the drivers had taken refuge, either in the ditch or under their machines, and as the *arrivés* were uncomfortably close I followed suit and crouched under the tail of my ambulance. As I sat there a jagged shell fragment, the length of my middle finger, struck and burrowed into the hard surface of the road. I reached out for it but it was still too hot to handle; when it had cooled I put it in my pocket. It would probably have penetrated my tin hat; I was thankful it hadn't but wished it had left its mark on the car.

The faster we pursued the Boche the further we drew away from the field hospitals until the gap was as much as 50 kilometers — longer anguish for the wounded, and more tension for the driver who knew that life was seeping away. We would be keyed up until our *blessés* were delivered, then on the solo ride back we fought against the cold night and drowsiness. I would bang my head with my tin hat and try to sing; twice I fell asleep at the wheel; the first time I had draped a blanket over my shoulders, the extra warmth gave me a momentary glimpse of the family in our living room, while, when my eyes closed, the car swerved to the left, narrowly missing a tree, climbed the bank and locked the front wheels in the narrow-gauge track supplying a French battery. The motor was steaming like a spent horse. Now, what the hell? In the morning fog I saw a dim blue figure emerge from an *abri* and take his morning's piss. "*Mon garçon,*" I shouted, "*venez, venez!*" He and his fellow artillerymen, when roused, literally carried the flivver back to the road, and with tire tape I repaired the ruptured rubber hose to the radiator. They gave me the water I needed and I gave them all the cigarettes I had. *En avant!*

The resourceful Bob Reaser, whom I was taking up to a forward *poste,* helped me out of a hot spot on the road to Parpeville, east of St.-Quentin. A Boche plane was overhead dropping bombs and we were in no mood to tarry, when my bands gave out. In total darkness Bob with those artistic fingers unbolted the crankcase and with my wrench tightened the damn bands in half the time it would have taken me. The relief and gratitude I felt as we drove off is still unpaid.

Bob could do wonders. When my wristwatch stopped running I showed it to him. He shook it, opened the cover, and looked grave. "Give you fifteen francs for it," he said and I accepted the offer. He then took it apart, found the trouble, put it together, and when it was keeping time, sold it for forty-five francs to one of the mechanics with a 90-day guarantee. On the 91st day it stopped again, for good. He knew his limitations.

7

Somewhere in all this, without my knowledge, my father submitted a collection of my war letters to the *Atlantic Monthly.* They were courteously rejected (I found the carbon copy in our files years later;

one such as I have written thousands of times on the same stationery). When the note was forwarded to me, I saw in one encouraging sentence a seed of hope. So did Dick. "After a thing like that," he said, "you've got to transfer to Harvard and study English. You'd be a fool not to!"

During the last weeks before the Armistice we moved camp almost every day, getting farther from the railhead. It was a good thing there were few wounded, for our cars were falling apart and the mechanics had all they could do to keep the cripples running. I was hung up for forty-eight hours on my way back to the Front. The town was La Fère with its six blown-up bridges; at the moment I was the only resident, I and my loaf of bread and can of sardines. The car simply stopped there like a mule and refused to start. I cranked and used every blandishment; I thought by this time I knew the Model T inside and out, but what I didn't know was that the tiny spring in my distributor had broken. In this lone state, I wrote letters, cranked repeatedly to make sure, and waited for relief. At night in my blankets I could hear the Annamites who were repairing the road: they would gather around the car, chittering like sparrows, and help themselves to the can of gasoline, strapped to the fender, to replenish their lighters. Only it held water; the extra gas I had taken to bed with me. After the long wait, Ken and the mechanic arrived and in two minutes spotted the trouble. When at last word reached us that the war was over, we were on the Belgian border in Hirson, a village as cold, forlorn, and as far from dancing and champagne as I had been at La Fère.

We had been going on our nerves longer than we realized and the starch went completely out of us at Hirson after the Armistice. In all, we had served 322 days at the Front. We were now living in the circular dormitory of what had been a German officers' club and they may have put the curse on it, for in varying degrees we all came down with the flu. We raised a feeble cheer at the lieutenant's announcement of those who were to receive the Croix de guerre, but this meant little to Brickley, who was dying. We would long remember with what grief his buddy, Paul Culbertson, sprinkled water into his grave. How does one equate such things: our two deaths against the more than 16,000 wounded we transported? Our Croix de guerre for duty performed against the Congressional Medal of Honor awarded to Don Call for bravery "over and above the call of duty" in the tanks? In war one does what one can.

When we had recuperated, as part of the French army of occupation, we began the long, slow drive into Germany, with twenty one-night stands. At Rambervillers in the Vosges on January 31, 1919, we paused and spruced up for a ceremony performed in a vast brick courtyard before a few unimpressed local women: the *médecin divisionnaire* decorated first the lieutenant for the work performed by the section in the past three months, and then twelve of us individually received the Croix de guerre. My pride in this was diminished by sadness: a letter from Mother told me that Ed Bonnell, who had gone into the infantry straight from Exeter, had been killed in October 1918. The Silver Star awarded to him posthumously spoke for courage beyond mine.

On we drove and at Alzey in Hesse I had a surprise. Back home one's twenty-first birthday was an event to be celebrated by the family, the time for a gold watch, or the opening of champagne. But as February 19, 1919, approached and the Algerians continued their slow progress up the Sous Valley, no one in the division knew I was coming of age, and I was not about to tell them. The day itself was dank, overcast, and Charlie Leonard, by good luck, managed to fry up some potatoes to brighten our slumgullion of carrots, beans and the occasional chunk of beef. Afterwards, a group of us, Dick, O'Brien, Vic Baum, Ken Norton, and some others filled a couple of tables in an *estaminet*. We ordered cognac, but before it was served, a purple-eyed prostitute appeared from nowhere, saddled herself in my lap, and began kissing me furiously. I was struggling to dodge — at such close range this was hard to do — when "Happy Birthday to you. Happy Birthday to you. Happy Birthday, dear Teddy . . ." told me that Dick had rigged the whole thing.

Our eventual cantonment was in the hills above Wiesbaden and there, save for an occasional sick call, our occupation was confined to gambling (with IOU's to be paid off on demobilization), fretting for home, and long bull sessions on what we would be doing a year hence. On nights off a party of us in one ambulance would coast down the mountainside into Wiesbaden to enjoy the opera or the wine and dancing at the Rheingold. In the town, work was at a standstill, the populace lived on army rations, and our general had commanded that the pleasures be turned on: the baths, the symphony orchestra, the opera, and the dance halls. In this forced gaiety the masked balls at the Rheingold, with its superb orchestra, brought out attractive German girls, whose escorts, some German veterans, were stiffly on the defense. On a wager I cut in on a pretty blonde with a turned-up nose who was dancing noticeably well with what I took to be a former German officer, judging from his dress trousers. After I faced their surprised and hostile glances, Tillie relented, and finding she could dance just as well with me, joined our table, where the bottle I had won was uncorked and Bob Reaser sketched her profile. From then on,

Ted.

"Tillie."

Tillie and I at Wiesbaden,
sketched by Bob Reaser

I spent every free night in Tillie's company, my high school German improved, and our devotion which could only end in parting was as happy as the moment. It is my experience that sex, abridged or deferred before twenty, can be relished as sweetly later. Up till now I had judged the Germans by what I had read of the Prussians and by the abjectness of the prisoners we had captured. Tillie showed me there was another, more human side. I should probably have enjoyed her more had I not been so sick for home.

As is the way in the army, rumors that we would soon be homeward bound long preceded the event. I had a forty-eight-hour leave in Paris, where I bought some perfume for Tillie and shipped off my belongings at the University Club. Then at last in late March we set out, making our re-entry at Metz, pausing at Paris, and then in the most enormous car-graveyard at Ferrières, parking those doughty, overworked buses in the mud for the last time.

On May 17, 1919, we boarded an army transport bound for Hoboken, Camp Dix, delousing, and discharge. It was a slow tub of 7,000 tons, a banana boat, the *H. R. Mallory* — "Hell Rolling Mallory," we called it — that took twelve days crossing from St.-Nazaire. There were 2,025 of us on a ship built for 45 passengers and crew; we ate in shifts, standing up at high tables, and in between the crap games and chow we stripped to the waist and were tanned by the sun. At the stern end of the boat deck was a compartment holding the shell-shocked cases and they, too, took their sunning, in a wire cage, morose or gesticulating.

At Hoboken those whose parents were in the vicinity were allowed ashore for a reunion. I heard my name read over the intercom, buttoned on my tunic, and ran for the gangway, filed down it, passed by two rows of expectant faces and hurried on with the others to the Red Cross hut. Inside nothing but strangers, each to his own. Disappointed, I turned back to the door and saw coming up the deserted street my parents. It was the first time Mother had held me in two years and she was silent, but Dad behind her was sizing me up. "Boy," he said, "how you've grown! You're as tall as I am. You must have walked right by us."

W's always come at the end of any line and at Camp Dix my impatience seemed unendurable as the clerks hunted for my misplaced discharge. The other members of the section shook my hand, wished me luck; and my intimates counted out my bridge and poker winnings before we said farewell. But the crisp green was poor consolation when I was left by myself. Two hours later that Sunday afternoon I stood on the Trenton platform waiting for the train to take me to Elizabeth.

It was well past seven when my taxi slowed into Clinton Place, where I could see my parents and the aunts and uncles having cocktails on the screened porch. The prodigal returns but once, and this was a heart-warming evening, if occasionally punctured by Uncle Jamie's realism. Uncle Jamie Brewster was in the insurance business and had the reputation of asking the blunt questions when others were hesitant. Going in to dinner he drew me aside. "Ted," he said, "I trust you're keeping up your veterans' insurance: it's the cheapest you'll ever get, and you never know." I assured him I was. Then before we left the table came the big question: what was I going to do next? "Well," I said slowly, "I think I'll go to Harvard and study English." To my Princeton-oriented family this came as a shock, almost as great a shock as if I had taken a hand grenade out of my pocket. Uncle Jamie was the first to rally. "Ned," he said, addressing my father, not me, "I'm not sure I'd let the boy do it. If he goes to Harvard he may get over it, but he'll never be the same!"

III

THE FOLLOWING Monday morning I went to see Maria Davidson. Everyone in town knew the Davidson boys, of whom there were six. Tall, rangy, auburn-haired and freckled, they were born leaders. The four oldest had been in uniform, three of them as pilots, one in the field artillery: Delosier, in naval aviation, had been lost in a submarine patrol over the English Channel; Crawford, the third son, was killed in training at Kelly Field, and Boardley, "Bud" for short, my contemporary who outstripped us all and who had been captain of football at Battin High School, received his wings at Kelly Field just two days after his brother's funeral. Mrs. Davidson, a widow, had mothered the gang who congregated in her famous "mud room" on Saturday mornings: each son had his locker for his athletic equipment and there we came with our baseball gloves or rubber noseguards to emulate the big guys in our pickup games. Now on the bosom of her dress she wore a narrow blue ribbon with two gold stars, and with the humility of one who had come back, I tried to tell her what "Dee" and "Torf" had meant to us who were younger. She took both my hands in hers as I rose to go. "My, how you have grown!" she exclaimed. "More than six inches," I said. "No longer a runt." Her eyes were full of tears.

Walking home I wondered what I had acquired in those twenty-three months away: a speaking knowledge of French, a liking for French wine, confidence in dealing with men and motors, a hunch that Harvard might help me, and a whole heart. Ellen had never written and Dick had cauterized that hurt with irony until it hurt no longer.

The next week I took a longer walk in the Welcome Home Parade. Elizabeth had its own regiment of the National Guard, but for the rest we were casuals wearing the arm patches of every outfit under the sun. Mine was a silver-threaded, defiant chanticleer against a maroon background, and on my sleeve I wore the gold stripes for my service overseas. We forgathered down at Elizabethport, where it appeared that there were three enlisted men who had been decorated — a bos'n with the Navy Cross, and a Marine sergeant and I with the Croix de guerre — and that we were to head the parade, marching behind the first band and directly ahead of the Colors; then came the mounted officers, led by Ned Olmsted, my old scoutmaster, now a brigadier, followed by more music and the ranks on foot. Marching to a good Sousa rhythm gives one a lift. At the outset we passed through a corridor of schoolchildren who sang and threw flowers in our path; we halted to unveil the memorial tablet at City Hall and then on through the center of town where the streets were massed with spectators, bareheaded, cheering and clapping. We were supposed to march eyes front, but the Marine, who was to my left, felt horny. "With this piece of tin," he kept saying to me out of the corner of his mouth, "I can lay any kid I want in this joint," and he pronounced the "oi" as only a Jerseyman can. I had my eyes on the cobblestones, not the girls, and it was a long walk to the Armory, where a luncheon of lobster salad and strawberry ice cream awaited us. I had forgotten that there were still so many horses about.

A soldier home from war, what does he want immediately? I was twenty-one and what I wanted were a hot tub and clean sheets, thin pajamas and the luxury of sleeping late. I wanted home-cooking, the chance to work up a good sweat at tennis followed by cold beer. I wanted leisure to read, white flannels, and some good-looking neckties. I wanted to drive the family car, a gun-metal Moon with a powerful motor, and I, too, wanted girls. Not just any girls.

So did Dick Salinger, who on his discharge had forgotten his threats of getting even with Sergeant Barrett; instead he had posted off to Montreal to get himself engaged to Dorothy Smart, the daughter of a Canadian general, whom he had first courted in France. He had abandoned his dream of playwriting for the surer money in advertising, and expected to get married soon. That was further than I wanted to commit myself, but I was ready for intimacy and freshly aware of how much more the high-breasted, long-legged American beauty appealed to me than those short-waisted, heavy-bosomed types in France.

In this impressionable state I drove the family down to the Monterey Inn in the Blue Ridge, where it was thought the mountain air would be tonic for my baby brother, Hendryk, born while I was overseas. The inn was a rambling wooden structure of three stories, whose long French windows opened on broad verandas and whose table served delicious hot breads, fricasseed chicken, home-churned peach ice cream, and tempting side dishes all set about in small white saucers. It had a history, too, for General Lee's ambulance train had used it as a hospital on the retreat from Gettysburg, leaving the hopeless cases behind when they pressed on to Blue Ridge Summit and the safety of the valley. We were the only Northern family at this old Southern resort, and as Dad came down rarely I was the man of the family. I pulled Tiger, our bulldog, out of fights, turned Mother's music when the ladies asked her to sing in the evening, established our credit at the little country club, where I found good tennis opponents in Tom Gregory and Sugar Voight, and donned my uniform with the other veterans for a memorial service on the Fourth.

I don't think I have ever seen so many pretty girls in so small a community — but then I was vulnerable! One of the first to tease me was Frederica Leser, the daughter of Judge Leser of Baltimore: she was a gay, witty redhead with a charming drawl. "Mr. Weeks," she said when I first cut in on her, "Everyone says you're a divine dancer!" and with that she closed her knees, and threw me out of step for half the length of the floor. I drew my head back, saw that she was laughing — and our friendship was to last for life. In the cottages, on the ridge of the "Summit" there lived a bevy of cousins from Norfolk, Richmond and Baltimore, the granddaughters of Walter S. Taylor, who had served before Appomattox as Lee's adjutant general. Long after the war, General Taylor, then a director of the Norfolk and Western Railroad, had purchased an old tavern, high on the ridge, which he converted into a summer home for his wife and eight children. It burned down, but its successor, the "Big House," — now presided over by Miss Bland, the General's daughter — with its white décor, polished floors, old mahogany and summer flowers everywhere, was easily the most stylish place in the Summit and I thought the same could be said for one of the granddaughters. Cornelia Tomlin was a tall, slender blonde whose figure and whose reserve intrigued me. I hoped to impress her by wearing my old Field Service tunic with white flannels (in fact, I had outgrown every stitch and had only enough cash for a blue serge suit), and perhaps I did, but with the caution of the subdeb she was giving nothing away. She listened as I talked; I tried to guess what went on behind her Virginia accent; we drifted together at the Saturday night dances and on one mountain climb to Key Rock we became so immersed that the rest of the party stole away without our knowing it. A kind of tentative, hands-off attraction.

To my relief, Harvard accepted me as an unclassified student, on probation until I demonstrated which of the upper classes I belonged in. Before departure my father and I had a frank talk about finances.

Mother had told me that on Armistice night he had said to her, "When that damn boy gets back he can have any damn thing he wants!" Now he said he could let me have $1,400 for the first year; it seemed a lot of money and I was sure I could stretch it or add to it if necessary. I was quite conscious of the fact that at twenty-one I was embarking on an expensive course, with five younger brothers and sisters whose school bills Dad also had to meet. The sooner I had my degree the better.

I had never seen Boston and did not see much of it on arrival as I shot through on the subway to what the guard called "Harvard Squaair." My first impression, as I surfaced, was of a drab, congested shopping center, noisy with traffic and, as this was the opening day of college, thronged with students. I got my breakfast at the Waldorf, a white-tiled, one-armed lunch, more remarkable for speed than taste, and left my suitcase in its care until I had found a room. To cross the street and enter the gate into Harvard Yard, a distance of fifty feet, was to forget the clanging trolley cars as one felt the quiet of a timeless place: the architecture was the mix of centuries, but what I would always remember were the old colonial buildings, square-ended, red brick, white trim, once used as a barracks by Washington's Continentals; the wine-glass elms, with their pools of shadow on the sunny turf; and, in the center, the classical granite façade of University Hall, where I had a ten o'clock appointment with Dean Chester Greenough.

Our meeting was brief. It was probably my cockiness as a veteran plus an underlying anxiety which prompted me to say that with my credits from Cornell and my idiomatic French I might take my degree in a year or a year and a half. The Dean punctured that bubble with one sentence. "Mr. Weeks, Harvard College never confers a baccalaureate for one year's work, and besides," he paused to look into a folder, "your performance at Ithaca leaves something to be desired. . . ." I flushed and he relented as he went on to explain that I had passed enough courses in science to satisfy what he called my "distribution," that I was free to concentrate in English and that after the midyear examinations they would assign me to a class, adding, "But I warn you, it may take three years!" I was conceited enough not to believe that.

After I had registered I went out in search of a room. Guided by the price list, I soon found out that I was a late-comer and the few I could afford were up under the eaves, at the end of three or four flights, and not inviting. Claverly and Westmorly, the handsome dormitories on Mt. Auburn Street (known as "the Gold Coast") were way beyond my reach and already full, but the rooming houses at the lower end looked more modest and at No. 30, opposite the newly built Catholic

Church with its handsome bell tower, I found a bedroom–sitting room with an open fire, and on the ground floor! Miss Phelan, bowed with arthritis, was kindly and she was neat. Seeing that I hesitated over the price, she led me upstairs. "Here is the bathroom, and these," opening the door of the suite directly over mine, "are our prize rooms. They belong to Mr. Hillyer, the poet. He teaches in the English Department." Prize rooms they certainly were; hardwood floor, birch logs in the fireplace, chintz curtains at the windows, his bookshelves, his engravings of Queen Elizabeth, and his tea table in the corner. Such civilized comfort decided me and that afternoon I moved in.

There were, as I soon discovered, two outs to Miss Phelan's: the gas jets, which gave off a flickering, uncongenial aura, and the campanile, whose bells, recording every quarter hour, were no comfort to a light sleeper. But the overriding advantage was the presence of Robert Hillyer. He was something of a legend to me, for during the summers at Bay Head I had watched him with the curiosity of a junior; he walked by himself, striding along the beach or at dusk on the board-walk, head thrown back and always alone. The older girls, attracted by his good looks, spoke of him as unapproachable. Now at Cambridge, before I had caught up with Harry Crosby and the others, it was Bob who made me welcome. He said he remembered me with my tennis racket and white tennis hat; we supped together at the Brattle Inn and beginning that evening he casually included me in his circle.

At close range I could appreciate what an animated being he was: he had a delightful sense of the absurd and in memory I see him in laughter, convulsing us as he talked, with his fine brow and high color, the short nose and the mouth softly molded, the full head of dark curls.

Bob was the first man I came to know intimately who lived to write, who put his poetry above everything: above money-making, above sex (he had already been divorced — "There's really not all that mystery to sex," he said mischievously, as we were walking, "only that small crease"), above scholarship — he had no intention of taking a Ph.D., although at Harvard the degree had become almost mandatory for promotion — above alcohol, of which a little was excitable, and more hurt him. We often went for walks, upstream along the river, or down-stream to Boston, to the old bookshops on Cornhill or the Italian restaurants in the North End, talking as fast as we walked. What amazed me was that his reading was behind him; his mind was stored, his bookshelves were packed with the poets he knew and could quote, especially the Elizabethans, and with such sources as Hakluyt's *Voyages,* Malory's *Morte d'Arthur,* and the Icelandic sagas. He seldom

The Harvard student, taken in Miss Phelan's garden

Robert Hillyer reading with his favorite cat, drawn by Beatrice Stevens

bothered with new books except those by his friends. He recited poetry superbly, from the vowel music of Chaucer to the creamy roll of Swinburne. With Miss Amy Lowell he was a favorite despite their differences, for he was an uncompromising traditionalist and she was not; he enjoyed her nine o'clock dinners in Brookline, respected her devotion to Keats, but never took her own verse as seriously as she wished.

Bob's friends, four or five years my senior, as they came and went, seemed to be of the same persuasion: Foster Damon, whose moustache made him look older and who was correcting the proofs of his scholarly work on Blake; Stewart Mitchell, the urbane managing editor of the *Dial*, a literary review; and Ronald Levinson, the classicist. John Dos Passos frequently figured in the conversation; he and Bob had been friends at Harvard; they had been ambulance drivers in the same section, and in their spare time had projected a first novel. "Dos," whom I was to meet later, was still in Europe working on a book about the war. My passport to this circle was the New Jersey applejack with which my father supplied me; and my status, that of spectator, quiet but listening. What it meant was that during the first months of uncertainty I had in Bob an unofficial tutor who took an encouraging interest in me. His enthusiasm, his devotion to letters, formed an incentive greater than I realized.

The only undergraduates I knew were my four friends of the war, Harry Crosby, Phil Shepley, Tote Fearing, and Stu Kaiser (Dick was working in New York), and I wanted to spruce up my rooms before we met. Except for a comfortable Morris chair, an empty bookcase, and a battered desk, the living room was bare. At an auction in a secondhand furniture shop, I bid on a tip-top mahogany table for $9; a Windsor chair for $6, and — my most admired piece — a mahogany cellarette for $14. It stood waist-high, had a movable top, an arm that swung out holding glasses, a drawer for corkscrew and opener, and a cabinet which would hold more liquor than I possessed. Custom-made, said the auctioneer; the owner was so infuriated with Prohibition that he practically gave it away. Dad bought his New Jersey applejack — from the sheriff of Monmouth County! — by the keg and my share was siphoned off in old bottles with gin, vermouth, or whiskey labels. Anyone helping himself in my absence might think he was mixing a cocktail, but what he got was a double portion of applejack, 90 proof. I also found a green and white chintz which Miss Phelan converted into window curtains, a writing board with an adjustable leg to use in the Morris chair and a romantic print of a medieval maiden standing at the foot of a craggy castle gazing longingly out to sea. To me it said the Crusades, and I liked what the wind did to her figure. The reaction of "the Hounds," as we called ourselves that winter, when they saw my surroundings was forthright. "Jesus, what a place to bring a woman!" said Tote. Harry was spellbound by the picture. "I've got to have that print," he said. "Pay you double what you bought it for," and took it away.

Before their coming, Harvard, islanded by the turgid Cambridge traffic, had seemed to me a cold and crowded community where what fun there was went on behind closed doors. There was none of the amiable loafing I associated with Princeton. Students, passing through the Yard, where the seniors had their rooms, were hurrying to lectures or to the Library, and though they might sit next to you in class, you could never be sure they would speak as they passed. The classes were overcrowded with returning veterans like myself, lecture halls were packed, and the Commons, where eating together, however dismal the food, might have broken the ice, had been closed. One ate either in cafeterias or in clubs, and to a newcomer the air of exclusiveness was noticeable. The riverbank was my solace: on fair afternoons I would foot the path along the bank of the Charles watching with a coxswain's eye the laboring efforts of the freshman crews and the more powerful rhythm of the varsity boats. I was now thirty-five pounds too heavy for the stern seat and tiller ropes, and ineligible anyway, but the shouts of the cox and the megaphoned instruction of the coach were familiar.

From such loneliness the Hounds rescued me and helped me find my bearings. They pointed out the clubs, interspersed with the dormitories along Mt. Auburn Street, in particular the Iroquois, to which Harry thought I might be elected "as soon as people get to know you." Having obtained a quick discharge in France, he had reached Cambridge in time to earn his freshman credits in the spring and summer, so he was now a sophomore, Class of 1922, and running on the cross-country team. To get me in circulation he invited me down to his family's country place, The Apple Trees, at Manchester for a debutante ball the last weekend in September. The invitation was a kindness in many ways, for at his mother's suggestion my name went on the list for the Boston parties. It was my first glimpse of New England autumn on the coast and in the crisp air the low sun seemed to gild everything: the blue sea, the white lobster boats, the scarlet and saffron foliage through which we drove.

We were never still, pausing in the lovely house — there were old apple trees in the meadow below it — just long enough to greet his parents and change into white flannels, then three sets of tennis on the grass courts at Essex — we were very even — then back to dress and drink a martini with Steve, Harry's high-strung father, followed by more at the dinner party, and then I was dancing with the girls Harry had grown up with — Betty Beal, his cousin, who remembered me from the *Espagne;* "Sister," a very beautiful blonde with brown eyes; Ella, a challenging gamine. I had snatches of them but not for long, they were too popular. . . . Prohibition had closed the bar; we drank raw liquor out of a flask. I got stuck with a young matron who had been at our dinner, and no one would cut in until Harry rescued me. "Never do that again, you rodent!" he said. After a short night and a huge breakfast the kaleidoscope continued. Tote Fearing picked us up in his Stutz Bearcat, and curving through the pine woods at 50 mph, his long arm grabbed my shoulder as I was about to slide out of the bucket seat into the underbrush. Our first stop was at Charlie's and he was still asleep. We trooped upstairs, Harry shook him, and as we came into focus, he sheepishly drew from beneath his pillow a long, slim, black silk stocking, he wouldn't tell us whose . . . Leaving Charlie to his eggs, we drove on to Larry Foster's; his family's house was perched above a cove, and from a narrow ribbon of turf between the porch and the rocks, Larry was driving golfballs, floaters, into the sea, to be retrieved by the gardener in a rowboat. We made side bets on who could hit the furthest and took turns until it was time for lunch. After thirty hours of this I returned to Miss Phelan's feeling giddy and ready for work.

2

I had studied no English at Cornell, and Harvard insisted that I begin with English A, freshman composition, a course so overcrowded that extra instructors were called in. Mine, in normal circumstance, was the Concord historian Allen French. This was the autumn of the Boston Police Strike, leaving the city open to thugs and thieves, when the governor, Calvin Coolidge, dispatched to Samuel Gompers that famous telegram: "There is no right to strike against the public safety by anybody, anywhere, anytime," which was to elevate him to the vice-presidency, and after Harding's death, to the White House. When Coolidge called out the National Guard to police the city, Mr. French, in his sergeant's stripes, lectured to us, off duty, in khaki.

He liked my short themes on France, gave me ten A's in succession and in November promoted me out of the course, with the advice to save my composition for Dean Briggs's English 5, in which the competition would be keener. When I went to collect my papers at the pigeon-holes in Warren House I stood beside handsome John Gaston, late of the Marines and now a tough varsity end, who was in my section. As he saw me riffle through my succession of A's, he exploded, "What in hell have you been up to?"

What I had been up to was spending an occasional Sunday in Concord with Mr. French, who had the keys to all the old houses and to the lives of those who had lived in them some eighty years earlier: here was the cupola in which Hawthorne wrote *Mosses from an Old Manse* and the ridge leading to the cemetery where he liked to walk; here the Alcott House, where Louisa May and her sisters lived *Little Women;* here the back door of Emerson's house, where on a summer Sunday Henry Thoreau, returning to his hermitage on Walden, would pause to pick up Mrs. Emerson's fresh-baked apple pie and bread; and here was the little bedroom at the head of the stairs, where Henry slept during Emerson's long absence abroad and where propinquity built up in him a mature passion for that same woman, the wife of his best friend. I was beginning to read the Concordians and taking them in by this osmosis made them so much less austere. Emerson occasionally spoke to me in passages like this one from "Behavior," which made me realize that in hot blood he had felt the more-than-casual glance — the eternal question — which passes between a man and an attractive woman:

Eyes are bold as lions, — roving, running, leaping, here and there, far and near. They speak all languages. They wait for no introduction; they are no Englishmen; ask no leave of age or rank; they respect neither poverty nor riches, neither learning nor power, nor virtue, nor sex, but intrude, and come again, and go through and through you, in a moment of time. What inundation of life and thought is discharged from one soul into another, through them! The glance is natural magic. The mysterious communication established across a house between two entire strangers, moves all the springs of wonder. The communication by the glance is in the greatest part not subject to the control of the will.

But for all his insight and perceptive phrases, Emerson with his marble detachment appealed to me as a man much less than the defiant, unorthodox Henry Thoreau. Gradually the truth was seeping through, that measured against Bob Hillyer or Allen French I was unread.

Cambridge that autumn was too exhilarating for self-doubt. There was wine in the air and plenty of bathtub gin available for those who defied Prohibition. The scarcity of good Scotch had not yet reached the point where drinkers were impelled to suck the bottle till it was dry. Some returnees were still in uniform: I saw a very tall figure with bony knees, in the kilt of the Black Watch, enter the portals of the Hasty Pudding Club and was told it was Robert Sherwood, who was writing the new Pudding show. The stadium was packed on Saturday afternoons. The Harvard varsity was scoring an unbeaten season that would end with the victory over Oregon in the Rose Bowl. Every Friday night there were coming-out parties at the Copley-Plaza, and the Boston Symphony on Saturday, if one could stay awake.

To my gratification I was elected to the Iroquois. The food was exceptionally good and there were some members of my age — Bill Dexter, George Reynolds and Henry Guild — with whom it was fun to play bridge after lunch. Harry called it "a waiting club."

"Waiting for what?" I asked.

"Why, to be looked over for a Final Club."

"I thought there was only one, the Porcellian."

"You goat," he said. "Sure the Porc is something special — it's the oldest. But they only take in six or eight. There are other good ones. You'll learn."

What I was learning in English 28 was disturbing. This was a year-long panorama of English literature from Chaucer to Masefield, in which the stars of the department lectured to us on their special fields. They were quite a galaxy: Fritz Robinson, whose bell-like voice brought out the meaning and music of Chaucer, and George Lyman Kittredge, a Harvard character with his white beard, gray flannel suit and bright-blue cravats, who left no doubt that he was an authority on Shakespeare and that we were to esteem them both. John Livingston Lowes expounded Milton in a deep bass, surprising in so small a figure; Charles Townsend Copeland, a great showman, introduced us to Johnson and his circle; Dean Briggs spoke admiringly of Browning; and Bliss Perry, formerly editor of the *Atlantic Monthly,* aroused our sympathy for the Romantic poets. Bliss had a verve rare in academic lecturers, a freshness of delivery that made one think he was saying these things for the first time about Shelley, Keats and Byron. For me it *was* the first time, and while I was impressed and attracted by men I wanted to work with, I was chagrined to discover how little I knew. Ben Lehman, later to be a celebrated figure at Berkeley, was the instructor in charge and near enough to me in age so that I could tell him of my dismay, which came to a head after a laborious assignment on Spenser's *Faerie Queene.* Dean Greenough was right: it would take me years.

The misgiving with which I went home at Christmas I confided only to Mother, but it was deepened by a glimpse I caught of my father at work. The cotton business was in the doldrums and Weeks, Sawyer & Co. was already in distress, with Dad's wealthy partner showing signs of wanting to retire. On a visit to New York I stopped by at his office at 63 Leonard Street. The afternoon was overcast and as I entered, between the tables with their big bolts of cloth, there was an aisle of light leading to the inner office where, at his desk, chin cupped in his hands sat Dad, glowering at a sheet of figures. It was the first time I had ever thought of him as in trouble — he was always so debonair — and I was shocked. How could I go on bleeding him for college? As the oldest of the kids, I had to get off his back and how was this possible in Cambridge? Mother made me promise to stick it out till June, and then, if there seemed no hope, we'd call it quits.

At midyears I was notified that I had been admitted to the Class of 1922 — Harry's class — and eligible to participate in college activities. This was official confirmation that I was still two full years away from a degree — and that to get it I would have to find work. I immediately applied at University Hall and was appointed a monitor, checking the attendance in all my classes, which meant of course that I could take no cuts. But this was chicken feed. I could probably net a couple of hundred by tutoring during the summer but if I was to return in the fall I would have to find some dependable income.

Bob Hillyer had no patience with my misgivings. "Show the best of what you've written to Dean Briggs," he advised, "and if he admits you to English 5, you'll have a great year." He was confident I'd be accepted and I was. Bob had published two books of verse and as I read his *Sonnets and Other Lyrics,* after some shy questioning, I came to appreciate his skill. He was a great technician who took pleasure in the music and variety of traditional verse forms — which was why he crossed swords with Amy Lowell and her free verse. Unused to poetry I found his meaning remote and wanted something more direct and powerful (at a soiree in Boston I had heard Vachel Lindsay recite his long poem "The Congo" and the alliteration and force of his delivery swept me off my feet). But I was learning to differentiate and noticing my concern for style Bob fed me the Elizabethans, especially Christopher Marlowe, and novels like Arthur Machen's *The Hill of Dreams.* As the snow melted we resumed our long walks and on one of them he regaled me with his mischievous account of a recent dinner party at Miss Lowell's. Among the guests was Maxwell Bodenheim, one of whose books had the adventurous title *Naked on Roller Skates.* He arrived at Sevenels in Brookline at 8 P.M., an hour ahead of time, when Miss Lowell's pack of sheep dogs were still on the loose; at his approach they bounced up to him and, terrified, he took refuge behind one of the Chinese urns at the entrance but not before one of the dogs had nipped the seat out of his gray flannels. Hearing the rumpus Miss Lowell threw up a window on the second floor and called down:

"Max, is that you?"

"Yes. Call your dogs off. And come down and sew me up!" Bodenheim saw nothing funny in it, Bob said, and was only soothed when Miss Lowell gave him a check for a new pair of pants.

At Bob's own parties I was often the barkeep. To one of them came Charles Brackett, a senior in the Law School who had just sold two stories to the *Saturday Evening Post,* and who was wondering whether to stay on for his final exams or pull out and write. "To hell with the Law," cried Bob. "Go on with your writing!" He did and eventually became Hollywood's highest-paid screen writer, though the decision was not settled that evening. Foster Damon was present and he and Brackett took an instant dislike to each other. Brackett had been on the Williams fencing team and Foster had fenced at Harvard; now in formal posture, using their right arms as foils they lunged back and forth at each other with Bob in a gale of laughter until the bout crowded into the tea table and one of his precious cups crashed to the floor.

On another evening a minister was present. He was some distance from his flock and whether it was the potency of the liquor or his light head it eventually became apparent that he was so tight we would have to put him up for the night, and what was more embarrassing was his desire to spend it in my bed, with me. Bob eased him down the stairs and left me to settle the matter, which I did by shoving him in the bedroom, having extracted the puff and my wrapper for my Morris chair. It was my first encounter with a homosexual, and I was surprised because my urge, when I had it, was in the other direction. Why did I attract him?

In April I got a break. A fellow veteran, with whom I had struck up an acquaintance in Modern History 1, fell in step with me as we were leaving the New Lecture Hall and suggested that we lunch together. I knew he had been in the artillery and been wounded; what I did not know was that his back had been ruined by a shell that had exploded right on his gun; that he had been going to the veterans' hospital three times a week for treatment, and that to augment his government pension he had been covering Harvard as the correspondent for the Boston *Evening Transcript.* The strain, he said, was just too damn much; he meant to finish out the term and then chuck it. Would I like him to recommend me for his job?

"Sure. How much is it good for?" I asked.

"About seven hundred. But it hurts me to type. You might make more."

"Boy," I said, "I'd love to do it."

There was my backlog. So when Bob told me that he had been

granted a Scandinavian fellowship that would take him to Copenhagen, Oslo, and Stockholm next year and would I like to move up into his room and take care of his things, I could tell him of my good luck, and, yes, now that I had the *Transcript* I could afford to do so. My benefactor had taken me into town to meet his boss, the genial Henry Claus, editor of the education page; he introduced me to the publisher and owner, Mr. Mandell, a sallow man with a squeaky voice; I seemed to pass muster and they arranged to send me the paper so that I could familiarize myself with the coverage.

On every available bulletin board in Cambridge that spring were posters reading

WANTED!

HARVEST HANDS

$7.00 A DAY AND KEEP

FOLLOW THE HARVEST FROM OKLAHOMA TO CANADA.

A bumper crop was evidently expected for a world no longer at war. Those posters started me figuring. By early June I might have just enough money left to get to Kansas City; harvesting from the time I got there to Labor Day, with Sundays and time off between jobs, should yield at least seventy days time seven dollars — more than I could make from tutoring and probably more fun. I applied, as directed, to the Boston Chamber of Commerce, where I was given a slip as flimsy as my qualifications, reading: "To the best of our knowledge the undersigned is entitled to serve as a harvest hand." With that guarantee I moved my belongings up to Bob's room, said farewell to Miss Phelan, and after purchasing my ticket to Kansas City, I had $20 left. I decided not to tell the family till I got there.

3

To one who had never been farther west than Princeton the country — what I saw of it after the sleeper to Chicago, where I changed trains — was wider, flatter and less settled than I had imagined. I was looking for vestiges of the frontier and from the taxi in Kansas City saw what I took to be Indians, though not with feathers. I checked my suitcase at the Muehlebach Hotel, sent the family a postcard telling them what I was up to, and set out for the Chamber of Commerce. The clerk gave a cursory glance at my tissue affidavit and turned to consult a large map. "Let's see," he said, "they're harvesting right now in the vicinity of Colby. If you'll present that slip to the head of the bank there — his name is Lauterbach — he'll tell you what to do."

95

"Colby!" I exclaimed. "But I thought the wheatfields were here."

"Brother," he said kindly, "you've got to go a hundred and sixty-five miles farther west before that piece of paper is worth a nickel."

That took figuring. At the station after I paid my fare to Colby — no Pullman this time — I had exactly $12 left. Back I walked to the hotel, pausing at an army surplus store where I purchased overalls, white socks, blue denims, shoes, cotton gloves, and a wide-brimmed straw hat, also a red bandana and a little canvas *musette* for my extras, such as we used in France. In the men's room of the Muehlebach I changed costume, packed my city clothes and raincoat in the suitcase, checked it and emerged in the regalia of a harvest hand. At least it was what a lot of other people in Kansas City were wearing. Then back I trudged to the depot, where I killed time with the Kansas City *Star*, had a bowl of bean soup for supper, and got aboard the night train with less than a dollar in my pocket. When I stepped down from the day coach at 6 A.M. the next morning into the bright June sunlight, I felt sleepy, hungry and overawed by the big, sunburned men who were everywhere — on the station platform, squatting on the curb, leaning against the shop fronts of the little crossroads village. The bank was not yet open so I inquired the way to Mr. Lauterbach's house, a white-frame dwelling not far up Main Street. Mrs. Lauterbach, smiling and German, answered my knock. She must have seen I was famished, for I was soon seated on the porch step relishing every mouthful of her ham and eggs and fried potatoes, mopped up with a slab of homemade bread. Breakfast can make the day and this one was flavored with kindness. Mr. Lauterbach appeared in his undershirt, dark pants and suspenders, gave me a refill of coffee, and accepted my thanks and my voucher. "Well, son," he said, "you go back and wait there with the others. I expect someone'll sign you up before noon, but if there's any trouble you let me know."

Main Street was in the process of being paved and on the facing curbs with their feet in the dirt sat two long rows of tanned, big-fisted men. I joined the end and listened. Most of them, it seems, had been harvesting for the past fortnight, twenty to twenty-five miles to the south; now as in an enormous checker game they were passing through — jumping over the sections which were presently being harvested to get at the new fields to the north. The look of me in my unstained levis said Easterner to my neighbor even before I opened my mouth and he volunteered a piece of advice. "Out here, Slim, it's best not to carry your money, not even in your socks. Buy an express check. There are too many guys will work you over while you sleep." Coming from one of his heft, quiet spoken, it wasn't kidding. As we were talking, clouds of dust approached on the flat horizon, Fords from which emerged a farm owner or foreman who walked down the line sizing us up. The rugged, competent-looking guys were the first to go and by noon, when I was beginning to wonder how much lunch I could get for a quarter, a car halted before me. "Looking for a job, Slim? Well, climb in."

My boss was Bill Carpenter, a neat tall figure in his thirties. He introduced me to the rest of his crew: next to him in front was Red, a cowhand from Montana; beside me in the rear, a high school boy from Colby and a bulky nondescript called Sandy. Carpenter must have seen at a glance that I was a greenhorn and I liked him for his willingness to gamble. It was ten miles to his place and as we drove past the limitless fields of corn and wheat he explained the setup. He was harvesting two and a half sections (a section is 640 acres): he would drive the reaper; his neighbor, old Pops, would stack, and we four would be paired off in the two header boxes. Dinner would be ready for us as soon as we arrived.

The Carpenter home was a newly painted white-frame farmhouse, shaded by maples and sitting like a lighthouse in a sea of wheat; back of it was a large red barn and behind that a corral for the horses. Jerry, the sturdy kid from the high school, as we stowed our stuff in the haymow where we were to sleep, explained that the Boss was one of three brothers who had married three sisters and that if we were to do their combined cutting it might run more than a couple of weeks. Looked as if I were in luck.

Promptly at one o'clock we trooped into the big kitchen for dinner. Mrs. Carpenter and her girls served — they did not eat till the hands were finished — and what they served was pork and mashed potatoes with gravy, vegetables out of cans, apple pie and buckets of coffee — good chow but heavy in the dry heat of 90 degrees. It struck me as strange that in the midst of all this growing there were no fresh vegetables. There may have been a truck garden somewhere but I never saw it.

That afternoon I got a taste of what was to come when we harnessed up and drove out to the first of the uncut fields. Pops, who at seventy-one was a sinewy, little bald eagle, would do the stacking in the center of the huge rectangle; the horse-drawn reaper as it cut its long swath back and forth would fill up our header box as it traversed the north end, turned and came back to the stack, and there, empty and waiting, would be the second header box ready to take aboard the wheat from the south end. In theory there should be no pause, one box pitchforking its wheat onto the stack while the other was being loaded.

The header box was a light wooden cradle on wheels with a high retaining wall on one side and a very low one on the other, where the incoming wheat was spewed up at us by the canvas elevator on the reaper. Jerry, my partner, drove the team, spacing the load and tamping it down at his end while I followed suit from the stern. There was one difference: he handled the pitchfork as rhythmically as a violin; I handled mine as if it were a snow shovel, digging, jerking and heaving at the in-pouring stream with a tight grip that raised blisters in four hours. A stone jug of cold water lay hidden at Jerry's feet and during the twenty minutes it took us to make our round trip and pitch the wheat off to Pops I could hardly wait to get at it. Under that blazing sun an undershirt was a wet blotter; the sweat ran off you everywhere.

I don't think I have ever lived so long on a hot day as I did on that header box. We awoke at five and caught the horses in the corral, ate a big fried breakfast, and were in the fields by seven. By midmorning, when the sun was rising to 100 degrees, I was burned to a crisp and aware of all the small miseries: the grain sheds tiny arrows which when embedded in one's socks chafe the ankles; the cotton gloves were no comfort to my blisters, which had broken; and the muscles in my back ached. The jug and I were dry when we came in for the noon break, and I had no zest for the heavy food but much for the shade of the barn, against which I lay back, legs outspread. Jerry paced himself and by midafternoon was trying to make up for my ineptness as I flailed away with that devil's instrument. By God's grace the reaper broke down that second day and as the Boss fussed over it I stretched flat out beneath the header box, and my grogginess receded; a light breeze had sprung up as the horses jogged home at five-thirty; my shirt ceased to stick to me, and the cold water I sloshed over my face and throat from the tank in the yard was reviving. After supper the locals took turns wrestling the cowboy, and I, head propped up on my elbow, had just enough juice left to cheer.

The cowboy was a stranger and a challenge but I was a novelty, and almost everything I did beginning with brushing my teeth at dawn ("You do that every day, Slim?") was accepted with curious attention. The third morning the Boss suggested I hitch up the team on our header box. The horses were patient as I backed them in and I did what I'd watched Jerry do but somehow when everything should have been in place, the whole contraption — wagon tongue, leather traces and all — had sunk to the level of the horses' hocks, a bare six inches above the earth. I was puzzling over this, wondering where Jerry was, when there came an explosion of laughter from every crack and cranny where the other members of the crew, joined by Mrs. Carpenter, were watching my performance. "Slim," she said, "you're a caution!"

The reaper broke down again later in the week, giving me a second reprieve, but not before it had become plain as the heat waves that by midafternoon I was dragging my feet, and our header box with Jerry having to do most of the pitching was slowing down the whole operation. Had I been a city cousin, beginning slowly and trying an hour more each day, I might have acquired the rhythm and hardened my sore hands, but there is no place for a weak sister in a twelve-hour day at harvest wages. Saturday afternoon Mr. Carpenter put it more kindly than that when he paid me off with $50, adding that he'd drive me in town early Sunday to pick up my replacement. Pops must have known this was coming, for he invited me over to take supper with his wife and himself that evening. I followed him across country, walking the bed of a dried creek, head down, watching where I was going, and so perfect was the camouflage that I didn't realize until my foot was raised that I was about to tread on a rattler, coiled on a flat rock; horrified I pivoted and then leaped ahead to the old man. He laughed it off: "Probably didn't know you were there; they get drugged with the sun."

Pops presented me to his gentle-faced wife, and before we washed they took me out in back of their small neat farmhouse to show me the sod house which they had shared half a century earlier when they first came to Kansas. We stepped down into that meager little hut, half underground, one room, perhaps twelve feet by twenty, with one window, a floor of hard-packed earth and a stovepipe through the roof. It looked so defenseless compared to the modern dwelling — what could it have been like in winter, with a baby, the lice and the cold? They kept it as a reminder and it was my first authentic glimpse of pioneering. Supper was delicious: the pork was tender and with it we had succotash with fresh corn cut from the cob and then lemon meringue pie with a collar two inches high. As we chattered afterwards, I noticed that they read the *National Geographic* as well as the Kansas City *Star;* they gave me a friendly send-off and I walked home, by road this time, between the fields of wheat, barley and corn, listening in the moonlight as the wind rustled through the corn sheaves with the sound of running water.

Back in Colby on Sunday morning with the $50 in my socks, I took a more inquiring interest in Main Street. The stores were closed but in the window of the Idlewild Café was a sign, DISHWASHER WANTED. As this was one salable asset I had acquired in the army I applied and in no time flat was behind the sink. From the evidence we were serving a hearty breakfast to the men still pouring through town: fried eggs, ham and chips, buckwheat cakes and coffee; or, as I counted, five (granite) plates and one cup to each man. The taps ran cold but I was told that midmorning and afternoon I could bucket in all the hot water I wanted from the bakery next door. Other times when the rush was on I swabbed off the syrup with cold pancakes and used a tin scraper, bent from a can, to assist the cold rinse. It was not a finicky business.

My hours were six to six; my take $2.50 a day, with bed, which I shared with the cook, male, and board. The cook, a morose two-hundred-pounder who was naturally called Heavy, seemed relieved by my presence; he told me confidentially that the Idlewild had been closed for sanitary reasons but that because of the harvest the authorities had allowed it to reopen. The bed we shared was not fresh, the pillow so gray that I spread my one clean handkerchief over the square I hoped to sleep on. What the cook did not disclose was his private addiction to Ed Pinaud's Hair Tonic, which he drank for its alcoholic content, Kansas being bone-dry. It affected his scent but not his disposition.

Eight men and one woman, in turn, washed and talked beside me at the sink during my weeks at the Idlewild. The men, on their way north to new jobs, would pause for a day for the sake of three square meals. The woman and her husband, a Swedish carpenter, were working their way east and while he attended to a small job she really cleaned the place up. After their departure things drifted back to normal. I remembered as a boy how I had envied the shop girls at Huyler's who could help themselves to any candy they wanted in those elegant counters, but there was no such illusion about our food here. One morning just after I'd put the kettle on, Heavy opened the door of the big, old-fashioned icebox, and drew back his head in disgust. "Boy!" he said. "Smell those sausages. They sure won't last." And without a change of expression: "Slim, chalk up on the board 'Special Today — Wheat cakes and Sausage'!"

Occasionally, after hours, I would treat myself to supper at the Colby House up the street. It was our rival; the setup was cleaner than ours and as I had nothing to do with it the food was more appetizing. Afterwards, I'd settle down in the lobby and read my way through the Kansas City *Star*, front page, editorials, sports, book reviews, hog prices and the well-chosen clippings from the national press. It struck me as an uncommonly good newspaper; I had no way of knowing that three years earlier a cub reporter, Ernest Hemingway, had been schooled on their style sheet and was never to forget what Pete Wellington, the assistant city editor, taught him.

When I had saved enough for my fare to New York I wrote Dad a note telling of my impending arrival, and boarded the day train to Kansas City, where at the Muehlebach I resumed my Eastern appearance. I'd been away just over a month and what I brought back were my Levi's, a six-month subscription to the *Star*, to begin in Cambridge, but no savings. It was humiliating to realize that I was so inept physically, yet I seemed to get along with people, dishwashing had healed my hands, and I had the makings of a story which I plotted as the miles clicked by: about old Pops, the sod house, and those limitless fields under the moonlight.

Dad, with whom I lunched in New York, was more concerned about my catching on with the *Transcript* than with my failure in Kansas. The family, as I knew, were again spending the summer in the Blue Ridge, and when I joined them at the Monterey Inn they accepted my explanation, in which I made more of the harvesting than of the sink. During my Western exposure I'd been too bushed to think of girls; now the distance from the inn to the Summit was about four miles and I drove it in the heavy, rattling Moon, as often as Cornelia would permit.

Since last summer Cornelia's slender figure had filled out in the right places; she did her blond hair in a high crest and the pastel shades she dressed in set her off. We took undemonstrative pleasure in being together; we challenged her father and older sister, "Tommy," at tennis, read poetry aloud, drove up to Buena Vista in the moonlight or down the mountain to picnic on the Gettysburg battlefield, parts of which — the two Round Tops, the Devil's Den, the Peach Orchard, Seminary Ridge and the High Water Mark — we would long remember; and at supper parties in Charmian, we danced well and often. I delighted in catching her by surprise, making her laugh, and in all of this, save once, was the unspoken understanding that I should come no closer than when we loitered in the car or in her Gloucester hammock, my arm casually resting on the back of the seat. Why did we hold back? In her case, I think, because she was unsure and wanted no beau to have priority before her debut; in mine, because I was penniless with a long future at Harvard. But desire feeds on denial. For every undergraduate there is a road not taken, a girl not taken, and Cornelia was mine.

4

The Boston *Evening Transcript* in the 1920's was the intellectual leader of the seven Boston dailies. In its typography, its editorials, Washington reports, sports page and book reviews, and particularly in the dramatic and music criticism of H. T. Parker, it was a stylish Boston product with a national reputation out of all proportion to its circulation. It glorified "the Hub," Harvard, the Republican Party, and all worthy charities; it was sustained by pages of financial advertising and by the more fashionable dress shops (and when these disappeared in the Depression, it was dead). Humor was never its strong point. Whether, in the announcement of President Coolidge's austere social program, the *Transcript* actually published the headline "One Ball

Enough for Coolidge," I have never discovered, but it is in character, and possible. This was the institution I was to serve with my second-hand, portable Corona. My sources were the university *Gazette*, the weekly schedule of events, the *Harvard Crimson*, which I soon learned how to digest, the handouts from University Hall, and such stories as I snooped on my own. I had a full column to fill on Wednesdays and Fridays (athletics excluded), and when something special broke like the *Harvard Lampoon's* scurrilous attack on Harold Laski, the English Socialist, then an instructor in government, an attack inspired by Attorney General Palmer's "Red Hunt" and hotly denounced by President Lowell, my copy might make the front page.

The official releases from the President's office were prepared by Frederick Lewis Allen, one of the two secretaries of the Harvard Corporation, a man of utmost charm and perspicacity. Fred, who had served his apprenticeship with the *Atlantic Monthly*, was a few years older than I; with his genial, brisk intelligence, he generated a personal warmth that was to make him later a fine editor of *Harper's Magazine*. It was my luck that he befriended me now, as he would when we became competitors. In his little office beside the furnace in University Hall he prepared mimeographed statements of Harvard's policy — as bland and noncommittal as President A. Lawrence Lowell wished them to be. One of the first things he did was to set me straight on how Harvard was run: the all-powerful, self-perpetuating Corporation of seven men, including the President and Treasurer, were the policy makers, and below them were the thirty members of the Board of Overseers, who were elected by the alumni, and served in an advisory, often rubber-stamp role, with a veto power over appointments, rarely exercised. The faculty had a voice, but under Mr. Lowell it did not have the final say.

In Harvard that autumn of 1921 one had direct access to one's teachers, as I had to Dean Briggs, who did more for my education than any other. I saw him in his course on composition, English 5; again, in a private session once a month at his office in the attic of University Hall, and at the informal evenings in his home, watching Jonathan the cat play with Mrs. Briggs's ball of wool as she knitted. I enjoyed the good talk; I noticed the skill with which the Dean kept the conversation from being monopolized by the graduate students, and was thankful for the cocoa and cookies that were passed around at nine o'clock.

Le Baron Russell Briggs was Dean of the Faculty of Arts and Sciences, which meant that he handled the tough disciplinary problems as well as the academic; he was the moving spirit in the Athletic Committee, which was striving for better relations with Princeton, and the author of a leaflet which was sent to every freshman as a thoughtful introduction

Dean L. B. R. Briggs

to the College. He was a tall, spare man, his coat usually streaked with chalk from his habit of tilting back against the blackboard as he lectured. Of sandy complexion with wispy hair and hooded eyes his face was a map of his emotions, the wrinkles expressing his amusement, his kindliness, or that pensive look when troubled. He spoke with a countryman's creak, like an old farmer from Cape Cod, yet his words were music when he was reading something of mine aloud. That was his practice, to expose without comment the short stories, poems, or essays we had submitted, and let the class judge them in a single-page criticism at the end. There were twenty-two of us who competed. Sex made him blush, and blush he did over the fleshy offerings of my classmate Virgil Thomson.

Good writing cannot be taught but one can learn from example. Over the years the Dean had amassed some common errors and uncommon howlers committed to print by well-known authors; he kept these on cards and would quote a few at the beginning of the class to get us alert. He taught us to be economical in our prose but to keep adding to our vocabulary (I carried slips of paper in my pocket with a new word on one side and its meaning on the reverse, to absorb on the subway). He taught us to shun superlatives and to watch for repetitions; he taught us that there was more muscle in adverbs than in adjectives and that to be precise in our use of pronouns we must never leave the antecedent in doubt. If, in time, I came to have an editor's eye for excesses, bad grammar, purple prose, and lazy writing, it is due to the Dean.

I missed Bob Hillyer, the more so as I was occupying his rooms, surrounded by his books and pictures. Stockholm, he wrote, was a gloomy place in winter with heavy drinking and a shocking number of suicides. A sophomore by the name of Donald Mitchell Oenslager had moved into my old quarters below: he fancied himself a stage designer — today he is one of the best — and hovered over a miniature stage for whose cardboard characters he devised backdrops and props. He was as intent with his doll's house as I with my Corona. Early mornings before classes I was writing my copy for the *Transcript* and after supper, stories and essays for the Dean. I wrote about France, about the wheat fields, the Blue Ridge, and occasionally about a stranger in Boston, and soon learned not to trust what I wrote after 11 P.M. That was when I turned on the required reading, and since I didn't have sense enough to eat a midnight snack, I often lay awake listening to those remorseless chimes from across the street.

The *Harvard Advocate* had announced a short story contest with a first prize of $25 and I won it with a piece I had written for the Dean entitled "Ink." I should have split with Cornelia, for she figured in it at that very still September sunset before we parted, when I broke control and pressing my face against her breast told her what I had been holding back. We were both speechless when I stepped on the starter of the Moon. Actually I never got the prize; they promptly elected me to the editorial board, and no money changed hands.

As a member of the *Advocate* I came into the company of two capable journalists: Roy Larsen, probably the ablest business manager in the magazine's history, who was to prove, next to Henry Luce, the most indispensable executive in the Time-Life empire; and, also in the Class of 1921, John Cowles, whose father published the Des Moines *Register*. John, in his serious way, scored three goals: in his freshman year he was elected to the *Lampoon*, as a sophomore to the *Advocate*, and as a junior to the *Harvard Crimson*, an ambitious prelude to his influential record as president and owner of the Minneapolis *Star-Tribune*. In my year were William Whitman III, the poet; Payson Rowe, whom Larsen wanted to take with him to *Time*; Berry Fleming, the novelist-to-be, and Francis Beidler II of Chicago, who wrote our reviews and cajoled advertisements from the reluctant Cambridge merchants. George Santayana, T. S. Eliot, and Conrad Aiken were numbered among the earlier editors of the *Advocate* and our task, like theirs, was in trying to maintain a sheet perennially short of cash.

At the board meetings, which I enjoyed, the fun was provided by Bill Whitman. Bill was a hulking, good-natured blond with powerful arms and a broad smile; he had rowed in the freshman boat and was slated for the varsity until a heart murmur diverted his energy to print and poetry. He and I liked each other; he was to be the new editor-in-chief, and together we gave time and encouragement to the manuscripts of two promising freshmen: Oliver ("Inky") La Farge, who wrote romantically about the sea, and the other, a square-built upstate New Yorker, Walter D. Edmonds, who was brimming with stories about the Erie Canal. With their help we put out a better than average college monthly; our chief rival was the *Yale Lit*, and though we jibed at the "Browning or Bust" style of their editors — a hierarchy of William Rose and Stephen Vincent Benét, John Farrar, Cyril Hume, and Thornton Wilder — privately we envied the distinction of their damned sheet.

The prize stories had been judged by the trustees of the *Advocate*, one of whom, Holworthy Hall, an author of popular fiction, wrote a most appreciative note on "Ink." With another, Arthur Johnson, I struck up a friendship that began at one of our functions. Arthur, who had published a volume of short stories, was a Boston lawyer whose deep husky voice and good looks commended him to the famous Mrs. Jack Gardner.

We fell to comparing the ostentatious magpie nest which William Randolph Hearst was assembling at San Simeon with Mrs. Gardner's Fenway Court, and it was Arthur, her last and youngest lawyer, who told me about her. He was speaking of the woman we see in Sargent's full-length portrait, which had prompted such scurrilous comments at the Somerset Club that her husband hotly resigned; in her low-cut gown with her rubies, the loop of pearls about her waist, and the triangle formed by her lovely arms and clasped hands, the artist has accentuated her corseted figure. Arthur told me of how she, an outlander from New York, challenged Boston's decorum and disapproval on all sides by the way she was spending her husband's money. He spoke of the years in which she filled warehouses with her treasures, and of how, when the museum was being built, she labored with the painters, who could not produce the sepia tint she wanted for the interior of the courtyard. Finally, in exasperation, she seized a sponge, dipped it in a pot of white, then in red, and flung it high against the wall. "There!" she cried, as the stain began to spread. "Match that!" Of how, at the opening reception, she received at the apex on the second floor, and of how friends and critics alike trooped up to shake her hand. Of how each year she picked two or three attractive Harvard upperclassmen to fill in at her parties ("Boy, I'd like to have been one of them"), demanding unfailing attention; but if they pled another engagement or were flirting elsewhere, they were dismissed. Of how she loved to spring surprises on her guests in the long green-tiled banquet hall: at the conclusion of one party a screen was brought in from the pantry and suddenly, there behind it, softly silhouetted, was Sandow, the strong man, in the buff and flexing his muscles. When the ladies applauded again and again, "Remove the screen," said the hostess. Of how the year the Red Sox won the pennant she appeared at the first Friday afternoon symphony concert with "The Red Sox" lettered in white on a red ribbon in her hair, and with a young debutante in tow. In the intermission the deb remarked on how close it was. "My dear," said Isabella, "when you are a little older you will realize that some of the nicest things in life take place in a close atmosphere." Of how she prized victory and of how year after year at the Cotillion Mrs. Gardner's bouquets were so numerous they overflowed the box where her party assembled and had to be displayed in the adjoining one; when her rival planned to outbid her, Isabella scored her final triumph by appearing with a demure bunch of violets. And now, said Arthur, she lives alone, frail and aging, in a small room on the ground floor of the Court, conserving her income for the endowment of the collection. She has moments of despondency, he added; the other night her housekeeper found her wandering in her nightgown on the second floor, dangerously close to the balcony, and telephoned to him in alarm. He hurried to the Court. "Mrs. Gardner," he said, "you'll get pneumonia! Come to bed!"

"I never in all my life caught cold in a ball dress," she said as they led her away.

It was not Arthur Johnson who presented me to the great lady but the girl I took to the Junior Prom, Margaretta Wood, whose father was Admiral of the First Naval District. When Cornelia turned me down, I invited Meg, who was near and willing, and now she was repaying me. Mrs. Gardner received us in the little room which had become her home, surrounded by her favorite watercolors by Sargent and Dodge McKnight. She reclined on a chaise longue, under an ermine robe. One arm in its lace sleeve gestured us to our chairs. Tea was served, and knowing of her affection for them I spoke of Colonel A. Piatt Andrew and Harry Sleeper and their leadership in the Field Service, but my mind was only half on what I was saying. To my right and close to where she lay stood a tall brass urn, filled to the brim with handwritten letters, elegant stationery of every tint, ripped in half. I could not help reading their salutations — "Dearest Belle" — and my editorial instinct was silently pleading, shouldn't some be saved, surely they had a story to tell? But I lacked the nerve. My one meeting with that gay withered spirit told me with what imperviousness she was discarding the past. It struck me, too, that with all its conservatism Boston still bred its rebels.

5

Junior year is the happiest. I was finding my friends and my confidence and enjoying the independence which is a side effect of what passes for Harvard "indifference." I saw Harry at parties — his mother gave two splendid dinner dances at 95 Beacon Street — but he and I were never in the same courses and now that he was in the A.D. Club, I seldom saw him at lunch. Harry's drinking was causing trouble. He kept in training for the cross-country team until the night before the Yale meet, then went on a bender and the next morning, still hung over, followed the race in a roadster, cheering, "Come on, you poor bastards," at the teammates he should have been laboring with. Afterward in expiation he ran the boards and persuaded me to buy a pair of spikes and longjohns and run with him. Round and round that wooden track we'd thump in the wintry air. "How does he look, Pooch?" Harry would call as we passed Donovan, the track coach, and I'd try harder to stay with him, but by four laps my lungs felt burned out and I'd begin to sag. "Pooch" was noncommittal and after ten days I'd had enough, and enough to know that Harry would have been a good miler had he been willing to train.

My Harvard life would have been much more somber had I not known Elizabeth Councilman. A popular party girl who did not take Society seriously, Lib inherited from her father, a doctor on the staff of the Harvard Medical School, his quizzical attitude toward life, and would, in time, follow him into the medical profession. She was a beautiful dancer and we shared a physical attraction which stopped just short of love. "There is," says Landor, "a middle state between love and friendship more delightful than either but more difficult to remain in," and for a time we were in it. I bless Lib for laughing at my self-concern, for our happy times, and for one of the most surprising compliments I ever received. "You'll age well," she said as we stood on the Pepper Pot Bridge, looking down at the Harvard crews. When I told Lib that I'd been elected treasurer of the Iroquois, she said, "Why do you want to take on that thankless job? You'll simply be a walking reminder of unpaid bills."

The clubs at Harvard were a network, with the Hasty Pudding and Pi Eta (both theatrical) and the Institute of 1770 on the periphery, and the Final Clubs, smaller, more homogeneous units at the center. The latter were recruited, though not exclusively, from the big boarding schools — Groton, St. Mark's, St. Paul's, Andover and Exeter, Milton, St. George's and Middlesex, to name a few. The athletes who went into the A.D. or the Owl had competed against each other in school, the socially elect of Porcellian had been rivals at Newport, Southampton or Bar Harbor, and together they formed a hegemony. Harry had done his best for me. I suspected I was being seriously considered for a Final Club and knew it when those members of the Fly with whom I had least in common began taking me out to golf or the theater as if to overcome their reluctance. The social part of me would have enjoyed belonging, the more reticent literary part was not so sure. I was not elected.

I found what I wanted in the Signet, a literary society of independents and clubmen who were fond of the arts. The Signet was different; it was housed in an early-nineteenth-century building and served meals that did not need to be disguised by tomato catsup, but what made the difference was one's daily affiliation with older men. To the three groups of seven elected from the junior class, the Signet added a fourth seven in the senior year and associate members from the graduate schools, like Wheeler Williams, the sculptor, from Architecture, Philip Barry, also from Yale, now producing his first plays in Professor Baker's workshop; Law School students like Jimmie Douglas and Ferdinand Jelke from Princeton, and what was most important, the Signet retained the loyalty of its members on the faculty. Those professors who attended our luncheons with some regularity were Charles K. Grandgent and E. K. Rand from Classics, Samuel Eliot Morison from History, Kittredge and John Livingston Lowes from English; Louis Allard from French Literature, and with them came the young deans Kenneth Murdock and David Little, and Fred Allen from the President's office. They came expecting to be baited; they were pleased if they got as good as they gave, and their presence added voltage to our table talk and initiation.

One recalls the ambience of good talk, rather than what was said, but I do recall the attitudes: Allard and his watch-charm ally, Yves Buehler, reminding us of how things were done in Paris; "Petty" MacVeagh, always querulous, demanding of anyone why Anglo-Saxon was mandatory for Honors in English; Edgar Scott and David McCord representing the *Lampoon;* Phil Barry and John Mason Brown deriding or applauding the new plays on Broadway; Bill Whitman and I deploring the lack of any lectures on the modern novel. The wit was usually critical. President Lowell attended the annual dinner and read to us each year a letter from a supposed friend on Easter Island, a quaint community where the government seemed as much out of joint as ours at home. It was this affiliation with our elders quite as much as our fondness for contemporaries that made the club in John Mason Brown's words, "Harvard's Conversational Paradise."

Fair, with a Scopas profile, John was the most entertaining of us all; his humor was quick and uninhibited and he emphasized his points with his chin, lifted when he was in earnest, lowered when in doubt, or in smiling acknowledgement that he had been scored on. He had come to Harvard to study English, bringing with him his Kentucky charm and his love for the theater. President Lowell did not approve of the stage — not in a university — and would not permit Professor Baker to build the little theater for which John had helped pledge the funds. This stubborn decision was ultimately to drive Baker to Yale, where a million-dollar playhouse was in readiness, but meantime his "47 Workshop" scintillated in its poverty, and John who, oddly, could not act, immersed himself in the theater, past and present. We loved him, and the Signet table was never happier than when he was at the center of it.

The initiation was formal. I was called for by a senior, in evening dress, who ushered me to the back door and upstairs into a tiny room under the eaves. In the general nervousness I grinned at the other six candidates and at the wallpaper, a sepia montage of the leading Parisian newspapers of the 1890's. Then, one by one, we were summoned down to the library to read and afterwards defend the part we each had written. The neophyte stood facing a high-powered electric bulb in a dazzling white reflector, which shut out any recognition of those in the long, darkened room. The heckling and laughter began before one had finished reading.

At one famous initiation in 1903, Kittredge, who was usually qualified to make a fool out of anyone, asked the neophyte, Harry Dana, confusing him with another candidate whose part had dealt with Lapland, "Mr. Dana, will you tell me the population of Lapland?"

"Exactly three Laps to the mile, sir," came the reply.

I was the first of my seven to speak and after my ordeal had the relief of listening to the others, particularly to Douglas Burden, who had chosen for his part an ancient dilemma: the crusader off to the wars leaving his lady locked in a chastity belt and her page searching high and low for the key. Doug had set this in Chaucerian verse and where the key was found and how the page applied it was a deft teaser that had everyone laughing.

The drinking at the Signet was light — only at initiation and at Strawberry Night, a waltzing party in the ballroom upstairs where the springy floor seemed to sway with the rhythm. But in many clubs the liquor was hard and the drinking heavy. Bathtub or bootleg gin was the staple; the war veterans, especially, resented Prohibition, and when pre-Volstead whiskey was available, they settled down to kill the bottle on the spot, a habit that was to result in deplorable casualties from speeding cars on narrow roads.

President Eliot had thrown out the fraternities but clubs had grown up in their place without giving the college "the solidarity" which President Lowell asked for in his inaugural address. Actually they accommodated less than fifty percent of the undergraduates. No one in Cambridge raised the question, as did Richard Cleveland at Princeton, whether such a division was healthy. Cleveland was a campus leader who could have had any bid he wanted; instead he chose to buck the system on the principle that there should be clubs enough for all who wanted them, or none. It was a bold position and I wondered at the time if he was right. (I now think he was.) Shortly after my graduation two leading members of the Harvard Student Council, Edward C. Aswell and Walter D. Edmonds, prompted a committee which brought in a plan to subdivide the Harvard community into houses: self-contained units of several hundred students and instructors. This blueprint was in President Lowell's desk drawer when an unexpected visitor, Edward Harkness, a wealthy Yale alumnus, made the offer (earlier declined by his alma mater) which converted the projection into reality. Someone has said that the ideal society is one in which the dividing line between the exclusive and the excluded is relatively painless. I think it is in

Cambridge today. As the houses developed, the clubs declined, in number and influence. Those that survive are largely supported by their alumni; the Signet is one of them, the first to elect black students and the first to elect women.

6

At the time I am speaking of, my conscience was more troubled by my relations to the church than to the clubs I belonged to. Students begin questioning the beliefs they have inherited when they run into a lot of people who don't believe the same thing. Harvard was nonsectarian and the preacher in residence, Dr. Edward C. Moore, was dullness personified, but the more forceful visitors in the pulpit like Dean Washburn of St. Paul's Cathedral, or Dean Charles R. Brown of the Yale Divinity School, aroused my respect for the intellectual leadership of the Protestant Church, even though listening to them did not quell my doubts about the Creed which as an Episcopalian I had recited unquestioningly until the war. Seeing so much of death in France had left me skeptical about "the resurrection of the body and the life everlasting" and now passages in *The Golden Bough* by Sir James Frazer made me question whether Christian missionaries were right in trying to impose their faith upon people as devout and as ancient as the Buddhists or the Polynesians. I was not happy in such skepticism for I am by temperament a believer: I believed that man was possessed of an inner spirit and that on rare occasions I had felt its uplift. Religious habits have a lasting grip: despite the hiatus in France I still felt guilty if I did not attend service on the Sabbath and just as I had once prayed for protection while under shellfire so I now prayed for repentance, as in the Lord's Prayer and for betterment, as in my own words I asked for "strength, simplicity and sincerity."

To keep doubts at bay I taught Sunday School at Trinity Church in Boston, the high-vaulted Romanesque beauty which Phillips Brooks had made famous in his day and to which Henry Sherrill was soon to bring his magnetic leadership. I was put in charge of a disorderly class of older boys, five from the Back Bay, six from the South End, who had been venting their class warfare in threats, sly kicks and hard pinches. I calmed the feud by announcing in the fall that each boy with perfect attendance would be given a scout knife in June and that if they paid attention and did the lesson quietly I would show them my war photographs in the closing minutes. This may not have been Christianity but it worked and I was complimented by Dr. Van Etten, the head of the school.

During my boyhood it was Harvey Officer — Father Officer, O.H.C. —

who first aroused my curiosity about the monastic life. With Father Huntington and Father Sill he was one of the three who founded the Order of the Holy Cross, an Episcopalian brotherhood whose monastery, built by Ralph Adams Cram, stood high on the west bank of the Hudson below Poughkeepsie. Father Huntington became its superior, Father Sill retained his association but departed the cloister to become the first headmaster of Kent School, and Father Officer, on countless missions to lethargic parishes, proved himself an impassioned revivalist. He was an old friend of the family, who had known him before he became a celibate, and when he was in our part of the world we went to hear him and brought him home to supper. Off duty he was a gifted musician and great fun. I see him on a Sunday evening after having preached to an overflowing congregation in Newark, a dark-browed vibrant figure in his brown habit, seated at Mother's piano, head thrown back, singing "Go Down to Kew in Lilac Time," with Tiger, our bulldog, to whose collar I had attached Harvey's cincture, howling an accompaniment.

Father Officer came back into my mind now because of the reading I was doing for Professor Charles Haskins's course, "The Thought and Expression of the Middle Ages." Our text was the ardent, scholarly two volumes by Henry Osborn Taylor, *The Mediaeval Mind,* with its glorification of the monastery as an intellectual stronghold. Toward the end of volume one a chapter entitled "The Spotted Reality" recounted the temptations and backsliding of monks and nuns. Harvey, alas, to the dismay of my elders, had deserted his stronghold, breaking his vows to marry an old flame in Paris, and when last heard from was supporting himself as a music teacher. This did not lessen my desire to experience, even as an outsider, the privacy and mysticism of the cell and when at midyears my examinations fell on the first four days and I was left with more than a week's freedom, I agreed to companion my friend, the Reverend S. Taggert Steele, on a retreat at the Order of the Holy Cross.

Tag had been intensely attracted to the Order, had passed through his novitiate, and then after soul-searching — and greatly to the relief of his family — had decided that his place was in a parish. He was now serving as one of the assistants at Old Trinity in lower New York and on the train trip up the Hudson he instructed me in the essential precautions: the order of silence prevailed throughout, and only the brother in charge of hospitality would speak to us on our arrival; I would be expected to attend the morning prayers and vespers, and since this was Lent, the Stations of the Cross; the library was a good one and there we would read after supper.

The place was deep in snow the evening of our arrival: I remember the shaft of light on the snowbanks as we entered the Gothic portal and how, after a cordial welcome, I was shown to the stone-cold cell of St. Louis with its Hudson's Bay cot, single chair, washstand, and chamber pot, and left to myself. In the black dawn the following morning there came a knock on the door and a voice proclaimed, "Brother, the day is with us." Not yet, I thought, and snuggled deeper into my cocoon of warmth. The statement was repeated and to show I was awake, I raised and dropped one of my shoes. A third time the knock came and emphatically, "Brother, the day is with us!"

"Okay," I said, "wait till I get my pants on." There was a snort, and the brother's heels retreated up the corridor. My response should have been, "Praise be to God."

We processioned to our meals in the order of our coming, with Father Huntington at the head, and were then read aloud to, which distracted me from my plate; as I have always been a slow eater, by the time I was ready for a second helping the platter was bare. We were being fed on twenty-seven cents a day, mostly it seemed to me on rice and stewed tomatoes; and after two days I was burping with a Lenten hunger. In the entry was a row of hooks holding the winter cloaks and labeled for each member of the Order; the cloak still hanging under Father Officer's name was a sad reminder. Here in the afternoon we donned overshoes and with Robin Hood staff trudged out in the snow, down the slope of the garden and vineyards to the glorious river. Now the brothers were free to talk, and much of what they said centered on disillusion with secular life, the rejections which had led some of them to their vow of chastity, what they had experienced at their mission in Liberia and, from one who chose to confide in me, the question of who would succeed the Father Superior.

If visions are in part the result of ascetic fasting I was well conditioned for one, but none came. In an earlier incarnation I might have been a monk but now in my self-communion in the library, where I was reading the life of St. Francis of Assisi, and in my cell, I realized that my place, too, was in a parish — I wanted more of life, not less; I enjoyed working with people, and I was fond of women.

The steak dinner to which I treated Tag on our return to Manhattan had a filling, mundane taste.

7

In February when the *Advocate* elected its new board, Bill Whitman became president, Payson Rowe, the treasurer, and I the secretary. Despite Roy Larsen's success in inducing freshmen to subscribe and Harvard Square to advertise, our cash balance was dwindling and our first priority was to get out a special issue which would start us off in

the black. The *Harvard Lampoon* at the time of the Versailles Conference had made money with an amusing parody of the Boston *Evening
Transcript*. We believed we could go them one better if we found the
right target and it didn't take much searching to convince us that the
Atlantic Monthly, Boston's literary darling, was our victim.

Before we could make fun of the *Atlantic* we had to familiarize ourselves with it — some of us for the first time. After a fairly intensive
study of the issues for 1920, it was apparent that the editor, Ellery
Sedgwick, had an addiction for certain writers: he favored, perhaps for
family reasons, the flowery, oh so English, short stories of Anne Douglas
Sedgwick, the florid botanical exploits of William Beebe, and the
"psychographs," the *Atlantic's* term for slightly Freudian portraits by
Gamaliel Bradford. These targets were definite and their style and
their names lent themselves to mockery: our lead story was "June
Dandelions" by "Anne Dugan Sandwitch," followed by an article "Pe-
tunia the Precocious" by "William Boobie," and, a little further down,
the "Portrait of Julia Stowe Fuller" by "Gabriel Breadfruit." Sedgwick
had shown a dilated interest in prison conditions, especially when reported by female inmates, and this prompted a paper in which I had
a hand: "Prison Cruelty" by "O. Joy Anlove."

Our ten-strike, written by Stedman Buttrick, was a take-off of a Sedgwick discovery which in our eyes was a fake: "The Diary of Opal
Whiteley," purported to be the confidings of a young woman, allegedly
the illegitimate daughter of a French nobleman, who had been brought
up in the American Northwest and whose diary had been torn to shreds
by an angry foster-mother. Sedgwick had imported her into Boston and
paid her to piece together the scraps in her trunk on a tambour frame (a
lawyer friend of mine estimated it must have taken the stepmother a
week of angry tearing to fill that trunk). The reconstructed diary, in
which Opal bestowed loving nicknames on all the creatures in her
neighborhood, was then serialized. No one could have invented a better
subject for derision; we called our version "The Story of Isette, the Journal of a Misunderstanding Heart" by "Isette Likely." The *Atlantic* poems
we reprinted much as they had appeared, simply altering the last few
lines for the lubricous effect we were after. With the buff cover of the
Atlantic superimposed on our regular logotype we were ready for
business.

Our first test was to show the result to Mr. Sedgwick. Bill Whitman
called for an appointment and he and I went in town to the office on
Arlington Street. We introduced ourselves, I laid an advance copy before
him, and we sat in trepidation, watching that ruddy face and those expressive dark eyes for a sign. He spent some time on the cover, digesting

the titles, and emitting a series of short barks: "Oh — oh — oh!" Then he turned in to the text with a grin, and we relaxed. We left with an order for a thousand copies, which he intended to distribute to the schools and colleges using the *Atlantic* in classwork. The first printing sold out, the last copies in New York fetching a dollar apiece; we put out a second edition (never done before or since) and might have needed a third had not a printers' strike cut short our bonanza. The sale and the ads procured by Payson and Frank Beidler put us — temporarily — on Easy Street.

My essays and short stories, and my criticism in class earned the A the Dean gave me; certainly I worked harder for it than for any other course in college. His comments had a Yankee flavor: "Too much porch for the meeting house," he wrote on one of my stories in which there was too much description, too little action. Each of us went to our conferences with him wanting to be assured that we somehow had a future in literature but that was a question I could never put in words. Instead he showed a concern for the present: observing the dark circles under my eyes he asked if I had insomnia and when I said yes, prescribed a glass of milk and ten minutes of James Thomson's *The Seasons* before I turned out the light — it was, he declared, the dullest long poem in the English language, sure to put anyone to sleep! Observing also that I was hard up, he suggested that I try out for the Boylston Prize in Public Speaking and when I trotted out my old warhorse and won the $30 with my recitation of Kipling's "Wee Willie Winkie," he seemed pleased. I don't know how many young men he carried on his conscience — the undergraduates in trouble, the would-be writers, the graduate students struggling for the Ph.D., the impoverished — fifty, maybe, yet he seemed to know what each needed and when to push. It was the Dean who told me I had been recommended for a scholarship in memory of William Meeker, which was designated for one showing ability in English. My prize, my checks from the *Transcript*, my monitoring, and the free lunches I earned as treasurer of the Iroquois grossed over $1,200 and with the scholarship I would do better than ever as a senior.

For the summer I filled out an application as a companion-tutor: the going rate, I was told, was $150 a month, and I asked for double that on the ground that I was a veteran "competent to teach French and English; a tested driver who could play tennis and golf, swim, and ride horseback." The last was an exaggeration: every horse I ever sat on knew who was in control the moment I put foot in stirrup. But audacity pays; I was signed on for the summer, and as my employer had a stable of horses I thought it might be wise to get in the saddle. The captain of the Harvard ROTC unit told me to tip the sergeant at the Commonwealth Avenue Armory $10 and he'd let me ride any horse on the picket line I wanted. In those days a bridle path led from the Armory through the back part of Brookline to the Jamaica Pond Parkway, and each afternoon for two weeks I followed the sergeant as he headed a detachment out for exercise. When I was on a docile beast I came back with him; when I rode one of those tough bastards who had worked the bit up into his teeth I came on ahead. In a hurry. With no pause for traffic lights, trolleys, cars or pedestrians we would hurtle home, shoot across Commonwealth Avenue and up to the picket line, where he stopped and I, free of the stirrups, shot over his head.

In the final exams that followed this equestrianism, I won honors but my butt was so sore it took a lot of squirming in those wooden seats to do it.

IV

A TUTOR, like a piano teacher, is paid by the lesson and leaves when his instruction is over. A companion-tutor, more like a governess, lives with the family and is paid by the month; he is included in most of their doings and teaching is only one of his duties. I had been engaged, after a single interview, by some wealthy New Yorkers who were spending the summer at Long Point on Lake Chautauqua and who had picked me, so I was told, because of my high price and the kind things Eric McCouch, a Law School student, had said about me.

My employer was Charles D. Wetmore, partner of the New York architectural firm, Warren & Wetmore, whose more conspicuous achievements were the Grand Central Station on Forty-second Street, the Ritz-Carlton and Vanderbilt hotels, and the restoration of the Louvain Cathedral in Belgium. In Cambridge I learned what little I could about him: that he had entered Harvard, Class of 1889, from upstate New York, with money and ability; when he was not invited to join the Porcellian, he became one of the founders of the Fly Club and had designed the clubhouse as well as one of the luxurious dormitories on the "Gold Coast." But instead of taking his degree in architecture he had graduated from the Law School *cum laude,* and only when deafness cut short his promising career as a trial lawyer did he revert to his first love, building.

On a Saturday morning, in mid-June, I stepped down from the Pullman at Jamestown, New York. There to greet me were Bill Wetmore, who was to be my charge, and Colby, the family chauffeur, a round apple of a man who stowed my golf clubs and suitcase in the tonneau of the royal-blue Pierce Arrow and strapped my steamer trunk on the rack. Together they made room for me on the front seat. Bill at fourteen was a good-looking youngster, a curly-headed blond, short but well built; voice was changing, and at the moment, he was snuffling with hay fever. "I get the damn thing when I ride," he said, a remark which gave me momentary relief — maybe we wouldn't do too much of it.

As we drove north along the lake shore, I pumped them discreetly. Lake Chautauqua — I could see that it was wide with heavily wooded banks — was eighteen miles long, very deep, full of muskellunge and bass. They had a cabin cruiser for picnics and fishing, and four horses. "I ride Wildfire," said the boy. "He's a Morgan and runs like a bat out of hell." And they played a lot of tennis. "I like it better than golf. Hope you're not too good for me." Now we were turning off the highway, through deep woods, down over the trolley tracks with its warning light, and so into the grounds of Long Point with its green and white stable and paddock, the clay court, surrounded by hollyhocks, a gazebo with white fantailed pigeons on the roof, and the green lawn under giant oaks sloping down to the dock. Coming to welcome me were Mr. and Mrs. Wetmore, and from the family resemblance, what must be Bill's older sister, a plumpish girl whose teeth were being straightened.

Charles Wetmore looked very sure of himself and very stylish. His complexion was florid (so, I was to learn, was his temper), his fine white hair was brushed back above his ears and with his high-ridged aristocratic nose, thin lips and light blue eyes he was clearly one who enjoyed authority. Mrs. Wetmore, in a creamy negligee trimmed with maribou — they'd been having a late breakfast — led me into the living room of the main house, a plaster and wood chalet which he had designed and she had decorated — my first impression was of white lace, green jade, gay chintz, flowers everywhere — and she won my heart when she ordered hot coffee for me and confided that Bill (who had disappeared), on learning that I was twenty-three and still unmarried, had remarked that I must be "either a saint or a devil." She added, "He's wild to play tennis with you, so get into your things as soon as you can." To the rear of the main house, opening on a boardwalk, were a row of spacious wooden-frame tents, four on either side, each with its separate bathroom; their entrances were screened from the lake by a high hedge of rose of Sharon, and in my quarters between the tents of Bill and his sister my things were ready for me to unpack.

It was lucky for me that the first inspection took place on the tennis court where I was confident of my credentials: in my white flannels and white buckskin tennis shoes with red soles, newly purchased from Brooks Brothers, I gave Bill a good workout — his reflexes were quick but in our rally it was clear that he relied too much on his chop stroke, so

Charles D. Wetmore

Mrs. Wetmore at Long Point

The château, the gardens, and the tents

I took the net and fed to his forehand drive. Then we played a couple of sets, giving him a lead of thirty points a game, and he made a match of it, darting from one side of the court to the other to keep the ball in play. Mr. and Mrs. Wetmore, watching from the garden bench, were obviously pleased. I passed a second test that evening after dinner when in a cleared space in the living room, Frederica Watriss, "Fritzy" as they called her, danced alternately with the tutor and her brother, with Mrs. Wetmore nodding her head in time with the Victrola.

The shyness on both sides began to rub off in the days that followed as I succumbed to the charm of my hostess. I realized that there had been a divorce, a thing I had never encountered at close quarters before, and it took time and discretion for me to fit the pieces together. Mrs. Wetmore alluded affectionately to Philadelphia: there, as Sara Thomson, and a beauty, she had made her debut, handsomely attended by her older brothers. Her marriage to Frederic Watriss swept her into the gaiety of Long Island, where their two daughters and Bill were born (Martha, the eldest, was now in Europe). Then ensued her divorce and her subsequent marriage to Charles Wetmore, who had adopted Bill. In a time when divorce was rare enough to be an embarrassment, Long Point was her refuge from the past.

And what a secluded and lovely spot it was. The point extended for a quarter of a mile south into the lake forming, on either side, a cove with a sandy beach; it was thick with shrubs and oaks, some, like those which overshadowed the house, more than a century old. Here, as a boy, Charlie Wetmore had come on picnics and it had been his dream to own the place and transform the refreshment stand into a chalet open to the breeze and the sun, as, with its tall French windows it certainly was. The living room was Mrs. Wetmore's creation: her laces she had collected in Europe and some were museum pieces; the wicker sofas on either side of the fireplace, with their bright chintz of roses and dark green leaves, the gay rugs, the lace lampshades, the jade bowls and the ornaments on the grand piano, all radiated color even on the gloomiest days.

This was my first experience of working in the lap of luxury and I found it as delicious as the Rhine wine cup which William Bollard, Mr. Wetmore's valet and steward, served with fresh mint at Sunday dinner. Bollard did the ordering, scouring the countryside for fresh peas, sweet corn, cantaloupe, and raspberries, and what delicacies he could not find were sent up from Shaffer's Market in New York. A short, bandy-legged Cockney, whose bald head and crooked nose made him the image of Mr. Punch, he had been trained in England in the Prince of Wales' set, before Mr. Wetmore, then a bachelor, brought him to

New York. On me Bollard cast a suspicious eye — he wasn't at all sure that I belonged.

Bill was to enter St. Mark's in the fall and it was my mission to remedy his deficiencies in French and English. Our lessons began in my tent on Monday morning, when we went right to work planning his theme "My Summer at the Lake," which I was sure he would be asked to write in the examination. He would write and I correct a paragraph; when it sounded natural he had to memorize it. After that French verbs and a mild dose of translation. Looking up from the drill I spotted Fritzy, feigning to read, sitting within earshot on the other side of the hedge. I suspected that she had been posted there to report, and as she had already passed her way into Bryn Mawr at the age of sixteen, it was just as well to have her approval.

Mr. Wetmore had left instructions with Bollard that we were to ride on Wednesday. For this ordeal I planned to wear my Field Service tunic and I had had buckskin knee patches sewn to my old whipcord breeches, to suggest my familiarity with the saddle. Bollard had the horses ready. Bill took Wildfire; Fritzy one of the brown mares, and I went up on the big black stallion Mr. Wetmore customarily rode. Bollard, not unimpressed with my ribbons, did not accompany us, for which I was thankful.

We went off at a restrained trot through the woods and we slowed to a walk across the highway, but once we hit the dusty roads that wound uphill and down through that lush countryside, the Morgan challenged the black in what was evidently a standing duel, the black responded, and we lit out in a wild canter that left Fritzy in our dust. For a quarter of a mile the Morgan led, then with no spurring from me the big black drew away and away. He had plenty of power, and after a while I thought it best to aim him at a red barn at the side of the road, whose door was closed. He accepted the halt and we stood there panting until the cavalcade came up. There was no recurrence on the home trip; none, that is, until we had stepped carefully across the highway and into our shady drive. Again despite my tight rein, the black broke away; he thundered through the woods, across the tracks — fortunately no trolley was in sight — and came into the paddock in a lather.

"You shouldn't work him so hard!" protested Bollard as I dismounted.

"It's the other way around," I replied, just as the kids rode in. Bill's nose and eyes were streaming and although I sympathized with him I couldn't feel too sorry.

We lived unto ourselves during the week, tennis and swimming every morning, golf after luncheon at one of the nine-hole courses along the lake, paddling and fishing in the canoe, a picnic supper (with hot dishes) at the tip of the point at sunset. But all went into high gear Friday nights, when Mr. Wetmore arrived with his guests, De Coursey Fales or Andy Dana or Mrs. Wetmore's brothers, Beau and George Thomson. Mr. Wetmore had taken up golf late in life, played a short game, remarkably steady for a left-hander, and won nearly every match with the handicaps he had demanded over martinis the evening before. Only Fritzy, with the long swing and pivot Jim Barnes had taught her at Virginia Hot Springs, was wise to him and beat him regularly. The matches would be played with special caddies at the Chautauqua links across the lake, and then on our return, bundled up in sweaters and polo coats, we'd sit out under the oaks watching the sunset on the water and drinking French 75's before we took hot baths. For those who don't know, a 75 is served — and replenished — in a tall glass: to two inches of gin you add three drops of grenadine and a wedge of ice, and fill 'er up with champagne. Recommended both for victory and the sting of defeat.

Instead of guests, on the Friday before the Fourth of July, "Unkie," as the kids called him, brought an immense carton of fireworks, Roman candles, pinwheels, rockets and bombs — the biggest and best. Bill and I spent the afternoon fixing pinwheels to trees with the highest branches and building the launching pad for the rockets on the beach, aimed for the open sky. We, Unkie included, could hardly wait for dark to fall. But Mrs. Wetmore was apprehensive from the start; the wind from the south did not abate at sundown and her timidity increased when Fritzy, casually handling her first Roman candle, set it off wrong side up and the angry pellets narrowly missed her legs. Mr. Wetmore calmed things down and there were no mishaps when the pinwheels started whirling. To the south of us at Bemus Point rockets arched into the dark sky with the showers of colored stars slowly drifting down toward the water. We felt it was our turn to respond. When our first bomb erupted at the end of the dock, a glorious cerise thunderbolt emitting bang! after bang! of blue and golden stars, Mrs. Wetmore screamed, I thought from excitement, though I could see that the final shower was blown in toward the trees. Bill had a salvo of rockets ready, and now as we touched the smoking punk to the fuse, the first two went up the troughs with a great whoosh! Up and up until, meeting the full force of the wind, they curved back and with a distant pfft! the stars like sparks showered over our heads, over the tents. "Charlie, you damn fool," screamed Mrs. Wetmore. "Stop it! You'll set the place on fire. Stop it!" And in her high-heeled mules she stamped toward the cartons of treasure. "Stop it, all of you! The wind's too dangerous. Come in by the fire and we'll have some family poker."

Chastened, our ammunition not half spent, we obeyed, carrying the armory back to the porch, the phalanx of rockets in one box, the squat, beautiful bombs in the other. It had been chilly out there and the open fire in the living room felt good. I busied myself unfolding the green baize table, Fritzy began sorting the chips, Bill, all hopes dashed, was gazing into space, Mr. Wetmore, in his favorite chair, had turned to the financial pages of the New York *Times*. Still muttering, still berating "Charlie," Mrs. Wetmore bustled in through the screen door with something in her arms and before anyone could stop her she emptied the open carton of bombs into the fireplace. There was a second, maybe three, before anything happened. Then the first bolt shot out past the *Times,* close enough for Mr. Wetmore to hear it; he took a quick look, "Good for you, Mama," he said as he sprang up to move her out of range, and to me, "Get Bollard. And a bucket of water. Hurry!" Colby and Bollard came on the run, and two pails of water from the kitchen dampened the fire and fireworks. The room was dense with smoke and ashes but there was surprisingly little damage thanks to Bill, who with a mop had jammed the fire screen against the hearth until I came back with the water. The first bolts that escaped had not set fire to the lace on the mantle or the lampshades and were suppressed by wet mops. When the night watchman appeared he was told to be on the lookout for embers and we went to bed. Bill had the last word. "Gee, Ma," he said, "it's lucky you didn't pick the rockets."

The lessons went smoothly because there could be no tennis until they were done. Paragraph by paragraph I had Bill describe our life at Long Point, including the mishaps, the fireworks and the picnic when Mrs. Wetmore insisted that he and I paddle her to the point in the canoe. She was tall and fairly stout but we finally got her settled in the center with a backrest and shoved off. The trouble was in getting her out: Bill had pulled the bow up on the sand but as she got to her feet she lost her balance. "Don't do —— " I started to say but never finished as we rolled over in six inches of water. This provided a paragraph Bill had no trouble memorizing. It was going to be a good theme.

He was an attractive youngster: he had no aptitude for books but was a natural athlete, quick and strong — he drove a golf ball further than I did — and when we threw long passes with the football I could see that he was fast and shifty on his feet. Bill's friend Henry Reeder came to visit and the three of us became absorbed in painting and rigging a model sloop. The jibs and mainsail, hauled up and down through miniature blocks, were sewn by Ellie, Mrs. Wetmore's personal maid; somehow a needle got misplaced in my tent, and when I stepped on it, it broke off in the ball of my foot. The doctor cauterized the spot but said not to worry, it would work its way through in the course of the summer, which it did.

Mrs. Wetmore was concerned and as solace she ordered for me from Charvet's a lavender shirt with French cuffs and pleated bosom. My admiration of her had grown: her abundant fair hair, parted in the middle, her lovely skin, her gay, deep-throated laugh; there were moments — sometimes at the piano — when I saw the charm of the girl emerge from middle age. She loved music and on fair nights we boated up to Chautauqua and dropped anchor to listen to the symphony concert across the water. She also came out in the motorboat to watch Bill and me make our initial performance on the surfboard; when towed at accelerating speed the performer, with a guide rope to steady himself, would crouch, then stand erect, on the stern of the board much as our water skiers do today. The trouble was that my blue flannel trunks with white canvas belt were a little large and in the speed of the operation, before I could get to my feet, were washed away.

"Get up! Get up!" came the cries from the launch.

"I've lost my trunks," I shouted back, which of course they couldn't hear.

Finally they got the idea and towed me back to our cove, where I swam ashore and they went looking for my bottom half.

Sundays were festive, and as the summer ripened, the chalet with its gay green-and-white awning over the porch and the flower beds with their delphinium, lilies, and the masses of white Killarney roses was an inviting spot. The Pierce Arrow was sent in to Jamestown to fetch Aunt Gertrude; and Mr. Wetmore's boyhood friends, the Sheldons, the Griffins and the Bradshaws, came to Long Point by boat or car for the midday feast. Aunt Gertrude made a ceremony of kissing Bill, to his disgust.

"What's your trouble? Cracked lips?" I asked him one Sunday as I caught him smearing his mouth with cold cream.

"Scaring off Aunt Gertrude."

For those repasts Bollard outdid himself. I declined the cocktails since they made me sleepy, but delighted in what followed: the entree of fresh, boned muskellunge with cucumber salad, the main course of capon or a rib roast with Yorkshire pudding, succotash of the tenderest corn and baby limas, the palate freshened by the Rhine wine cup, and dessert — raspberry mousse or Bill's favorite, baked Alaska — still to come. Such food tranquilized the party and it was a shock to all when on one occasion two of the fantails — we could hear the idiot birds strutting on the roof — lost their balance and tumbled down the chimney, landing in the unlit fireplace, where they were promptly set on by Sport, Fritzy's Sealyham terrier. The fuss and feathers of the untanglement was soothed by a second helping all around.

Bill and I would ask to be excused after coffee and would keep out of sight, for brandy led to stories about Jamestown, and to reminiscences, with gales of laughter, and to singing; and on it would go until it was time for a fresh round of cocktails and a light supper. After one of these marathons, when dark had fallen and the last guest departed, an altercation was heard at the end of the dock. There in a rowboat was Mr. Wetmore striving to row down the lake for a nightcap with the Sheldons, and Bollard, none too sober himself, holding the painter while he tried to dissuade the oarsman — neither apparently aware that the rope was securely lashed to the dock.

Mrs. Wetmore's pet, a bright-hued, vile-tempered macaw named Bonita, was jealous of Mr. Wetmore and would scuttle after his bare feet trying to impale him with her beak. On Sunday nights "Charlie" was tipsy vulnerable, and once when she had impaled his slipper he flung himself backward on the bed, waving his leg aloft, thrashing at the bird with a newspaper and shouting for help.

Never had I encountered such a combination of intelligence, will power and contentiousness as when I tried to hold my end up against Mr. Wetmore. He was an implacable Republican and twitted me about my admiration for Woodrow Wilson; he had no use for contemporary writing, seldom read a book, was a stickler for facts, and depending on how sure he was, would bet me five or ten dollars that I was wrong. Since he scorned a hearing aid our arguments were carried on at the top of the voice. On anything to do with building or finance he was sharp as a buzz saw. (The only bet I recall winning was when he disputed my claim that there were at least a dozen houses in Boston with private ballrooms. I named them.) To him a challenge was the quickest way to test a man, and he once admitted that his closest friends were those he had angered at the outset. He had achieved renown in his field without a degree in architecture and he scorned *Who's Who* and jury awards — "Who are they to judge me?" was his attitude. We had our differences but he was passionately devoted to Harvard and that was our common ground. He believed that the presidency of Harvard was second only to the presidency of the United States, and while still a student he invested part of his inheritance in a Pool, known in time as the Harvard Riverside Associates, which disputed the judgment of President Eliot. The president believed that the future expansion of the university would be to the north, in the direction of Arlington and away from the Charles River, a tidal stream whose banks were odiferous when the water was low, and the new buildings of the Eliot administration were all planted to the north of the Yard. The Pool believed that when the river was dammed its banks would become immensely desirable for the college and that the time to purchase the river shanties and real estate was now when people were looking the other way. Which the members of the Pool did, quietly. Their expectations were completely realized in 1910, when the river, dammed at the Boston outlet, formed the Basin and Esplanade, and when the Pool's holdings on the Cambridge side (site of the future Harvard Houses) were turned over to the incoming president, A. Lawrence Lowell, at cost.

At the beginning of summer my letters to Blue Ridge put out feelers for at least a week's reunion with Cornelia there or anywhere before I had to return to Cambridge. She wrote that a group of them were going to the Poconos and to come along. But in early September as the twilight shortened and the wind across the lake turned chill, something I hadn't counted on occurred. The three of us — Fritzy, Bill and I — were sitting on the steps of the boardwalk as the sun set and every leaf of the old oaks seemed outlined in gold. My days were numbered and I'd been ruminating about the Dean and my hope that my love for writing could carry me somewhere and Fritzy said, "I believe it will," in such a way that I turned and looked at her. Had propinquity done something to us, to me and to this kid Bill and I had been teasing all summer about her "cootie cages," those buns covering her ears which she stuffed with false hair, bobby pins and scraps of lace, or so we said; the girl the family was sending to Foxcroft for a year because they thought she was too young for Bryn Mawr? She and I rose at six the next morning and met at the Crow's Nest, the summerhouse that faced away from the camp. I had my answer and we were back in our tents before breakfast — a disturbing one, for companion-tutors are not supposed to court the daughter of the house. But what about my distant love? Had luxury as well as propinquity turned my head?

A letter from Bill Whitman in Canada put the kibosh on my Blue Ridge reunion anyway; he and his father were on their way to the woods and would I mind coming to Cambridge a week early to set up our first issue of the *Advocate?* On my departure Mrs. Wetmore gave me a small gold matchbox engraved with my initials, Bill gave me his promise to pass those exams, Fritzy the pressure of her fingers and a grin.

Fritzy with her cootie cages

2

Summer for indulgence but give me a New England autumn for enterprise. By senior year the fortunate have secured their place in college; the fever of competition even among athletes has been tempered
and one is beginning to look beyond the present to the future. I was
two years older than many of my classmates and had already made one
false start, but Harvard, Hillyer, and the Dean had shown me where I
wanted to go though not how to get there. That Fritzy and I were attracted to each other was an unexpected complication, but it would be
years before I could get married and she was too young to be engaged.
We had reached an understanding and in tender moments I wanted it
to deepen.

In the 1920's a Harvard class spent freshman year in dormitories
down by the river and as seniors moved in a body to the Yard. Bill
Whitman and I, who were rooming together, had drawn a suite on the
top floor of Hollis Hall, one of the oldest of the pre-Revolution buildings. In the week before college opened I moved up my furniture from
Miss Phelan's, laid in a supply of logs for our fireplace, telephoned
Henry Claus of the *Transcript* that I'd bring in my first column for the
Friday edition and, alone in the *Advocate*'s office, began laying out our
first issue for the fall. Bill had warned me that I'd have to write or dig
for most of the contents and he was correct: the filing cabinet, which
was our treasury, contained the wet-drip poems we hadn't wanted to
publish the previous spring and one short story by Robert H. Chambers,
'23, which to judge from its professional touches had probably been
doctored by his father, a highly paid writer of popular fiction. I needed
help and found it in the Dunster House Book Shop, where the proprietor and Pierre La Rose, a literary poseur, both promised to give me
book reviews. At dusk after an early supper I sauntered along Brattle
Street, past the old houses whose lighted windows gave me a glimpse
of Cambridge elegance, and so home and up three flights to the window
seat where I sat gazing into the elms as my thoughts wavered between
a love letter and an unwritten editorial for the *Advocate*. Fritzy's letters from Foxcroft told of Miss Charlotte, the sparky headmistress, of
her own horse, Ginger, and of how she had been thrown at one of the
jumps, landed on her head and suffered a mild concussion which was
not discovered until she tried to take a shower while still in her riding
clothes.

Our rooms in Hollis held vestiges of the long past in addition to the
window seat: the coil of thick rope hanging in the corner which would
be our fire escape, the fireplace which would soon have its winter bed

of ashes, the wooden shutters on which former occupants had carved their initials, and, framed in black, the long list of those who had preceded us, and their class. It delighted me that Ralph Waldo Emerson and Henry Thoreau had lived in Hollis, and had sat, perhaps, by this same window. This embrasure with its view through the trees of the classic white façade of University Hall was never to lose its spell, not even in winter when a tipsy classmate, returning late from town, would shout to the moon, "Oh, Rinehart. Stick your head out!" There was no Rinehart now but there once had been, so lonely and neglected that he used to bay that way under his own window. Now, at the cry a dozen sills would be thrown up and the call would be flung back and forth until things sobered down.

With Bill Whitman's return, not only 30 Hollis but the whole Yard came to life with the tramp on the stairs as our neighbors moved in: across the hall was Berry Fleming, a Southerner who wrote and painted, and who, despite his craving for privacy, I came to know well; and next to him Robert Hopkins, the youngest-looking and certainly the most modest man in the class. Sharing quarters with Bill was delightfull. Big, gay, and generous, fond of women and needing them, Bill with his broad smile stands in memory always in sunlight, one who would never be more sure of himself as in that year on the threshold. I envied his talent; he found his inspiration in Yeats and Synge, and his verse came in spurts whether he was writing a piece for the *Advocate*, or the Class Poem, or that longer effort that won him the Lloyd McKim Garrison Prize.

From the beginning of our friendship Mrs. Whitman and Bill's older sister Peg had made me welcome at their comfortable home on Commonwealth Avenue, at Thanksgiving and for Sunday supper when it was a joy to taste good food and share in the family banter. Bill's father — "Phyd," as children called him — was a yachtsman, and that fall his forty-foot yawl *The Spalpeen*, was still at her mooring in Marblehead when on an autumn Saturday after the football game, Bill drove his brother Loring and me down for an overnight cruise. The supper Tom, the steward, cooked for us as we left the harbor was a glory: venison steaks which "Phyd" had brought down from New Brunswick, hashed-brown potatoes, and homemade apple pie, preceded by real House of Lords martinis. I remember every detail, even the brown gravy flecked with currant jelly, for I reviewed them at length, so to speak, the following morning when in an oily swell we anchored for some deep-sea fishing and I was too sick to care whether I had a boot or a cod at the end of my line. What I best remember after that supper was the cool breeze on my forehead as we came within hail of the Eastern Yacht Club.

It was not until my last year that I realized how generous a part Boston played in a Harvard education. My love of music, fostered by my mother, drew me in town on Sunday afternoons to listen to a string quartet or a soloist at Fenway Court, and afterwards to visit with my favorite paintings: the Vermeer, Rembrandt's "Self-portrait," Titian's "Rape of Europa," and the Sargent watercolors. The members of the course in musical appreciation, conducted by Edward Ballantine, I discovered, had access to a block of six seats at the Saturday night concerts of the Boston Symphony; they were rarely asked for so, as the monitor of the course, I formed the habit of requisitioning two of them whenever I was free.

I was seeing less of Harry Crosby, as he had taken a war degree and had withdrawn from college to work in a State Street bank, a job he loathed. "I recite *The Rubáiyát* as I jog across the Common to State Street," he told me, "the only bright spot in my day." He had fallen hard for the appealing Polly Peabody, who was seeking a divorce from her alcoholic husband and was then living in New York City. Harry commuted for love every weekend, to his parents' dismay, and when I chanced to draw the berth opposite him on one return trip on the Owl, he gave me a snort from his flask, loosened his tie, removed his shoes and coat, and slid into the blankets the same impulsive, unorthodox kid. Steve, his father, did everything to break up the affair, promising Harry a new car if he'd drop it; after one angry exchange Harry came out to spend a few nights on our spare cot in Hollis.

Below us in Hollis and in the same entry lived "Copey," Charles Townsend Copeland, a short wisp of a man with a domed forehead and a precise and resonant voice. Copey's lectures on Johnson and his circle were packed, he taught English composition to a select few, which had included Walter Lippmann and John Reed, but he educated others by the cultivation of his reading aloud: in his lamp-lit, book-lined living room with its colorful memorabilia, on Tuesday evenings he read from the Bible, Shakespeare, John Donne, or Robert Benchley, to as many students as could hunker down on the floor, and quite often he had a guest, seated across the table from him — William Morton Prince, the psychologist; Maxwell Perkins, the editor; or Heywood Broun, the columnist — who would talk and answer questions.

I attended regularly through the year and I got into the habit of auditing other courses than those in which I was enrolled. I heard Irving Babbitt lecture on comparative literature — erudite, full of brilliant quotations, but not my meat; I appeared so repeatedly in B. A. G. Fuller's course on Plato that he said he'd give me a C if I took the exam (which I didn't); and I listened to Bliss Perry on the critical essay, more pedestrian than his Poets. What stayed with me was the work I did for John Livingston Lowes. In class he read to us chapters from the book he was writing on Coleridge, *The Road to Xanadu,* and out of class, by implication, we were supposed to make the same approach in a thesis about a poet of our choosing. When I called on Mr. Lowes I proposed to write about "The Love Influence on the Poetry of Byron and Keats."

"Isn't that rather a large subject?" he asked without a smile.

"Yes," I said, "I guess it is. Which one would you prefer?"

"Keats."

John Keats is above all a young man's poet. I read his poems in conjunction with his letters, those valiant, eloquent, self-mocking letters in which he is confident of his power, so generous to his brothers and his friends, so unaware of his courage. I read the great books about him — Severn and Sydney Colvin — and the yardstick was always there: how little I had done compared with how much he had accomplished at my age. My Riverside edition of Keats's *Poems and Letters* by the marginal comments shows the lines and the truths I took to heart. This was the academic reward one does not lose.

I was so preoccupied, writing, listening, and assimilating, that I heard only faintly, as if from offstage, the news of larger consequence. But one thing did impress me: Woodrow Wilson, touring the country to win support for the League of Nations, had been felled by a stroke in California, and returned to the capital in pitiable condition. One of my boyhood idols, he appealed to me as an architect of a peaceful world; I took his defeat personally, becoming more firmly committed to the Democratic Party and contemptuous of the scandals that soon came to light in the Harding administration. It was something of a shock when I heard Professor Robert Howard Lord critically discuss the Treaty of Versailles. I knew he had served as one of our consultants, but now he seemed deeply depressed, and crossing the Yard afterwards, I fell in step with him and asked why. "Danzig!" he exclaimed. "The Danzig Corridor undoes all we had hoped for — I am deeply dismayed by that partition. It can only make trouble for the future." Danzig? Poland? How will they affect the United States? were the questions I wondered but did not ask.

A senior's concern was not so much for the body politic but for his own immediate destination. Long gone were the days when half of Harvard's first ten went into the ministry. The graduate schools — Law, Medicine, and Business Administration — now took their pick, the athletes drifted into stockbroking, where their reputations opened doors for their salesmanship, and individuals as uncertain as Robert Benchley, the humorist, tried and lost a dozen jobs before finding the right one.

But all that lay months ahead. The immediate objective in the fall of 1921 was to beat Yale. Fritzy's family did not approve of her leaving Foxcroft, so I invited a Radcliffe senior, Marian Vaillant, whose brother George, a classmate and a delightfully ironic cuss, was already engrossed in archaeology. We had an early buffet luncheon together at the family home on Commonwealth Avenue and over drinks Mr. Vaillant Senior began to reminisce. "In my day," he mused, "it used to be said that when a man escorted a girl to the Yale Game it meant that —— "

"Pa," said George, cutting in, "watch your language."

The walk from the Square to Soldiers Field was quick with expectancy, the band was serenading the Elis as we climbed to our seats and we just had time to wrap the blanket about our feet before the kickoff. The teams were very even, victory could have gone either way, it was a battle of captains, each a natural leader. Keith Kane, the Harvard captain, soon to be elected First Marshal of my class, had been a star all the way: as a sophomore he had played tackle in the Rose Bowl; now with his speed downfield and his courage he was a standout. Malcolm Aldrich, the Yale captain, was their best passer and ball carrier, and a danger every time he got the ball. In the second half, with Harvard leading 7 to 3, Aldrich led the Yale attack deep into Harvard territory, and on an end run to his right, he suddenly spun and shot a long pass to his left end, hightailing it toward the goal line. Vinton Chapin, Harvard's fastest sprinter, was defending that zone; he intercepted the pass and had a clear field down the sideline, but Aldrich, cutting across on the diagonal, nailed him at midfield in a tackle so desperate it flattened them both. It was the turning point and Harvard held on to win, but there wasn't a man in the stadium who didn't admire Aldrich for his spunk in defeat.

After the celebration, 30 Hollis was noticeably low in liquor, and on an impulse Bill and I drove out toward Concord in search of cider. We found better than that, for on the road to Stow was a large red barn, set about with jugs and festooned with a sign reading, "Champagne Cider! Come in and try it." It was delicious, cold, bubbles and all, and the proprietor explained how to make it: hang yeast and some raisins inside the jug in this small cotton sack; cork the jug tightly, keep it at an even temperature for a month, and the cider will become sparkling. We purchased two full jugs and the sacks and, back in Hollis, once they were corked and the yeast beginning to work we had a disposal problem. For one jug we appropriated an empty closet of Bob Hopkins' in exchange for a share in the wine; he protested that a hot-water pipe ran through it and he didn't like champagne anyway, but it was empty and available. The other jug we placed in the bottom of our coldest closet, first removing the clothing. . . .

A. Lawrence Lowell, Harvard's autocratic president, was a familiar

A. Lawrence Lowell, President of Harvard, 1909–1933

sight to everyone living in the Yard. He was in his mid-sixties when I first knew him, a trim figure with the broad brow, fine eyes and square-cut features of the Lowells. When he wished to see members of the faculty he called at their office or home ("It's easier to leave that way," he once explained). As Elliott Perkins, one of the house masters, has said, "Harvard was still small enough, but only just, to be run as a one-man show. . . . He seemed to be everywhere, to know everything, to have his finger in every pie, and as far as the college was concerned, he was and he did." Mr. Lowell's attire few others could have worn with such style: the morning coat, striped trousers and starched white shirt with turn-down collar were set off by the Harvard touch: a crimson or red necktie and tan shoes. The best miler in college in his day, he still liked to exercise those long legs: at track meets, which he never missed, he would be all over the inner circle of the Stadium, watching and congratulating. He walked everywhere, accompanied by his fawn-colored spaniel, Phantom — to the practice fields, to see the buildings in progress, to appraise the old elms in the Yard — with a "Good morning, gentlemen," to us as we passed. From my window seat I could see him return to University Hall, leaping up the steps two at a time, coattails flying.

He and Mrs. Lowell had no children and it was to Harvard that he gave of his wealth, anonymously. He was the greatest builder in the university's history but his deeper concern was to raise the academic standards of the college ("We teach everything, you can learn any-thing," was Samuel Eliot Morison's characterization of the elective system under President Eliot), and to bring "young men of promise of every kind from every part of the country" to live together in a society whose divisions would not be "on the basis of wealth." This he did and it has not changed.

Thirty days is a long time for the thirsty to wait. After ten had passed we bought a length of rubber tubing, uncorked and tasted the brew in Hoppy's closet. We could hear the fermentation working before we began to suck and that raised our hopes, but what came through the tube was warm and not something you wanted to retain in the back of your mouth. Premature of course. So we wedged the cork back, not tightly enough perhaps, for two nights later Hoppy came running in to say that the cork had been blown out and would we for God's sake clean up the stinking mess! It was too sticky to be removed with toilet paper, and judging from the odor the taste had not improved. Evidently the place had been too damned hot, we thought as we scrubbed.

There was a sudden cold snap in early December, which gave Bill a bright idea: if we hung our surviving jug outside and some of the liquid froze, the alcoholic content of the inner portion would certainly rise. We lashed it securely to the sill and for three days rejoiced as the temperature hovered below freezing. Then at dusk came a knock on the door and when I opened it there stood the President.

"Gentlemen," he said as he entered, "I wish you'd tell me what you have in that suspicious-looking jug hanging from your window."

"We think it's champagne cider, sir," said Bill. "Won't you sit down?"

"Might I taste it?"

"Well . . ." I began hesitantly.

"Only a little," said Mr. Lowell.

We hauled in the jug, placed it on the floor, and tugged out the cork. Bill had produced the tubing. "Wouldn't it be better . . ." he began, but the President had already cleaned off one end of the rubber with his linen handkerchief and was preparing to inhale. After a brief pull his expression was not reassuring. He wiped his lips.

"You might stomach it," he said, "but I think it better for the entry if you flushed it down the toilet."

As his footsteps receded down the stairs, Bill looked at me, tears of suppressed laughter in his eyes. "What a man!" he said. "What a reprimand!"

As it happened, President Lowell at this time had got himself involved in a situation the seriousness of which it was certainly not Freddy Allen's duty to reveal to me. A rumor circulated that the President, noticing the increase of Jewish students in the college, was thinking of setting a quota. The reporter for the Hearst paper was suspicious and was sure that Lowell would have to deny the charge at the State House, but when I questioned Fred he said to forget it, nothing to it, the talk would all blow over in no time. The incident is not alluded to in Lowell's biography and it was not until years later that I learned the truth. The President had indeed proposed that a quota be set, and I believe that 15 percent was the figure he had in mind, the same quota the Czars permitted in the Russian universities. The proposal created a storm in the governing boards. Mr. Lowell's predecessor, Charles William Eliot, then in his eighties, was called in to intervene, and no formal action was taken. At the time, the rumor created much anguish among Jewish students, and it is not to my credit as a reporter that I was unaware of their suffering and its cause.

3

Commencement was only two months away and the decision of what to do afterwards, hard enough for me who knew the direction I wanted to take, must have been harder still for those who heard no calling. I was determined to go on with books, and a year of graduate study abroad seemed possible: the American Field Service was awarding scholarships for study in France, with first preference for veteran drivers — why not a year at the Sorbonne? At this point Dean Briggs intervened: the Fiske Scholarship, he told me, had recently been established at Trinity College, Cambridge, in memory of Charles Fiske, Jr., of the Class of 1919, who had been killed in action, and he would be glad to recommend me for it if I was interested. (When would I ever again have the chance to live for a year in England?) Yes, I said without hesitation, I'd be most grateful. On June 1 came the formal notification from Dean Chester Greenough, the same man who had warned me that I would not be able to get my degree "in a year or a year and a half," stating that my nomination had been approved by the Corporation, and that Mr. Fiske would like to talk to me.

What a prospect! I wrote Dad, playing up the honor, not the cash, and sent a gay wire to Fritzy. True, in English money the grant looked meager (it is three times larger today): the college fees and my room were covered, but there was only a paltry amount for food and clearly I should have to earn enough to keep myself afloat during the five-week vacations at Christmas and before the spring term. I went in town to the *Transcript* to tell Mr. Claus my news and to ask if I might continue to write for the paper "on spec," sending him short articles which, if he liked, he could pass on to the editor of the Saturday edition. And would he object if I sent a carbon copy to my home-town paper, the Elizabeth *Daily Journal?* Perfectly all right, he agreed, and why not try the New York *Evening Post,* which regularly printed descriptive pieces? Such became my syndicate.

Charles Fiske, with his brown Vandyke and kindly dark eyes, was one of those elders who enjoyed the young; he had obviously been wrapped up in his only son, whom I had never known. He told me how young Charlie had spent a year at Trinity before entering Harvard and what it had meant to him. The letters from Charlie's English friends at the Front had impelled him to enlist early. "Now, I have a special assignment for you," said Mr. Fiske. "I want you to write an account of your year in Cambridge which I can show to the Scholars who come after you, and I'm giving you a camera so that you can illustrate it."

The project took on more color at his supper table that evening, when his frail wife and two attractive daughters, Nella and Roxanna, whom I had met before, chimed in with their remembrances and suggestions. They had visited Cambridge; the lovable and eccentric traits of the dons who had taken an interest in Charlie were described, and I was promised letters of introduction. As I returned to the Yard, I was flooded with a feeling of gratitude toward those Boston families who had befriended me and added such warmth to my Harvard education — the Crosbys, the Whitmans, and now the Fiskes.

Spring in New England does not come slowly as in New Jersey. The magnolias are the messenger and when the windy April rains bring on a warm spell in which the tulips, then the azaleas and lilacs explode, the effect is enough to bring anyone's romance to a head. Bill had been out on a good many evenings and I kept hearing more about Marjorie Warren, "Pargie," as he called her, whose mother was a celebrated beauty and local poet, and whose father, Fiske Warren, was an anomaly, the controlling director of the S. D. Warren Paper Company and an ardent disciple of Henry George (Warren financed in the village of Harvard, Massachusetts, a vast enclave, run on the Single Tax principle). I might have guessed when one midnight Bill came back from town carrying in a brown paper parcel a quart of Johnnie Walker. As he told me his news, he turned pink and seemed to glow with happiness. He and Pargie were engaged. He uncorked the Scotch and poured us each a long one. The wedding would take place soon after Commencement, and they wanted me to be an usher. After their honeymoon they'd sail for England where he'd work through the winter in the London office of Curtis Brown, the literary agents. This had been arranged by Houghton Mifflin, whose editorial staff he would join in the spring. "Finish that off and we'll have another. . . ."

The moonlight beckoned us out into the deserted Yard and we strolled over to Sever Hall where we sat on the steps. I recall the emotion and a little of what Bill said: "I'm really very fond of you, Ted. . . . This has been a great year we've had together. . . . Pargie likes you. . . . We'll both be in England and you must spend Christmas with us in London. . . . I'm beginning to feel blissfully tired." And with that he tilted over on his side on the bottom step, propping up his head on his elbow and continuing to talk. "Come on to bed," I said. "This stone is getting cold."

After that things came with a rush. The class elected its permanent officers, headed by Keith Kane as our First Marshal, Bill was our Poet, and I missed being Class Orator by a single vote. We were the first to take the General Examinations and the last to enjoy a Senior Picnic, which fell on the hottest day in June. According to tradition we all donned white overalls on which friends wrote obscene sentiments. It really is not agreeable so soon after breakfast to drink fruit punch of grapefruit juice and bathtub gin, which slipped down the throat like a steel file, but we did, and then, standing in open trucks under the blazing sun, we were transported to Lake Suntaug. On the Revere Beach Parkway two of the trucks got to racing side by side and an adventurous

William Whitman III

Marjorie Warren Whitman ("Pargie")

classmate who tried to jump across fell between and broke his leg. At least he was spared from what followed. We swam; but the lake was like warm sarsaparilla, and as the punch wore off so did any appetite for the dismal lunch. It was all so depressing that Bill slipped away to the phone booth and asked Pargie to drive down and pick us up at the nearest crossroads, which, bless her, she did.

Commencement, with the faculty in their robes, the President ensconced on his throne, a curiously wrought old wooden chair, and the girls in light frocks, is intended for sunlight; ours was preceded by heavy rain which did not let up until the conferring of degrees. The Spreads were held under dripping canvas and the Senior Prom in the lugubrious vastness of Memorial Hall, where Fritzy and I danced to the tunes from *Sally*. From the whirl two memories remain: the wet afternoon when Fritzy and I, she clad in my plus fours and tweed coat, went for a walk in the Belmont woods. We were spattered from above and the path was much too moist for any sitting but there was plenty of privacy. There are times when the hands inform. The other moment was when we seniors crowded up to the platform as President Lowell admitted us "to the company of educated men."

I stayed on alone in Hollis, packing and preening for Bill's wedding, a gay affair for which I rented a cutaway. At the ushers' dinner, with its toasts, we gave Bill the traditional square silver cigarette box with our signatures inscribed on the cover, and for each of us he had gold cufflinks, his initials on one oval and ours on the other, links which might so easily have been lost, but mine have not been.

4

I needed money for England, at least $500, and the quickest way to earn it was, again, as a companion-tutor. I expected it would be a letdown after last summer. An invitation came from a Mrs. Andrew Robeson Sargent, a widow, who asked that I drive out to her farm in Harvard village to see if her young son and I could hit it off. I borrowed a car, smartened up in my starched Charvet shirt to impress her, and arrived at the white-and-green, shuttered farmhouse in time for tea. Mrs. Sargent, very chic in cream knitted jersey, and her friend and companion, Miss Miriam Shaw, ushered me into their living room, and one look at Proust and D. H. Lawrence on the table, with the *Atlantic* and the *Nation,* told me that they were bluestockings. The tea was Earl Grey, the cinnamon toast and the frosted walnut cake delicious. But no boy. Mrs. Sargent, who from her questions knew of my writing for the *Advocate* and the *Transcript,* spoke of their plans for the summer: to be here through June, and then she and Peter, but not Miss Shaw, would spend two months at York Harbor, Maine. "Now, Peter," she said, addressing the piano at the end of the room, "come say hello to Mr. Weeks," and from the shadows where he had been squatting, my charge emerged. He shook my hand shyly and muttered, "Come on out back and show me what you can do."

Peter was an uncommonly big boy for his nine years, tall and sturdy. He led me away from the house toward a pine from whose lower limb hung a pair of those rings on which gymnasts perform; they were too low for my height and anyway I was having none of that. I picked up a stone from the driveway. "I like to throw," I said. "What do you want me to hit?" He pointed to a slender pear tree and, with God's grace, I plunked it in the center. "It's fun to skim flat ones across a pond," I added, "sometimes they skip six or eight times. Ever try?" He shook his head.

"What else do you like?" he asked.

I thought for a moment. "I like brooks," I said. "It's fun to wade up them, to build harbors, and to whittle small boats to race."

He seemed more interested as we strolled back to the house. Propped against the wall was a painter's ladder reaching up to a small window. "Sometimes," said Peter reflectively, "when there's nothing else to do I climb up there and watch the maid take her bath."

"When I'm here, you won't," I said.

"Sure I will," he said, "and you'll do it, too."

I was installed in a comfortable bedroom in a nearby farmhouse at Harvard with a Ford runabout in which Peter and I explored the countryside. We found our brooks, a pond for skipping stones, and a deep sandpit with quite a drop from its rim. "I dare you to jump it," said Peter. I did, and was just recovering from the jar of the landing when I heard his thud behind me. Peter, christened Ignatius, was the grandson of Charles Sargent, the famous horticulturist; the Sargents were big men and Peter's father, who had played football at Harvard, was building his reputation as a landscape architect at the time of his early death. The boy, so long in the company of women, was courageous, very inquisitive, very thorough in what he put his mind to; he did not know his own strength and tended to bully his smaller contemporaries. Very different from Bill Wetmore but in his own right as interesting.

It was roaring hot the morning we moved into the cottage at York Harbor and as soon as we had unpacked our bathing suits Peter and I headed for the bathing beach. The water was arctic cold but the beach of firm sand was ideal for dabbling. I had brought along a tennis ball to play catch, but as I saw Peter, in his reserved way, sizing up the boys of his own age my mind went back to a game we used to play at Bay Head. I drew Peter away from the crowd to an empty stretch and together we dug six small pockets in a crescent just above the water line. "Now, Pete," I said, "you stand behind the holes and I'll roll the ball down toward them. I'm free to run and duck while it's rolling but the moment it falls into a pocket and you pick it up, I've got to freeze and if you hit me I'm 'It' and it's your turn to roll." I didn't run far; twice he hit me in the rump and once I stung him in the back — and that was enough to attract some youthful spectators.

"What are you doing?" asked the boldest, a boy named Hugh Chisholm.

"We're playing Baby-in-the-Hat," I said. "This is Peter Sargent and I'm Mr. Weeks. Want to join us?"

In no time we had a boy behind each pocket, ducking or laughing off the momentary sting of the wet ball. In the days that followed, the beach was the meeting place of the "Gang," in which Pete became a natural leader without having to push the kids around. I had my accolade when one of the mothers asked if I would accept a fee for keeping my eye on her Tommy, too. "If he's in the gang," I said, shaking my head, "you don't need to worry."

Peter's single-mindedness surprised me. In our reading aloud I began with *Dr. Dolittle's Circus* and when we had finished switched to Robert Louis Stevenson. But Peter wouldn't stay with *Treasure Island*. "Let's go back to *Dr. Dolittle*," he insisted. We read it three times. Nor could I check his inquisitiveness. One Sunday morning when the beach was crowded Peter had lagged behind and I was dressed and combing my hair when somewhat sheepishly he entered the bathhouse we shared. "Hurry it up," I said as I left, and ran smack into an outraged woman. "Do you know where your boy's been?" she demanded, "on the roof of the bathhouses, watching me, and I don't know how many others, dress!" To which I could only reply that I was sorry.

For the Gang I had persuaded Mrs. Sargent to rent a fourteen-foot skiff, in which on calm days I rowed them about the harbor in their life preservers, one boy seated in the bow, one on the thwart, one, rarely two, in the stern. The tide in the York River is very powerful, as I found when I got caught upstream, trying to get my passengers back for their six o'clock suppers. Only when the tide was with me or at about the turn did I dare cross the inlet to a tiny cove on Rocky Neck where, opposite the Marshall House hotel, at the entrance to a cave we made a fire of driftwood in which we roasted potatoes. On one fair day, the tide going out, I made for our cove with three aboard. What I did not realize until it was too late was that the east wind had kicked up a choppy sea even at the foot of the inlet; I was all right so long as

I kept us bow-on in the outgoing current, but to turn broadside was to ask for trouble. Yet it had to be done if we were not to be swept out into the rougher chop ahead. "Everybody down on the floor," I said. "We may ship water as we turn in." Backing with my left oar, pulling hard with the right we slewed around into the trough, and out of the corner of my eye I saw a man in dark clothes on the Marshall House lawn watching us, transfixed, a witness, a judge of what I was doing. God help us! I thought. The boat rose and pitched as we shipped water with the first two bites of my oars, and again with the next, and the next, then we slid out of the current and into the slack. I looked back over my shoulder; the man was gone. Was he ever there? With our backsides wet we beached, tilted the water out of the skiff, and began collecting the driftwood. The boys were laughing and oblivious by the time the potatoes were done but I had no taste for them that morning, my heart still being in my mouth. On our return I hugged the shore, the wind at our back, and the tide, now incoming, sped us to the landing. But I had taken a risk I was never to forget.

As Labor Day approached Mrs. Sargent offered me a tempting dividend if I would stay on for an additional fortnight. I needed the money but I needed a week with Fritzy at Long Point, if we were to be parted for ten months. Pete ducked his head to keep back the tears when we said good-bye. But we did not lose touch. Later, as a Harvard freshman Peter spent every weekend learning to fly; as a test pilot in France his message, relayed by his mother, told me how defenseless the French air force was in 1939, and I was to take pride in his magnificent record as a captain in the 19th Bombardment Group: he flew more than fifty missions, and not a man of his crew was killed or wounded. He remarked once that he did not want to be known as the best living pilot — just the oldest.

V

LONG POINT was as lovely as I remembered. I unpacked in my old tent, recently vacated by my successor, the new tutor, the sunpoints were dancing on the lake, the old oaks stirring in the morning breeze just as a year before. Bill Wetmore, whose progress, especially in athletics I had observed on my visits to St. Mark's, was glad to have me back, Mrs. Wetmore kissed me, and Mr. Wetmore with a smile asked if my golf was any better. I was "Ted" to the family now, only the critical Bollard maintained the "Mr. Weeks." But there was a subtle difference: young lovers are quite incapable of concealing from older eyes the glances that tell their secret. Bill may have been unaware, but Mrs. Wetmore was not; she had decided that Fritzy, who was the first girl from Foxcroft to pass the exams for Bryn Mawr, should be held out until she was eighteen and that in the interim she was to go on a world cruise chaperoned by an elderly spinster cousin, one motive being, so I surmised, to distract attention from an impecunious Harvard undergraduate. Fritzy, who had been rather plump for her height when she went off to boarding school, was "beginning to shape up," as I told her the first evening when she appeared in a most becoming jade-green tea gown. Mrs. Wetmore overheard me and chuckled. But Fritzy did not take it as a compliment until I was more explicit. Our one chance for privacy occurred on a sunny morning when, Bill having gone to Jamestown, we paddled across the lake in our bathing suits, went swimming on the little shingle before a dense grove of pines and then explored their shade for a hidden spot to embrace. As we were leaving Fritzy spied a heart-shaped piece of lichen, scratched on it the initials "E. A. W. III" — my namesake to be — and we buried it under the moss-covered log on which we had been sitting.

I intended to work my way across the Atlantic on a cattle boat. A business friend of Father's in Montreal had secured a berth for me on the first outgoing ship after September 15 on condition that I consign my pay to the foreman. I was to be packed, ready to take the sleeper, when he telegraphed. This gave me a few days to catch up with Mother and the kids. She told me how disappointed she and Dad had been not to come up for my graduation and added ruefully that Dad's business was no better: Charlie Anderson, his junior partner, was a very sick man, and Bill Sawyer, the partner with the capital, wanted to pull out.

"Gosh," I said, "I wish I could help. Can he keep the firm going alone?"

"Yes," she said, "with Henry Caesar's backing. And you're going to make good on your scholarship."

Still I did feel guilty, more so when on the day I left for Montreal Dad presented me with a draft on Baring Brothers, London, for $600 and another hundred in English money. I knew he must have stretched to do it, with things as they were — Rufus, my next brother, and Frederika, my sister, in boarding school. I was sure I'd be a weak reed in his office, I had no heart for the cotton business, but all I could say was: "This is the last time, Dad. I'll be on my own next year."

At the Montreal station I checked my belongings and caught a taxi to the docks to make sure of my sailing. Beside a pier with a railroad track down its center I found the ship, a black-and-white new-looking freighter whose winches were swinging aboard bales of hay and bags of feed. And in a shed alongside I found the foreman, a burly Irishman with a flattened nose who called me "Kid," had me sign a paper releasing to him my pay of $4 a day, and told me to be back at noon when the cattle train from the West was due. We would sail for Glasgow on the outgoing tide that afternoon.

When I returned to the pier after thanking my Canadian benefactor, the cab driver piled my steamer trunk and suitcase beside the gangway with my Corona on top. No other cattle hands were in evidence and I needed help. Leaning on the rail, spitting in the crevasse between the ship and the dock, were four Scottish seamen, black-haired, ruddy-cheeked, and silent. When I crossed the gangway and sidled up to the nearest man, he shifted his weight to glance at me.

"So ye write for the papers, do ye?" he said in a Glasgow burr, "and ye're looking for local color?"

"Aye, he'll find it," came from his neighbor, "plenty of color and all brown."

With that they helped me stow my things in a small deckhouse at the stern, where I preempted a lower berth, changed into gray flannels and an old sweater, and went looking for the rest of my gang. I had not realized that there would be such a class difference between the crew and the cattle hands. But there was.

In the foreman's office I met the other members of the team as they signed on and two of them I liked on sight. George was a tall, raw-boned Australian who had served beside the Algerians on the Somme and since the war had worked with cattle in South Africa and Canada. He had competence written all over him and so did Alf, a Yorkshireman turned Canadian farmer, who was hoping to get home before his father died. The unknown quantities were " 'Enry," a plump Cockney, and myself.

The cattle train backed in at one o'clock, and we were all at the rail to watch the steers come aboard. Prodded by Canadian cattlemen, the big animals lumbered out of their cars and onto the high-arched bridge that fed down into a circular, unpartitioned runway on the lower deck. In the rush a 1,600-pound bull got caught backwards; he was borne along by his fellows until he reached the steep incline; there he described a somersault, hit the deck like a falling meteor, and scrambled to his feet, snorting but unhurt. There were no stanchions below. The runway, which completely encircled the deck like a race-track, was enclosed by a wooden headboard, four and a half feet high, in which holes had been bored at regular intervals. The steers were hitched to this with their rumps to the hull and enough leeway to lower their heads for water and feed. The manure lay where it fell; there could be no thorough cleanup till after we docked. I could soon smell why the crew did not want us in their mess.

Each steer carried a length of knotted rope around his throat, and with this the men from the train were expected to secure the beast to the headboard. But our skipper was in a hurry to catch the tide, and before the drivers had tied up a third of our cargo — we were carrying 170 head — he ordered them off and we got under way. Then it was our turn in the oval; there was a bellow from the foreman to get below and tie up "them goddamn steers." The cattle knot is a combination of bow and slipknot, strong but easily untied, for if the animal falls to his knees or gets his head crossed with his neighbor's, he must be rescued from choking. If you want a steer to go right you hit his nose on the left, and you propel him by twisting his tail. Obviously not a one-man job. The unattached steers were milling around in the indoor track and the foreman, who had been drinking and reeked of Irish whiskey, took me with him into the maelstrom. He was to twist the tail and I at the end of the line would wave my arms and flag them in, while in the alleyway outside, the other men made fast the ropes in the headboard. One by one we tied them up until we came to one stubborn critter who lowered his head and backed up, treading heavily on the foreman's corns. With painful obscenity the Irishman removed himself, the Australian took his place, and the game went on until supper and all the following day, while we pursued our way down the placid St. Lawrence. There was one small black bull with a stout rib cage, no neck, and the soul of a devil. He had broken his headrope and kept backing away with his little eyes gleaming. We could not catch him until we put buckets of water temptingly out of his reach and at last brought his head into line. In the strenuous work we got to know each other, and the suspicion grew that the Cockney was dodging his share. On the first night out the foreman, who was laid up in his bunk, sent word through George that we would have to stand watch on the cattle to make sure that none of them fell down, and we solved this problem by giving the Cockney the job. He could patrol the alley or chin with the cook, and we three would do the housework from four in the morning until lights out. 'Enry took no offense at our decision. I think he was pleased at the prospect of spending half the day in his bunk. Gazing reflectively at the ceiling as he got ready for his night watch, he remarked, "An' 'ere's a bloomin' fly hexpatriating 'imself."

On our pastoral voyage down the St. Lawrence, between the flat farmlands and tiny white villages of French Canada, we learned our routine. The Cockney roused us at 4 A.M. and in the chill dark the hot coffee he brought from the galley stopped my teeth from chattering. In sweaters we went out into the dimly lit alleyway, where heads were thrust between the bars, moist noses beckoning. The steers' breakfast consisted of water — as much as eight buckets to an animal, for in their greed they would knock the pail over — and a couple of flakes of hay. Down one alley and up the other we went; it was my job to fill the wooden buckets from the high tuns of water and pass them to my two teammates. I started counting the pailfuls I lifted out, and had passed five hundred before the last steer was replete. George growled, "They aren't cattle; they're bloody camels!" At nine o'clock we distributed their lunch of cornmeal, a second round of water and hay followed at four in the afternoon, and between meals we cleaned up the fringes with pitchfork and shovel. For relief we went up on deck where the salt air swept away the reek from below. So passed our day.

The foreman was a bully and his voice was like a whip. Now three of us had served in France; we were used to discipline and not unwilling. "Tell him off," said George, and I spoke up to the Irishman.

"Look," I said, "there's work to be done and we'll do it. But we don't like your nagging at us. Right, George?"

"Ar-hhh," said the old pugilist, for that's what he had been. He looked

147

as though he wanted to break me into pieces, but except for the unusual he was quieter after that.

From the Laurentian Mountains, whose brown slopes were stippled with evergreens, the river widened into the broad sweep of the gulf. We passed the rusty wreck of the H.M.S. *Raleigh,* piled up on the rocks of Belle Isle. Icebergs were sighted, the air grew colder; and as we came into the open sea the sky turned lead and we were caught like a chip in an equinoctial gale. With the North Atlantic at its roughest, life took on a darker aspect. Our bunkhouse rose and fell with nauseous regularity. The crew from the first had refused to let us mess with them; our food was sloshed into three pannikins which we carried across the heaving deck to our close compartment. The ship climbed and plunged in the mountain seas; sheets of water came over the side and poured into the hatches; steers had to be moved from drenched areas and freshly bedded down. Three of us were seasick but the feeding went on in the tumbling boat and the circus stench. I could hold nothing down, I nibbled at the slice of cold mutton on bread for which I paid the cook a dollar. The steers were seasick, too, but they could not dramatize it; they simply drank more and more water. My tonic was a remark of the foreman's which George, our only hale member, reported to me. "Sure the Kid's sick," said the pug, "I seen him spittin' out his heart. But he don't quit; he's a tryer, all right."

On the fifth day I had my sea legs even if they were hollow like my belly. The book I had brought with me in my suitcase was *Old Junk,* H. M. Tomlinson's sketches of the sea, and as the wind slackened and sunlight poured over us, I stretched out on a dry bale of hay in the open hatch to hear how that great seafarer described what we had just been through. Tomlinson like Conrad was a painter of storm. From where I lay I could see the blue sky and the green crests as we dipped. Sunlight and calmer water revived our appetites; we swallowed the finnan haddie and spuds and hankered for richer food. I went up to the bow as we passed through the Devil's Hole, that much feared stretch to the north of Ireland, and the bell buoy was riding serenely. Then on our last dawn we entered the Firth of Clyde. The sun sparkled on the water; the stone cottages shone; the white dots on the uplands were sheep, grazing uphill. We were in the Clyde now and slowed down to take aboard the pilot. A liner passed us, outward bound, and I was glad I was not aboard; we made our way through a fleet of submarines, anchored, and then in the distance saw the black derricks of the Glasgow shipyards. The steers had scented land and were stamping and lowing in impatience. The foreman said they would all have put on about fifteen pounds on the voyage across and, thank God, that it was not our responsibility to get them off. Handshakes all around, a pat on the shoulder from George, and a surprisingly affectionate "Take care of yourself, Kid," from our tough boss. In our discharge papers was the reminder that we were entitled to a free trip back on a cattle boat anytime within three months.

I came ashore ravenous, never so hungry, and had the taxi take me to a good hotel, the Queens, in the center of town, where for two days I concentrated on the best the menu had to offer, including a huge tea with Scotch scones and strawberry jam. On the table by the window of my bedroom I began typing a piece about the cattle boat, the first for my syndicate, and for exercise I rode about town in the yellow and green busses and stretched my legs at the Glasgow Museum of Art. My English money still seemed abundant but when I called at Thomas Cook and Sons to get a seat on the daily express to London, I was dismayed to find that I didn't have quite enough to pay for the ticket and my hotel bill.

"You *have* been improvident," said the clerk looking me over.

"Yes, but I have this draft on Barings — "

"Which cannot be drawn on until deposited."

"Good Lord," I said, "what shall I do?"

"Though it's strictly against the rules," he said, "I'll make you a personal loan, enough to get you to London. But understand, it's at my risk."

In a strange country one instantly notices what is different from home. I noticed the profusion of wild flowers bordering the railway, and the tidy cultivation of this ancient land, in which the fields and roads were so clearly defined by hedges. The express was not as swank — at least where I was sitting — as the special-fare trains on the New York–Boston run but it was just as fast and the roadbed smoother. Passing through Carlisle I noticed the little flower gardens which gave individuality to the hundreds of identical sallow brick homes.

When I arrived at Euston Station shortly before midnight I had one shilling left in my pocket. Suitcase in one hand, Corona in the other, I walked out and up to the police officer directing traffic, and while he waved his white gauntlets, I explained my plight.

"My relief will be along shortly," he said. "Then we'll see what can be done." I waited on the curb and a few moments later he led me down to a side street, knocked on one door which did not respond, knocked on a second, and when the landlady opened, asked if she'd be willing to take in this American for the night. She did, and next morning fed me a hot breakfast of egg, bacon and tea. Bed-and-breakfast, it appeared, was the usual deal. This was my first lesson in British civility, on the part of the clerk, the bobby, and herself, a quality I have never ceased to admire.

As I had no money to pay him, I had the taxi driver wait until my draft was deposited; then, money in the bank and pounds in my pocket, feeling as free as air, I told him to show me a little of London. "Right you are, Governor!" He had me get out for a moment at Trafalgar Square, where the crouching lions, Napier on his charger, the glittering fountain, the pigeons, and Nelson on his sky-high pedestal struck me as a splendid British affirmation. We went down Whitehall to the Houses of Parliament and we paused again at Westminster Abbey. Just a taste — I'd come back again in earnest later. Meanwhile I had a call to make on Fleet Street before paying my landlady and collecting my luggage for Cambridge. At the London office of the Associated Press, I inquired if they had an American correspondent at Cambridge. It appeared not; the last one was in 1914. I pointed out that more Americans were enrolled in the university now; I mentioned my *Transcript* connection, and asked if I could serve them in a similar capacity, and at what rate? Yes, that might be a sensible arrangement: they'd pay a shilling a line for any story of mine they put on the wire. It would be on spec, of course, how it worked out would be up to me.

2

The anticipation with which I traveled down to Cambridge was somewhat subdued by my first glance at my lodgings on Portugal Place. My room on the ground floor was narrow, with barely enough space to stand between the cot lying against one wall and the bureau opposite; by the window were a small table, set before a tiny coal grate, a basket chair of wicker, and a straight chair facing a rickety desk. A chamber pot beneath the bed completed the furnishings. Tea for two would be about the limit of my hospitality.

Still it is only a short walk to Trinity, I thought, as I set forth on my first duty, a formal call on my tutor, Gaillard Lapsley. In the mist the college was more impressive than I had imagined: I passed through Great Gate with the weathered statue of Henry VIII, the founder, above the portal, and getting my directions from the porter, went on across the immense Gothic quadrangle of Great Court into the more classic serenity of Nevile's Court with its rug of green turf and lovely cloisters. The ancient gray stone buildings, the walks of flint and flagstone, the steps which centuries of scholars' feet have hollowed — this was the monastic stronghold of learning which I had read about, and here it was so little altered. Mr. Lapsley's rooms were on the north side, close to the Wren library, which overlooked the River Cam.

I was not sure what to expect. Mr. Fiske admired him but the daughters had reservations, thought he put on airs. I knew that Lapsley was an American, a Harvard graduate and a bachelor, a scholar who had made himself an authority on British medieval history and the *Domesday Book,* an admirer and friend of Henry James and Edith Wharton. He sounded formidable. The outer door to his suite was open and I knocked. "Come in!" said a high peremptory voice.

The Lapsley who greeted me seemed hesitant, and soon explained why. According to the regulations governing those *in statu pupillari,* a copy of which he gave me, I should have presented myself in academic dress, and when I acknowledged that I hadn't even bought it, he suggested that I do so and return. When I reappeared in the dark-blue and black Trinity gown with its short tails, and my mortarboard, he was more cordial, and as he poured us each a glass of sherry I studied him and his elegant study, book-lined from wainscot to ceiling: he was tall and broad-shouldered, had a hook of a nose and a long jaw, was stylish, not casual in his dress, and talked with that ultra-English accent which was what the girls thought affected.

"My dear Weeks," he said, "you are to be here for three terms of eight weeks each. How do you propose to spend them?"

"I'm twenty-four," I said, "and this is my last chance to fill in the chinks. I want to listen to some lectures, read English authors on their native ground, and write some descriptive pieces for the Boston *Transcript.*"

"You'll have two month-long vacations for the writing. But I wonder if it wouldn't interest you to attend my lectures and those of Kenneth Pickthorn on British constitutional history. It's really the struggle for political freedom, and the origin of our law. I take it from the Conquest to 1485, and Pickthorn from 1485 to the present. We'd expect you to read Bishop Stubbs, but I shall excuse you from doing the weekly papers. I do wish you would think about it, for it's not a subject to be worked up by yourself."

"I like that idea," I said. "I hope I'll also have time to listen to Quiller-Couch and some of the other literary people?"

"Good," said Lapsley. "I'm glad you approve. Yes, certainly time for the others, too. And you must exercise regularly. *Mens sana in corpore sano* — it's the only way to survive in this beastly Fen country." He cleared his throat with a great hawk.

"I'll play tennis." And added as I rose, "Sir, that little room of mine on Portugal Place is pretty dismal."

"I dare say," he said. "But all first-year men are obliged to live in digs. You'll have to bear it for this term and then perhaps at Christmas we can make a shift."

Before I could enjoy life I had to do something about the cold. The

Fen country surrounding Cambridge was originally a dank morass of marsh and stream, and even now, though the marsh had been drained, the mist, sharp as a knife blade, often did not burn off till mid-morning. I had not thought of myself as cold-blooded in New England, but my cotton underwear and American suit were no protection here and I swallowed my pride as I purchased woolen longjohns and a heavy suit of English tweed, whose nap grew overnight. So encased I needed no outer covering save my Trinity gown, which was mandatory for all lectures, the library, for dinner in Hall, and wherever I went after dusk. Some students took the stuffing out of their mortarboards with a lop-eared effect; I learned to fit mine at a comfortable angle and didn't bother.

All locomotion was by bicycle — undergraduates were forbidden to have cars — and as I intended to use mine for sight-seeing I bought one with two gears, which was essential for long runs and helpful on hills. Everyone rode "push bikes" in Cambridge, even the stylish Lapsley, and the girls from Newnham and Girton, especially those with good legs, like the beautiful Miss Webber, had a way of patting down the skirt just as the right knee came up, quite inviting to the eye. Driving or riding on the left side of the road is a habit not easily acquired by Americans abroad, and one evening when dark fell early I broke all the rules in the book. I was on my way home and had not troubled to light my lamp. Approaching me with his light showing came a solitary old party in his proper lane. I suppose it was my native instinct which prompted me to cross the road, ram him, and in the collision split his trousers. He was quite annoyed. In court the following morning I was admonished, fined, and obliged to pay the victim the price of a new pair of flannels.

Trinity, the largest and richest of the eighteen colleges which then made up the federation of the university, has enjoyed the special benevolence of the Crown ever since Henry VIII. The Prince of Wales, when he studies at Cambridge, is traditionally at Trinity, and its seven hundred undergraduates for all these reasons dine well. My landlady served me breakfast — eggs and bacon, kidneys, sausage, or kippered herring, at which I drew the line — but my other meals I took in the resplendent Great Hall with its raftered ceiling fifty feet above us, the glee gallery with its gilded screen, the Master and dons seated on the dais beneath Holbein's portrait of Henry VIII, and along the wall the paintings of the Trinity "Great": Byron and Balfour, old Butler with his vast beard, Macaulay and Thackeray, on and on. In such medieval splendor the food was tasty: the soups, thick and heartening; the mutton tender with crisp fat; the deep-dish apple tart or Trinity's specialty for

In my Trinity cap and gown, and a heavy
English tweed, at the entry to P-4, Great
Court

Gaillard Lapsley of Trinity, tutor, lecturer
par excellence — and occasional chaperon

private dinners, *crème brûlée,* the perfect dessert. Our chef could make even the turnips and Brussels sprouts acceptable.

We were required to dine in Hall five nights a week and the marker, to make sure that we did, checked off our names on a long scroll as he paced between the tables. At the outset I had no temptation to eat elsewhere, for in Hall I was beginning to find my friends; but this restriction and the others I had observed seemed to me a peculiar paternalism for so sophisticated a place. I did not realize that they were rituals hung over from the past, and that an Englishman clings to tradition. For instance, all students were expected to be off the streets and in their own colleges by midnight. It did not matter how late they read or talked in their rooms but they must not be out of the college. This statute, a precaution against the town-and-gown riots of earlier times and, incidentally, against whoring, still stood: if I returned to my room on Portugal Place after 10 P.M., my landlady, acting as if she were the college porter at Trinity Gate, chalked up a fine of a penny; if I returned after eleven, the fine rose to tuppence; her door, like Trinity Gate, was bolted at midnight and should I knock after that or stay out all night, I might be "rusticated," that is, sent home for the remainder of the term. In the colleges this "gating" was enforced by moats, iron pickets to shut off the easy climb to an abutting tree, and in some colleges by broken glass embedded on the tops of walls — and of course, it was defied by bold spirits who found unsuspected footholds for entry after hours.

Discipline in the streets of the university was administered by a Senior and a Junior Proctor, faculty members who ranked next to the Vice-Chancellor in authority. When the "Prog" patrolled the darkened lanes in his academic robe, he was attended by "bullers" or "bulldogs," two porters in frock coats and high hats, selected for their speed. The culprit, if captured, was brought up to the Proctor, who put the traditional questions, "Your name and college, sir?" The next morning the student would make a formal call on the Proctor and, before hearing his sentence, usually a fine, would be proffered a glass of port. Oh, hallowed tradition!

My only contemporary to incur a proctor's wrath was William Wallace at Oxford, who had graduated ahead of me at Harvard. His father was a Mormon and a former governor of Utah, and Bill had been well drilled in the Scriptures, an accomplishment which led to his becoming, inadvertently, an officer of the College Bible Society. But Bill inclined to the bottle, and one evening before midnight he got to drinking with a friendly cab driver and overstayed. The cabbie, in attempting to drive Bill to his lodgings, broke a wheel on the Martyrs' Memorial, and there being no further solution, went home leaving the occupant asleep in the back seat. This was an infraction so public that Bill was sent packing. I had no such run in. It was Lapsley who gave me permission to go dancing and to attend the annual Pilgrim's Dinner held in London on Thanksgiving (and I had to return to Cambridge that night!). In short, the English undergraduate is more closely watched during term than his American contemporary.

In Britain's golden age under Queen Victoria it was said that to be happy at Cambridge one must "read, ride or row." The introduction of football, golf, and tennis in the 1870's widened the choice of sport, but the first requirement, "to read," is still mandatory for those who wish to graduate with honors. In the fascinating first volume of his autobiography, Bertrand Russell gives the best account yet written of the intellectual life in Trinity. He inherited a head for ideas, and he spent a secluded boyhood studying under private tutors in the home of Lord Russell, his grandfather. Russell styles himself "a shy prig" when at eighteen he came to Cambridge on a scholarship in the fall of 1890; yet in the course of his first week in Trinity he made the friends of a lifetime. Alfred North Whitehead had been one of his examiners and had passed the word that this was an extraordinary prospect. Admittedly, I knew no student of Russell's precocity in Trinity, but his book speaks for the intensity of intellectual curiosity which continues to draw together the brilliant scholars.

At the opposite end of the spectrum was the varsity eight. Rowing has from the beginning been the sovereign sport at Cambridge and Oxford despite the fact that at neither place is there to American eyes a river fit to race on. The Cam, from which Cambridge takes it name, is a placid little stream winding its way through meadow and town and rarely wider than thirty yards. Since it was quite impossible for crews to race abreast, the English solved the problem by lining them up and encouraging the faster boats to bump the slower. There are eight crews in a race; the boats start a length and a half apart; in the course of a mile and five-eighths are three tricky curves, and at Grassy Corner, where the pace usually tells, the coxswain of an overtaking crew will cut the Corner so as to bump with his prow the tiller or stern of the tortoise ahead. The instant this occurs, the defeated crew and the "bumper" pull over to the bank and the other pursuers move on amidst the wild cheers of those running on the towpath. "Up! Up! Up! Trinity!" "Up! Up! Queens!" (Very rarely, a fast crew will attempt a double bump.) The scene would be ludicrous if it were not for the fervor of the spectators and the desperation of the oarsmen. Trinity, because of its size, was divided into two boat clubs, the First and Third Trinity, the latter being restricted to graduates of Eton and Westminster; between them there must have been at least twoscore oarsmen who competed for the top boats. Every college boated at least one crew — while I was there Trinity trained four — the races were held on four successive afternoons, and those few crews that achieved four bumps were awarded their oars, and their victory banquet was wet and noisy. Pembroke College was "head of the river" in my time, and Trinity, in second place, could not displace her.

The varsity oarsmen stand apart. They have either won their Blue (at Oxford, a dark-blue blazer and scarf, at Cambridge, the same in light blue, are the equivalent of a varsity letter in America) the year previous or are new men coming up with a reputation from Eton or from Harvard like my classmate R. Keith Kane, who had rowed for two years on the Harvard Varsity. When I knew Keith was going to Balliol I asked him what he planned to study. "Roman law," he replied. "All I can get of it before law school. And no athletics!" But when I saw him at Balliol College in the autumn he had been hooked.

Keith rowed for Balliol in the bumping races at the end of Michaelmas term. His performance attracted attention, for in the south of France where he spent Christmas a telegram from the Oxford captain recalled him before the opening of college to compete in the trial eights, the two crews from which the final varsity and the spares are picked. Out they went for two practices a day until courses were resumed. Professional coaches are of course taboo, and in this preliminary period the crews were under the eye of Dr. Bourne, an old Blue. In the final selection two Americans were seated: Keith at No. 4 and "Pussy" Mellen, formerly of Middlesex School, at stroke. The idea of having two Americans out of nine in the boat caused such a furor in the English press that Keith offered to withdraw, but the Oxford boys said no.

March, as Keith recalled for me later, was the period of accelerated training, leading up to the race with Cambridge on March 24. Early in the month they commuted to Henley, thirty miles distant, where under a second amateur, Coach Horsfall, they practiced at a slow stroke, getting accustomed to each other on a three-mile stretch between the locks. Then for the final fortnight they departed Oxford for an old inn at Putney on the Thames, where they rowed twice a day inspired by Harcourt Gold, a London broker who had stroked the Oxford boat of 1909. "Tarka" Gold used to tell them that if an eight ever gets together they feel as if they are just rising out of the water and taking to wings but this happens none too frequently and lasts only for a week at the most. As they practiced their sprints at forty strokes a

Straining for a bump at Grassy Corner, Cambridge, 1922

R. Keith Kane and William P. ("Pussy") Mellen, Putney, March 1923

minute, he was aiming for this magic get-together, and they found it.

The race took place on Saturday, March 24, 1923, and as always it emptied London offices and halted all river traffic on that part of the Thames until it was over. Half a million or more watched it from the many vantage points — I in the crowd at the Hammersmith Bridge. The course, which covers four and a half miles, is in the shape of a giant horseshoe and the coxswain of the crew that is leading as they approach the big bend at Harrods can force his opponent to row wide. Cambridge had won every race since the war but now the odds were on Oxford. This was one of the few times either varsity had been stroked by an American, and Mellen, after a fast start, soon took the lead at a lower stroke. He called for a sudden spurt at the Hammersmith Bridge and they shot out from underneath us three-quarters of a length ahead; Cambridge, much the lighter crew, made a brave challenge at Duke's Meadows but Oxford had found that "magic rhythm," and held that margin to the grueling finish.

Someone has figured that in those three months of training a crew will have rowed one thousand miles. As if this were not enough, Keith, now twenty pounds heavier than when he left Harvard, went back to pull an oar for Balliol and to row for Leander at Henley. "Too much rowing!" he exclaimed.

3

It did not irritate me as it did several of my compatriots that the English had a tendency to patronize us; individually we were acceptable, collectively we were still Colonials, unpredictable in our wealth and power. (At a luncheon for us all at Corpus Christi, Sir Geoffrey Butler, a don who had married an American wife, intended a compliment when he said, "We feel as if you were almost one of our Colonies.") When Stephen Runciman, a brilliant scholar, certain to become a Fellow, asked if I had brought my "shooting irons" with me, he smiled but would not have been too surprised if I had said yes. Their feeling toward us came out in their talk, and what spicy, graceful talkers the best of them are! The English relish conversation and it differs from ours: they embellish absurd happenings with an understatement as we do with exaggeration. (In the men's lavatory of the British Museum was a sign reading, "These basins are for partial ablutions only," and when I asked the attendant why, he responded, "Why, sir, in the old days persons used to come here for their baarths.") English wit is mischievous, and in describing anything they disapprove of, even in a close friend, they can be murderously funny. In Trinity a comic debating society known as the Magpie and Stump enjoyed pairing a Briton and an American (sometimes me) against an American and a Briton on subjects such as "Resolved: When in Rome One Should Do as the Americans Do." We could hold our own in such informality, but it was a different matter in the Cambridge Union, where the discussion was mainly sober and where the Question Period gave the newcomer a chance to be heard. The American, it seemed to me, tried to clinch the argument by slugging his opponent with a sockful of facts, whereas the English debater tried to persuade you into accepting his interpretation of the facts.

British constitutional history was proving to be a surprisingly engrossing subject, though without aid I doubt if I would ever have plowed through the three solid volumes by Bishop Stubbs. It took an effort to divide my attention between the two periods: the medieval, which Lapsley illuminated in his clear, stylish lectures, so well attended that they overflowed the classroom and had to be given in the Great Hall of Trinity; and the later period, which Kenneth Pickthorn expounded, pungently, to a much smaller audience. Pickthorn was closer to my age and I liked him. A short slender blond, he had come through hard fighting in the war and a head wound had left him prey to insomnia. This would show in his brusqueness: he could not tolerate interruption, and when a girl from Girton came late to class, he barked at her and she fled in tears, and did not return. "It costs me five pounds when I do that," he said to me ruefully after class. "I envy Gaillard the fees he gets from his harem." We used to enjoy playing bridge together and after I went down it cheered me to know that Kenneth had been chosen to represent the university in Parliament, where his ability to cut through nonsense and red tape made him one of the most respected backbenchers.

Again it surprised me to discover that there was no English department, that until the coming of Sir Arthur Quiller-Couch in 1912 there had never been a professor of English at either Oxford or Cambridge. It was not thought necessary: English was syntax drilled into a boy at school, as Winston Churchill discovered; after that, one formed a style or used the commonplace. In my time Sir Arthur, who now held a university appointment at Cambridge, gave a series of ornamental talks, very popular, on his favorite Victorian writers, and one evening a week, welcomed a select group to his library at nine o'clock, where after the serving of coffee and biscuits we discussed and applied the meaning of Aristotle's *Poetics*. I say "we," though actually it was he, reeking warmly of brandy, who did all the talking. To the meetings he brought his experience as a playwright, as the editor of *The Oxford Book of English Verse*, as a critic and essayist. He hoped to stimulate us to supply contemporary illustrations to Aristotle's truths, but the group was evenly divided between Britons and Americans, both afraid to show off or make fools of themselves, and when Paul Fenimore Cooper, who liked to annoy the English, made some derisive statement we all clammed up.

The intercourse was far more lively in the experimental seminars conducted by I. A. Richards and C. K. Ogden on "The Meaning of Meaning" — they preferred to use Americans almost exclusively as their guinea pigs and under their probing inhibitions vanished. It was King's College that now flaunted its intellectual supremacy, with E. M. Forster, Lytton Strachey, and the banker-economist John Maynard Keynes frequenters of their High Table, but they were accessible only to the elders. The Fellow of King's I most enjoyed was Dr. John Sheppard, who brought such felicity and enthusiasm to his lectures on the Greek dramatists. He reminded me of Harvard's Kittredge, though his eccentricities were different: in the excitement of re-enacting a play, the emotion would cause him to thrust both hands in the vents of his gown and suddenly raise the garment over his head. He was a good coach and inspired several undergraduate productions in the Amateur Dramatic Club; under his direction Dennis Arundell played the leading role in *Oedipus Rex.* It was the first Greek tragedy I had seen and I was amazed that through the masks and the translation I should be stirred so deeply. After the final line, "Call no man happy . . ." the lights went out and there was complete silence. How often have a play — and an actor — achieved that?

Walter de la Mare, a good poet, came down to deliver the Clark Lectures and I hoped he would allude to his friendship with Rupert Brooke, but he spoke in a voice so melodious and so muted that I heard only half he said and after a second try, gave up. The poet who cut deeper was Wilfred Owen. *Poems,* the single volume of his work, published posthumously, was a lyrical, powerful protest against the brutality and wastefulness of the war. Owen's verse was a far cry from Brooke's six sonnets of 1914, which I knew by heart:

> *If I should die, think only this of me:*
> *That there's some corner of a foreign field*
> *That is for ever England. There shall be*
> *In that rich earth a richer dust concealed;*
> *A dust whom England bore, shaped, made aware,*
> *Gave, once, her flowers to love, her ways to roam. . . .*

Those sonnets exalted the patriotism that swept young England into the cauldron, and now here from another grave was the answer. The brevity of Owen's career was reminiscent of Keats, whom he had worshipped: a young infantry officer, he was invalided home in 1916 with a bad concussion; in his slow convalescence in a mental hospital he was joined by the officer and poet Siegfried Sassoon, who had been committed as a punishment for his denunciation of the war. Their friendship gave Owen the confidence to release his verses, the first of which were published in a small magazine edited by Edith Sitwell. For a time it seemed as if someone in high place was shielding Owen's talent, but in 1918 he was ordered to return to his old battalion; he crossed to France that summer, was decorated with the Military Cross for his gallantry, and finally met his death in action one week before the Armistice. He was twenty-six and his *Poems*, edited by Sassoon, especially the piteous "Mental Cases," mark him as the finest of the war poets, one who might have given so much more had he survived. "Mental Cases" reminded me of those victims of shell shock who returned on the transport with me, caged on the upper deck, and I instantly responded to the compassion in this superb, shorter lyric:

FUTILITY

Move him into the sun —
Gently its touch awoke him once,
At home, whispering of fields unsown.
Always it woke him, even in France.
Until this morning and this snow.
If anything might rouse him now
The kind old sun will know.

Think how it wakes the seeds —
Woke, once, the clay of a cold star.
Are limbs so dear-achieved, are sides
Full-nerved — still warm — too hard to stir?
Was it for this the clay grew tall?
— Oh, what made fatuous sunbeams toil
To break earth's sleep at all?

This deepening revulsion against the war I found in the poems of Robert Graves and in Edmund Blunden's essay "Overtones of War," which I read in the *Adelphi,* and I accepted it because of what I had seen of the mutilation of men; it became the basis of my judgment of books about the war. Yet I could not forget, as some did, that the love of country and one's sacrifice for it, so ardently expressed in Rupert Brooke's sonnets, was as true of England in 1914–1915 as it had been at the time of the Armada. I read with sympathy a volume of essays,

Disenchantment, by C. E. Montague, one of the abler young writers for the Manchester *Guardian,* who had been a correspondent at the Front. The book was much discussed at the time, for it deplored the loss of youth and of leadership for which the greedy terms of Versailles could never atone. How pervasive was this loss in Britain I had no idea, though a single incident bore witness. On a trip to London I shared a compartment with a well-dressed weather-beaten elder who took one look at me when I spoke to the conductor and then retired behind the protection of *The Times.* When he could bear the silence no longer, he snapped down the upper half of his paper and exclaimed, "Mind you, we'll get it back!"

"What, sir?" I asked in all innocence.

"The sovereignty of the seas!" he glared at me as if I should have known. "You'll never keep up your fleet!"

My acquaintance with my English contemporaries came casually, at the meals in Hall, at lectures, and on the tennis courts where I worked my way into the finals of the Trinity freshman tournament to face a handsome, long-legged Scot named MacInnes. After I had won the first two sets, I became overconfident, and he began to solve my service: his raking ground strokes caught me out of position and he went on to win in five sets. My trophy was a cable-stitch, white sweater with Trinity colors at the V neck and waist.

The Englishman with whom I found I had most in common was H. R. Creswick: three years my junior, he had been too young for the war but he had matured early and had worked effectively in his father's London office so that his elders asked him why he need take a degree. But Dick had a passion for books and would not be denied. He too lived in diggings and was as eager as I to get out of them; we walked the towpath, watching the crews in training for the Lent races or we rode our push bikes out to Grantchester, sacred to Byron and Rupert Brooke, or to see the famous country houses like Madingley, where Edward VII had lived when he studied at Trinity. In November an upperclassman was forced by ill health to leave college and his fine set of rooms next the Queen Anne Gate in Great Court was "thrown on the screens," that is, offered for occupancy. The suite came under Lapsley's jurisdiction and Dick and I asked if we might share it, moving in at the beginning of the next term in January, to which our tutor agreed. It meant that I would exchange my dingy cell on Portugal Place for a living room, twenty-nine by thirty-two feet, with a fireplace wide enough to sleep in, and that I would share the grandeur of Great Court with this short, trim, dark-haired Englishman, bright-eyed and meticulous, who with his quiet sense of humor would teach me about English ways and the rare books he fancied. (In time to come, Dick would be the first Englishman to serve successively as Bodley's Librarian in Oxford and then as the University Librarian in Cambridge.)

Meanwhile I had my writing to do. My piece on the cattle boat had brought me two modest checks, I had sent the "syndicate" a second on the bumping races and would try a third one on the Oxford-Cambridge rugger match in early December. For the Associated Press I made a card file of the Americans in residence and their home-town newspapers. There were 52 of us spread among the 7,000 and I got a line on each of them, with particular attention, naturally, to those who were likely to excel in athletics. In Trinity, for instance, were Ted Hilles, who had been Yale's best miler, and three men who were already playing in test matches for the varsity golf: Webster Todd and Ed Pulling of Princeton, and my Harvard classmate Arthur Gardiner. Harry Atkinson, the Fiske Scholar who had preceded me, had stayed on in hope of making one of the trial eights, perhaps the final crew. At Christ's College was Jimmy Van Alen of Newport, the best singles player in the University, and at Jesus was James Johnson Sweeney, a red-haired, broad-shouldered shot-putter from Princeton. When he did win that event in the intercollege track meet, my piece with the head "Sweeney Wins Shot-put for Jesus" went on the AP wire and earned me a handful of shillings.

4

London on ten pounds a week, could I do it? On the train going up for the Christmas vacation I found in the "personal" column of the *Daily Mail* an address in Chelsea advertising "Bed and Breakfast for a Guinea a Week." A guinea was only one pound and one shilling, so that seemed the place to stay. The house, clean but shabby, with its fine staircase and molding, wore an air of faded glory, and as I climbed the four flights to my room under the eaves, I expressed my admiration to the landlady.

"Oh, yes, sir," she said. "Royalty lived here!"

"Royalty?"

"One of King Edward's favorite lydies lived here."

I put in coppers to heat my little room and was instructed where to put more if I wanted hot water in the bath, but the cot was springy and the skylight adequate for my typing so I paid in advance and went out to see that glorious city of which I can never have enough. I traveled everywhere on top of the red busses, to the Abbey and the National Gallery that first day with a late lunch of beefsteak and kidney pie at

The interior of P–4, Great Court, with its black-walnut paneling and the fireplace which kept our breakfast warm

The American "club," May 1923, after a luncheon at Corpus Christi College. Standing, left to right: Nev Bartow, Monk Hackney, Webster Todd, Anson Stokes, Ted Hilliard. Seated, left to right: Ted Weeks, Ed Pulling, Harry Atkinson, Ev Case, Ted Hilles

Simpson's, then back to spruce up for dinner with Bill and Marjorie Whitman. I called for him at the Curtis Brown office in the late afternoon and he told me the news on the train to Wembley. He had had his fill of reading second-rate manuscripts and had learned all he wanted to know about literary agents. He would enroll as a special student at Oxford beginning in January, and for the Christmas holidays Marjorie's uncle, a wealthy Oxford don, had offered them his well-staffed house in Lewes, Sussex — and I was to come with them. Pargie, he added, had had a miscarriage but was well over it, and never mind their present woeful surroundings, which he referred to as "Mud's End."

Their house was one of a half-completed development, forlorn in a raw red sea of mud; the plaster was so new it sweated and the gas heaters were no match for the dampness. "If love can stand this," I thought — and it clearly could. The Scotch was cheering and over the bottle of St. Emilion I had brought we talked of our days-to-come in Sussex. The uncle, it seems, was a bachelor and a classicist, living on the proceeds of the Warren Paper Company and indulging his tastes in wine, poetry, and the fine arts. He would be off to Italy on the twenty-first, leaving in our care his adopted son, Stephen, fifteen. "But he'll be no trouble," said Bill, and when Pargie kissed me as I departed, I felt I was really wanted.

My first duty was to attend the Oxford-Cambridge rugger match at Twickenham. English football, by which I mean rugger, not soccer, seemed to me a better, faster game than its American offshoot. It is played with a team of fifteen: eight in the "scrum," or line as we would call it; two scrum backs, quick small men who feed the ball to a backfield of four speedsters; and a fullback, the safety, who does the punting. They play in shorts, with no padding or helmets, there is no substitution, and since downfield blocking or interference is illegal, there are very few injuries. The ball is in constant motion, and if a man has his wind knocked out or twists an ankle, the team plays on without him while he recovers on the sideline. The Cambridge scrum was led by Wakefield, a monster of a man and an inspired captain. I had followed the early games, had lunched with Arthur Young, one of the scrum backs who gave me pointers, and I was confident Cambridge would win, which it did. When that article was written and posted, I was free as air.

My love of history drew me to the National Portrait Gallery to see how the great ones looked; thence to Kensington Palace and down the Thames to Greenwich; I spent hours at the British Museum, took the bus to Hampstead, to the small double house in which Keats lived with his friend Brown on one side and his passion, Fanny Brawne, on the other. I walked the Heath to get the view he so loved of London, with

St. Paul's in the golden Turner haze, and stood beside the propped-up, aged mulberry tree under which he sat writing "Ode to a Nightingale." Balcony seats were cheap, and from on high I watched *Charlot's Revue,* starring those three incomparables, Jack Buchanan, the dancer, Gertrude Lawrence, and Beatrice Lillie. "Bea," with her sleek seal head and her clear impudent voice, singing and acting "Rule Britannia" or "There Are Fairies at the Bottom of my Garden" or in her parody of a lady attempting to order "A Dozen Double Damask Dinner Napkins" was, I thought, the funniest woman in the kingdom.

In London I purchased the back issues of a new monthly, the *Adelphi,* to which I had subscribed in Cambridge. It was edited by John Middleton Murry, and each issue contained the work of writers I wanted to know more about: D. H. Lawrence, Edmund Blunden, H. M. Tomlinson, and chief among them, Katherine Mansfield, the wife of the editor. I admired the luminous quality of her work and the feeling with which her characters were charged; it seemed to me that this little magazine in its canary covers, with no illustrations and few advertisements, was in a class by itself.

In the novelty and adjustment of Cambridge, Fritzy had drifted far away, as indeed she was; even a clipping from a San Francisco paper about the cruise ship S.S. *Resolute,* on which Fritzy had won the diving contest and been promised a bath in champagne, did not pique my jealousy. But now as I entered the intimacy of young marriage with Bill and Pargie, their physical delight in each other and their confiding to me, after Stephen had gone yawning to bed, that I would never taste real bliss until I was married made Fritzy seem more desirable than she had been in the Orient. Bill, blushing in his asides, could not repress the delicious discoveries of the connubial bed.

The big house at Lewes was enchanting: books everywhere, a few fine paintings, and in the bicycle shed Rodin's "Lovers," the pair seated in entwined rapture but far too large to be lodged in any room. The wine was excellent and, bemused, I came up to read and drowse in my tower room, the open fire flickering as I drifted off, and on the shelves the Elizabethan poets and dramatists, some of whose sentiments began to color my letters to the *Resolute.*

Happiness never comes cheap and the price we paid was Stephen, who was with us every waking hour. He was big for fifteen, did not care for books, and longed to excel. His two accomplishments were Japanese wrestling, at which his wrist was no match for Bill's, and Maskelyne's magic tricks, no one of which had he quite mastered, though he tried them on us each a score of times. Together we four walked the tawny Downs; we watched the hunt gather on New Year's

Day, and to work off Stephen's energy we would bet him five shillings that he could not climb to the top of the great slope seen from the library and signal to us within fifty minutes, a bet we gladly lost for the quiet that followed. Poor Stephen, for we were wrapped in a love from which he was excluded.

It was a different life which Dick Creswick and I were treated to when we moved into P-4 Great Court. His parents, whom I visited in Hertfordshire and who gave me my first country appetite for jugged hare and blood sausage, had sent up the linen, silver and furniture for our comfort and Dick had purchased a convertible sofa on which he would sleep in the big room while I occupied the tiny bedroom. Now in the prime months of the British calendar we became part of the color of Great Court. It is, I believe, the largest quadrangle in any British university; only a swift runner like Lord Burghley could sprint around its four sides while the chapel clock strikes twelve. Through our open windows we heard the splash of the fountain in the center, Trinity's principal water supply until the nineteenth century, and our ears grew accustomed to the chapel clock, which ever since the eighteenth century had been chiming the quarters and each hour twice over. We watched our spry Master, the eminent J. J. Thomson, hurrying toward the Lodge, the once brilliant philosopher McTaggart, now grown old and eccentric, or a waiter from the buttery, balancing on his head the wooden tray with the dishes for a private dinner. We lived in creature comfort, each day heralded by the stir of the "bedder" who cleared the ashes from the grate, built a fresh fire, and placed before it the hot covered dishes of our breakfast.

History for me is personalities and it was fun to locate those who had dwelt here before us. For our baths, we padded forty yards in the open to the southeast corner of the Court where tubs, that modern convenience, were installed. In the attic directly above, Byron, in defiance of the ban on keeping dogs in college, had housed a tame bear. There was no regulation about bears, so he took his walking on a chain, though, I suspect, not for long. According to Louis T. Stanley in *The Cambridge Year*, Byron's other extracurricular activities in 1805 included "swimming by the weir above Granchester, a place now called Byron's Pool; riding; boxing under the training of his pugilist-friend, Jackson; shooting with pistols," and no one can doubt that he read. Diagonally across from us was the entry where on one side dwelt Sir Isaac Newton, who matriculated in 1661 at the age of eighteen, and departed, world-renowned, at fifty-three. In the same entry, to the right, were the ground-floor rooms in which Thackeray in 1830 lost so much of his patrimony to two professional gamblers that he was sent down without a degree. The list is endless; I picked out those I liked: Tennyson, ever grateful to Trinity, roomed behind us in New Court; John Donne, a Catholic too bright to be denied, matriculated in 1587, but departed without a degree; so did Dryden in 1650 — he was "discommuned for contumacy to the Vice-Master."

Dick and I fared well as roommates: he withdrew to the Wren Library when I was typing, and now that I could entertain in style, made allowance for my occasional bridge parties. We frequently lunched together in the big room — sliced ham, Bass's ale, currant buns from Matthews, and tea of which he was a master-brewer — and the talk was often of books. I had introduced him to David, the secondhand bookseller, whose barrow in the market place was a treasure trove. David, as he bid in the libraries of estates on the market, had his eye on the rarities; the more familiar volumes, and broken sets, however fine the binding, he offered at ridiculously low prices. My Boswell's *Johnson* in tree calf, much annotated, with the owner's name torn out of the title page, cost me two shillings a volume, my quite elegant Francis Bacon I got for four. Dick was primarily interested in incunabula, but he kept an experienced eye on my needs, and wherever he found the handsome, beautifully illustrated Malory's *Morte d'Arthur* he gave me, it could not have been cheap.

In the Lent term throughout the academic world animal spirits grew restive. Cambridge had cultivated the pose that it was a place for men without women, and although the girls from Newnham and Girton were underfoot and to be seen in the front rows of any lecture, the Cambridge Senate steadily refused to grant them degrees. A certificate should suffice. But Oxford had already capitulated and when the Cambridge Vice-Chancellor showed a tendency to surrender, the students demonstrated their disapproval. The small sports car that he drove was seized and disassembled in the dead of night, transported by hoist and ladder to the roof of the Senate House, where it was put together again and left on view as a public remonstrance. Such "rags" were usually organized by the students of Gonville and Caius College, known as "Keys," and quite apart from whatever bribery was necessary, this one called for engineering skill and extraordinary agility.

As the spring vacation approached, Morley Dobson of Corpus Christi and I made plans for a bicycle trip that would take us in a circuitous way to the Lake Country and to Derwentwater. I had liked him as a shy poet at Harvard, where his lyrics had appeared in the *Advocate*. England had enchanted him — he was to become a British subject — and in his soft-spoken way he wanted to share his pleasure in it with me.

Fair, nearsighted, with very pink coloring he was much tougher than he looked, especially on a push bike. His love of poetry was combined with a love of height and he had ideas of doing some climbing which I did not take seriously. Wordsworth and Coleridge went with us in our knapsacks.

The Roman roads were a joy; like smooth straight dikes pointing north, they were graded for the swinging cadence of the legions, and we too limbered our leg muscles as we rode from Cambridge to Ely, and from Ely to Lincoln, where we took our time in the beautiful cathedral. At York we spent the night the better to see the Minster, to walk the old ramparts, to poke about the little streets and bookshops, and to treat ourselves to a dinner of mutton. We were living on six shillings a day — $1.50 in the currency of that time — and that meant a double bed in the Temperance hotels, the cleanest and cheapest hostelries, and if Temperance wasn't available, then we would try for a spare room over the local bakery. Fresh bread in the early morning gives one a good send-off. Morley was on the lookout for the Roman tile, the Norman tower, the crusader's tomb, the battle flags and inscriptions in the village church that told of the reigning family; I, for the ancient fig arbor in the rector's garden, for any quaintness in this rural life about which I was unabashedly curious: as a team we enlarged each other's view.

From York we headed northwest to Richmond with its great medieval Keep dominating the river, and nearby the ruins of Easby abbey, best seen as we walked to it through the woods by moonlight. After Richmond we came to the Vales and Dales, now pushing the bikes ahead of us as we slugged up the unridable hills, and now sweeping down the long deserted roads. Wild, sparsely inhabited country, numbering more sheep than people, with rocky streams that looked like trout, and little stone farmhouses or tiny hamlets miles apart.

Our big meal of the day was breakfast — eggs and sausage, fresh rolls, strawberry jam, and buckets of tea. We'd be on the road by eight; would slow down to look at any ancient barrow, Roman ruin, or tempting churchyard; and would knock off at noon for beer and cheese at the local pub. I remember that during one day's ride in Yorkshire we were passed by two automobiles, while we in turn passed four farm carts and one old surrey. We took in the country through all our senses, and we learned that the reward of sight-seeing is in inverse ratio to the speed: the slower you go the more you appreciate. We could cover fifty miles by three-thirty, and then it was time to find a spare room, stow our knapsacks, and sight-see.

At Keswick, where the daffodils were nodding, we made our headquarters in a comfortable room over the bakery, and rejoiced in the suppers of thin sliced ham, fragrant loaves, and comforting tea with which the baker's wife stoked us on our return from a day on the wet and windy heights. Here Morley acquired a handbook on mountain climbing by Mr. Abraham, the seer of the Lake Country, also a rope and the calked boots which, he said, we needed for the scree on the upland slopes of Scafell, Great End, and Helvellyn. Morley had been here before, and each morning he guided me to a convenient farm at the base of one of these peaks. Because he knew the rock faces, he led, and with my faintheartedness about the task, I followed — which was not easy. We used the whole day for climbing, our lunch was a bar of chocolate — chocolate, and water from one of the tarns, was our fortifier — but the real reward was when, tense and panting, we scrabbled up the last twenty yards of crusted snow and rolled over on the crest with the world at our feet.

On one warm day's climb we disobeyed Mr. Abraham, who had laid down firm injunctions against following the bed of a brook in the spring. But it was temptingly easy to kick a footing in a snowy little runoff, and not until we had reached the upper rock face, the more treacherous for the film of ice which coated the toeholds left by an earlier ice-pick, did we realize why Mr. Abraham had said no. Then it was too late. The rope braced us, and I think we did the last fifteen yards with the strength of our fingernails. We were so winded (and I so terrified) when at last we pulled ourselves over the top that we lay there longer than usual, munching the chocolate and reviewing our conquest. At this moment, up the path on the safe side (there is always a path) came a severe, retired colonel and his obedient terrier wife. "Did you see the pair of idiots below you," he asked indignantly, "messing about on that ice face? Really too sickening. Wonder they weren't killed!" We said we hadn't noticed.

I made the home trip alone, Morley having decided that he wanted every last minute at the Lakes. Fountains Abbey, so green and gold on that lovely afternoon, gave me the eerie feeling that I had been there in another incarnation: I all but recognized the cell I had occupied. I came down through what remains of Sherwood Forest; I saw Nottingham, and then I found myself pushing along through the cinders and smokestacks of industrial England. How I wanted to get out of it!

I finally did at Peterborough, but by that time I had run out of cash and out of air. Both tires had developed slow leaks, and had to be blown up alternately every three miles. I was down to my last sixpence and Cambridge seemed a long, long distance in the future. So I took a gamble. With my sixpence I bought a platform pass to the Peterborough railway platform; there I waited for the next train to Cambridge, on the chance that among the Peterborough passengers I would find at least one student from whom I could borrow the price of a return ticket. I found him in a Trinity don, George Kitson Clark, who after being surprised by my predicament happily bailed me out. We had supper that night in his rooms — mutton, wine, and *crème brûlée*. A happy ending.

With new tires I continued to bicycle for the remainder of the holiday. From Southwark Cathedral in London I followed the way Chaucer's pilgrims had taken to the shrine of Thomas à Becket and I traced Mr. Pickwick's adventures in Kent. Whenever I was in the vicinity of Sevenoaks and weary of being alone, I threw myself on the mercy of Arthur Gardiner's family: his father, a shipping magnate and a Gloucestershire man who looked like Jove; his mother an American and a dear friend of my Aunt Liz. They always made me welcome, asked where I'd been, fed me up, and after some Gilbert and Sullivan at the piano I'd totter off to the guest room. On these trips to Kent I tried to imagine what it was like to have lived in the old luxury of Knole or in Penshurst, the lovely home of Sir Philip Sidney. After visiting Warwick Castle I spent the night in a roadside pub. Mine evidently was the only spare room and the partition being thin I listened for what seemed hours to the wife's entreaty with her husband to give up the liquor business, which was taking too much of their friends' money and getting them into bad habits. I had never heard that side argued before and it put me in mind of an article on Prohibition which I wrote for the *Granta* on my return to Great Court.

5

In the spring the slumbering Cam came alive. The crews multiplied: there must have been twoscore of them, the varsity oarsmen now adding strength to their college boats, all reaching and straining for the rhythm that would be needed in the bumping races in May Week, a euphemism for the terminal festivities that actually take place in June, and last a fortnight. The punts emerged from hibernation and were ready for hire. A punt is a narrow, ten-foot scow with a flat bottom and blunt ends, wide enough for a couple to lie full length on the cushions, safe enough for flirtation on placid water; it is propelled either by a paddle or more expertly by a pole wielded from the stern in gondolier style. But if, in a show of strength, the pole is shoved too hard into the oozy bottom, one may be faced with the choice of abandoning it or of being hung up (and doused) as the boat slides out from under your feet. Now the attractive girls from the women's colleges came under closer inspection. I confined my attention to two Americans: the dark-haired Alida Bigelow, who came from St. Paul, Minnesota, and had known Scott Fitzgerald, and Betty McVicker, from my home state. For safety's sake I employed the paddle, not the pole. The art of punting is to avoid collisions as one talks of the Future, while creeping past King's Chapel with its green meadow, under Clare Bridge, called "the bridge of uncountable balls" because of its decoration, under Trinity Bridge, with its famous old avenue of limes, past the busy tennis courts of St. John's, and under its Bridge of Sighs to the lower reaches, where the down-dripping willows offer seclusion and the chance in Rupert Brooke's words

> *To smell the thrilling-sweet and rotten*
> *Unforgettable, unforgotten*
> *River-smell* . . .

And early in May came Fritzy. I had word from her that she was leaving the cruise in France, detaching herself from her chaperon, and if I could find someone to assume that function in Cambridge, she would like to pay a six-day visit. Lapsley seemed my best bet as he and her father had been Harvard classmates; when I asked him he looked at me gravely and said that he'd be delighted to accept the responsibility and that Dick Creswick could be his deputy when he was otherwise engaged. I reserved a room for her at the Blue Boar, the nearest hostel to Trinity and began to plan.

She surprised me by flying, not boating, across the Channel — that was audacious in 1923 — and surprised me further with her Paris wardrobe, particularly her suit of beige wool, the skirt of which was simply wrapped around her shapely thighs: when she walked the slit on the right gave a good view of her calf and knee, and when she rode the bicycle I had hired for her, the view went higher. It was a rather heavy machine with a small gear, so the opening and closing of the skirt was frequent and beguiling. She had not ridden for years, and when following me into the narrow twisting street with cyclists flying by in both directions, it was small wonder that she ran squarely into the bobby directing traffic opposite the Round Church. "I saw you coming, miss," he said, "but you really should keep on the left." On the towpath, where we went to watch the crews, the reaction was more predictable: as we approached an eight, resting on their oars and listening to their coach, all eyes would suddenly shift to Fritzy and her skirt; the coach, on his horse and unaware, would look up and cover his embarrassment by shouting, "Eyes in the boat! Come forward! Ready! Row!" It happened twice.

A long engagement is only supportable by the rediscovery that comes

The Wych-Elms and the mounting block

after separation. We had not seen each other for eight months and there was no distraction. After a decorous tea with Mr. Lapsley we strolled out through Nevile's Court, leaned on the parapet of Trinity Bridge to watch the punts and then continued along Lime Row and into the Backs. One of the glories of the Backs was the row of wych-elms, nearly three centuries old, creating their pools of black shadows in the sunset, and in their midst, like a small gem, was a white stone mounting block, each step worn down by the myriad of riders who had used it in the past. A second glory is the Trinity Fellows' Garden, where in the fragrance of lilacs we heard our first nightingale. I took her to the varsity courts at Fenners, and in a three-set trial I won my Fenners blazer, as consolation for not winning a Blue. On a picnic in the woods of Madingley, we got off to a bad start when I seated us on a bed of nettles, but things improved: she began telling me of the incredible beauty of Peking which I hushed with my kisses.

We were served dinner every night in the big room before the cozy fire, but not until I had appeared in Hall in my gown and tipped my cap to the marker. Usually we were joined by Dick, and we always had wine; I knew I was running up a large bill and didn't care. The climax came on May 11, when Dick introduced us to his girl, Agnes, a comforting person with a sharp sense of humor whom we both liked; she had arrived with Dick's parents and his uncle to celebrate his twenty-first birthday. In the big room the spring flowers and candlelight shone against the dark paneling. The refectory table was large enough for us all; Trinity's kitchen sent up its best and the champagne and toasts pledged a friendship that has never faltered.

The next noon before her departure Fritzy asked if I could loan her five pounds. I could just make it, and after I put her aboard her train I walked the long way back to college. The formal notification from Lapsley that I had exceeded my allowance for wine and food from the buttery was no surprise. Anyway I was broke.

Only news-notes for the Associated Press could provide relief in the less than the thirty days that remained, and I wrote up those Americans who were figuring in the spring activities. Next to Trinity my favorite college was the smallest, Corpus Christi. Among its one hundred undergraduates were two good friends: Morley Dobson, who was finishing a long poem that came within one vote of winning the Chancellor's Medal, and Everett Case, formerly of Princeton, and like myself a fringe member of the tennis squad. Of the dons, two had been particularly cordial, Kenneth Pickthorn and Arthur Goodhart; twice the latter had taken me as his guest to the Quinquaginta Club, for which I had to have special leave, where our partners were Rosamond Lehmann, the prettiest girl at Girton, and Arthur's bride-to-be, Cecily, who held the same honor at Newnham. Now, as our stay shortened, Goodhart gave a luncheon for ten Americans who he hoped would be on the lookout for likely candidates for Cambridge, and afterwards we had our picture taken in Corpus Old Court. Of the ten, only one I believe, Ed Pulling, knew precisely what he wanted to do: teach in a boys' boarding school until he had raised sufficient capital to found one of his own. (But from that picture frame there emerged in time a headmaster, a college president, a judge of the juvenile court, an Episcopal bishop, a builder of Rockefeller Center, a professor of English, and an editor.)

I knew I was headed for journalism or publishing and the choice was narrowed for me by Alice Duer Miller. She was my cousin and she was visiting her son, Denning, my classmate at Harvard, now at Christ's College. Elegant, witty, fine-featured, she had turned to writing social comedy when her husband lost his stake in Mexico. She knew all of literary New York. Alice came to have tea with me, alone — Denny was rowing — and as she remarked the beauty of the room and turned for the view of Great Court, I found myself wondering where I would be in three months' time.

"Alice," I asked, "if you were looking for some kind of literary work, where would you begin?"

She thought for a few moments. "There are three men in New York," she said, "all young, for whom it would be fun to work: Nelson Doubleday, son of the publisher, who is on his own and has just brought out a successful book on etiquette. Then, Harold Ross, editor of the *American Legion Weekly* — he's raising money for a new magazine. And thirdly, Horace Liveright, who has put together an incredible list of authors in five years. I'd look up each one of them." When she left she dipped into her handbag and came out with a five-pound note which she pressed into my hand; whether it was her innate kindness or that she detected my financial strain I could not know, but I told her it would come in mighty handy and I would repay her later, as I did.

The last days sped by. There was an evening of folk dancing with spectators crowding the four sides of Nevile's Court in the lingering silver dusk, and we were so carried away by the frenzy of the Scottish Sword Dance that it had to be repeated. I took my farewell of Lapsley, whom I had come to admire, and presented him with my handsomely bound copy of Bacon's *Essays*. I saw the pavilion for the Trinity Ball go up beside the river, and knew I could never afford it — and then while I packed my trunk, Dick boxed my books and, unknown to me, placed in their midst, wrapped in tissue paper, a knife, fork, and spoon with the Trinity hallmark such as we daily used in Hall, explaining in a note that it was traditional to take home a set as a reminder.

It had been a memorable year with kindly people. My admiration for the English and my appreciation of their humor were a priming more valuable than I realized in my eagerness to be home and on my own. When I cleaned up my bills, the balance was too little to pay my return passage; Arthur Gardiner's parents had invited me to motor with them for a week in Cornwall and Gloucestershire and after that I would try my luck "on the beach" in London. We drove to Mr. Gardiner's home place, wove our way in and out of the fishing villages on the west coast, feasted on strawberries and Devonshire cream and speculated about the sea-washed ruins of Tintagel, which may have been King Arthur's stronghold. Then good-bye! Good-bye!

To go "on the beach" in any foreign port one must be under the necessity of working one's passage home. Herman Melville was literally on the beach in Tahiti when he signed on as an ordinary seaman in an American frigate. In London, those of us needing a berth gathered each morning in the cellar of the American consulate where a bored clerk had us fill out cards giving our qualifications (mine read "dishwasher, steward, ordinary seaman"); then we sat, awaiting the daily report from homeward-bound passenger liners requiring extra hands for the return trip. I palled up with a couple of clean-looking A.B.'s who had been too drunk to get aboard their freighter when she sailed. They were busted and repentant and, over the beer and cheese I paid for, they promised to show me the ropes if we drew the same ship. At last the S.S. *President Polk* of the United States Line showed up; she had a big passenger list, was taking on immigrants at Queenstown and needed a dozen extra men. Armed with our cards, which I took for a promise, we all went down to Limehouse together but not before I spent my last pound bribing the freight agent to get my trunk on the boat.

We were directed aboard and down to the stern where the First Officer was looking over the prospects. Alas, the word had gone out to every pub in Limehouse, and here came stokers, oilers, stewards, A.B.'s, all with an experience that outclassed a cattle hand. When the field was reduced to three, bidding for the last job of Ordinary Seaman, I spoke up with a confidence I did not feel, and suggested we draw straws. God was kind and I drew the long one. I would not have had money for a night's lodging had I lost.

"You're on the First Watch," said the officer. "Get into the clothes you'll find on your bunks and report on the forward deck. We're sailing shortly." In my dark jersey with s.s. PRESIDENT POLK in white letters and my blue denims, I went up to the bow. The warping, I believe that is the word for it, of a liner out of the Limehouse docks began with the taking in of the wire cable, which like a giant cobra came inching over the winch. I stood at the rail watching, fascinated. There seemed to be some hullabaloo on the bridge. A voice from a bullhorn shouted, "Tell that goddamn fool by the winch to stand away!" As there was no one else in that position, he must have meant me, and I obeyed. "If that cable ever broke and you were within range," said Harry to me later, "the whiplash could kill you." Harry was the more talkative of the pair I had fed. He slept in the bunk above and was constantly confiding bits of his experience. "After I've been at sea for awhile," he told me, "I feel like taking things easy ashore and I can always find a widow to sleep with. No problem there. Now, if I'm working when I live with her I lose weight. But if she's just taking care of me, I put it on."

It was an agreeable voyage. At Queenstown I watched the Irish immigrants as they came into the steerage, weeping and lamenting. An hour later when land was out of sight someone struck up a jig on his accordion, and the deck was full of dancing couples.

The food was excellent, the work not onerous, and I was being paid. When I wasn't painting I was swabbing the deck, scrubbing a holystone across the white wood promenade. There were a couple of Hollywood beauties amidships and those on the early watch went slowly by their cabin, hoping for a glimpse in negligee. Midway across, a cable warned us that the *Mauretania* was also homeward bound with a load of immigrants, and if we were to get ours under the quota, our only chance was to dock ahead of her at Boston. We made it by a narrow margin, and while the Irish disembarked, I stood by the rail in my sailor's garb enjoying my first view of home.

VI

THE NOISE and humidity of Manhattan in mid-July of 1923 were quite a change from the tranquillity of Great Court and the cool English rain. Elizabeth was quieter but just as sticky. My English tweeds were too heavy; I put them away and spent my pay from the *President Polk* for a light linen suit. Mother and the family were in a cottage on Lake Champlain but I was not going anywhere until I had a job.

My brother Rufus, five years my junior, had graduated from preparatory school and gone straight to work for my father; Dad told me he was learning fast and would make an excellent salesman. We three kept bachelors' hall: Rufus and I took turns frying the breakfast eggs and bacon; we commuted together and occasionally got back in time for some tennis at the country club before supper. The old man, when he felt like it, could cook up a tasty meal for a hot night.

There were a good many college graduates in New York that summer in quest of a job and it did not take me long to shed the illusion that editorial work was to be had for the asking. My old friend Frederick Lewis Allen, who used to feed me the handouts at University Hall, had become the assistant editor of *Harper's Magazine;* he knew my credentials better than anyone, so I began with him. Their editorial staff, he assured me, was a small one and there were no openings at the moment, but he would keep me in mind.

Next, with a letter from Alice Duer Miller, I applied to Harold Ross in the rather shabby office of the *American Legion Weekly* on West Thirteenth Street. A lean, high-strung guy with a bottle-brush haircut, he skimmed the note and looked me over with his keen eyes.

"Did you like England?" And without waiting for a reply, "As Alice may have told you, I'm trying to raise the capital for a new magazine. I might have a place for you six months from now . . ."

"Sorry, but I can't wait that long," I said.

Then I tried three leads on my own. Carl Van Doren, tall and considerate, heard me out and seemed genuinely sorry that the *Century's* editorial staff was full. Frank Crowninshield, the dapper editor of *Vanity Fair,* said he'd like to think it over, and a few days later wrote that I seemed "too serious for the position he had in mind." As Edmund Wilson, hardly a lightweight, was at that time his managing editor, I accepted this as a polite evasion. Finally, I tried my favorite newspaper, the New York *Tribune.* In my interview with the managing editor, Julian Mason, I told him how much I admired the sheet, and I sensed that there was a chance.

"Will you go on the rewrite desk?" he asked.

"Sir," I said, "I'm really a better reporter. I'd much rather be on the street."

"Well, come back and see me a week from today."

That was my single ray of hope as I kept knocking on other doors and generally the brush-off was that I "lacked experience." In dismay I returned to Elizabeth, rumpled and sweaty, at the day's end. A couple of sets of tennis revived me — perhaps tomorrow I'd get a break. On the day appointed I went back to see Mr. Mason and to my joy received a definite assignment as a reporter to begin the following Monday at $35 a week. Dad shook up cocktails for the three of us to celebrate (we had them only on special occasions). But that was the weekend the *Tribune* and the New York *Herald* merged; the last to be employed were the first to be cut, and I was released before I ever began. Once more to the pavements.

My letter from Cousin Alice got me into the sanctum of Horace Liveright, a surprisingly gay and decorative room for such a sober brownstone front on West Forty-eighth Street. Tall, well tailored, with a carnation in his buttonhole, Liveright had something of the actor about him, but what attracted me were his dark eyes, which seemed to enlarge with animation.

"Do you think you could persuade Mrs. Miller to bring her books to us?" he asked, after reading her note.

"I'm not sure," I said.

"Well, that's beside the point," he said. "We need a salesman. Do you think you could sell books?" I knew by now that I had to get my foot in the door.

"I would sure like to try!"

Mr. Liveright buzzed for a Mr. Messner and Dick Simon, a towering, long-armed man of my age with a likable smile. After the briefest of formalities, it was agreed that I should be given a tryout as Simon's understudy, and while he rounded up some advance copies for me to read over the weekend, Mr. Messner, in a kindly way, described my job: I'd be selling in the city; $35 a week as a start; and we worked on Saturdays only during the fall rush. "You'll go out with Dick Simon at first," he said. "He'll introduce you to the buyers. Be sure to familiarize yourself with the books he gives you, you'll be selling some of them next week." After all those days of dismay, I had landed a job.

I had known a little about Boni and Liveright before my call. The firm had put together an extraordinary list of authors — Eugene O'Neill, George Moore, Theodore Dreiser, Rose Macaulay, Sherwood Anderson — in less than six years. They had a reputation for publishing bawdy books like the *Satyricon* at a high price and in limited editions, to avoid the watchdogs of the New York Society for the Suppression of Vice. Their backlog was the Modern Library, reprints in a linoleum binding smelling like cod liver oil, that were edited by Albert Boni before he left the firm. It was said that Liveright, now the boss, would gamble on any promising writer, as he had gambled on Wall Street before he entered publishing. The catalogue which Dick Simon included in the package he gave me I studied as carefully as I did the four glossy volumes I showed to Dad and Rufus as evidence of my new trade. The first one I read, *Strenuous Americans* by Roy F. Dibble, a Columbia professor, was a collection of profiles of outdoorsmen like Teddy Roosevelt and Amos Pinchot, which I thought pedestrian; of the novels there was *Flaming Youth,* a fleshy account of undergraduate life by Warner Fabian, which was sexier but not so good as *This Side of Paradise.*

Monday morning I was given a desk on the third floor and my order book, and then Dick introduced me to the key people. There was Manuel Komroff, a jolly pipe-smoking original who had been in Petrograd with John Reed at the time of the Russian Revolution, and who while nominally in charge of manufacture, was a very shrewd editor as well. Komroff with his wheezy laugh appealed to me, and brown became him — brown moustache, brown hair brushed over his high forehead, brown suit and twinkling brown eyes. There was Isadore Schneider, a poet who spent his days laying out the Boni and Liveright advertisements, sketching with his thick black pencil the firm's colophon of a monk bent over his tablet, the trademark for the least monastic list of authors in America. And on the fourth floor there was Beatrice Kaufman, the black-eyed intelligent wife of the playwright George Kaufman. Thoughtful and sympathetic, "Bea" read manuscripts, but so I soon learned did anyone else who wanted to. The firm was small enough for everyone to know what was going on: the day's reorders were placed

Dorothy and Frederick L. Allen, on
Marlborough Street, Boston, 1923

Manuel Komroff, Paris, 1926

on a round table in what must have been the dining room of the old house and we all riffled through them to see if *Black Oxen* by Gertrude Atherton, our best seller, was still at the top of the list. T. R. Smith, the editor responsible for so many of our foreign importations, was in Europe and I got the impression he had a free rein.

Tuesday a friend had invited me to play tennis after work and stay overnight at his home in Forest Hills, so I took my racket and tennis clothes in a small bag to the office. I spent the day reading our new books and as the afternoon was waning Dick Simon stopped by and proposed that we make an introductory call on the Scribner Book Store, one block away on Fifth Avenue. "Let's show them *Strenuous Americans*," he suggested; "they ought to take twenty-five copies. Don't forget your order book." Figuring that after the call I could take off for Long Island, I gathered up my racket and bag as well. Dick eyed them but said nothing.

Scribner's and Brentano's were then the two elegant bookstores in New York. Dick piloted me through the counters and upstairs to the mezzanine, where George Whitworth, the book buyer, had his desk. The conversation went as follows:

"Mr. Whitworth, I'd like you to meet our new salesman, Ted Weeks."

"Hello," he said. "What have you got there, a dirty book?"

"No," I said, putting down the racket and bag on an empty chair. "It's a collection of sketches about naturalists and outdoorsmen like Teddy Roosevelt. Scribner's should do well with it."

"Have you read it?"

"Yes."

"Do you like it?"

"Not very much."

"Better put us down for five copies. And come back and see me anytime."

I wrote down the order, we shook hands, and Dick and I departed. At the corner of Fifth Avenue and Forty-sixth Street, Dick paused and looked down at me. "Ted," he said, "go on to your game. But next time, leave the racket in the office. And if you don't like a book, try not to be so blunt about it."

After that inauspicious beginning, thanks to Dick's patient example I learned to do better. He was a superb salesman because he believed so genuinely in what he was selling and was so honest about its possibilities: if it was commercial fiction he said so; if a book had literary merit he praised it; if it would appeal to a limited readership, he pushed it in the small, personal bookshops. I watched his technique with Miss Gage, the smart-as-a-whip buyer for Macy's who rarely allowed you more than three minutes for any single title: he excited her interest and she trusted him. I was given the long shots, the first novels and the literary gambles; I worked hard over *The Sacrificial Goat,* a novel, perhaps libelous, said to be based on the unpublished love story of George Bernard Shaw, and when I came back with an order for one hundred from Lord and Taylor, Dick and Jules Messner took me to lunch at the French restaurant next door. (After Christmas we had to give them credit for fifty copies that hadn't moved.) I did well with a much better book, Doughty's *Travels in Arabia Deserta,* which we imported in two expensive volumes from England and soon had to reprint. I earned the confidence of the buyers at Wanamaker's as well as Lord and Taylor, went as far afield as the department stores in Brooklyn, and was very attentive to a classy uptown shop with a fine clientele known as "The Sunrise Turn." In this apprenticeship I became very fond of Dick Simon. He could calculate discounts and profits with a swiftness I lacked, but privately he was dedicated, as I was, to the literary value of what we were doing and there was an understanding between us I prized. I was sorry he was leaving to start a firm of his own with an idea man named Max Schuster, who was very good at public relations.

2

There was neither time nor money for a weekend at Long Point, so my first reunion with Fritzy was when she came to town early in September to freshen up her wardrobe for Bryn Mawr. Remembering our English picnics I asked Dad if I could borrow the car for her last Saturday: she would come out on the early morning train to Elizabeth, we'd picnic on the way to Seabright, go for a swim with my friend Bob Sanderson, and then ease back. She had a dinner party with her family at eight. I thought my parents reacted strangely. "The road to the shore is more crowded than you remember," they said. But this seemed to be our best chance to be alone and we started off with our packed lunch and a Thermos. The road was indeed crowded; then we were detoured into a two-lane crawl and finally in the vicinity of Perth Amboy were obliged to cross a bridge, if ever our bumper-to-bumper line could reach it. By the time the damn bridge was behind us, it was one-thirty, so we pulled into a field and ate our lunch sitting with our backs against a roadside advertisement. The scraps I buried, keeping a hard-boiled egg and a jam sandwich if things were as bad coming back. Too late for a swim when we reached Seabright, we had just time enough to wash up, have a drink and some small talk before we started home. Bob told me of a better road but evidently others knew of it too; we could never make Elizabeth in time for Fritzy to catch her train, so

I shoved her off at the Rahway railway station with a kiss and the waxed paper of leftovers in case the local to New York was late. She wrote me that what she opened on the train was a mess of egg shells and bread crusts. I had buried the wrong packet. We were subsisting on our love letters and the remembrance of this fiasco added to our longing for next time.

Now that I had the security of a job I was determined to live in New York. The commuting from Elizabeth involved three changes — the train to the Hudson Tunnel, change there, and change again on the New York side to an uptown express to Forty-second Street — over an hour with the best of connections, and sure to be longer at the five o'clock rush. I loathed it, but wondered what better I could afford on my salary. I was catching up with the family now that they had returned from the lake: with Frederika, a tall girl who of us all most closely resembled Mother; with Eliza — "Tiny" to me — whose looks and generosity reminded me of Aunt Liz; and with Jack, who on the q.t. did side-splitting imitations of Dad losing his temper. But the nest was crowded and I had to get out.

I obviously needed a roommate to share the cost and I wrote to Berry Fleming, that witty, slow-speaking Southerner who had lived across the hall from me in Hollis and who was now working on the Augusta *Chronicle:* I knew he wanted to write and it turned out that he had sold a few short pieces to *Life* and was eager to free-lance in New York if I could line up something cheap. The living room of the Harvard Club on Forty-fourth Street with its portraits and backgammon tables was a clearinghouse for those who did business uptown and in it I encountered another classmate, Eliot Cabot, whose mournful dark eyes and long upper lip cast him as the ideal rejected lover: he had been a leading man in the Hasty Pudding shows and now had an excellent part in *White Cargo* which seemed destined for a long run. I told him of my hope that Berry would come north and it was agreed that he would join us when his present lease ran out if an inexpensive apartment could be found. On my selling trips downtown I began to search.

What I found was in Greenwich Village, a third-floor walk-up at 105 West Eleventh Street: two fireplaces, one in each of the "large" rooms, small bedrooms at the front and back of the hall, kitchen with gas range, and the use of the bathroom on the floor below — all for $75 a month. There was no electricity at first, but the landlord promised it would be installed. It is true that our east wall faced the Sixth Avenue Elevated and the whole place trembled like jelly when a train went by, but one could get used to that and there weren't many trains after midnight. I wrote a slightly exaggerated description to Berry and we took it.

Our landlord was a Greek doctor whose prosperous practice over-flowed the waiting room on the ground floor. On the second floor in dusty gilt and faded velvet lived the "Countess of Castelvecchio" (who said she liked to hear Berry's typing, it kept her company) and the "Professor," her husband, who was the Italian translator at a munici-pal court. We shared the bathroom with them. The "Countess" did their cooking on a gas ring, he had taught the doctor English, and I think they were given the place in gratitude. My family sent over some cast-off furniture, including a battered couch easily converted into a guest bed, and to help us move in was a janitor named Jesus Christ because of his preface to every remark:

"Do you suppose you could find us a small rug to go in front of the fireplace?"

"Jesus Christ, you'll have it tomorrow!"

"For not more than fifteen dollars?"

"Jesus Christ, sure."

We never knew whether he stole it, but it appeared as promised and in surprisingly good condition.

It was an amiable Box and Cox arrangement. I was uptown all day and seldom returned before Eliot had left for the theater; Berry held the fort alone, doing his writing and making a weekly foray to *Life*'s office to show his new pieces to Oliver Herford, the assistant editor. He and I usually took supper together in one of the basement restaurants, a candle on each table and a greasy menu with French or Italian special-ties depending on the cook. Berry told me that Mr. Herford would read his manuscripts on the spot, retaining what he wanted, rejecting the others. As the old gentleman's memory was not too active, Berry found it expedient to include a reject in each offering: the new pieces would often seem better by comparison and its presence would help Mr. Her-ford to decide. A more difficult achievement was the acceptance of his longer pieces by *Punch*, a periodical not cordial to American contribu-tors, but they took a liking to Berry's humor.

Sundays we slept late and had a leisurely breakfast together. At the French bakery on the corner I bought croissants, sweet butter, and large crispy rolls with caraway seeds on top. These latter when heated in the oven with melting butter in the center were a nest for a lightly boiled egg, with paprika to taste, and plenty of coffee. It was our intent-ness on our own concerns and our respect for the others' privacy that made it work so well. No whiskey, a cocktail rarely, if Dad had given me one of his bottles of applejack, and never a woman in the place while I was there.

Except for the Irish telephone operator I was the only church-going gentile in the Liveright office, which was why I was summoned to a conference in Mr. Liveright's office about Hendrik Willem Van Loon's *The Story of the Bible*. This was the sequel to *The Story of Mankind,* which with Van Loon's striking illustrations, some in color, had sold over fifty thousand copies. Sight unseen, our salesmen on the road had been taking orders for *The Story of the Bible,* and now the manuscript, which had been written in Utrecht, was here, our big book of the winter.

"Ted, do you have any friends in the clergy here in New York?" asked Mr. Liveright.

"Yes," I said, "two of them: Taggert Steele at Old Trinity and Dr. Vesey, one of the canons at St. John the Divine."

"Well, I wish you'd call them both and see if they can arrange to read this manuscript and let me have a report by next Monday. I'll pay them each a hundred dollars. It's terribly important to know what its effect will be on believers."

Taggert and Vesey were quite willing and it was agreed that Vesey would deliver the joint report on Monday morning. Meantime I learned from Komroff that paper had been ordered for a first printing of forty thousand copies and Schneider showed me a rough of the first full-page announcement for the newspapers.

Mr. Liveright asked me to be present at the meeting on Monday morning; he sat at his desk by the window facing you as you entered. B and L books in their bright jackets filled the shelves, and in the wall opposite the desk were two doors gaily illuminated with flamingos; one door, as I knew, led to a washroom, the other to a small bar. Handshakes all around and the affable Vesey took the chair indicated.

"Well," said Liveright, "what's the verdict?"

"Sir, Van Loon's treatment of the Old Testament is truly remarkable, condensed and vivid history. I couldn't ask for anything better for our Men's Bible Class. But in Dr. Steele's and my judgment his treatment of the New Testament is appalling. When he implies that Jesus was of illegitimate birth, when he scoffs at the Miracles, omits the Sermon on the Mount, and makes no reference to the Resurrection, or to St. Paul, those of us who are Christians — "

"My God," said Liveright. "Will you have a drink?" And he walked over to the door to the bar where he poured himself a whiskey.

Neither the canon nor I were drinking. "This is very serious; we've invested heavily in that book," said Liveright. "Of course we shall have to cable the author for revisions. Would you before you leave give Ted a list of those changes you think imperative?"

Tom Smith was still away and it was in the privacy of his room that we composed the first of several lengthy cables to Van Loon in Holland. The author compromised reluctantly and in this, my first professional editorial job, I could never eliminate the agnosticism which permeated his chapters on the New Testament and which would turn Christians of every denomination against the book. For several weeks I divided my time between the galley proofs and my sales trips, and the doctoring, futile as it proved, earned me some encouraging words from Liveright and a $10 a week raise. Despite the unfavorable reports the firm went right ahead with its confident promotion of the book, and there was an advance sale of over thirty thousand copies, which at a $5 price was big for those days. But they never moved out of the bookstores and most of them, as I learned later, had to be exchanged for a more salable title.

At about this time a newcomer joined the firm and was given a desk beside mine in the sales department on the third floor. Bennett Cerf, two years younger than I, was a graduate of Columbia and of the Columbia School of Journalism; he and Dick Simon had been friends in college and now for a brief period the three of us worked together in the same room. Sleek and dark, with very bright eyes and a ready laugh, "Beans" was addicted to punning. He remembered and retold every story he heard; the jokes bubbled out of him but did not disguise how much he was learning about books. He was more shrewd in his judgment than Dick and with his independent means he was used to thinking in larger sums than I. With the purchase of $80,000 worth of Boni and Liveright stock he had acquired the title of vice president, but not for a while a commensurate authority. Like myself he was set to reading the galleys of forthcoming books and among them a novel so cheap and pornographic that he went down to Liveright to complain.

"Do we really have to go through with this wretched job?" he demanded. "It's a disgrace to the imprint. Can't we buy out?"

Liveright mollified him and said he'd see what could be done. Bennett was away for a few days on his first selling trip and shortly after his return there on his desk appeared the bound pages of the novel. Nothing had been changed. Looking over at me Beans held his fingers to his nose and dropped it into the wastebasket.

The firm often paid for such impetuosity, and a pretty girl may have been involved in this particular case, but, in the main, Cousin Alice was right: Liveright was the most adventurous publisher in New York City and it was fun to work for him. On the narrow stairs of the old brownstone on Forty-eighth Street or glancing into the reception room one saw glamorous figures: the striking brunette, Djuna Barnes; the ponderous Theodore Dreiser; the good-natured Sherwood Anderson. Liveright had the reputation of paying large advances, but I am sure it was the personal persuasion of those luminous dark`eyes that helped. To acquire the work of Dreiser, Liveright had to stand off the New York Society for the Suppression of Vice while he lobbied for a change in the statute on book censorship. The law in New York, as in most states at that time, was a "containing phrase" indictment aimed at any book, periodical, pamphlet, and the like that *contained language* that was obscene, indecent, or impure. Under it, *Sister Carrie*, Dreiser's novel about a prostitute, had been banned and his publisher attempted no defense. The novelist agreed that if Liveright could relieve the pressure he would bring all his work to B and L, and according to the office legend Liveright drew $1,000 from the till and went up to Albany prepared to play poker with the minority whip, Jimmy Walker, and his cronies by way of persuading them to broaden the bill so that the whole book rather than excerpts from it would stand trial. Jimmy Walker and his clever partner, Arthur Garfield Hays, were Liveright's lawyers.

After a long night of gambling, when the amended statute came up for a vote, Jimmy Walker burst into Hibernian oratory: under this bluenose law any book, even the Bible and Shakespeare, could be prosecuted. Those were the only two books his mother had in her home and anyone voting against such a reasonable change would be violating her memory, God rest her soul! Liveright returned without the $1,000, but the law was amended, a change which was to give judges and authors a new latitude, and in the upshot Dreiser brought his novels, old and new, to B and L.

Sherwood Anderson, a new voice from the Midwest, whose early work had been published elsewhere, was captivated by Liveright's generosity. *Winesburg, Ohio,* Anderson's collection of short stories, was a sensation critically but not a big money-maker, and between books, Sherwood, now in Greenwich Village, lived on a narrow margin. Liveright perceived this at once when he traced Anderson to his rooming house, and for the novel Sherwood was working on, *Dark Laughter,* he proposed an advance of $100 a week until the book was finished.

"You mean one hundred dollars every Monday?" asked Anderson.

"Every Monday," said Liveright, and the contract was signed.

What followed was confirmed for me by Anderson sometime later when he was a guest on my radio program: the first Monday morning, when the mail came through the slot he was waiting for it, and there was the envelope with his check; that week he and his friends ate well but he wrote only a few pages; the second week he paid some bills, ate well and did little work; and at the month's end, having decided that this regime was too rich for his blood, he went uptown with his contract.

Robert Reaser, Greenwich Village, 1923

Horace Liveright

"Mr. Liveright," he said, laying the form on the desk, "I want you to give me back my poverty."

"Why?" asked Horace. "What's wrong? Who's offered you more?"

Anderson explained what was troubling him and at his insistence the agreement was modified.

3

New York has an exciting beauty, never more so than in November, when on cloudless afternoons, just before the lights go on in the great towers, the sky above the canyons turns a clear, cobalt blue, and people hurry with expectation to their homes, their supper and their loves. At such times I often rode downtown on the Sixth Avenue El: I could get a seat — impossible to do on the subway — and I enjoyed the intimate glimpses into the tenements or apartments like our own, and of the swarthy Italian women, who gave back my stare as arms akimbo they leaned on the sill. It was the airy way to return to the Village, and when I got off at Eighth Street I descended the stairs into a covered way where restaurants and shops were warm with life. Berry and I would sup at the Checkerboard or the Russian Bear over on Second Avenue and were often joined by Bob Reaser, my war buddy, who was working hard at his painting and had got in the habit of spending at least a night a week on our sofa. It was Bob who took me to see the Swedish ballet, with sets by Léger and music by Honegger, Milhaud and Kurt Atterberg. Very *avant-garde*. New York was agog, so were we.

Sundays, when not reading I idled about, exploring the Mews, the former stables now being converted into dwellings, or walked past the red-brick eighteenth-century buildings on the northeast side of Washington Square, in one of which lived a stylish Weeks, my second cousin John from Oyster Bay — would I ever have that kind of money? — or at dusk I went down to Brooklyn Bridge and strolled across it for the view. If we were flush, Berry and I might blow ourselves to a meal at the Lafayette, with its delicious French cuisine. Sometimes I dropped in for a chat with Olga, a bachelor girl and an avid reader. One evening when she had been deriding James Branch Cabell's *Jurgen*, a pretentious, sexual fantasy, the talk turned to free love — "free love," like "self-expression," was a possibility much talked about in the Village and to some extent, practiced. Olga had the looks of an intellectual: her hair parted in the middle and drawn tight back, her steel-rimmed spectacles and the gray, flat sweater. Now when she told me she had tried having an affair with a decent guy, I hope I did not show my surprise. "But it was too awkward — I just didn't want to go on with it," she added. We left it at that.

Free love, if there was desire on both sides, I thought preferable to what you paid for. Harry Buxton, my mother's old beau, who had watched over me at Princeton and with whom I had sailed so often at Bay Head, was concerned about my sex life. Harry was a bachelor with an apartment off Washington Square and one evening when we were dining together he remarked that if I ever wanted a girl — perfectly normal, most men did — he'd be glad to take me to a clean, attractive place. I thanked him; I did not want to seem priggish, so I told him that with Fritzy in mind the urge was not that insistent.

In this city of easy money, where the stock market was now being "played" by the lambs who had made their first investment ever in war bonds, where my barber confided that he had cleared \$3,000 on a tip from a customer — I, with little to spend and nothing to lose, was having fun. There were invitations to tea dances and, more unusual, Bea Kaufman invited me to accompany her to the opening of George's new play, *The Deep Tangled Wildwood;* I dined with them before the theater, noticing how pale and tense George seemed and we were prompt in our seats, the playwright having detached himself to prowl in the background when the lights were dimmed. I am easily smitten by comedy and sentiment and enjoyed myself but Kaufman knew before the final curtain that he had no hit. We went on to Twenty-one, a new speakeasy where one had to be recognized; George's wit concealed his anxiety but the reviews next morning confirmed the worst.

Much more unnerving for me was the evening when I first played bridge with Kaufman as my partner. We played in Bennett's apartment and I cannot remember the fourth. Kaufman was the next thing to a professional and had placed the cards after the second lead. When he was dummy he would get out of his chair, freshen his drink, and stand behind me: every finesse I tried went wrong; when I overbid, the opponents forced me out of trumps and I went down four doubled, and in my loss of confidence I made things worse. A miserable performance. They had reduced the stake for my benefit to half a cent a point, and that was the only mercy.

On rare occasions I lunched with Liveright and the others at the Algonquin, that unassuming hotel on West Forty-fourth Street which, perhaps because of its tolerance of slow-paid bills, had become the literary showplace. Writers, actors, illustrators, critics, and publishers came there to lunch and be seen; Kaufman, Franklin P. Adams, and Alexander Woollcott were regulars at the Round Table, which the *New Yorker's* tribe would later dominate, and at night there were poker games at high unliterary stakes, which made it hard for the newcomer. I never asked to play but little John V. A. Weaver, the poet, who did, lost in one session the royalties on his new book, *In American*. Liveright, compulsive gambler that he was, loved to play there and when he lost, as he often did, would the next day sign a voucher for the $500 or whatever, and charge it to the firm.

The critics one saw at the Algonquin were men of influence, who appreciated what would appeal to many people and who were not afraid to be wrong, particularly Robert Benchley, who reviewed the plays, as Robert Sherwood did the films, for the original *Life*, and Alexander Woollcott, dramatic critic of the New York *Times*. One day as that trio came toward us on Fifth Avenue, so easy to spot because of Sherwood's towering height, Freddie Allen said to me, "Here come the Three Fates," as indeed they were, for their praise when quoted sold theater seats and moved books. The one play Benchley could make no dent on was *Abie's Irish Rose*, a low comedy poking fun at the social aspirations of the Irish and the Jews; both groups loved it, and it packed them in week after week, month after month (for five years), despite Benchley's derision, lampooning and sarcasm.

The great mansions, like the red and white French château of Cornelius Vanderbilt's, which occupied the entire block between Fifty-seventh and Fifty-eighth streets opposite the Plaza, were show-pieces, and a few were Victorian relics, like the large house on the corner of Fifth and Forty-eighth with an enclosed brick yard running a third of the block and an old-fashioned stable at the end of it. This was occupied by the Wendel sisters, who were elderly and seldom ventured out, to judge from the condition of the vestibule leading to the locked front entrance on Fifth Avenue — it was cluttered with torn sheets of newspaper and cigarette butts looking as if it had not been swept in a year. As we passed it one day Dick remarked, "That place will eventually be sold for millions." So was born my daydream: the Misses Wendel must have a fortune if they could pay such taxes, and clinging to the past as they seemed to do, they must be lonely: if I could find the right way of presenting myself, might I not become — might they not be persuaded to endow me as an adopted nephew? But how could I get past their housekeeper and with what few words could I touch their sympathy? I never rang.

One weekend of long walks and home-cooking I spent with Freddie and Dorothy Allen in Scarsdale, and when I remarked that "autumn was the poignant time of year" they burst into peals of laughter and wanted to know why. I could not tell them that my envy of their happiness was sharpened by the beauty of the fall, and "poignant" became a tease word for those two days. My courtship of Fritzy was in a state of suspension. When the family had rebuked her for her stopover in Cambridge she had declared that if she could not marry me she would wait until she found someone as like as possible. She put her foot down against making any formal debut, said she was much too interested in her courses but that she wanted to come back for the debutante parties of a few close friends like Rita Delafield. As her escort I was welcomed back to the armistice that prevailed at 8 West Fifty-third Street.

The interior of that high-stooped brownstone, across from St. Thomas's, was of great charm. The parlor, like most outer rooms, was seldom used: it was dominated by the piano, and in the corner beside it, Bill's drums and traps which he exercised during vacations. The parlor sofa was where, after a party, Fritzy and I briefly retired for our intimacy. (In the spring Mrs. Wetmore remarked dryly that she had to have its wicker seat repaired.) One passed through Venetian doors into the living room, the heart of the house, holding the laces and flowers Mrs. Wetmore loved, the piano where she played after dinner, and the handsome, comfortable old furniture her architect husband had collected. On the east wall shelves of dark walnut reached to the ceiling with his books, solid and lustrous in the lamplight; sofas of crimson damask were on either side of the fireplace; by the window, the splendid inlaid desk from Spain; and covering the wall behind the piano, a wide gilded French mirror that added depth to the room. Gone now but with its memorabilia once so perfectly reflecting the taste of the couple who had planned it.

Here Fritzy and I had cocktails with the family before going on to our dinner party or on those few occasions when we had seats for the theater. The theater was always a problem: because of his deafness Mr. Wetmore would seldom go and he was inflexible that dinner should not be served before eight. When I took Fritzy to Baliev's Chauve-Souris, we slid into our first-balcony seats thirty minutes late, and when she in return took me to *Back to Methuselah* by George Bernard Shaw, an interminable historical fantasy at the Theatre Guild, we arrived at nine-fifteen for a play that had begun at five, with a brief intermission for supper — and we were still confused when the curtain came down.

In the living room or at the dinner table my arguments with Mr. Wetmore were resumed. "Book publishing is in a blind alley!" he would declare in his high carrying voice. "You ought to get into something safe like banking or real estate. People are too busy driving, dancing, going to the movies, listening to the radio; they're never going to read books again!"

"Who do you think is reading *Babbitt?*" I shouted back. "Or Wells's *Outline of History?*"

He did not know, not having seen either; like so many successful professionals his book reading was behind him. But that he was concerned I took as a point in my favor. Mrs. Wetmore tried to quell these outbursts; however, since we were each set in our beliefs they went right on.

It was during the Christmas holidays that Fritzy and I once more were united. She came back from Bryn Mawr, blond, slim and assured. In the physical tests she was reported to have the strongest right arm in her class, a fact impressed on me at home when in reproof of her smoking so much I removed from her lips a cigarette she was about to light. She spun around with clenched fist, hit me in the solar plexis and I went down in a heap with my breath knocked out. Despite such prowess she was absorbed in her studies, especially the course in fine arts by Miss Georgiana King and one in psychology by that superlative teacher James Leuba. She told me that in a lyrical aside Georgiana King had remarked that "crushed violets was the odor of love."

"*Miss* King," I laughed, "is ethereal. How the hell would she know?"

Fritzy's clothes set off her figure. She scorned the new style with the waistline around the hips and the flat unfitted blouse; instead she wore long black velvet, cut low, with a rhinestone border. I was taller by a head but we danced well together and I was conscious of the beauty of her breast; I may have held her too close, for when we got through dancing to "Margie" at Rita's ball, the satin lapels of my full-dress coat were so lacerated by those rhinestones they had to be refaced.

On a clear Saturday afternoon I proposed that we take the subway down to Brooklyn Bridge, and walk across at sunset. The BMT at the Forty-second Street station was crowded with Christmas shoppers and in my hurry to jam us aboard the express I failed to notice that it was the express to Flushing, Long Island, and we zipped over the great span in seconds, instead of arm-in-arm, as I had planned. No matter: on arrival we changed to a local inbound, got off at the bridge and did things properly, though by now it was dark. "You are an adorable idiot," she said, as she took my arm, "and I love you."

Between us we had a surprising new prospect not yet disclosed to anyone. In the second week of December Freddie Allen invited me to lunch at the Coffee House, a genial club I was hoping to join. I suspected he might be planning to introduce me to members of the Election Committee, but no, at the big round table I was seated next to a middle-aged biographer from Boston with a dreadful stutter who was introduced as Mr. Howe — M. A. De Wolfe Howe. He showed a solicitous interest in my work at Boni and Liveright, but my attention to his laborious inquiry was distracted by the taunts being exchanged between John Jay Chapman at one end of the table and Heywood Broun at the other. Chapman was intensely anti-Catholic and anti-Semitic, and Broun was leading him on. I was all ears and when after coffee Mr. Howe was appropriated by Mr. Chapman, I made my exit with Fred and thought no more about it.

A week later I found on my desk a crisp handwritten letter from Boston which in my hurry to get over to Brooklyn I did not open. When I did, in the basement of Abraham and Straus, waiting my turn to sell the spring books, what I found was an invitation from Ellery Sedgwick to join the editorial staff of the *Atlantic Monthly*. I had been recommended by Mr. Howe and Fred Allen, and if interested could I arrange to see him the following Wednesday at the Century Club?

There is no elation quite like that of a surprise offer when one is young. The drawback was that I had come to respect the quality and daring of the publishing on West Forty-eighth Street. In assimilating our backlist I had cruised through *A Story Teller's Holiday* by George Moore (in a limited edition it, too, avoided the censor); *Sticks and Stones* by Lewis Mumford; parts of the *Intimate Journals* of Paul Gauguin, a rather querulous book; *The Enormous Room,* by e e cummings, an ambulance driver who had been abused by the French; *Upstream* by the critic Ludwig Lewisohn; and *The Waste Land,* a long poem by T. S. Eliot, an American expatriate, parts of which left me puzzled after two readings. Most of those titles as well as our best sellers by Rose Macaulay and Gertrude Atherton were gathered by Tom Smith, with an able assist by Komroff and the allure of Liveright's generosity. I was not sure where I fitted, certainly not as a long-term salesman, though I knew I was in better standing. Horace said complimentary things when I took Sunday dinner with his family in New Rochelle, and when I came suddenly upon Bea Kaufman in Manuel's office, I sensed that they had been talking about me as I overheard her say, "He'll be making good money before too long."

That was several light years away from the figure Ellery Sedgwick mentioned as we sipped our sherry in the awesome upstairs of the Century. A short, solid man with high coloring and a strong jaw, he exuded confidence and he spoke with such affection about the *Atlantic* that I felt charmed and honored to be included. He, too, had begun his career in New York and his dark eyes sparkled as he told of editing the old *Leslie's Monthly Magazine* on a shoestring. He seemed pleased with my interest in war books, and the work I had done for the *Transcript* and at Trinity, and grinned when I reminded him of the *Advocate's* parody of his magazine. As we talked, the job he wanted me for, that of "first reader," began to appeal. I said I would let him know within a fortnight and came away believing that I could up the salary.

I said to Fritzy that it was a gamble but that I was tempted to go to Boston and explained why. She agreed but she was the only one to do so. Mr. Liveright, when I told him of Sedgwick's offer, scoffed at it — I was off to a good start, he would pay me more to stay than Sedgwick offered and promised that hereafter I could devote part of my time to editing. But I knew that was the rub: Tom Smith on his return from Europe had shown not the slightest interest in having me as his understudy, and with Bennett Cerf outranking me as an executive I had no place in which to grow. When my father heard of Liveright's raise he said I would be a fool to think of leaving and later, in the midst of Christmas festivities, drew me aside to tell me that he had made inquiries and had been told that Sedgwick never kept his young assistants for longer than three years. "So you'd be out on your ear in Boston, having passed up a good chance down here . . ."

Maybe the odds were against it, but I believed I should enjoy working with Sedgwick, and might prove to be the exception to his rule. On New Year's Day I wrote him my acceptance and added what was intended to be jocular: "I am disappointed in the coined recompense. That matter, however, is extrinsic. I like the promise of your work and am sure that we can arrange its particulars agreeably when they have been fairly judged."

I little knew my man.

VII

THE *Atlantic* offices, like Liveright's, occupied what had once been a brownstone, high-studded town house, and there the resemblance ceased. On my initial visit as an undergraduate I had been impressed by its unhurried decorum. Now, as I presented myself on a Monday morning in mid-January of 1924, I was aware of the quiet, of the prevalence of women, and of doors that were shut. The excitement of the business was not in the air for all to share as it had been on West Forty-eighth Street.

Mr. Sedgwick's sanctum, which if my friend Komroff was right would someday be mine, was flooded with light from the windows overlooking the Public Garden. I like good clothes and so, I observed, did he: the dark-blue cheviot he was wearing, with the white piping on the waistcoat, had surely been fashioned in London. His hooked nose and the muscles in his jaw spelled decision; with his crisp black hair, graying at the temples, his heavy lower lip and ruddy complexion he had a piratical Spanish look not without distinction. He sat at a worm-eaten refectory table and its companion piece, a huge chest at the end of the room, bound by iron hinges and locked by enormous key, was evidently of monastic origin. The marble fireplace, the large charcoal portrait of the bearded James Russell Lowell, the *Atlantic*'s first editor, hanging above the mantel, and in the corner on a pedestal, a marble bust of Charles Eliot Norton, Sedgwick's favorite teacher, were austerities of the past very different from the flamingo panels and half-concealed bar of Mr. Liveright's. The antique chair on which I was perched, listening, was hard and uncomfortable enough to cut short any long-winded visitor.

Having sketched my duties as first reader, Mr. Sedgwick introduced me to three women: to Miss Berkefeld, his discreet secretary; to Miss

Ellery Sedgwick

8 Arlington Street, 1924

Fitzpatrick, very short and brisk, who bossed the circulation department — all those women — on the top floor and who was, as I soon learned, most efficient; and to Miss Florence Converse, who conducted me to the room we were to share.

"F.C.," as I called her, a trim little figure in her tweeds and flat heels, was a Wellesley graduate of middle years behind whose steel-rimmed spectacles dwelt a first-rate critic who was also a poet. She had been the first reader under Bliss Perry, the previous editor, and Sedgwick, when he purchased the magazine, had wisely promoted her to be his understudy. When he was abroad she made up the magazine, and except in the most sensitive relationships, as with Edith Wharton or Gertrude Stein, had the power to accept or reject. Manuscripts she handled with dispatch, and whether she was removing purple passages from a descriptive essay or operating on the proofs of a book, cutting and tying together the excerpts for a three-part serial, no surgeon with his scalpel was ever more sure. Our desks adjoined and at a V angle to each other with the windows at our backs, and I learned by watching her. We shared a secretary, and listening to F.C. dictate her letters of rejection I came to respect the firmness of her judgment and also her power to encourage revision. Surprisingly, she and I, Mr. Sedgwick, and one buoyant and resourceful proofreader, Caroline Church, who had taken honors at Radcliffe, comprised the entire editorial staff.

In the center of our bare room with its empty hearth was a round mahogany table holding three tin breadboxes which Miss Converse had labeled "TODAY," "YESTERDAY," and "THE ABYSS OF TIME." They held our fodder and, after my first month, if neither of us was diverted, we could dispose of 150 manuscripts a day. I had never been a fast reader in college, and when I clocked myself on Bishop Stubbs at Trinity, I only averaged thirty-five pages an hour. Now I learned to step up the pace. In two pages one can usually determine whether the offering is stylish, thoughtful, mediocre, hopeless or perhaps a diamond in the rough. To cope with the latter, by narrowing my gaze to the center of the page and by reading straight down instead of across I could get an understanding at double the speed. Articles that had been commissioned or were from old contributors were separated from the "generals" and were read as soon as possible. Miss Converse did not have to impress on me that the *Atlantic* prided itself on "discoveries."

I arranged my day's reading as if it were a diet, beginning with the hardheaded articles on foreign policy or economics in the morning, then the essays, short stories after lunch, the poems when I felt like a change. At the outset, until I had more confidence I deferred to F.C.'s knowledge of poetry as she deferred to me on war stories. A friend in

The First Reader, on the steps of No. 8

the paper business helped me avoid tedium: he gave me a thousand three-by-five blank sheets and a leather box to hold a large clump; on them I kept a daily tally, copied quotations I wished to remember, and checked the source of divinely inspired or "nut" manuscripts — California led the Union in those — and I jotted down and sometimes embellished verses that were amusing in a way the author had not intended:

THE SPIRIT OF A DEAD EAGLE ADDRESSES ITS STUFFED FORM

> *So that was I*
> *Feathers and claws and beak*
> *And with such poor equipment*
> *Did I seek*
> *To match the great round orange*
> *Of the sky*
> *Which always swang amazingly too high.*

Of the other seniors in the office I was most drawn to M. A. De Wolfe Howe, who had scouted me in New York, and who devoted part of his time to the Atlantic Monthly Press books. Mark was one of the kindest men in the world and I turned to him in difficulties. He was a charming versifier and the author of many books, chiefly biographical; the best of them were *Memoirs of a Hostess*, the reminiscences of Mrs. James T. Fields, wife of the second editor of the *Atlantic,* and *Barrett Wendell and His Letters*, which won the Pulitzer Prize. John Bakeless, a bright-eyed graduate student who had befriended me in Cambridge, was my nearest contemporary; he had a precise, far-reaching mind; he envied my days in France, I envied his scholarship. John worked on the floor above me as the assistant editor of the *Living Age*, a fortnightly digest of the international press which Mr. Sedgwick had purchased on an impulse and was publishing at a deficit. From Howe, Bakeless, and from MacGregor Jenkins, the tall, bald publisher and part owner of the *Atlantic,* who would anecdote you to death if given the chance, I got my bearings.

Ellery Sedgwick, whose forebears had long been the squires of Stockbridge, Massachusetts, had entered publishing in New York after graduating from Harvard in 1894: he had worked for D. Appleton and Company, one of the old-line houses, served not happily as an assistant to S. S. McClure, the meteoritic magazine editor of his day, and had boldly revitalized *Leslie's Monthly,* converting it with his initiative and bank loans into the *American* magazine, which he sold at a profit.

With his earnings and what he could borrow from his inlaws, the Cabots, he came up to Boston to make a bid for the *Atlantic*.

That famous monthly had begun to peter out after its first fifty years. The circulation had declined and its proprietors, Houghton Mifflin Company, who had given up hope of a dependable profit, were wondering if they could market it in an exclusive limited edition, priced at $10 a year (instead of the current $3), when Sedgwick made his offer. He bought the magazine for $35,000 cash and 150 shares in his new company, with the right to call in those shares in the future. Put the total at $50,000.

The *Atlantic*, which at the beginning had been a firebrand for Abolition, had lost its spark and become genteel; Sedgwick intended to restore its robust controversial nature without losing its literary quality, and the magazine responded to his powerful personality as it had, briefly, to the editing of Walter Hines Page in the late 1890's. I had been reading Page's *Life and Letters* by Burton J. Hendrick, to glean what secrets I could, and it was plain how much Page and Sedgwick had in common: each believed in our expanding destiny as a world power, each was an ardent admirer of England and did not hesitate to draw as much as forty percent of a single issue from British writers, each battled strenuously for higher standards in American education, and each was a Wilsonian Democrat, though they maintained the *Atlantic* as a nonpartisan sheet. Sedgwick had over thirty thousand subscribers by August 1914, and under his brilliant editing during the war, with his curiosity about the changing world and his ardent support of the League of Nations, that figure had nearly trebled when I joined the staff.

The early twenties were a fertile time for periodicals. In 1922 De Witt Wallace and Lila Wallace launched the *Reader's Digest* on a capital of $1,800, mostly borrowed from his father and brother, after Hearst and half a dozen other publishers had turned it down as nonprofitable. In the same year *Time*, the news magazine, was projected by Henry Luce and Briton Hadden, with Roy Larsen managing the circulation. Harold Ross had found the capital he wanted from Raoul Fleischmann and his friends at the Algonquin and the *New Yorker* made its bow. For us a new challenger appeared when Alfred A. Knopf published the *American Mercury*, edited by Henry L. Mencken and George Jean Nathan. Mencken was the works — Nathan soon withdrew — and he promised to be a more formidable rival than some of the other editors of the Quality Group. He was an iconoclast: politically as sympathetic to Germany as we were to England (it was at his urging that Knopf published the novels of Thomas Mann), and I found it impossible not to admire the way he whacked heads and ridiculed pomposity. He was intentionally bellicose and peppered his text with amusing epithets: a professor was usually a "bunkum professor"; ministers were referred to as "high priests" or "psalm singers"; political commentators, as "soothsayers"; for politicians, "the Honorable" became a term of contempt; Billy Sunday, the revivalist, was "America's celebrated pulpit clown" — Mencken was constantly revising this glossary of endearments for the "booboisie." He did most of his editing at his home in Baltimore, which he much preferred to New York, and as I followed the *Mercury*, it seemed to me that he was devoting too much time to book reviewing, pungent as the reviews were, and not enough to scouting, that his choice of short stories and poetry left much to be desired, and that he was overplaying his style. I remember how surprised I was when Granville Hicks showed me a manuscript of his which the *Mercury* had accepted and then had returned for his approval with such Menckenisms as I have quoted, inserted. Hicks acquiesced though I think he would have preferred to have his piece printed without the additions. By such imposition the contributors in time came to sound like Mencken's younger cousins, and this sameness, this lack of variety in style, must have contributed in part to the magazine's undoing.

Mencken presented his compliments to the *Atlantic* when he wrote: "All the more pretentious American authors try to write chastely and elegantly; the typical literary product of the country is still a refined essay in the *Atlantic Monthly*, perhaps gently jocose but never rough — by Emerson, so to speak, out of Charles Lamb." Certainly, we had them. But it was due to Sedgwick's superiority as an editor that we had so much more. His curiosity was far-ranging. He was, for instance, very curious about mass production, which was then being introduced, and what its effect might be in human terms. The man I replaced, Charles R. Walter, a Yale classicist, had worked in heavy industry after the war and the articles depicting his experiences in a steel mill were featured, as was a much-quoted series "The Iron Man in Industry," in which Arthur Pound described the impact of the assembly line in Detroit. Again, in every issue Sedgwick reserved three places for papers about the realignment in Europe and Asia. Japan fascinated him, and after repeated visits he illustrated in fine articles the contrast between Japan's recent medievalism and its immediate and highly potential industrialization.

Sedgwick injected a personal note that had been missing in the *Atlantic*'s columns: he had an inexhaustible interest in the first person singular — the more singular the better — and when he found an adventurer, man or woman, who could write, he paid them and pressed for more. James Norman Hall of Iowa was one of his prizes. Hall, a young Grinnell graduate, was on a bicycle trip in England the summer of 1914, and when war broke out, he promptly enlisted as a Canadian and became a machine gunner in the British Expeditionary Force. When he transferred to the Lafayette Escadrille, the *Atlantic* featured his war letters, which were published in book form, entitled *High Adventure,* and at the war's end when Hall and another pilot, Charles Nordhoff, were searching for a place in which to live cheaply and write, Sedgwick diverted them from Bermuda to Tahiti and helped to subsidize their setup. A different prize was Hans Coudenhove of Vienna, a naturalist and philosopher, who renounced his title in favor of a younger brother — in partitioned Austria there was not money enough for both — and went off to live in Nyasaland beyond the furthest settlement; the papers he wrote about his hermitage and the wildlife — *My African Neighbors* — were true and continued until a search party found him dead on his camp cot, mourned by the monkeys on the roof whom he once had fed.

Autobiography takes many forms and there was one field in which the *Atlantic* was alone. Mr. Sedgwick had a predilection for Roman Catholic priests who had recanted: an ex-Jesuit or ex-Dominican who had put aside his vows and was seeking a new start was sure of a welcome. Such contributions were usually shrouded in secrecy and printed anonymously; to a readership largely Protestant they were engrossing, and I should add that the editor knew just how far to go without infuriating the Boston hierarchy.

I followed with wonder Mr. Sedgwick's correspondence with a German dentist who, wearied of his family, had secured a divorce, and enchanted by a new soul mate, was having her and himself fitted with steel teeth for the Garden of Eden they expected to find in the Galápagos Islands. He was eager to write a philosophic account of their hand-to-mouth existence and Ellery staked him modestly, with self-addressed envelopes to be sent to Boston by whatever whaler or passing ship came within hailing distance. In time two such envelopes did arrive in German script, turgid with philosophy but disappointingly devoid of sex or hardship. Then after the silence of many months we heard the rumor that a castaway had appropriated the German wife and killed the dentist.

The girls came from everywhere, from the Kentucky mountains and the Ozarks. Jean Kenyon Mackenzie on her African farm was sturdily authentic; so too was Hilda Rose, that mite of a woman who with "Daddy," her aging husband, and their plucky son, was carrying on a desperate struggle for life on their Stump Farm in the Barren Lands. Hilda's "Letters from a Stump Farm," which ran through several seasons, brought forth many gifts from tenderhearted readers, some of whom did not realize that electric toasters were no use without electricity.

Serials such as these built circulation, and to get them Sedgwick took chances. As I said earlier, there were many questions about Opal Whiteley: was she in fact the daughter of a pretender to the French throne, begotten when her father was big-game hunting in Canada, and was her diary torn to bits by her furious foster-mother? All I can attest is that Opal's diary was a spellbinder in the magazine, and later in book form.

Mr. Sedgwick's letters, the carbons of which in a Manila folder, came to my desk each week, were a revelation. His fees were low, as he knew — $400 was the top price — but he wrote with such warmth and persuasiveness as to cause a busy statesman like Balfour, or a writer of Walter Lippmann's or Galsworthy's prominence, to interrupt his work to do the paper Ellery had suggested. And he could discriminate without angering the writer. A letter from Amy Lowell told me some surprising facts about her beginning as a writer and, also, how much she deferred to Mr. Sedgwick's judgment:

> Brookline, Mass.
> 3 March, 1924
>
> Dear Ellery:
> Here are the six sonnets. . . . Perhaps you do not know my experience with Madame Duse to which these poems refer all the way through. In order to make the sonnets intelligible to you in judging them, I will tell you the story, although I think they stand up by themselves perfectly well in reading. . . . For years, as a girl, I had tried to write various things and had came to the conclusion that I was not born to be a writer, to my great sorrow. Poetry I had only tried as a child and had entirely abandoned. When Madame Duse came here twenty years ago, I went to see her many times. I have always believed that great art fecundates art. After her visit here, to my intense astonishment, I found myself trying to write poetry, knowing noth-ing about poetry. I began to write, not specifically about Madame Duse, but simply out of the fullness of the vision of poetry which she had given me. From that day to this, I have not ceased, and you published the first poem of mine which ever came out in print — a sonnet, you will remember — which appeared in 1910. These sonnets are my reaction to her twenty years later. . . . Under the circumstances of your printing my first poem and her inspir-ing it, it seems as if the "Atlantic" were eminently the place for these sonnets.
> Sincerely yours,
> AMY LOWELL

Ellery did not agree and the sonnets were declined. Back she came with a more amorous poem, which was accepted.

2

It was good to be back in Boston and to be welcomed by dear friends like Bill and Marjorie Whitman, who with their first-born daughter were living on Beacon Hill. As it proved, I was soon in need of their food and their care. Bill had arranged for me to stay with his mother-in-law, Mrs. Fiske Warren, until I had found a furnished room to my liking, but unfortunately I arrived with an unsuspected case of German measles (I had already had it once as a child), and when shortly the high fever drove me to bed I needed nursing. As soon as I could get back on my feet, I sent my hostess the largest azalea plant I could afford and moved my belongings to the fifth floor of a rooming house at No. 10 Joy Street. All bachelors should dwell for a time on a Joy Street, but the four flights were a far climb for one as shaky as I, for that pesky attack had left me with colitis, more dependent on milk than on alcohol and with little appetite for dancing girls. We all have to learn to doctor ourselves, but this was a hard lesson when I wanted to be at my best. I ate in the small restaurants that dotted the Hill: breakfast of poached eggs and raisin bread, toasted, at One Step Down on Anderson Street; dinner across the way at the Old Gray House, where the proprietress served good chicken dinners and the student-waitresses would sit down and chat between courses. There were evenings when everything disagreed and I would deposit the meal I had just paid for in the can at No. 10 on my way to bed. To strengthen my diaphragm I stretched out flat in my pajamas, trying to balance a ten-pound shot on my thin belly, listening to the mice scurrying in the attic overhead — the little devils had already eaten holes in the Irish linen handkerchiefs Fritzy had given me for Christmas — and remembering Dick Salinger's old war cry, "Jesus, lover of my soul!" Now it was my turn to suffer.

Pargie Whitman pulled me out of all this by feeding me a bland diet while Bill and I caught up with each other. It cannot be easy for a possessive wife to see her husband re-enter the intimacy of a close friendship, but Pargie was sympathetic and she needed my help, for Bill was restless. He was writing the blurbs and promotion for Houghton Mifflin books, and he told me that in advance of Amy Lowell's new volume of verse he had gone out to Sevenels to butter her up in an interview for the *Transcript*. She smoked one of her long cigars as she answered his questions, they got along well, and in his full-page spread he used the comparative throughout: "Miss Lowell, one of the leading Imagists," "one of the first to discover," and so on, and then sent the proof to her for approval. Back it came, with every comparative turned into a superlative. "Miss Lowell, the leading Imagist . . ." Bill laughed but I could see it made him impatient to fuss over other people's work when he wanted to be writing his own, and when I urged him to send us some of his new poems, he flushed at my confidence in him.

We three attended a banquet in honor of Miss Lowell's long-awaited biography of Keats. It was my first full-dress literary affair; John Livingston Lowes of Harvard presided and I was impressed by the turnout and the number of celebrities on the dais, twelve as I recall, the majority from New York, come to praise Boston's most eminent writer. Miss Lowell had not been well and arrived an hour late; dinner was being served as she entered, a square solid figure in black, very pale. The speaking was interminable and to me surprisingly dull: while ostensibly telling how Miss Lowell had helped her with her poetry Elinor Wylie managed to pin several dozen roses on herself and A. Edward Newton fell asleep waiting to be called on. But in her response Miss Lowell summoned the force others lacked: she concluded by reciting two of her poems, "Lilacs" and "Patterns," and I remember the impact of her last line on that hushed audience: "Christ! What are patterns for?"

Joy Street runs up and over the crest of Beacon Hill, only half a block away from Charles Bulfinch's red-brick, white-porticoed State House, whose golden dome had long been the town's landmark. The Hill was a village within the city, with its own shops and restaurants, whose master architect, Bulfinch, had set an enduring style. The homes he built for clients like Harrison Gray Otis, of brick and marble, with their curving stairways, hand-carved mantels and decorative fenestration were a monument to Federalist Boston, its taste and its seafaring prosperity. On the eastern or Beacon Street slope the original mansions had gardens, elms, and carriage houses at their rear; the back side of the Hill, known as "Whoredom" when the British troops occupied Boston, was more raffish and Bohemian.

I had a seven-minute walk down the Hill and through the Public Garden to my office. Returning at nightfall before the curtains were drawn I loitered, gazing into the softly lit libraries or dining rooms, window-shopping for where I should live when my ship came in. Which at the moment it showed no sign of doing. After six months I had hoped to be raised to what Liveright had promised me; without putting it in words Mr. Sedgwick implied that I was earning valuable experience. Such mundane details were not in mind when I was invited to dine at their home on Walnut Street. Mrs. Sedgwick in her shy and gracious way was solicitous about my health and pleased with my interest in their house. It was said to be the oldest on the Hill, and the French windows of the drawing room opened on what was left of the original garden with flowering shrubs and one old elm. It also retained in winter a good deal of the original cold and only those within range of the fireplaces were really warm. My boss was a charming host and I came away disarmed.

There were dinner parties on Louisburg Square; Serge Koussevitsky, the new conductor, added vivacity to the Boston Symphony; and when the Metropolitan Opera Company came up for its fortnight in April, the magnolias were in full bloom in the Public Garden and the promise of spring was in the air. I was enjoying a Sunday supper in Cambridge with Billy and Alice James and their Harvard friends when a voice down the table remarked:

"I hear that Freddie Watriss's daughter is engaged."

"I hope she's as attractive as her mother. Who is the man?" asked the host.

"I forget his name," said the first voice, "but I think he works in Boston."

It seemed to me this had gone far enough. "He does," I said. "In fact, he's right here." Blushes and congratulations all around.

It was true: the family had capitulated. My ill-health — there had been the threat of appendicitis at Easter — may have weakened their resistance, that and Fritzy's determination that we were to be married at the end of her sophomore year. I came into the living room on family terms on my rare trips to New York: Fritzy's mother had become "Sara" and Mr. Wetmore "Unkie." Skirmishes were avoided, although obdurate Democrat that I was I could not resist rubbing in the scandal of Teapot Dome.

"Why did you vote for a man like Harding?" I shouted.

"I vote for the candidate of my party."

"Damned if I will," I said. "In Boston I'm quite ready to split my ticket."

"How the hell do you think you're qualified . . ." he shouted, dander beginning to rise, but Sara intervened.

Accompanied by her older daughter, Martha, Sara came to Boston to inspect the living quarters I had in mind for us. She balked after once toiling up the stairs — protesting at each flight — to what the agent termed "a fourth-floor complex." "No daughter of mine . . ." Sara began, and with those words my hope of living on what I earned went out the window. Fritzy would have an allowance sufficient to cover the rent. My salary — Mr. Sedgwick at the announcement had raised me to $50 a week — would stretch for the rest. Once that understanding had been reached, the agent with a gleam in his eye led us to the top of Mt. Vernon Street where an old bow-front, high-studded brick house had been subdivided. When he unlocked the third-floor front the girls, all three, had what they wanted: the living room, whose two big windows looked across at Mr. Sedgwick's, was a beauty, with a marble fireplace, tall bookshelves and enough depth for a dining alcove. There was a small guest room, and the corridor leading to our big bedroom in the rear was lined with cabinets and closets. "Actually," said the agent, "this was the suite occupied by Edward the Seventh when as a young man, traveling as Lord Renfrew, he visited Boston in 1861." That clinched the deal.

So began my losing struggle for economy. I had been saving every penny I could for an engagement ring and what we would need for a wedding trip. Sara had the agent take the measurements for the draperies she intended to give us but the envelope was mislaid and I was asked to get a tape measure, record the height and depth of the windows, front and back, and telephone.

"Oh, is that you, Ted," said Sara when I called. "Now wait, I have to get a pencil."

I waited and waited, so long I thought the connection had been broken; but no, there she was. "I can't find a pencil, Ted dear. Call me again in half an hour."

"Please deposit $2.15 for your overtime," said the toll operator.

For the two principals the honeymoon is more memorable than the events leading up to it, or so it was in my case. I do recall the strange mood of reluctance that settled on me just before I came down to New York for the wedding — after these many years of waiting was I sure? Was this passion that flared up between us enough to build a life on? This uncertainty lasted through the haze of the ushers' dinner and until I saw Fritzy coming down the aisle of the chapel of St. Thomas's — she had simply walked down the steps of the house and across Fifty-third Street to the door of the chapel — and her eyes said this was right. I recall the momentary stiffness as her father and his third wife came up in the receiving line and swiftly departed, and then as the champagne took hold and I responded to the toasts and took Mother's proud farewell kiss and changed into day clothes for our getaway I knew my solitariness was over.

We were married in late May and our plans were to drive south in the little Dodge which was Unkie's present; it was arranged that the car would be delivered to us at the Ritz Carlton in Philadelphia where we would be spending the night. Fritzy wanted me to see Foxcroft and meet Miss Charlotte Nolan, the headmistress, and I who had been reading Henderson's *Stonewall Jackson* wanted to show her the battle-fields at Gettysburg and on down the Shenandoah Valley, perhaps as far as Charlottesville. We got more ribbing than encouragement at home. Bill came up with the joke "Why does a bride wear fur around the bottom of her nightgown?" "To keep her neck warm." And Sara said she didn't see why we bothered to go at all; she had gone on two honeymoons and hadn't enjoyed either. But ours would be different.

I think the less said about the First Night the better. Both partners are nervously spent and the extra bottle of champagne before bed is a vinegary stimulant; the hands once so subtle with clothing are now too hurried. One does not discard reticence or achieve the art of satisfying love in one night.

My reactions were not too sharp the next morning as the grinning bellhop loaded our gear into the car and the man from the agency explained that the gearshift of the Dodge was different from the standard model — the Dodge reverse was where I was accustomed to shift into first speed. He had me practice it several times and then Fritzy and I drifted out into the Market Street traffic in our shining black chariot with its primrose-yellow wheels. We were held up by fire apparatus screaming across town and when at last the cop gave us the come-on I reached down, shifted gears, and backed straight into the protesting taxi at our rear. Got out, no damage, apologized, quite an impatient line behind me, got back, corrected the error, and at the signal crept forward. As he drove past, the taxi driver called to me, "Brother! You're going to hurt yourself with that thing!"

We made it safely to the Devon Horse Show that afternoon, where I was shown off to some of Fritzy's friends, and that night we stabled the Dodge and ordered our dinner at the little hotel in York. I looked over the menu and spotted, "Specialty: York County Snapping Turtle Soup," and with just a touch of patronage said it was always fun to try the *spécialité de la maison*. Fritzy would have none of it but I did and it was turtle soup all right but with a peculiar flavor that kept reasserting itself far into the night.

"Try some bicarbonate," muttered Fritzy in the dark.

"I have; I'll take some more."

The plains of Gettysburg were broiling hot and crowded on Memorial Day. We paused at the High-Water Mark of Pickett's charge, at Seminary Ridge and the Devil's Den, but Fritzy was not in the mood for battles. "Come on," she said, "let's get going," pointing up to the Blue Ridge. We were the first guests of the season at the old Monterey Inn;

it was only half open but they gave us a big comfortable bedroom, made fragrant by the white lilacs we had found at an abandoned farm on the way up the mountain. One of my ushers had given us three bottles of Scotch in a wicker case. We had the nine-hole golf course almost to ourselves and when we tubbed after our round — two in a tub, there should be a song about it — and had polished off a couple of long drinks on the veranda outside our room, we were ravenous. I could not suppress my delight in seeing Fritzy walk about so unabashed and lovely in the nude. The reading of *Stonewall Jackson* was put aside, and as dark fell and the cool of the mountain drifted in through our door to the porch we were at last at ease with love.

The June days came on like midsummer, people said we were in for a record heat wave, and as we moved down the valley the temperature rose into the nineties; at the tearoom where we stopped for lunch the butter was melting, the salad limp, and our conversation, like the fried chicken, drying up. Afterwards we drove in silence until Fritzy broke it: "If we see any attractive stream with shade, let's stop and cool off." Maybe ten miles later as we approached a bridge, I slowed down and there it was, a good current of clear water over rocks and a narrow overgrown lane leading into the woods on the further side; we turned in and drove about a mile, passing a disused sandpit but no habitation, and came eventually to the lip of the stream, with trees at our back and across the water a high grassy bank merging into the densely wooded slope. No picnic leftovers, a sandy bottom, but not deep enough for a swimming hole. "Never mind the suits," said Fritzy, "we're alone. Let's get in quick." We did, she sitting in a shallow pool below me and I leaning back against a flat-faced rock above the water line, the water coursing over us cooler than the air. I had fetched Rupert Brooke's small volume to the rock and now began to read aloud his poem "The Fish":

> *In a cool curving world he lies*
> *And ripples with dark ecstasies . . .*

My eye had reached the bottom of the page when on glancing up I saw the trees at the lower end of our vista begin to toss their branches. There wasn't that much wind. "Go on," said Fritzy. But I didn't, for coming toward us out of the greenery was the afternoon train from Washington. The heat-drugged faces at the windows that whirled by forty feet above us suddenly came to, jerked around for a second look, and were gone, leaving us in the culvert like Adam and Eve in their first embarrassment. "Total strangers," said Fritzy in her laughter. "Go on and finish it."

214

The little Dodge was jouncy on the country roads, but the gearshift was no mystery by now and I enjoyed driving. Because of the unbroken heat we made an early start, found our lodgings for the night and took a long siesta after lunch. At Berryville, where we got black looks because the sight of our Massachusetts license plate interrupted their memorial parade for the Confederate Dead, there was a refreshing thunderstorm which cleared the air by early evening and the moon came out. But our room was still close. "Let's put on our bathing suits," I suggested after supper, "and see if we can find a stream to wade in." Everything was rain-washed and the creek we discovered was unmolested, with a bank of high moist grass on a little knoll as if placed there for our benefit. In the moonlight we stripped off our suits and used them for a mattress. "If we keep on doing this," said Fritzy, "my precautions will be no use." We had agreed on no children for two years so that Fritzy could take her degree at Radcliffe, and now I felt guilty.

After that we were better behaved. "Miss Charlotte" had mint juleps and a really delicious dinner ready for us when we reached Foxcroft and she herself was everything Fritzy had foretold — the perfect combination of a cavalry colonel and a woman of charm, her love of horses and her air of command in perfect keeping with her handsome clear-cut features. She guided us through the stables, told us of her early days in Boston — at the Sargent School she had been one of the pioneers in physical education — and she roared at my account of the railway culvert. Then despite the heat we pressed on to Charlottesville, where we roamed about the Rotunda in the cool of the evening, and early next morning began the long drive back to New York. Rumpled and road-weary we rang the bell at 8 West Fifty-third Street in the late afternoon and it felt good to enter the cool interior. Mr. and Mrs. Wetmore were in the library.

"What did I tell you!" cried Sara, who was in negligee. "You poor kids must have melted. It's been perfectly awful here; why didn't you come back sooner?"

Unkie in white ducks and a shirt of Canton silk was seated before a punch bowl in which one small chunk of ice remained. "We've been mixing a fruit punch for your return," he said. "But we kept tasting it and now there isn't much left." Even so it was delicious.

The drive to Boston along the old Post Road went smoothly, and when we reached our apartment on Mt. Vernon Street, it was to find the lamps turned on, flowers in the vases, food in the icebox and our bed made up, as if a housekeeper had just stepped out. As indeed she had: Martha, Fritzy's sister, whose thoughtfulness I was beginning to appreciate, had come to town in the heat, unpacked our wedding presents, hung up our clothes and laid in supplies including a bottle of Scotch, and gin and vermouth — and then thirty minutes before our arrival, she had vanished. We savored the place, which would never look more inviting, until from our rear window I espied my old carpet slippers and the red fez I had worn with the Algerians thrown out on the top of the ash barrel in the service alley. Never! They may not have been treasures in Martie's eyes but they were in mine and I dashed down to rescue them.

It was a most happy summer in which the disclosure of each other's tastes and humors led as often to laughter as to passion. Having picked up the rudiments of cooking at home, Fritzy contrived to make me feel healthier, although at the outset there were some oddities. She did her shopping at the Faneuil Hall Market and the butcher, who had spotted her as a bride after she had ordered lamb chops for the third successive day, asked innocently, "Doesn't your man sometimes like a change?"

"Why, yes," said Fritzy. "What would you suggest?"

"Pig's knuckles," said the butcher, tongue in cheek, and gave her a careful recipe for cooking them. What I got resembled hard brown doorknobs with a skin so tough it resisted the sharpest knife. The next day, when she related the result and admitted she had forgotten to boil them, Butcher & Co. were convulsed.

Fritzy at this time was experimenting with a rubber girdle, although in my view she was so slim it was quite unnecessary. Fresh peas, corn on the cob and our fruit she purchased at the Italian market in the North End, and one morning as she was footing it home with her string bag full, she felt the rubber girdle begin to rip. She told me she took shorter steps hoping to reach the apartment in time, she even tried shuffling, but when she reached the top of Mt. Vernon Street the split was complete and down came everything, leaving her no choice but to drop her shopping bag, undo her garters, pick up the two halves of pink rubber, and with her stockings about her ankles trudge up the walk to No. 67.

Had I been wiser I should have taken this as a warning, but I wasn't. Midmorning in late August the office boy placed on my desk a sealed envelope of *Atlantic* stationery addressed in Fritzy's handwriting. Opening it I read, "Poops: Barney Google, Jr., is expected sometime in February." I sat there gazing into space. I knew she had an appointment to see Dr. Tom Goethals, the obstetrician, and after his verdict she had evidently written this at the desk in our reception room. Well, sure I was pleased, but so soon? Life was running away with us with no respect for our planning. After making the supreme sacrifice for our wedding, Mr. Sedgwick could hardly be expected to kick through with an-

other raise now. There was no way around it: Fritzy's allowance would
have to go up and I should have to earn money on the outside. I had
already published two papers in the *Atlantic:* "Christmas Underground,"
a humorous sketch of our Christmas in the Vosges in 1917, and "A Crim-
inal in Every Family," in which I hit hard at the reckless and alcoholic
drivers who were multiplying under Prohibition. Now I would have to
do more. Somber and elated by turns I went home to shake up a martini for us both.

3

When the English novelist, H. G. Wells, then in his early thirties, visited Boston in 1906 he experienced a disappointment which he later expressed in his book *The Future in America:*

One feels in Boston as one feels in no other part of the States, that the
intellectual movement has ceased. Boston is now producing no literature except a little criticism. Contemporary Boston art is imitative art, its writers
are correct and imitative writers, the central figure of its literary world is
that charming old lady of eighty-eight, Mrs. Julia Ward Howe. One meets
her and Colonel Higginson in the midst of an authors' society that is not
so much composed of minor stars as a chorus of indistinguishable culture.
There are an admirable library and a museum in Boston, and the library is
Italianate, and decorated within like an ancient missal. In the less ornamental
spaces of this place there are books and readers. There is particularly a
charming large room for children, full of pigmy chairs and tables, in which
quiet little tots sit reading. I regret now I did not ascertain precisely what
they were reading, but I have no doubt it was classical matter.
I do not know why the full sensing of what is ripe and good in the past
should carry with it this quality of discriminating against the present and
the future. The fact remains that it does so almost oppressively. . . . The
capacity of Boston, it would seem, was just sufficient but no more than
sufficient, to comprehend the whole achievement of the human intellect up,
let us say, to the year 1875 A.D. Then an equilibrium was established. At
or about that year Boston filled up.

This was still embarrassingly true. No one could say that Amy Lowell
was "imitative," but she certainly stood alone as Boston's innovator. The
outpouring of novels in New York came from everywhere except Boston. Were Yankee novelists bred out? Why had no angry young writer
emerged from the Boston Irish? There were four of us at Arlington
Street who used to chew this over at lunch: Quincy Howe, who had replaced Bakeless on the *Living Age,* and whose crisp, decisive mind I
admired; Theodore Morrison, a poet with a nice sense of satire, and our
new manuscript reader; Donald B. Snyder, a former teacher of English

whose editing of the *Scholastic* had recommended him to Sedgwick as an understudy for our ailing publisher; and myself.

One of the sorry aspects of Boston "equilibrium" was its acceptance of censorship. The censoring of books in New York City by the Society for the Suppression of Vice under Anthony Comstock and his successor, John Sumner, which I have mentioned in connection with Dreiser, was reinforced by the Watch and Ward Society, with reputable and wealthy supporters like Godfrey Lowell Cabot and with a formidable ally in the Roman Catholic hierarchy.

Massachusetts was hamstrung by the same "containing language" statute that until recently had existed in New York. Boston booksellers, having no wish to be hauled into court and fined for books they had neither read nor published, welcomed a tipoff from the police or the district attorney's office and Richard F. Fuller, owner of the Old Corner Bookstore, saw that they received such tips. Call it censorship by intimidation. The censors were either self-appointed, like the retired Protestant clergyman, with time on his hands, who took pleasure in warning a branch librarian of the vicious fiction he was reading, or they were of police training. The D.A.'s office soon wished it could wash its hands of the whole business. And the community was compliant. In 1925 these were among the books which Boston booksellers had either stopped from sale or were selling under the counter: *Galahad* by John Erskine, *Happiness in Marriage* by Margaret H. Sanger, *Manhattan Transfer* by John Dos Passos, *The Plastic Age* by Percy Marks, *The Hard-boiled Virgin* by Frances Newman, and *The World of William Clissold* by H. G. Wells. Fuller of the Old Corner Bookstore, who did read books, never hesitated to advise his fellow booksellers of titles he thought might be jumped on.

The target was made to order for Henry Mencken and twice in the autumn of 1925 he turned the guns of the *American Mercury* on the subservience of Boston, first in the article "Keeping the Puritans Pure," heaping scorn on the Watch and Ward, its director, J. Frank Chase, and its accomplice, the cautious Dick Fuller, and followed this up with an attack on the "Irish-Catholic Anthropoids . . . who have no more interest in ideas than a guinea pig has in Kant's *Critique of Pure Reason*."

Chase saw his chance to counterattack the following winter when Mencken published "Hatrack" by Herbert Asbury, the story of a prostitute in a small town who was maligned by the very people who patronized her. Chase tipped off the New England News Company that the sale of that issue would constitute the grounds for legal action and in a whisker the *Mercury* disappeared from sight. Mencken accepted the challenge and came up to Boston with Arthur Garfield Hays, the lawyer who had successfully defended Liveright in the case against the *Satyricon.* By prearrangement a meeting took place at the corner of the Boston Common close by the Park Street Church (where the Watch and Ward was founded). Reporters and a mass of spectators including many Harvard undergraduates cheered as Mencken publicly sold Chase a copy of the disputed issue and shouted when Mencken bit the proffered fifty-cent piece to make sure it wasn't lead. Mencken was immediately arrested and booked at the station house by a lieutenant of the vice squad, but to our intense delight the following day Judge James P. Parmenter, a Yankee Unitarian, found Mencken not guilty. Zechariah Chafee, Jr., and Felix Frankfurter of the Harvard Law School escorted the editor to the Harvard Yard, where Mencken spoke to six hundred students; and that night at the St. Botolph Club, to which I had recently been elected, Ferris Greenslet, the editor of Houghton Mifflin, and I gave him a dinner. We had procured a case of genuine German beer and, so inspired, Mencken opened up his incredible store of barroom ballads which he and Samuel Merwin sang back and forth across the table until the whole club rang.

Mencken's lawyer, Mr. Hays, filed suit in the federal court for an injunction against further harassment of the *American Mercury* and it was granted by Judge James M. Morton, Jr. But simultaneously a district judge in Middlesex County found a Cambridge bookseller guilty of selling the "Hatrack" issue and fined him $100. This underscored the absurdity of what was going on: books banned by intimidation in Boston were sold openly in Cambridge three miles away; "Hatrack," which was now cleared in Boston, was forbidden in Cambridge. Mencken's boldness had forced the issue into the limelight and whatever happened from now on would be played up in the nation's press.

4

Dr. Thomas Goethals' father had wiped out the threat of yellow fever in the building of the Panama Canal and Tom, like his old man, was direct, military in his bearing, and accurate. Fritzy liked him and right on schedule she produced our daughter Sara, named for her grandmother, and though like most fathers I wanted a boy, I must say I found the baby in her pinkness and blond topknot beguiling. She and the interim baby nurse, old "Aiah" who was old enough to have diapered many of my Boston friends, filled up our guest room and placed an additional strain on our budget which my boss did nothing to alleviate.

My predicament was similar to that of my Harvard classmate Joseph Alger. Joe had been the able editor of the *Harvard Lampoon,* and when he went to work for that booming advertising agency Batten, Barton, Durstine, and Osborn, he took along his sardonic humor. In a time of cheerful slogans Joe hung above his desk the sign he had hand-lettered: "When they said, 'We couldn't do it,' we never even tried." Perhaps this aroused some skepticism. In his vast shop when someone had done exceptionally well with a new account an American Beauty rose would be placed on his desk, by way of congratulation. Joe was very good at the piano and at the company party at Christmas when his turn came, with the high brass smiling in the front row, Joe sang a ditty of his own with the refrain:

> *When you gave me a rose*
> *Instead of a raise*
> *You sure got a rise out of me.*

With Mr. Sedgwick's rose I also received increasing responsibility. I wrote the biographical notes about our contributors. I wrote sometimes as many as seventy-five letters of rejection a week — and sometimes the revised manuscript was accepted. I assigned the book reviews, occasionally did one myself, and insisted that the reviewer should sign his full name instead of his initials. (No one signed any contribution in the *Atlantic* at the outset. Amy Lowell declined to do any reviewing for us until this last vestige of anonymity was abolished.)

When Mr. Sedgwick was indisposed or did not wish to see who was below I was sent as his delegate to the reception room. Thus on one occasion I took into my hands a book manuscript entitled "Coolidge-grams," epigrams by Calvin Coolidge, two or three of his terse, laconic remarks to the page, with a picture of the President as a frontispiece. Nonplussed I turned the pages and when I began to smile the delegate assumed that I was laughing not with but at his hero and departed in a huff. I had to be more respectful in my handling of Mr. John Farwell Moors, elderly and a member of the Harvard Corporation, who brought in a huge scrapbook labeled "Ananias." Within, as he showed me, were newspaper clippings, supposedly tracing every false statement Theodore Roosevelt had ever uttered from the time he entered public service — with appropriate damnation by Mr. Moors. There was a second volume at home. Would the *Atlantic* be interested in publishing them in book form? This was my first but not my last encounter with the vitriolic hatred of T. R. in Boston, "an enemy to his class."

It was in the recruiting of new writers that I was most eager. At my invitation we had published the poems of Bill Whitman and Morley Dobson and John Crowe Ransom, and essays by three who had impressed me at Cambridge: J. B. S. Haldane, H. M. Tomlinson, and

Gaillard Lapsley. A letter to my friend Douglas Burden, who was after big game in Indo-China, fetched two fine articles, the first on elephants, the other on tigers, by that famous French hunter Defosse. Defosse's account of the elephants he had observed caught the eye of a young ex-army officer, now lumbering with elephants in Burma, Captain A. W. Smith, late of the Gloucestershires, and in the approved British tradition he wrote in to explain how different were his pachyderms from those hunted by Defosse. His letter was long and so vivid that it was converted into an article almost without a change, the first of his many contributions. In fiction I took special pleasure in the stories we published by my friend Manuel Komroff.

If what they said was true, 1927 was the year my head was to be chopped off, but it opened auspiciously with a raise that put me over $3,500. That spring Mr. Sedgwick scored three master strokes. The first was the publication in the March issue of Felix Frankfurter's extended article "The Case of Sacco and Vanzetti," a "case" which had been before the courts for more than six years "in a state where ordinary murder trials are promptly dispatched." But this one was not ordinary. On April 15, 1920, Parmenter, a paymaster, and Berardelli, his guard, carrying two boxes containing the payroll of a shoe factory in South Braintree, were shot to death by two men on Main Street at three in the afternoon. The murderers threw the boxes holding in excess of $15,000 into a car driven by their confederates which had drawn up alongside them, leaped in themselves and disappeared. The holdup suspiciously resembled an earlier one in the neighboring town of Bridgewater. In both cases a gang was involved that made its getaway in a car and, in each, eyewitnesses believed the criminals to be Italians.

The Braintree murder was committed at a time when Attorney General Palmer was rounding up and deporting Reds and anarchists, some of them Italian, who had been fomenting trouble. The trail led to the arrest of Sacco, a shoe worker long employed, and Vanzetti, a fish peddler, both admitted radicals; and in a highly charged atmosphere in a trial lasting seven weeks, they were found guilty of murder in the first degree. But belief in their innocence carried far beyond the Commonwealth: the testimony of the witnesses was disputed, so was the propriety of the conduct of Judge Webster Thayer; there were demonstrations here and abroad and when a member of the Morelli gang of Providence, who was already in prison, finally confessed to taking part in the crime and thereby absolved Sacco and Vanzetti — "I seen Sacco's wife come up here with the kids and I felt sorry for the kids" — the appeal for a new trial stayed their execution. But the Supreme Court of Massachusetts was not then empowered to demand the retrial and Judge

Thayer was adamant in his "No!" It was at this point, before the men went to the electric chair that Frankfurter wrote his paper. Why he did so he explained to M. A. De Wolfe Howe years later in the following letter, the carbon copy of which he sent to me:

September 25, 1957

Dear Mark:

Thanks to Arthur Schlesinger, père, I read your reminiscences about the publication of my Sacco-Vanzetti piece in the *Atlantic*. You may care for the following comments.

You know what a hard-bitten and coercive editor — these are complimentary adjectives — Ellery Sedgwick was. When he phoned me to say he had heard I was writing a piece on Sacco and Vanzetti and that he wanted it for the *Atlantic*, I thought I would derive pleasure from making him woo me as he probably never in his life had to woo a contributor. The fact of the matter is that Herbert Croly had agreed to print my prospective piece as a supplement to the *New Republic* and when I asked him was, of course, characteristically generous in releasing me because of the greater public value of having it appear in the *Atlantic*. But I did have fun, as I have already indicated, in making Ellery be more than precatory and almost obeisant.

Secondly and more important, about the question you again raise regarding the propriety of publishing the article while the appeal was pending in the Supreme Judicial Court, there is all the difference in the world in discussing a case while it is being tried before a jury and discussing the legal questions of a case that is pending in an appellate court. And so while I think I fully appreciated and respected the questions that were raised about the propriety of publishing my article while the case was before the Supreme Judicial Court, I never had and do not now have the slightest doubt about the propriety of my doing so. The final word on this aspect of the matter was said by Lawrence Lowell in the fall of 1927 at the first meeting of the Board of Overseers. A number of Overseers were in high dudgeon about my conduct. They felt outraged that a professor of the Law School should have published that article while the appeal was *sub judice*. Several judges and lawyers then on the Board defended my conduct, but I was told that the devastating answer was given by Lowell. In closing the debate and addressing himself to my assailants, he said to them: "Would you have wanted Frankfurter to wait in expressing his views until the men were dead?"

In April 1927, Ellery baited a trap. Governor Al Smith of New York was the leading candidate for the Democratic nomination and Mr. Sedgwick had heard of a New York lawyer, Charles Marshall, who was publicly airing the question of whether the Governor's loyalty as a Roman Catholic did not disqualify him for the Presidency. The issue was a hot one, especially in the South. Mr. Marshall complied in "An Open Letter to the Honorable Alfred E. Smith," quoting pointedly from those papal encyclicals which he believed to be irreconcilable with the Constitution. It was certain that Al Smith would reply but it took all of Mr. Sedgwick's persuasion to forestall his releasing the answer to the press until we could print it in the *Atlantic*. The Governor's statement, "Catholic and Patriot," which he wrote in collaboration with Father Duffy, chaplain of New York's "Fighting 69th," was a ringing affirmation of his faith in this country and did much to clear the underbrush from his path and that of John F. Kennedy later. We ordered paper for 160,000 copies, the largest edition ever up to that time, and took the added precaution of copyrighting every page of the Smith article.

But the Boston *Post* with its many Catholic readers had no intention of waiting until we were on the newsstands. They sent a reporter to Concord, New Hampshire, who bribed the nightwatchman at the Rumford Press to give him access to the galley proofs of what Smith had written and they then broke the story eight days ahead of our release date, thus making it available to every other daily in the country. What this cost us in newsstand sales I cannot guess, but the Boston *Post,* I am happy to say, was on the downward path. It eventually disappeared, but not before it .paid us $20,000 in damages for breaking our copyright.

While all this was going on I made a couple of what seemed to me praiseworthy efforts to strengthen our *Atlantic* fiction. The first chance occurred when Manuel Komroff sent me a long story entitled "Fifty Grand" by a young American living abroad, Ernest Hemingway. They had met in Paris, where Hemingway showed him the narrative, which *Scribner's* thought too long but that they might take it if it could be cut. Hemingway said a fresh eye was needed and asked Manuel if he could cut out five hundred words, which he did with approval. Then after a long silence the manuscript was forwarded to Manuel in New York with the word that *Scribner's* did not want it after all. What did he think?

"Fifty Grand" is told in the words of a professional boxer, the welterweight champion, in training to defend his title. He is past his prime, so sure he is to be beaten that he bets $50,000 with the gamblers that he will lose. The climax of the fight when they try to double-cross him is a rugged, punishing piece of prose and I was not sure Miss Converse would like it but she was enthusiastic. Mr. Sedgwick was a vocal reader: when reading a manuscript on which he had set high hope — and even paid an advance — and it was proving to be a lemon, he could be heard moaning, beginning on a low note and swelling in volume. When he was discovering something he liked, a rising crescendo of short barks: "Oh-oh-OH-OH" told of his delight. We heard them as he read "Fifty Grand"

223

and the story was accepted without question or change. And put in the icebox for the July issue when the schools which used the *Atlantic* in their English classes would no longer be in session.

What neither Komroff or I knew was that in the long silence before it came to us "Fifty Grand" had been rejected by the *Cosmopolitan*, the *Saturday Evening Post*, and *Collier's*, as well as *Scribner's*. No matter. It stands as one of Hemingway's best and we were lucky to have it.

My other success — as it might have been — was when Thornton Wilder in response to my admiring inquiry about his next work sent me the first two thirds of *The Bridge of San Luis Rey*, with this letter:

New Haven, Conn.
June 3, 1927

Dear Mr. Weeks:

I am sending you under separate covers two very untidy portions of *The Bridge of San Luis Rey*. Of course I should be prouder than I can say if the *Atlantic* could use some of it. As you see there are two separate novelettes there, but the process in surgery would be beyond me. When I was in London Mr. Squire wanted to run the chapter on the Marquesa de Montemayor (a treatment of the life of Mme de Sévigné) but at that time I didn't see how the piece could be extracted from its "theological" frame. If you saw possibilities in the story of the twin brothers, then to retain some of the poignancy I think the portrait of Madre María del Pilar should be somehow lifted from the preceding chapter and inserted at the beginning.

The whole book will be very short. (you have two thirds of it there; the Uncle Pio section *excerpted* would be a little strong for the *Atlantic*) and I should be dazzled at your liking the whole. But Boni's and Longmans Green want to bring it out simultaneously (there is a copyright law about that) in the early fall, and I suppose your tables of contents are pretty well packed for many months to come. I don't mean it to look pretentious when I ask you to let me have the script back as soon as possible, because Boni have begun setting up already and Longmans are jealous of the time advantage, and that is their copy that you have. I haven't quite finished Parts Four and Five and am all flustered.

Whether you feel it suitable for your magazine or not, please write me an editorial-advice letter about it; I am eager for suggestion and if you found certain parts too sentimental or too didactic, I should be very indebted to you for saying so. I am not haughty about alterations in matters of "taste" either!

I hear that you are doing Ernest Hemingway's *Five Thousand Grand*. That's fine.

Well, whether anything comes of my ambition for the *Bridge* and yourselves, thanks very much for writing me, and excuse all this careless typewriting.

Very sincerely yours,
THORNTON WILDER

But I was the only enthusiast — it elicited no approval from my two seniors and despite my remonstrance and pleading for a deferred decision until we had the whole I was faced with the mortification of sending it back. In doing so I made a friend and we lost a superb serial.

I was being paid to make decisions and I probably argued too heatedly over this one. When a little later I was called in and sat in that damnable chair before Mr. Sedgwick's desk, I knew my sentence was to be pronounced. My time was up. I let my gaze wander into the Public Garden as I thought, Back to New York? and heard the words ". . . want you to make a more permanent place in our organization. I propose that you take over the editing of Atlantic books as your own department . . ."

I thanked him and said I'd want to think about it.

VIII

W HEN SHE FAILED to find what she wanted in the shops or was annoyed by the delay in the subway, Fritzy dismissed Boston as "a one-horse town." But now, faced with the possibility of leaving, we both hesitated. We had become more attached to the place than we realized: it had a quiet style and a distinctive beauty — the Public Garden with its tulip beds and magnolias, the long vista of elms on Commonwealth Avenue; the Esplanade when the crews were rowing in the spring; Symphony Hall and the splendid art museums in the Fenway — all were within easy reach and made city walking a delight. We both enjoyed the intimacy of our supper parties and theatergoing with Bill and Marjorie Whitman and the country weekends with new friends, George and Katharine Batchelder, who had revived the old Phillips estate on Wenham Lake, a show place whose great trees and banks of rhododendron, laurel and azalea had been originally laid out by Frederick Law Olmsted.

Besides, I was one of a young group injecting new life into the St. Botolph Club. The brownstone clubhouse with its bouquet of cigars, its massive mahogany and well-worn rugs, was only two blocks from my office. The cuisine naturally specialized in chops, scrod and steak, and in summer the generous members brought back the fruits of their gardens — fresh peas, green corn and raspberries. In addition, the wealthiest of them all, Henry Sweet, made us welcome at his private nine-hole golf links, carved out of the woods and pastures of Dover, where one carried one's bag and occasionally surprised a deer on the fairway. The spring and fall tournaments, in which everyone, even members as old as George Agassiz, took part, were an amusing blend of competition, comedy and alcohol.

We had our eccentrics: old Tom Fox, the architect, sunk in his chair, glowering at the noisy backgammon table, and white-maned Jake McGrath, the medical examiner, who liked his steak raw ("Just pass it over the coals, Fred!"), and who could take the edge off any appetite with his description of the female bodies, hacked and stuffed into old trunks, which it was his job to exhume. But we were part of that ageless fraternity that is club life: the elders gave us their experience and we gave them our high spirits in the Twelfth Night Revels, as when I played the part of Alice in "Alice in Botolphland," the text and lyrics by David McCord, who was Lewis Carroll.

The scenes were in pantomime, with David reading, and his verse was a skillful parody, as witness these opening stanzas to "Father William":

> *You are old, Father William, the young man said,*
> *And yet you are fearfully nimble.*
> *A drop of this bottle goes straight to your head.*
> *Pray, can I not pour you a thimble?*
>
> *In my youth, said the sage, as he twisted his beard,*
> *I told the best jokes in the hub;*
> *But now that I'm older, it's just as I feared;*
> *I tell them again at the Club.*

I lunched at the Botolph regularly, hoping to find any one of these three at the Round Table: the wise, florid Leslie P. Thompson, an artist, whether painting a still life or casting a fly, invariably dressed in gabardine with a Madras tie as pink as his cheeks; Robert Greenough, the great-hearted specialist on cancer, who took a dozen of us to his place on the Cape for the spring opening of golf and trout; and my particular favorite, Ferris Greenslet, the editor at Houghton Mifflin. Ferris, or "the Duke" as he was called, was a Latin scholar before he entered publishing. He studied for his doctorate at Columbia under George Edward Woodberry, and in his early twenties, as the literary critic of the *Nation*, wrote such brilliant columns that the poets and elders he criticized elected him to the American Academy of Arts and Letters. He came to Boston to be Bliss Perry's assistant on the *Atlantic*, and ripened as a gifted editor and biographer. Earl Gray and John Buchan were two of his English authors whom he much admired and I loved to hear him talk about them. The Duke looked out for me and I was ever grateful: he nominated me for the Century Club in New York, he counseled me like an older brother, and he eventually made me a convert to the fly rod. Give all this up for the costliness and the commuting of New York? "Have another talk with E.S. before you decide," said Fritzy.

In my dismay at being released from the magazine, I had not listened

Alice in Botolphland. The March Hare, Lovell Thompson; the Dormouse, George Goodspeed, Jr.; the Mad Hatter, Bill Kirkpatrick

A St. Botolph weekend on the Cape. Seated, left to right: Hardwick Stires, Jim White, Arthur Spear, John Hawes, Bill Smith, Dick Fuller. Standing: Ferris Greenslet, C. F. Weed, Harry Sherburne, Weeks, Bob Greenough, and Willie Chase

Photo by David McCord

attentively to the alternative. In the ensuing talk I did, and Mr. Sedgwick was candid. The Press, he explained, in its first decade had run up a deficit of $110,000 — we had published only one novel in that time and far too many collections of essays, garnered from the magazine; our biographies were distinctive, but too highly priced, and our single traveling salesman was inadequate. (I knew it, I had seen his dejection in my rounds in New York.) To change all this we had recently entered into an agreement with Little, Brown and Company, which would clean the slate. We would retain the initiative and the editing of Atlantic titles, our colophon would be preserved on the title page, but from now on all Atlantic books would have the advantage of the experience and full collaboration of Little, Brown. He looked to me to bring in new authors, novelists especially. "You have a flair for short stories," he said. "Use the *Atlantic* as a dragnet for bright fish." Put in this light, it was a challenge, not a cutoff, and I accepted.

"I hope, sir," I said, "that when the Press turns the corner I may be permitted to share in its earnings." He smiled and we shook hands.

I began with a staff of three: myself, scout and editor; my secretary, Miss Frances Bates, who read manuscripts in the intervals between dictation; and one antique proofreader, white-haired Miss Emery, who in slippery weather came to the office wearing steel clogs and who, as I soon found out, had to be restrained from expurgating all profanity from our fiction. I was so eager to get the engine started that I used my latchkey to the office at any hour of the weekend to keep abreast of the manuscripts.

We were soon overwhelmed. An Atlantic novel contest with a prize of $10,000 (Little, Brown to chip in $7,500; the *Atlantic*, the balance for the serial rights) had been announced some months earlier and now as the closing date approached the heavens opened. We were confident that the prize was large enough to attract new writers and those who had published but had not yet found a large readership. Wooden tables on trestles had been set up in the largest office available and on them reposed thirteen hundred book-length manuscripts, some of over a thousand pages!

The judging, as announced, would be done by the Atlantic staff, but first came the winnowing by Ted Morrison and myself, ably assisted by our wives and Mrs. Lovell Thompson (at $1.00 an hour). To speed things up I arranged to send one hundred manuscripts to a highly recommended staff member of the Boston Public Library with instructions on how to report: a large *D* on those that were worthless; *D* with a brief comment, on those that had some good points; an *R* with full comment, on the few that merited further reading. In three weeks back they came and as I unpacked them one by one from the cartons I could not find an *R* among them, nothing but *D*'s and mostly without a word. I could not believe it, so I started reading. She was right about the first four, but the fifth, which I could see at a glance was professionally typed, had the strange title *Jalna,* and on the report sheet beside the *D* was the comment: "The story of a quarrelsome, love-making family in Canada. It smells of the stable." I went on with my reading, took the manuscript home that evening, and my opinion of it was quite different. As it was passed from reader to reader, *Jalna* by Mazo de la Roche emerged as "the best so far," and then the book to beat.

When the field had been cut to eight, everyone took turns: F.C., Mr. Sedgwick, Mr. McIntyre, the president of Little, Brown, and their editors; for a time it was a tossup but eventually *Jalna* was proclaimed the winner. It is indeed the story of a passionate Canadian family, the Whiteoaks, dwelling and feuding in their country place on the shore of Lake Ontario, protective in their loyalty, downright in what they disliked. The grandmother, old Adeline, who ruled over them and was ninety-nine when the book began, seized the imagination in her indomitable way the instant she appeared on the page (as did Miss Ethel Barrymore when she played the role on the stage). Canadians have always denied that the Whiteoak family was "typical" and they are right. What cannot be denied is their universal appeal; translated into twelve languages, as popular in France and in Britain as it was in America, *Jalna* was a best seller such as we had never had before.

Miss de la Roche was a native of Toronto, and in appreciation of her victory the city had presented her with a silver service. Now a banquet was planned in her honor and I went north to speak for the Press. The check had already been deposited in her bank, but I carried a blank in a sealed envelope which I would present for theatrical effect at the conclusion of my remarks. I expected to praise Canadian writing — Bliss Carman, the poet, and Stephen Leacock, the humorist, had both appeared in the *Atlantic* — but I needed some spark. Just before I left Boston I stopped by the desk of our head proofreader, Caroline Church, who was copyediting the first installment of *Jalna* for the magazine. Were there any points she wanted me to take up with the author? She thought for a moment. "Mr. Weeks, frankly I've been troubled about the size of that house, Jalna. I just don't see how they all fit into it, especially when Eden, the married son, brings his wife there to live. There aren't enough bedrooms! Why don't you see if she has worked it out."

Before the festivities I took tea with Miss de la Roche and her cousin-companion, Caroline Clement, in their small apartment crowded with family heirlooms. Caroline was a delicate little blonde with Wat-

Mazo de la Roche

teau coloring; in contrast Mazo was tall, slender, aquiline, with soft auburn hair and dark eyes. She was nervous at the thought of the evening, and when she trembled she seemed as taut as copper wire.

At the banquet when I was called on and had delivered my *politesse*, I turned toward Mazo and remarked that we had been having a good deal of trouble with the Watch and Ward Society in Boston and I hoped they wouldn't ban *Jalna* because of the scarcity of bedrooms in that rambling old house. She blushed at the laughter, and later as we were standing together in the receiving line, she whispered, "It was wicked of you to mention those bedrooms! But your proofreader is right — there aren't enough. We shall have to make changes in the proof." A week later she sent her corrected galleys to Boston, having added two bedrooms in the attic, and making sure it was understood that the Grandmother slept on the ground floor!

Mazo had already published a collection of short stories and two novels before she turned to us and on this first of many visits I learned how much she trusted Hugh Eayrs, the head of Macmillan in Canada. It was Hugh who advised her to try for the prize when the American branch of Macmillan failed to show the enthusiasm which he felt *Jalna* deserved. She wrote in longhand, which usually results in a tight style; there were few surface blemishes in her text and it was only in the matter of bedrooms or of keeping her straight with the ages and birthdays of the numerous Whiteoaks that we could help.

Writers who had been through the war had a special hold on me. Not the generals now defending their careers, nor elder statesmen like Lloyd George, but younger men whose talent for writing had not been burned out in the fighting, such as T. E. Lawrence of Arabia. It was John Galsworthy who called our attention to one of Lawrence's friends, Henry Williamson, a young infantry officer who at the war's end had found for himself a hermitage, a one-room stone cottage deep in the Devon moor. Here through the seasons he lived to himself, quietly observing the falcon, the fox, the deer and the badger, above all, the otter, that fascinating inhabitant of land and water. His only diversion was on Saturday nights when he walked in to the hamlet of Georgeham to drink small beer with the villagers and to master the complexities of their Devonshire dialect. Galsworthy wrote that he had been "much struck by his writing. He has vision and feeling and, I think, a future." Sedgwick sent an inviting letter to Skirr Cottage, North Devon, and the nature sketches and stories which came by return post to Boston so delighted him that he read them aloud to Mrs. Sedgwick and in his acceptance wrote this to Williamson:

We do appreciate your skillful art in giving us, as it were, all England in a day. Your knowledge of the oldest races on the Island and your assurance that they still live until the present is very heartening to us city dwellers who have to motor fifteen miles to see a rabbit. I don't know how you were ever admitted to such intimacy with the beasts, but I speak for two Americans when I say that I sincerely envy your friendships.

Such praise and the check broke a long famine and Williamson's gratitude was touching:

Many thanks for your encouragement. It is indeed a comfort, for if ever an author was in the trough of a wave — a wave being about seven years so far — I am that wight. Here I am, working and working on essays and stories, most of which don't fetch so much as a grunt from the well-nourished swine who reject the pearls. . . . I want to be considered normal, as I am; but the sub-normal seem to predominate and so form the standards of the world.

I have written a book about an otter. . . . I can promise you there has never been anything like it; you ought to read it. The epithet Mr. Galsworthy used is "inspired."

Meanwhile I am as poor as a mouse in a black-frost winter.

No book of Williamson's in the seven years since his demobilization had sold more than a thousand copies — I doubt if his yearly income reached $700 — and the first edition of *Tarka the Otter: His Joyful Water-Life and Death in the Country of the Two Rivers,* sold only half that number on its first appearance in London. We had no chance for the American edition, which had been placed before we knew him, but when *Tarka* was awarded the Hawthornden Prize, England woke up — the English have always had a liking for naturalists — and began comparing him to Gilbert White of Selborne. In remembrance of Sedgwick's push, he gave us the American rights to his later books and, in time, we were rewarded with his second extraordinary novel, a narrative of river life and ocean depth, *Salar the Salmon* (which with *Tarka* was to have a formative effect on an American biologist, Miss Rachel Carson). He and I were to be friends for three decades.

I have mentioned Mr. Sedgwick's paternal interest in Nordhoff and Hall; now I was privileged to assist in their partnership, which was unique in American letters. In Paris in 1919 Charles Nordhoff and James Norman Hall had together written the history of the Lafayette Flying Corps, in which they had both been fighter pilots, and in the doing they had formed an enduring friendship. Physically they were a contrast: "Nordy," Harvard 1910, an ash-blond Nordic from California, tall and reserved; Jim, a graduate of Grinnell, slight, the most modest of men, his black hair close-cropped, his eyes gentle, his nose a long aquiline beak that had been broken on the control board when his Spad had crashed behind the German lines. Hall had already published two books, *Kitchener's Mob* and *High Adventure;* he was an ace, had escaped from a German prison camp, and received every decoration France could bestow; he had not lost his idealism and now what he most wanted was an inexpensive private place in which to write. So did Nordhoff, and with $1,000 from Harper and Brothers and an advance from the *Atlantic* they found their workshop in "Paré's Retreat," an old ramshackle hotel overlooking the lagoon at Papeete, Tahiti, where they shared two rooms opening on the upstairs veranda, with brass bedsteads, mosquito nets, crockery, and a tin bucket for slops. They paid off the debts with a volume of descriptive essays, *Faery Lands of the South Seas,* the chapters written individually but unsigned; then went their separate ways, Nordy publishing with us two successful books for boys, *The Pearl Lagoon* and *The Derelict,* Jim living more precariously on the fees from his poems and personal essays that appeared in the *Atlantic.* Nordhoff's blondness and austerity endowed him with an almost godlike attraction for the daughters of Papeete and he was the first to marry and settle outside the village, but he would still bicycle in to compare notes in the privacy of their workshop.

It occurred to Nordhoff that the young hero of his first two books had reached the age when he might conceivably have volunteered in the Lafayette Escadrille. Why not try a war novel? It would embody the daring of Tommy Hitchcock, one of the youngest and most dedicated of the original flyers, and the fortitude of Harold Willis of Boston, who had been shot down and on his third try escaped from the German prison in which he had been languishing. He evaded the border guards, swam the Rhine, and found sanctuary at a Swiss farmhouse at 3 A.M., stark naked, except for the bacon grease which had protected him from the chill of the water. For this book Nordy needed Hall's collaboration, both for Jim's much greater flying experience and for the miracle of Jim's survival when an antiaircraft shell buried itself in his motor but did not explode, and his spinning plane crashed into and hung in the branches of a great tree. This was their first venture together in fiction — I could tell who was writing by the difference in the color of the typewriting, Nordy's was a rusty gray, Jim's black and new-looking — and what coordinated the style was their familiarity with the subject and the vernacular. The chapters were evenly divided and read aloud to each other in Paré's Retreat; the only difficulty I spotted was the tendency to spend too much time re-identifying the characters before each embarked on a new episode. They hesitated at first to surrender their identities; the suggestion was made that their initials be printed beside each chapter in the table of contents. This I vetoed on the ground that it would detract from the unity of the book. Nordy thought of calling the novel *Huntsmen of the Skies;* probably it was Henry Williamson's story of a peregrine falcon that suggested the better title, *Falcons of France.*

For *Falcons of France* we paid the meager advance royalty of $600; it was serialized in *Liberty* for $10,000, and when the book sale passed seventy thousand copies the boys at last had folding money — much of which Mr. Sedgwick persuaded them to entrust to the treasurer of Harvard University, Henry Shattuck, for investment. Flushed with that success they cast about for a second project. A creative partnership such as theirs is a rare thing in literature and seldom lasts long.

One could never be sure about a prospective author till the typed pages were in hand, but it paid to be encouraging. A Miss Boylston came in asking to speak to an editor and I went down. A redhead with a New England accent, she had poise and the look of competence. Said she'd been writing short stories for a year and had only sold one. What had she done before? Nursing. Trained here in Boston at the Massachusetts General, served two years in their unit attached to a British field hospital in France, after the Armistice transferred to the Red Cross and nursed in Poland in the undeclared war against the Russians. Had she kept a diary? She flushed; yes, but it was very personal. Perhaps it might be cut for the magazine, I said. And then out of the blue there popped into my mind the recollection of *The Little Colonel* books my girl cousins used to read when I was a boy. Why don't you write a book for older girls about the training you and your friends went through at the MGH, I asked, and her eyes widened. That was the beginning of *Sue Barton, Student Nurse,* the first of seven entertaining, professionally accurate novels about nursing by Helen Dore Boylston. I did my best to keep the heroine a virgin, scornful of interns, through the first four, fearing her readers would lose interest after she married, but I was wrong, and when Sue found the right young doctor the series went gaily on, as popular in England as in America.

Sometimes I was tantalized. Dr. Harvey Cushing, who was the most eminent brain surgeon in the world, could speak and write with eloquence. For his biography of William Osler, his great teacher, published by the Oxford University Press he had been awarded the Pulitzer Prize and as a follow-up Mr. Sedgwick had persuaded him to let us publish

235

a volume of his collected papers entitled *Consecratio Medici*. It fell to me to carry manuscripts and proofs to Cushing's office at the Peter Bent Brigham Hospital and be patient while he fussed over them. He was a perfectionist with a swift, critical, eager mind, fiery when aroused, as hard on others as he was on himself. While waiting for him I grew familiar with his office. The glass-fronted bookshelves encasing his old and valuable medical library stood about five feet high and on their top was an array of war souvenirs that made me shudder: tin hats that had been pierced by shell fragments (which Cushing had later removed from various skulls); field glasses which a French officer had used at the Battle of the Marne, one half intact, the other a mass of tiny particles the bullet had driven through the eye and close to the brain. In extracting them Cushing for the first time had used the magnet and a long nail to withdraw the metal from the deeper incisions. The officer lived and here were the scraps to show what one brain could do to save another.

When type and paper and binding were at last to Dr. Cushing's satisfaction, he showed me to the door, pausing to point to a row of large black-bound volumes on a lower shelf. "Weeks, there's the makings of a good book but one that can't be published till I'm dead."

"What is it?" I asked.

"My war journals. More than a million words and full of indiscretion. Well, thanks for your help. Good-bye."

Six months later I called his office; he wasn't busy and when I heard his voice I said, "This is Edward Weeks. I want to know how you're feeling."

"Weeks? Why, I'm feeling all right. Why do you ask?"

"Well, you said I couldn't get at your war journals until you were dead and I wondered if my chances were improving."

I thought I could hear him chuckle. "You go to hell," he said, and hung up.

2

We were in the high tide of American fiction. The work of Sinclair Lewis, F. Scott Fitzgerald, Theodore Dreiser, Thornton Wilder, John Dos Passos, Ernest Hemingway, Thomas Wolfe, and William Faulkner — it seemed to me that never before had our novels been so versatile and so vital. Three of the heroes in those books spoke directly to me: Jay Gatsby, the outlaw, bucking the heartless extravagance of Long Island; Frederic Henry in *A Farewell to Arms*, with whom I relived my wartime experience, and whose passionate devotion to Catherine moved me to tears;

and Charley Anderson, Dos Passos' supersalesman in *The Big Money,* whose success and false hopes typified what I knew of my father and feared for my brother Rufus. Most of those writers were only a little older than I and, of course, I envied them in my admiration.

No Bostonian was among them. In fact, Bostonians were not supposed to read some of those books. My allusion to the New England Watch and Ward Society may have sounded facetious in Toronto, but it spoke for trouble at home, where Puritan and Roman Catholic set aside their antipathies to form a united front against the new literature. The district attorney, in warning booksellers not to touch *Elmer Gantry,* reminded Boston that the obscenity law of Massachusetts barred books endangering "the morals of youth," and the police chief went further. "I have read these books, and I think they are bad," he said. "I have a duty to protect the morals of the people of this county . . ." When the list of books restricted by the police department and those intimidated by the Watch and Ward, novels mostly, had mounted to over eighty, the tag "Banned in Boston" became a national joke. New York book clerks showed it smilingly to their customers.

An American Tragedy, the only major work to be tried, was found to be obscene by Municipal Judge James T. Devlin, and Liveright's representative, Donald Friede, was fined $100; on appeal to the superior criminal court, Liveright's lawyer, Arthur Garfield Hays, was in full cry. Dreiser took the stand briefly and Clarence Darrow was permitted to read a chapter of the book to the jury. But only excerpts of this essentially moral book were allowed to be heard and when Assistant District Attorney Doyle quoted the references to birth control, he won his case and the conviction stood. *Oil* by Upton Sinclair was more quietly banned for the same reason — it, too, had referred to birth control, anathema to the Roman Catholic Church. When in June of 1929 the Boston police chief banned an issue of *Scribner's* because it contained a serialized episode of Hemingway's *A Farewell to Arms* and when, that September, Mayor Malcolm A. Nichols refused to permit the Theatre Guild's performance of Eugene O'Neill's *Strange Interlude,* forcing the production to be transferred to Quincy, ten miles away, the temper of the community that had once listened to the unorthodox Emerson at last began to boil.

In the early stages of the resistance I acted as Mr. Sedgwick's deputy. In 1928 a citizens committee, with the backing of Mr. Sedgwick, A. Lincoln Filene (whose discriminating customers were now ordering their books from New York), eight librarians and a few booksellers, filed a bill to broaden the obscenity statute, by deleting reference to "the morals of youth" and requiring that a book's "language" be considered "in connection with its entire content." This was in the right direction but we did not have Richard Fuller of the Old Corner Bookstore with us and when he filed a rival bill leaving the obscenity clauses untouched and seeking more protection for the bookseller, the two knocked each other out and the legislature took no action. A year later the bolder librarians, headed by Hiller Wellman of Springfield, submitted a revision of the first bill with the added proviso that only a person who sold a book "knowing" it to be obscene should be prosecuted. I was among those who testified before the Joint Committee on Legal Affairs, quite nervously I might say, and we were all elated when by a unanimous vote the bill was reported favorably. Unfortunately we underestimated our opponents: they brought political pressure to bear, we did not, and the "Massachusetts Library Club bill" went down to a narrow defeat in the Senate, 15 to 13 votes.

I was angry and I must have shot off my mouth at the meeting called to decide what next, for at the end of it I found myself chairman of the "Massachusetts Citizens Committee for Revision of the Book Law." I had had my nose rubbed in the mess long enough to know that we had to keep the cautious booksellers, represented by Dick Fuller, with us, balancing their fear of the police and the Church against the courage of my liberal trio: Henry Burnham, a solid lawyer, Lawrence O'Toole, a loyal Catholic who wanted the nonsense to stop, and Herbert R. Burgess, a bookseller in Back Bay who feared no one. We agreed on a simpler revision, substituting for that damning phrase *"containing language* that is obscene, indecent, or liable to corrupt the morals of youth" the words "a book, magazine, pamphlet, etc., which considered as a whole is obscene, etc.," and with it I went to see Henry L. Shattuck.

Mr. Shattuck was our ace, the most respected Protestant in the State Legislature; he had spearheaded our two earlier tries and I wanted him again to do so in the House. He accepted our revision of the statute, although he frowned over the phrase "considered as a whole": "I wonder what the judiciary would make of that." Then he went on, "This time you cannot afford to fail. You must not let it become a party issue. Some member of your committee must interview every member of the Legislature to show them how this is damaging Boston and the Commonwealth. You must raise money, distribute leaflets, send speakers wherever they can get a hearing."

We got the money we needed in unexpectedly generous amounts, because, as I said, people were indignant, and I personally signed up the sponsors who would give us state-wide respectability: Mr. Sedgwick and Mr. Howe from the *Atlantic;* Bliss Perry from Harvard; Bishop Lawrence (who had resigned as a director of the Watch and Ward), the head of the Episcopal Theological School; Hiller Wellman and Walter Pritchard Eaton from the western part of the state; and the presidents of Mount Holyoke, Smith, Tufts and Wellesley.

Fifty Harvard professors had protested the ban of *Strange Interlude,* but President Lowell was silent. When I called at his office in University Hall, he seated me, and as I pled my case he began to circle the room as if it were a running track, hands behind his back. "Who are some of the reputable authors who have been banned?" he asked.

"Sinclair Lewis, H. G. Wells, Ernest Hemingway, Warwick Deeping, Michael Arlen —" I began.

"Rotters, all," he said. "No, I don't think I can sign your petition."

Sedgwick opened the columns of the *Atlantic,* first to the president of Smith College, William Allan Neilson, who derided "The Theory of Censorship" and then gave me the chance to relate the absurdities resulting from our blue-nose statute and to stress that only a revision of it could end "the hypocrisy of the present situation, the injury which it does to literature, the notoriety which it too often bestows on cheap books . . . the contempt for law which it encourages."

From mid-September of 1929, when our bill was filed, to mid-March, when it came up for vote, I spoke forty-two times at meetings of Rotary Clubs, chambers of commerce, PTA's, and wherever I could find a soapbox. I was sometimes referred to as "the man on dirty books," and on the program I was usually preceded or followed by the Commissioner of Health, who was campaigning in behalf of clean milk. I listened to him so often that I knew his speech by heart, just as I suspect he knew mine.

I also lobbied in the traditional way by taking reactionary members of the legislature to lunch at the Parker House. There, after a good meal we would sit while I dilated on the integrity of American publishers and authors. I remember one particularly stubborn session in mid-January. My guest was Martha Brookings, the woman member from Gloucester, and it did not appear that I had been making much headway. "You can say what you please, Mr. Weeks, but I still think there are authors who write dirt for dirt's sake. Why only this Christmas," she went on, "I gave my sister a book which had been highly recommended, and you know what happened? She told me she was so disgusted that she had thrown it in the furnace."

"What in the world was its title?" I asked.

"*John Brown's Body,*" she said, "by that man Benét." And she made a face.

There was a small volume obtainable at the State House containing the photograph, the personal background and political appointments of the members of the Legislature, and my committee and I checked out every one of them, sometimes calling on those known to be friendly and influential in the member's district.

Before the vote the Watch and Ward went further to incense our sympathizers. A pirated edition of *Lady Chatterley's Lover* by D. H. Lawrence had been distributed in New York; the Vice Society raided the warehouse and the bills of lading disclosed that five copies had been shipped to the Dunster House Bookshop, a most respectable shop in Cambridge. The Watch and Ward, when tipped off, sent an agent by the name of Slaymaker, who represented himself as a collector of D. H. Lawrence and who on repeated visits sought to buy a copy at a premium. When Al DeLacey, the proprietor, repurchased a copy for Slaymaker's "collection," he was arrested and in the ensuing trial received a jail sentence and a fine of $1,000. Now Cambridge like Boston was up in arms.

I was used to being called "the dirty-book man" by program chairmen but still I was on edge when I testified before the Joint Committee on Legal Affairs; once on my feet things seemed to go well and when they again reported unanimously in our favor my hopes rose. Then in March, the evening before the House was to vote I had a telephone call from Henry Shattuck. "I have sounded out the representatives," he said. They won't accept that wording, 'a book considered as a whole.' The judges don't like it. Will you accept 'a book which is obscene'? I think with that change the bill will pass."

"But will that do away with the 'containing language' limitation? We must have the whole book considered."

"I think so," said the heavy voice. "The judges are bound to consider the change and why it was made."

"Go ahead, then," I said.

I never doubted that we should win in the Senate but in the visitors' gallery of the House I was nagged by the apprehension that some opponent of our bill might try to defeat it by reading from *Lady Chatterley's Lover* and I was right. After Mr. Shattuck had spoken there were questions and discussion and then a representative whom I did not know rose, with what I took to be D. H. Lawrence's novel in his hands. "Mr. Speaker," he began, "the member from Brookline, a bachelor, would rather take to his bed a dirty book than a chaste wife . . ." Down came the gavel, the Irish tirade was cut short, ruled out of order; they proceeded to a vote and the "Weeks Bill," as it had come to be called, was passed with a majority of 121 to 89.

It would be unfair to leave the impression that Boston was the only victim of an outworn morality. The federal authorities were just as erratic. In April 1929, a copy of Rabelais being imported by the book collector A. Edward Newton of Philadelphia, was confiscated by a New York Customs inspector "acting under Section 305A of the Tariff Act." In his letter of protest to the Customs, Mr. Newton (who enjoyed publicity) wrote:

"The action of your representative is positively glorious! Rabelais is one of the world's classics: it is no more obscene than are Shakespeare and the English Bible. In order that you may not be the laughingstock of the world, I beg that the volume be sent to me immediately; but for no other reason, for one can secure a copy at any well-ordered bookshop or library in the United States."

The struggle we began in Boston was terminated four years later in the United States District Court of New York with the trial and exoneration of James Joyce's *Ulysses,* a novel published and defended by Bennett Cerf and one which has probably exerted more influence on twentieth-century fiction than any other. In his historic decision Judge John M. Woolsey set a reasonable precedent by which one should review the unorthodox books of the future. The door that was opened then has been pushed right back against its hinges.

3

What brought Harry Crosby and me together again after a lapse of three years, while he was living abroad, was his surprising determination to become a writer. Harry's rebellion against Boston reached the breaking point in 1922, when his mother appealed to her brother-in-law, J. P. Morgan, to find a job for Harry in Morgan et Cie, in Paris. He was no happier as a bank clerk there than he had been in Boston, but he was at liberty, with plenty of spending money, and at Auteuil was winning or losing more on a single race than he could earn in two months. His family hoped that France would cure him of his infatuation with Polly Peabody, but that autumn he cabled her that he was coming over steerage on the *Aquitania,* had reserved the bridal suite for the return voyage, and would she marry him in New York in the forty-eight hours while the ship was refueling? She had obtained her divorce, and the answer was yes.

They lived for a time in three crowded rooms on the Left Bank, with Polly's two young children by her first marriage; Harry had no patience with them, called them "the brats," and wanted them out of the way. Then as the family in Boston relented and funds became more plentiful, they moved eventually to a spacious apartment of three floors at 19 rue de Lille in the Faubourg St. Germain. Harry insisted on a new name for Polly, which reminded him of the past, and he found it in "Caresse." Under that signature in 1925 he published a limited edition of Caresse

Crosby's first book, *Crosses of Gold,* pleasant, facile love poems of minor quality. His letter and the French books he sent me showed how seriously he was studying Baudelaire, Mallarmé, and Rimbaud; he tried to curb his gambling and to believe in Huysmans's phrase: "that art is the only clean thing on earth except holiness." He who had so resisted discipline now struggled to discipline himself as a poet under Caresse's coaching, and with the stimulus of his elderly cousin Walter Van Rensselaer Berry.

Harry spoke repeatedly of Walter Berry during our meetings on the North Shore and the picture I got of his sixty-six-year-old mentor was of a tall, thin, elegant, with a bird-like head; a close friend of Henry James and Marcel Proust, and an intimate admirer of Edith Wharton. She frequently stayed at Berry's apartment in Paris where there was a concealed stairway connecting his library with her room on the third floor. On one such visit Mrs. Wharton came down with measles and when the fever abated her host spoke to her through the quarantine-door:

"Edith, how are you feeling?"

"Better but bored."

"Why don't you amuse yourself by writing a short story in French?"

What was begun as a dare was continued in earnest; such, Harry told me, was the origin of *Ethan Frome.* (This was later confirmed for me by Mrs. Winthrop Chanler.)

Like all beginning writers, Harry was in a hurry to publish, and bombarded us with his "Sonnets for Caresse" (a collection of which he had privately printed in 1926). Neither Miss Converse nor Mr. Sedgwick liked them — nor did I. In my letters I tried to explain why they had failed of acceptance; he was perfectly cheerful about it and, undaunted, kept sending me more. His versification was not as smooth as Caresse's and one had to sort through the confection and the clichés, for any glint of originality.

We saw a good deal of each other in that summer of his return, sometimes at parties and more casually after Caresse had taken the children to visit her mother at Nantucket. Harry was lonely in his old haunts. Fritzy and I had rented a little cottage in Ipswich and from there he and I roamed Coffin's Beach or the Essex Woods, talking of writing and the future while I tried to separate the man from the legend he was beginning to create. He was reputed to be a great lover, yet his devotion to Caresse seemed unshaken and he always came back to her. His philandering did not square with my idea of fidelity but if she ignored his swordsmanship, why shouldn't we? Paris had cultivated his taste for wine and he was a steady drinker; he was still gambling — and losing — heavily at the races, and, of course, there was talk of drugs. These extravagances concealed from old friends how serious was his intent to be a writer and how often he struggled against his dissipations. But as I studied him to see what had changed, I felt again his physical magnetism: his clear skin, the color of old ivory, the way his eyes lit up when animated, the slight tremble of his lips when he was emotionally stirred. Always on our walks we were accompanied by his black whippet, Narcisse Noir, a lithe, beautiful creature whom our friend, the sculptress Katherine Lane, was modeling. Narcisse was a champion and we would pause to watch his grace and swiftness on the beach.

Harry was as curious about my work on the *Atlantic* as I was about his life in Paris. He had been promoted at the bank but finance bored him; it was in writing and reading that he found satisfaction, reading not only the poets but cruising through the *Encyclopaedia Britannica,* searching for new words and ideas. The *Britannica* had led him to Frazer's *Golden Bough,* the source of his religious approach to sun worship to which he shyly alluded. He was getting to know the American expatriates in Paris: Archibald MacLeish, who had thrown up a promising legal career in Boston to turn poet; Kay Boyle, the short story writer; and Eugene Jolas, the editor of the esoteric little review *transition;* through Jolas, he hoped to meet James Joyce, whom he revered. In all this he had the approval of Walter Berry. Berry believed in Harry (and was planning to make him his heir though this I could not know); when Berry had learned of Amy Lowell's death he immediately counseled Caresse to send Houghton Mifflin her new manuscript of verse, on the chance that they would be looking for another woman poet. They were, and her second book of verse, *Graven Images,* was accepted.

He and Caresse were now planning to launch a series of recherché books in expensive limited editions, and he asked my advice. There is a good market for them here, I said, the sonnets of Edna St. Vincent Millay in a numbered edition with her signature fetched $25 — what title would they begin with? Harry suggested the selected poems of e e cummings. Humbert Wolfe, the Englishman, is better known, I said, but I thought Sterne's *Sentimental Journey* a safer bet — besides there'd be no royalties to pay. He saw the point; whatever they decided, would I act as their agent in America for a share of the proceeds? I agreed. When we parted he urged that Fritzy and I come to visit them in the spring when they hoped to be in business. But there was no prospect of our going abroad in 1927. Mr. Sedgwick did the traveling for the *Atlantic* and in any case Fritzy would have been unwilling to leave our baby, Sara, who was hardly a year old, even if the money had been available.

Harry resigned from the bank. He wrote that they had found in

Roger Lescaret the ideal printer, who did exquisite work on a hand press, and that they had decided on Poe's *The Fall of the House of Usher* as the first title for their limited editions. It was to be printed on special paper with four-color plates by the Hungarian artist Alastair. How many could I dispose of and at what price? We agreed on an edition of 308 (250 for the United States), priced at $7.50. I suggested an introduction by Arthur Symons, but I calculated that after we had paid Mr. Symons and the artist, and the import duty of 15 percent of the list price, and the bookseller's discount, there would not be much left for jam. When the books arrived, I spread them around in the more select shops — the Centaur in Philadelphia, the Brick Row in New Haven, Brentano's and Scribner's in New York — and as reorders came in, there was little doubt that my quota would be exhausted, so I called for some of the copies in Paris. At this encouragement the firm's imprint was changed from Narcisse to the Black Sun Press, because, as Caresse said, black was Harry's favorite color and he worshipped the sun.

I was tallying up our modest profit at the year's end when in came a letter from Harry asking that I send him part of his share in twenty-dollar gold pieces. He and Caresse had been traveling in the Middle East; in Egypt he chanced on a copy of *The Plumed Serpent* by D. H. Lawrence and was immediately stirred into action. From their boat on the Nile he dashed off by camel a compelling letter to Lawrence telling of his own belief in the Sun God and begging Lawrence for a sun story that they might bring out in a limited edition, to be paid for in twenty-dollar gold pieces, symbolizing the eagle and the sun. Lawrence's manuscript, *Sun,* was waiting for them when they returned.

It was forbidden to export gold and my problem was how to get the gold pieces across. It was solved by Bill Sykes, an eager young littérateur, bound for France: he secreted the gold pieces in the lining of his shoes, and so freighted, walked into their apartment on the rue de Lille, and when he undid his laces out rolled the hoard.

Including Lawrence's *Sun, The Birthday of the Infanta* by Oscar Wilde, the *Poems of Lord Lymington* and *The Letters of Henry James to Walter Berry,* the Crosbys had scheduled a total of ten titles for 1928. As this was obviously more than I could cope with, they found a New York bookseller, Harry Marks, who became their distributor. The list included new volumes of verse by each of the proprietors and *Shadows of the Sun,* a selection of entries from Harry's journal, a document which in its candid, nervous style was much more true of him than his verse. He offered excerpts of it to the *Atlantic* and I liked it for the picture it gave of the man in his medium, as witness:

JUNE 11. *With C to the Rue des Beaux-Arts to see the marble tablet we have placed on the Hôtel d'Alsace in honor of Oscar Wilde.*

OSCAR WILDE
Poète et dramaturge
Né à Dublin
Le 15 Octobre 1856
Est mort dans cette Maison
Le 30 novembre 1900

and we drank a toast to him in absinthe (he loved absinthe) from my silver flask and then went home to read Dorian Gray only we didn't read Dorian Gray for people came to tea.

---

13. This is how Baudelaire symbolizes the sonnet: "Avez-vous observé qu'un morceau du ciel aperçu par un soupirail, ou entre deux cheminées, deux rochers ou par une arcade, donnait une idée plus profonde de l'infini que le grand panorama vu du haut d'une montagne?"

---

17. Tea at W.V.R.B.'s [Walter Berry's] and we met Edith Wharton and everyone sat in the dining-room (where she wrote Ethan Frome, poor Ethan as she called him) — and there was Paul Morand of Ouvert and Fermé la Nuit and he was heavy and oriental with a pale opium face and there were the young Count and Countess (not the Countess) de Noailles, and a pretty Comtesse de Ganay and a Mrs. Hyde and last but not least a delightful Abbé Meugnier who said he wished that someone would invent another sin, he was so tired of always having to listen to the same ones, and who remarked when he saw Narcisse: "Mon coeur, c'est tout un jardin d'acclimatation."

---

18. Preparations for the Quatz Arts and the students are building an enormous serpent in the Rue Allent, and tickets are being distributed "Femme donne ton Soleil en adoration aux Incas" and costumes are being prepared and C tries on hers and she is passionate with bare legs, bare breasts, and a wig of turquoise hair.

Many people undressing and painting for the ball. Ellen B in her garters, C in her chemise, Raymonde in a peignoir while Lord Lymington (Gérard) and Vicomte du Vignaux (Gérard) and Croucher and a Foreign Legion Man and two or three students and Mortimer and my-

self all naked rubbing red ochre all over ourselves. (My costume a frail red loin-cloth and a necklace of three dead pigeons.)

At eight in the Library eighty students with their girls, and supper and a tremendous punch (forty bottles of champagne, five whiskey, five gin, five cointreau). And mad yells of Venez Boire and then pandemonium and more drinking and more and more and C and Raymonde were the most beautiful and C won the prize (twenty-five bottles of champagne) for the Atelier by riding (almost nude) around the ballroom in the jaws of the serpent while myriad students roared approval. I was ossified and was rescued by Raymonde who found me sprawled against a pillar and who was afraid of the mad antics and asked me to take her home or I her and there was a red blanket and the reek of dead pigeons and then complete oblivion.

---

19. A hot bath to scrub the paint off, then a cold one in an effort to revive, and a reading aloud from Beardsley's Venus and Tannhauser of the Ecstasy of Adolphe and the Remarkable Manifestation Thereof (Adolphe was the Unicorn — and what an ecstatic time he had!) and later on bacardi cocktails ("and lapped her little apéritif") and they give one a faraway (my thousand francs on Faraway) forest breath.

Luncheon at W.V.R.B.'s and the Ned Holmes are there and they have been scouring Italy for paintings for the Boston Art Museum and W.V.R.B. argued that the Museum should also buy modern paintings and I was lost with the Degas Girl and there have been times that I have lived with her in some experience of the mind. Suns within Suns.

Ever since I shifted to the Press, Mr. Sedgwick had been declining Harry's verse, courteously and at greater length than in his brief disposition of Caresse's work. But the journal he asked me to send back. I labored over the letter and I am sure this return hurt Harry more than the earlier rejections.

I next saw him in November of 1928 when he came over for the excitement of New York, which he was beginning to prefer to Paris, and that of the Yale-Harvard game at New Haven. He and Caresse stayed briefly with his parents at 95 Beacon Street. Their friends, Pete Powell, the photographer, and Gretchen, his wife, were also in this country and Harry had given them a blanket invitation to a spare room. They turned up unexpectedly at 95 with much luggage and a dog. As no spare room was available Harry announced that the Powells would sleep with Caresse and himself in their double bed — they had done it before.

Father Steve said no to that, angry words followed; there was a taxi strike on and Mrs. Crosby was out in the family car, so Harry hailed an ice wagon that was passing and in they piled, dogs, luggage and all and took off for the Statler. In the room they did share there was a radio with headphones and Harry experimented in making love with them on. Said it was distracting.

Despite the show-off Harry had plenty of serious news when we lunched together. Walter Berry had died in October and as his heir Harry was given his library "except such items as my good friend Edith Wharton would care to choose" (she chose five hundred volumes). Harry was thinking of writing the life of Rimbaud, as Berry had suggested, and his immediate job for the Black Sun Press, which was booming, was to translate the letters of Marcel Proust to Berry. He had put money in *transition,* was now an associate editor, and frowned when I said its symbolism left me hanging in mid-air. I thought he seemed more taut and later, in the drinking party with his friends, we did not reach each other as we had on our walks. I was to see him only once more before his death.

4

Our Sara was a plump, beguiling child. Being much in our company she picked up her vocabulary fast and the nicknames she bestowed on those she loved, stuck. Her grandmother, the elder Sara, became "Go-Go" and my golfing partner, James N. White, who took potluck with us and stayed on for backgammon or poker afterwards, was "Mr. Fudge." Since Jim was as generous as he was successful, this showed acumen. Another of our intimates whom she appropriated was David McCord, the poet, who became "Uncle David."

Since she was the first grandchild in my family, she had to stand up to no end of endearments when we took her to New York and Elizabeth for Christmas. It was a repeat performance and exhausting. The opening of presents at 8 West Fifty-third Street began after a very late dinner on Christmas Eve — fresh caviar, green turtle soup, turkey, champagne, plum pudding with the brandy blazing on the platter. Sara, wound up with excitement, was put to bed surrounded by her New York gifts sometime after eleven, but Christmas carols, Bill Wetmore's affairs — he was now football captain at St. Mark's and pointing for Harvard — family banter (but no arguments) kept the rest of us going until 2 A.M. Next morning, sleepy and satiated, Fritzy and I would have to pull ourselves together, dress Sara in her finery, and be downstairs ready for my father at an early hour. Dad drove us out to New Jersey and time had not made him any less competitive. A car ahead was a car to be passed, with scurrilities if necessary. Fortunately there were not too many contestants on the highway at that time on Christmas morning. Perhaps the ride keyed us up for the new round: the loving welcome, more presents to be opened, the cocktails, the delicious feast, the Chablis and the toasts. Then as the afternoon wore on and Sara had gone through her catechism seated beside Grandma Weeks on the sofa, the cousins all trooped in and I disappeared to help Dad into his Santa Claus costume and push him in the back window for his gift-giving beside the tree in the library. Somewhere in all this I always had time to tell Mother how the work was going in Boston; her pride in me was sustaining. But we were a weary trio when we returned to New York.

The symbol of our pilgrimages was a huge black suitcase of patent leather, cloth-covered, with straps for reinforcement, in which we carried our loot home. We first used it on our trip to Long Point for Martha's wedding. She was marrying a much older man, Sir Henry Thornton, American-born and now a British subject, whom she had met in France when she was nursing and when he was a major-general in charge of the railways of the British Expeditionary Force. Henry, as hearty as he was huge, was now head of the Canadian National Railroad, and wherever he traveled in his private car was Canadian soil, a fine thing for all of us in Prohibition as his gifts took the form of House of Lords gin and Haig and Haig. Hence the big black bag.

Perhaps I should add that Fritzy and I involuntarily supplied the comedy for the wedding. Martha and Henry were to take their vows on the lawn against a high screen of white lilies and after the rehearsal, drinks, and a light supper, the moonlight turned the Point, with its old oaks, into a place of shadowed beauty. We were sharing one of the tents and when the household had quieted down I suggested that we steal down to the tip of the Point in our wrappers. I seem never to have much luck as a forest lover and the spot I picked happened to be a lair of poisoned oak. The rash that broke out on Fritzy's bottom could not be concealed from her mother and Martha, and how they hooted!

Our brownstone complex at the corner of Arlington and Marlborough streets had become a hive of magazines. At No. 9 Arlington Street Christian Herter and Richard E. Danielson were editing a weekly, the *Independent,* and had plans on the drawing board for a much more expensive illustrated monthly, the *Sportsman.* At No. 8, Mr. Sedgwick presided over four periodicals: the *Atlantic,* his darling, now netting upwards of $100,000 a year; the *House Beautiful,* not much more than

Richard E. Danielson

a pamphlet when he purchased it, but now with its many photographs on coated paper, a solid rival to *House and Garden* and a money-maker earning close to a quarter of a million annually; the *Living Age* was sold; in its place was the *Scholastic* which could never be forced beyond a modest profit; and the *Youth's Companion,* which was losing money and which Sedgwick had taken under his wing in the hope that it could be revitalized. Even with our new brick annex we were short of space and I in my cubbyhole with my staff of two was the small tail of a large dog.

It is a reflection of our carefree days that we arranged a tennis tournament of the Boston publishers. Ellery and I represented the *Atlantic* and after we eliminated the editors of the *Youth's Companion* we were scheduled to play Chris Herter and Powell Cabot of the *Independent,* who had defeated Houghton Mifflin. The match took place on the exhibition grass court at the Essex County Country Club; staff and secretaries drove down to watch and there were side bets and cheers. Ellery had a wicked backhand chop and he could volley; I posted him at the net and went in to kill when I could. Our opponents came on the court wearing high-crowned Mexican hats — which were soon discarded. We won the first set and in the third broke Herter's booming serve for the victory. At the dinner afterwards I sat beside Dick Danielson and was altogether charmed by his humor and by his intimate knowledge and admiration of George Washington.

The *Youth's Companion* with a circulation of 260,000 had lost its grip. It had retained its readership by making every inducement for renewals and by ingenious offers of catcher's mitts, footballs, even bicycles to those eager beavers who could persuade their friends to subscribe. As a result by the time it reached its hundredth anniversary, its readers, many of them, were "youths" no longer but still content with simple fare; the magazine had been deserted by its advertisers and was losing half a cent on every copy printed.

The two editors called in to doctor the *Companion* were Harford Powell, Jr., a confident, saturnine veteran in advertising, and Eric Hodgins, an M.I.T. graduate who had been ably editing the *Technology Review.* Watching their efforts at resuscitation was to give me a preview of what was to come. The *Companion's* inventory of unprinted, old-fashioned stories was huge, and when Powell and Hodgins combed it looking for specialties for their Centennial Issue, they were delighted to find two lively pieces by Ben Ames Williams and Henry L. Mencken, which for some reason had been put aside for years. I particularly remember Mencken's because he made such a squawk trying to buy it back. It was the story of a diamond thief, long suspected but elusive, who secreted his gems in his molars and had to be strapped down in a dentist's chair before his guilt was revealed. Mencken offered to pay three times the original fee to get the story back but the boys wanted it.

I liked Eric Hodgins, so breezy, competent, and quick-witted, and I persuaded him and his friend Francis Magoun, also of M.I.T., to collaborate in the writing of *Sky High,* a sprightly history of aviation for older boys; Carleton Coon, a Harvard anthropologist who had been measuring skulls in the Riff (and protecting his pretty wife from the attention of the officers of the Foreign Legion) brought us his first novel, *The Riffian;* Owen Lattimore, linguist, traveler, and veteran of the camel caravans, was writing *The Desert Road to Turkestan;* and Walter D. Edmonds had finished *Rome Haul,* the first of his books about the Erie Canal, so descriptive of the towpath, the great locks, and the coziness of the cabin when the canaller has his girl aboard. The prize contests were our drum to attract new contributors. We published, in all, six books submitted for the novel prize of 1926: *Jalna* by Mazo de la Roche was on the best-seller list for two years, and the runner-up, *Red Rust* by Cornelia Cannon, sold forty thousand copies a year later. Thereafter we offered $10,000 for a novel on the even years, $5,000 for a work of nonfiction on the odd.

In June 1928, a letter came to my office from Wilma Frances Minor of San Diego, California, saying, "I have finished the true love story of Abe Lincoln and Ann Rutledge" and asking whether her manuscript would be eligible for our nonfiction award of 1929. I walked it straight down to Mr. Sedgwick; we knew nothing of Miss Minor and we were naturally incredulous ("Interesting, if true," was E.S.'s comment) but one could not shut out the possibility of what the letters would mean to the magazine and the Atlantic Press if they could be proved genuine. Mr. Sedgwick took over the correspondence and wrote to Miss Minor, asking to see photostats of the originals. She sent a half dozen and of course we concentrated on those signed "Abe." They appeared to be ragged and fragile. The handwriting, admittedly, was more angular and crudely formed than the small, rounded script of Lincoln's presidential years, but these were dated 1834, when he was twenty-five and, if they were to be believed, written in the rustic surroundings of New Salem, perhaps by firelight — and as everyone knows, handwriting changes with the years! Miss Minor was invited to send us her collection and to come to Boston at our expense.

She brought with her her mother, tall, beady-eyed, with surprisingly black hair, who somehow reminded me of a fortuneteller, and a plump, younger sister named Pearl. Wilma herself was lithesome, comely, with large Hollywood eyes. They were put up at the Ritz, only two blocks from the office.

The full board of directors were present next morning when Miss Minor unveiled her treasures. They covered most of the large table: a map of New Salem as it was when the lovers lived there in 1834; examples of Ann Rutledge's needlework; a diary by Matilda ("Matt") Cameron, Ann's cousin and best friend, depicting how the courtship developed after Ann had been deserted by her suitor from the East; a rusted breastpin which Abe had given Ann and the small Bible she had given him, with both their signatures; Kirkham's *Essay on Elocution,* third edition, with Lincoln's annotations; a chain of letters, some from well-identified persons, showing how the collection descended from Frederick W. Hirth of Emporia, Kansas, a Civil War veteran; and, finally, the fragile, rust-tinted love letters, twenty-seven in all. When she placed them in Mr. Sedgwick's hands he was visibly moved, spoke a few words about the solemnity of the occasion, put them on the table, and turned to the window to regain his composure. Wilma capped the drama by saying that after their publication she would present him with one of the originals.

That afternoon Fritzy and I drove the trio out to Concord. They seemed totally uninterested in Emerson, Louisa Alcott, or Thoreau, stowed away a big tea at the Concord Inn, and on the ride back complained of how hard it was to get any domestic help in California. Toward the end Miss Minor asked me if I didn't think there would be movie possibilities in the book whether or not it won the prize.

The girls returned to San Diego with a contract for the book, an advance of $1,000 and $4,000 more to follow on publication. Mr. Sedgwick assured them that serialization in the magazine would be contemplated as soon as we had had time to edit the material.

In the publication of letters much depends on the matrix which frames them and elucidates what may not be clear to the reader. Miss Minor's account was not entirely satisfactory and Mr. Sedgwick turned over to his assistant, Theodore Morrison, the task of checking and clarification; my job was to see how the material could be illustrated and the text amplified to fill a moderately sized book. Ted and I worked together and the lay of the land was confirmed for us by *The Prairie Years* by Carl Sandburg and *The Women Lincoln Loved* by William Barton. New Salem, Illinois, on a bluff above the Sangamon River, was a village of a dozen families, about the size of Chicago, when Lincoln arrived there in 1831. At the age of twenty-two he was very tall, strong, and lanky, and soon made himself useful in several ways. The founding

THE ATLANTIC MONTHLY

has the great honor to announce the publication of the

Original Love Letters

which passed between

Abraham Lincoln and Ann Rutledge

*A*T last, after nearly a century during which their existence was always suspected and hoped for, appear the priceless documents which lift the veil shrouding the love affair between Abraham Lincoln and young Ann Rutledge.

No longer need the biographer spend years of research, or the romancer dream of the idyll as it might have been. Here, for the first time, is revealed in Lincoln's own words, the tender love he bore for his "Dearly Valued Ann."

To the *Atlantic's* care has been confided the invaluable package inherited by Miss Wilma Frances Minor. Here are Lincoln's letters to Ann, and Ann's to Lincoln; letters from Lincoln to his friend and benefactor, John Calhoun; letters from the twenty-year old Ann to her cousin Mathilda Cameron, describing Lincoln's wooing ("he talks to me just like poetry," wrote the gentle, untutored girl); Mathilda's simply written revealing diary; the Bible Ann gave to Abraham; the little book of rhetoric with characteristic marginalia, which was the young Abe's daily companion through the days when he lived out the idyll of New Salem.

To those already privileged to see this collection, these documents seem the most moving personal mementoes in our history. Their deposit in the Treasure Room of the Congressional Library in Washington has been invited by the librarian.

Our first question, like the reader's, was,

of course, But, can this be *true?* Where have these letters been hidden all these years? When Lincoln scholars, students, lovers of his name, have eagerly searched for the proofs of this romance just hinted at in a few casual references and meager records of a scattered group of places and people, why have they not been discovered and given to the world before?

If there is one life of which the American people wish to know everything, it is Lincoln's, and his is the one life about which it long ago seemed impossible to unearth any new material.

And what have Lincoln scholars to say about this find? The leading Lincoln biographers and the country's most distinguished chemist who scrutinized the paper to determine if it were authentically of the period,— do they all accept these documents as the living record of the fragrant romance?

The answer to every question will be published in detail in the *Atlantic Monthly* beginning in December.

Miss Minor's story, with all its wealth of original, invaluable and long-sought Lincoln material, will begin in that issue. This feature alone, the first printing of these documents, will make an *Atlantic* subscription for the coming year a life-long keepsake—and incidentally a most appropriate Christmas remembrance.

The Lincoln story will be surrounded by an editorial program of true *Atlantic Monthly* standard.

The Lincoln serial will begin in the December Atlantic Monthly

A discovery that went wrong

families, the Rutledges and the Camerons, had built a dam and grist mill which attracted farmers from miles around; Abe clerked in the general store, split rails when trade was slow, helped navigate a flatboat in the shallow stream, put down the local bully, studied Kirkham's *Grammar* by the light of the woodchips in the cooper's shop and told stories that convulsed the community. He boarded with the Reverend John Cameron, who had a house full of daughters — eleven of them — but Abe had eyes only for Ann Rutledge, the daughter of the tavern keeper. Ann was thought to be engaged to an Easterner, who under the alias of John McNamar had run a store and bought property in New Salem; he had been recalled to New York, promising Ann to return. But he had not reappeared and it was in this dilemma, according to legend, that Lincoln began his clandestine courtship.

Miss Minor supplied the missing links, the letters in which the lovers confided secretly what could not be said openly in the close little community, and presumably they were conveyed by hand, through Ann's closest friend, "Matt," short for Matilda Cameron. Was Ann really as illiterate as her spelling suggested?

The testing began by our sending thin snips of the love letters to the Arthur D. Little Laboratory for analysis. Then Sedgwick approached the historians. Worthington Ford, previously head of the Manuscript Division of the Library of Congress, and now editor of the Massachusetts Historical Society, was the nearest at hand, and he was completely skeptical: he had just finished editing Senator Beveridge's life of Lincoln, left unfinished at the Senator's death, and said he did not understand how the letters could have escaped the vigilant search Beveridge had made for source material. Ford was written off as an unbeliever. Oliver R. Barrett of Chicago, whose famous store of Lincolniana Carl Sandburg was drawing on, was known to be skeptical, and we had no help from that quarter. When Herbert Putnam, the Librarian of Congress, made a special trip to Boston to see the papers, the most he would do was to show us how they tested dubious documents in Washington, enlarging the handwriting by photography and then comparing it, letter by letter, with authentic samples of the writer in question. He would give us no assurance, though he left the way open for a display of the letters at the Library after publication. When we made the handwriting comparison on our own, the letter *J* seemed to have a family resemblance in letters signed by Abe, Matt and Sally Calhoun, one of Ann's correspondents.

William Barton, the author of *The Women Lincoln Loved*, was more hopeful: he was ready to believe in the love affair, which had been terminated by Ann's untimely death and which might explain Lincoln's subsequent spells of melancholy. Carl Sandburg, who spent an overnight visit in Boston, was even more positive:

November 25, 1928

Dear Mr. Sedgwick:

These new Lincoln letters seem entirely authentic — and preciously and wonderfully co-ordinate and chime with all else known of Lincoln. Students of Lincoln's personal development will prize and love them for several known reasons and for intangible and inexplicable reasons. Thank you.

CARL SANDBURG

This was the signal for E.S., who had pretty much convinced himself, and he and Morrison laid out a three-part serial — "The Setting" (New Salem); "The Courtship"; "The Tragedy" — this to be preceded by a statement of the editor in the November issue of 1928, describing the find and embellishing its significance. If there was any skepticism within the office, it was confined to M. A. De Wolfe Howe on the general grounds that the trio gave no evidence of being historically minded.

The sharpshooting began with the appearance of the second installment in January 1929. The most accurate and devastating shot was Paul M. Angle, the secretary of the Lincoln Centennial Association, who hit not only the flaws in the handwriting but, what was worse, the historical discrepancies which neither Miss Minor nor Mr. Sedgwick could defend. Angle began by pointing out that according to J. C. Power's *History of the Early Settlers of Sangamon County,* John Calhoun had no daughter named Sarah or Sally, and that the Calhoun family had never lived in New Salem. Well, but Sally Calhoun was one of the two eyewitnesses verifying what was going on between Ann and Abe. Angle then riddled the letter Lincoln was alleged to have written to Sally's father, John Calhoun, on May 9, 1834: first, his statement that "the Bixbys are leaving this week for some place in Kansas." How come? Kansas was not organized as a territory until 1854. In the same letter Abe referred to a controversy "concerning that North East quarter of Section 40." But in the federal system of townships six miles square, there are only thirty-two sections. How could there be a Section 40? Ann makes a casual reference to Spencer's copybook, when in fact Spencer's first publication on penmanship did not appear until thirteen years after Ann's death. When Angle was joined by Barrett and Ford, the firing grew hotter, the absurdities more glaring.

Hoping things were not as black as they appeared, Mr. Sedgwick and Nelson J. Peabody had gone to the West Coast to talk with Miss Minor. But the criticism continued to be withering. Carl Sandburg recanted, so did Barton with less grace. On the way back to Boston a confrontation

255

with Lincoln experts took place in Chicago, which Paul Angle has described:

I do not remember the date, nor do I remember who arranged the meeting, but I remember everything else very clearly. We met at the Union League Club. Present were Sedgwick, Logan Hay, a very shrewd lawyer who was president of the Lincoln Centennial Association, Oliver Barrett, Dr. Otto L. Schmidt, president of the Illinois State Historical Society, Henry Horner, then judge of the Cook County Probate Court and later governor of Illinois, and I. For hours we pressed Sedgwick relentlessly; he gave ground grudgingly. Finally, late in the afternoon, he said to me, with something pretty close to a sneer, "Since you consider yourself an expert on Lincoln's handwriting, will you take a test?" "Of what kind?" I asked. Whereupon he handed me a sheet of paper on which he had pasted short words (like *an*, *the*, and *a*), and one- and two-digit numerals. Some, he explained, were photostatic copies from indubitable Lincoln letters; others came from the Minor documents. Would I distinguish between them?

I can't imagine a more unfair test, because anyone who has ever dealt with questioned documents knows that one should have a bigger sample than two or three letters. But in those days I really knew Lincoln's handwriting, and I was cocky. So I said, "Let me have it." And I ran down the list without any hesitation, distinguishing the good from the bad without a single error. That did it. Sedgwick folded, and asked me to write the article that appeared in the April, 1929, *Atlantic*.

But I believed then, as I believe now, that if I had said, "Mr. Sedgwick, perhaps I have overstated things a little today: I'd like to think about your invitation," he would have reverted immediately to his conviction that the Minor letters were genuine. In a long life I've never seen a man more impervious to reason.

The first two articles were in print and vulnerable, the third on press and impossible to change. On January 22nd Mr. Sedgwick issued a statement to the New York *Times* withdrawing our confidence in the letters and wrote to Miss Minor that we must defer the publication of the book.

In self-defense we employed detectives who discovered among other things that Wilma, as the sob sister for a San Diego newspaper, had published some years earlier an interview with Scott Greene, an old-timer from Sangamon County who had been slated to deliver a Lincoln's Birthday address only to be laid low with the flu. Scott was the son of Billy Greene, Lincoln's friend in the early days, and, as the interview disclosed, an ardent believer in the Ann Rutledge affair. From that point things happened fast. I took the train to Springfield, Illinois, prepared to meet Scott Greene, and read aloud the three installments so that he could identify what had come from him. Miss Fitzpatrick, our doughty circulation manager, went to the Coast to confront the girls. She departed before I did, just before we received a handwritten letter from Wilma's mother, saying that all this controversy had driven Wilma to her bed and would we please desist. It was the first specimen of her writing we had seen and in it was that letter *J* which we had found so peculiar in the documents.

Scott Greene, hale and in complete self-possession, sat me on his porch, and as I read, kept remarking, "Yes, I said that," "No, that's not what I believe." No question that he was a sincere and impressive narrator. Miss Fitzpatrick, to whom I wired that we had certain proof of the forgery, after a long session in Los Angeles, emerged with a confession signed by Wilma. It reads:

CONFESSION OF WILMA MINOR

Los Angeles, Cal. July 3, 1929

We have sat at the feet of the Master in our family.

Mr. Ashe said to me if that man, Scott Greene, knows anything about Lincoln and Ann Rutledge, get all you can of it because the world doesn't know the half of it.

I went to see Scott Greene and got his story and went home to Mama and said to her, Mama at last our faith of a lifetime has led to something. It has been given us for a divine purpose. On another plane those people (Lincoln and Ann and those other people) must exist. We have talked to many others, our family and close friends, and I said to Mama, Don't you think I have earned the right to be the channel to tell that real story to the world? Mama said, I don't know darling, we can try. Mama had always been the medium through whom the spirits had spoken. During these periods of mediumship Mama's face has broken out, her eyes have lost the power to focus. I asked the spirits through my mother why this was so. They answered that their handling of her caused such a rush of blood to the head. She always goes into a dead trance. One reason I am sorry for Mother is because as a medium she has never known how to handle things on this material plane. I have always taken care of her. She has been my child rather than my mother.

I was living at this time in East San Diego and only saw Mother on Wednesdays. On the next opportunity a few days later I asked through my Mother, who at that time was in a trance, the guide, — I believe it was my uncle who came, if I might have the divine privilege of being the instrument through whom the real story might come to the world. He answered he would find out and let me know the next week. The next week when Mother came again she went into her trance and the guide said he had asked the people (Lincoln, Ann, etc.) and they said they would give the story to me, provided I was willing to tie myself down to months and months of systematic labor. I agreed. I then began to prepare a series of questions. I would write out the questions. I would hand them to my Mother then in the trance; the spirit would come, whoever it might be, and fill out the answers. For instance, I would ask the ages of the two when Ann and Abe first met, and in the blank left under the question which was typewritten on a large sheet, the guide would answer through my Mother. My Mother would be seated at a table during this period. I asked what sort of a home they lived in. Ann drew a crude little sketch; she said this is very difficult for me, and said you must go to the books. This was the first idea I had of research. I had hoped they (the guides) could give me everything. In a talk they said that even on this plane many full years had elapsed, and over there one loses that direct contact with things here, so that incidents stand out and important matters, but not details, — dates grow hazy.

Every word in Matilda Cameron's Diary is verbatim as given by the guide. Every word written through my Mother as the medium. All this continued for a long period, but we had to stop for three or four weeks as my Mother was threatened with blindness. By this time I went to her home frequently. She would phone me that a "message come through last night," and I would go to see her, and she would give me the message she had received in her handwriting. I didn't have to be present when the handwriting message came, although I was at times. But I always had to be present when I put her into a trance, — no, not always. Sometimes in a great emergency she could go into a trance without material aid.

I asked where I would get the paper to write this on, the guide answered (oftentimes it would be Marie Corelli) that I could get it from old books and gave me a list of books that Lincoln used at that period of his life. I went to old bookshops and had no difficulty in picking them up. Then the guide told me for my continuity that I must look up written books for well known facts which were available to everyone. During this time, the guide drew the map through my Mother, who was in a trance. Mr. Ashe told me about the Atlantic Contest and although I had offered it to Harpers, I wrote to the Atlantic offering it as original Lincoln letters. I would die on the gallows that the spirits of Ann and Abe were speaking through my Mother to me, so that my gifts as a writer combined with her gifts as a medium could hand in something worthwhile to the world. This lay solely between my Mother and me, — I might really say me, my Mother was such a negligible part of it. During that time Ann Rutledge sent through this message to me, "I want in the next three years' time, for you to tell the world exactly how you got this." She thought it was a wonderful test case.

I have given this true and honest account of my own free will, and sign my name.

Wilma Frances Minor

Grace A. Downs ⎫
Harry S. Brill ⎬ Witnesses.
Teresa S. Fitzpatrick ⎭

I asked the guide if this was their handwriting and they said we can only go so far, we must in speaking use a medium's vocal chords and in writing they use the accustomed muscles of the hand of the medium. I knew nothing of Elizabeth's Uncle Fred's sister, the guides told me all about her. The guides gave me the story of just how to give the sequence of how the letters came into Mother's possession. I have suffered terribly for my Mother was really a negligible quality in the whole matter, — it seemed as though I was doing it only for my own aggrandizement. I had no fear in giving it out. I felt it was a holy mission. There was no craftiness in it at all. The idea of selling the letters was entirely obnoxious to me. You said one thing to me today that hurt me more than anything, when you said, "I guess you and Mother had a good laugh on the train home."

W.F.M.

Mama was indeed a fortuneteller.

The confession cleared up other points. The paper of the letters, which proved to be of the period, came from flyleaves of books which had been published in the appropriate year; the flyleaves were steeped in tea, then ironed, steeped again until of the right fragility and color. The paper of the map and of Matt Cameron's diary (neither tested) was of wood pulp, not manufactured prior to 1880. The ink was watercolor. Lincoln's textbooks had been purchased in secondhand bookstores, a couple had belonged to a woman, now deceased, who had actually taught in Illinois.

The humiliation took years for the *Atlantic* to live down and along with the embarrassment two questions persisted: why was the forgery foisted upon us and who was the mastermind? The first is the easier to answer: if the documents stood up in the *Atlantic,* there would almost certainly be a sale in five figures to Hollywood. The answer to the second is guesswork. I doubted if Wilma or her Mama had the ingenuity to put all this together or indeed to compose a diary as lively as Matt Cameron's, for all its theatrical misspelling. The only other forgery of even more compelling skill was the fabrication of *The Memoirs of Li Hung-Chang,* which fooled Houghton Mifflin Company and Constable of London, was serialized in the New York *Sun,* and quoted at length in Lytton Strachey's *Eminent Victorians.* That was the work of William Francis Mannix, America's ablest forger of this century. Did he also have a hand in the Lincoln letters? He died before I could inquire.

(There is a postscript. Twenty years after this black eye, my partner, Donald Snyder, and I were checking out certain expenses when he asked, "Ted, do you know what's in that safe deposit box we've been renting at the Shawmut?" I hadn't the foggiest, but the key was found, and when the box was opened, there were the Lincoln letters.)

5

That was an inauspicious beginning for 1929, a year that was to demolish the hopes of so many.

The war novel I had dreamed of finding turned up in the hands of our ally, Little, Brown and Company, when their editor, Herbert Jenkins, read in the Sunday book supplement of the New York *Times* that a story by a German veteran was breaking all records in Berlin. He cabled their European agent to make a bid for the American rights with an advance of $1,000. G. P. Putnam's had an option on the book but did not take it up — for whatever reason, they were to regret it — and as a result of Jenkins's shot in the dark *All Quiet on the Western Front* by Erich Maria Remarque gave Little, Brown a bonanza. *All Quiet* spoke for all who were disillusioned by the war, more powerfully than either Siegfried Sassoon's *Memoirs of a Fox-Hunting Man* or the front-line episodes in the novels by Ford Madox Ford. The book was a runaway from the start, the first printing was of 100,000 copies, and the jacket a triumph: the accusing eyes of the German soldier in his coal-scuttle helmet arrested literally millions of readers.

When Sinclair Lewis was awarded the Nobel Prize, he said in his speech of acceptance at Stockholm, "I know of only three educational institutions in America which teach literature as a living art — of these the Bread Loaf School of English is one." He was speaking as a neighbor and one who had lectured there. Bread Loaf Mountain and the thirty-four thousand acres of forest surrounding it, the rambling old inn and its guest cottages, trout stream, barnful of Morgan ponies, and two tennis courts, were bequeathed to Middlebury College by the philanthropist Joseph Battell, on condition that no trees be cut for a century and no automobiles be allowed. The Vermont Supreme Court permitted the felling of enough trees to cover taxes; the college relaxed the restriction on motors and turned the place into a summer school for English: six weeks of courses for college credit, followed by a two-week writers' conference. In the summer of 1929, Dr. R. M. Gay, the director, invited me to give a course on the essay and the magazine article at the conference. To do so meant sacrificing the whole of my summer vacation, but the experience proved to be worth it (and was to bring me back as a lecturer for at least one weekend over the ensuing decade).

Fritzy and I shared the small cottage with Dr. and Mrs. Gay, their daughter and their wire-haired fox terrier, Judy. One of the remaining guest rooms was occupied by Gorham Munson, the critic, and the last by

Joel Spingarn, the philosopher from Columbia. In such intimacy I soon came to admire Bob Gay, especially the gentle firmness with which he dealt with the literary temperament.

The faculty, of which I was the youngest member, was a versatile group. In addition to those I have already mentioned there were Edith Mirrilees, head of creative writing at Stanford and a gifted exponent of the short story; and Hervey Allen, that broad, hulking figure who still limped from the leg wounds he had received in the Argonne and who in his big, deliberate way reminded me of Doctor Johnson. Hervey was lecturing on the novel and at this point was halfway through a vast sprawling narrative of his own, from which he read us chapters in the evening sessions. He had been working on it for two years in Bermuda. The Guggenheim Foundation had turned down his request for a fellowship — they thought his book too involved — and John Farrar, his publisher, had advanced him $14,000, but he needed every penny he could pick up to keep the story going and his family fed. It was his first novel and it was to be called *Anthony Adverse.* We had the New York critic Grant Overton; Sinclair Lewis might drive over the mountain to spend an evening; John Farrar arrived for weekends; and several of our evening sessions were enlivened by Robert and Mrs. Frost. I found Robert impressive, wry, and delightful: some of the gleaming asides he tucked into his recitals had surely been uttered before, but they were as true as what came forth spontaneously. He liked to watch our tennis, especially the doubles with the quick volleys and overhead smashes. He borrowed a racket and had me feed him lobs, which he missed or smashed into the backstop in great swings.

We lived on mountain air and almost uninterruptedly in the flow of words: the first class began at 8:45, when the clanging of a dinner bell called us away from our last bite of breakfast; the same bell summoned us at 2:00 for the afternoon session, and our early supper was immediately followed by a public lecture or a reading or a play. After three days of this, Fritzy, who had nervously audited my class and was attending some of the others, found the regime a little less than a holiday. "They don't even give you time to go to the john," she whispered as we hurried out of the dining room.

Not until the evening performance was over did I relax. Then, with the guest of honor in our midst, we stretched out before the open fire to talk. It was good talk, sparked by Robert Frost; there was never any problem in getting him started, the problem was to get him to stop. He was a nighthawk who loved the stars, and he and Hervey would go on and on until two or three in the morning unless Mrs. Frost put her foot down. A flare-up occurred when John Farrar in a rambling lecture remarked that he liked to read poems aloud to his children and that his five-year-old responded much more eagerly to the music of Shelley than she did to Frost. He said it facetiously but it was tactless and Robert was miffed — it took all of Bob Gay's diplomacy to bring about a temporary reconciliation. For two years thereafter Frost would not attend.

Some forty students were in attendance, ranging from undergraduates to a grandmother in a wheelchair — Queen Victoria I called her — whose reminiscences I tried to put in order. There was no star comparable to Catherine Drinker Bowen, who a few years later came up to work with Bernard De Voto; my ablest were career women nearing retirement, a superintendent of nurses, an able teacher with a long experience in Harlem. I tried to help them be less reticent.

There came a renewed invitation to visit Harry and Caresse at the Moulin, the bizarre mill they had renovated outside Paris which Stuart and Minnie Kaiser had told us about: the donkey races; the tower room where Hart Crane had written "The Bridge," and on the top of which Harry would sunbathe; the champagne and the "riots" on weekends, when writers and freeloaders would descend from the city. I should like to have had a taste of Paris Denied, but there was no way and I cabled our regrets.

Harry had sent me copies of all his books but not *Mad Queen*, the volume of tirades he had written on their return from Egypt, feeling probably that I would resent his allusions to the *Atlantic* in his revilement of Boston; it was the first time he vented his bitterness on us as well as on his hometown.

None of this was in evidence when we met in Boston the week after Thanksgiving, 1929. I took him to lunch at the St. Botolph and we sat late. He mentioned the delivery of the gold pieces and that D. H. Lawrence felt he had been overpaid; said they had been promised three fragments of James Joyce's *Work in Progress*, which Caresse was handling most diplomatically. But for all this activity I had the impression that his life in Paris was beginning to sour and for the first time he spoke disparagingly of the French. He told me he had been taking lessons in flying and had done his first solo. I wondered if this explained why he seemed wound so tight; I asked about his health and he said he'd been to see a doctor who had found nothing serious; he added that he and Caresse had driven around Essex looking for a secluded place should they return. He adored his mother and the idea might have been hers. I wondered if it would work. We parted affectionately, and that was the last time I saw him.

On December 10 in Stanley Mortimer's apartment in New York, in a suicide pact, Harry shot his enchantress, Josephine, and then himself. Archibald MacLeish went quickly to the scene and was present when the medical inspector finished his examination.

"I pity that poor devil," said the doctor.

"Yes?" said MacLeish.

"Yes. After shooting her he sat here for five hours before he turned the gun on himself."

At the time all I was aware of was pity. *Why? Why?* I thought as I went over to 95 Beacon Street to see his parents. Steve alone came down the big stairway, holding one of Harry's miniature volumes, tears on his cheeks. "See how exquisite . . ." he said. I put my arm around his shoulder.

We learned part of the explanation three years later when in an edition of forty-four copies Caresse bravely published the third volume of Harry's journals, *Shadows of the Sun.* The old scar from Verdun had never healed. The feeling that he should have shared the fate of the older men he so admired, Oliver Ames and David Weld, had become a death wish, which appears again and again in the journal and became apparent in 1927, when he and Caresse fetched from the Montparnesse cemetery and had planted in the Moulin courtyard their tombstone, carved with their names and the date of their departure, 1942. But it was always Caresse who would accompany him. What he could not anticipate was the effect of opium on a system already overwrought by alcohol, gambling and sex. Caresse, perhaps for stability, overpraised his poetry, but I think that the closer he came to talented writers, the more he suspected that his verses could not stand comparison. Publishing and patronizing were not enough, and if I am right, this feeling of inadequacy further weakened his resolution. His infatuation with "J." had brought her to New York in early December. There were clandestine meetings usually ending in the journal's word "Fight." The final entry on the day before his death reads, "And again my invulnerability is put to the test." But he was not invulnerable.

It remained for Caresse to tell us in her memoir, *The Passionate Years,* published in 1953, that on the morning before the end, in the hotel bedroom twenty-seven floors above the street, in the early dazzling sunlight, Harry said to her: "Give me your hand, Caresse, our window is open wide. Let's meet the sun death together."

But she was frightened at his earnestness and held back.

IX

I T TOOK the country over a year to realize that the collapse of the
Hoover bull market on Tuesday, October 29, 1929, was more than a
temporary decline. Before he assumed the Presidency Hoover had
spoken hopefully of the abolition of poverty, and "Don't sell the United
States short" had become almost a patriotic motto. True, a rare skeptic
like Roger W. Babson, the Boston investment counselor, had predicted
that by September there might be a decline of as much as sixty to
eighty points, but people thought he was crying wolf and, besides,
things were running so true to form in that lovely autumn: Tilden had
won his seventh (and last) singles championship at Forest Hills, Bobby
Jones had again proved he was the best amateur golfer in the game's
history, Babe Ruth was slamming out home runs for the ninth successive
year, and contract bridge and backgammon had never been more
popular. The Coolidge-Hoover prosperity seemed resilient, and when
the first shock of the market's collapse had subsided, Secretary of the
Treasury Mellon gave us his reassurance and Thomas W. Lamont of
J. P. Morgan and Company, spokesman for five eminent bankers, each
of whom had put up forty millions to stop the leaks, uttered what
Frederick Lewis Allen in *Only Yesterday* has characterized as one of
the most remarkable understatements of all time: "There has been,"
Mr. Lamont began, "a little distress selling on the Stock Exchange and
we have held a meeting of the heads of several financial institutions to
discuss the situation. We have found that there are no houses in difficulty and reports from brokers indicate that margins are being maintained satisfactorily . . ."

There were worried men on State Street but this did not show at the
private luncheon held at the Somerset Club for the benefit of some
of the major investors in International Match and Kreuger and Toll

stock. Mr. Ivar Kreuger of Stockholm had come to Boston in search of further loans and his American bankers, notably the directors of Lee, Higginson and Company, thought it would be expedient were he to appear and speak. The Napoleon of finance had no prepared statement, he simply fielded questions, which he had trained himself to do very well. Professor Ralph Barton Perry of the Harvard Philosophy Department, one of the few present with nothing at stake, told me afterwards that had he had $10,000 within reach he would have entrusted it to Kreuger on the spot.

Kreuger's parting words as he waved farewell to those who saw him off to Europe were, "Gentlemen, buy Kreuger and Toll!" Indeed there was an optimistic recovery in the market during the spring of 1930. Henry Ford announced that he and his son "were buying common stocks," and when prices began tumbling again in the summer, the head of one of Boston's most eminent investment trusts circularized his clients, saying, "This is the opportunity we have been waiting for . . ." But this time the decline was not halted and the *New Yorker*'s sardonic comment was the cartoon of a banker in a high silk hat and cutaway, lying flat on his back, and beneath, the caption "The Upturn."

During the long uncertainty Boston society maintained its gaiety and decorum, and it seemed to me that the talk, perhaps because of an undercurrent of tension, was better than ever. Boston from the earliest times has produced famous talkers, the habit of dining together for an evening of conversation and drinking was a male prerogative inherited from the English. But when Cotton Mather forbade the theater, a prohibition momentarily broken by the amateur dramatics in the British army of occupation in 1774, then reinforced until early in the nineteenth century, talk became not only the communication of faith but the vent of criticism, and the source of entertainment. The earliest of the small dining clubs — the Wednesday Evening Club (1777) and the Boston Library Society (1794) are two of them — originated when men were deeply concerned about independence and the Constitution, and the China Trade, the opening of the West, the financing of the railroads, Abolition, the Civil War, and Reconstruction were reason enough for good conversation to continue.

The great talkers in Boston in the 1930's, present company excepted, I can characterize by the temper of their minds and the diversity of their experience:

Hans Zinsser, the best. A good poet and first-class pathologist, a classicist, brought up in the European tradition, at ease in German and French (he lectured in French at the Sorbonne), an ardent horseman, sparky, dangerous when aroused, with a glorious capacity for outrage.

Langdon Warner, interpreter and defender of Oriental art, a far and dedicated traveler in China. His letters were illuminating and despite his protests to the contrary he was a critic and appraiser of the first rank.

Thomas Barbour, a gigantic, gusty naturalist, fond of reptiles, full of adventures as odd as the caverns he explored, irrepressibly curious, liking to be henpecked, always the butt of his own stories. One of a kind.

Charles P. Curtis, Jr., bubbling like champagne, a classicist widely read who remembered. I can hear him stuttering, "Wait-a-minute, wait-a-minute, wait a min . . ." as his mind raced toward the new topic; an admirer of President Lowell, and the youngest member of the Harvard Corporation. That diverse anthology, *The Practical Cogitator,* is a monument to his taste and that of his collaborator, Ferris Greenslet.

Charles R. Codman, a Francophile whose French was so perfect he served as our translator at the Casablanca Conference; the best judge in Boston of French wines and the theater; ambulance driver and pilot in the First World War; George Patton's deputy who kept that irascible commander out of trouble in Morocco and France in World War II; a man of utmost charm who held the confidences of men and women.

Abigail Adams Homans, inheriting the courage and common sense of her namesake, educated by that extraordinary trio of uncles, Brooks, Charles, and Henry Adams; with her own insight and love of the absurd she was the best company a man could wish.

Fritzy and I were among the younger members of the Contemporary Club, which met four times a winter to cheer up Boston's Sunday evenings. These were full-dress, white-tie-and-tails affairs, preceded by champagne dinners, then the lecture or entertainment (forty minutes, but no longer) at one of the big houses, the Montgomery Searses' or the Edwin Websters', whose ballroom could seat upwards of a hundred and twenty guests, then a pleasant mingling with more champagne. Mrs. Homans was chairman of the program committee and when she appointed me to it I fell under her spell.

We were after speakers or performers not readily accessible: Bertrand Russell on trial marriage; Harlow Shapley soaring off to his outermost galaxies, the first mind-shocking exposure in space for many of us; and Dr. Archibald T. Davison leading forty picked members of the Harvard Glee Club from the earliest folk songs to the most sophisticated chorus, were all good evenings. But there were two programs, for both of which I was personally responsible, that ran a more checkered course. J. B. S. Haldane, a biochemist, was one of the most brilliant men I had listened to in Cambridge. Learning that he was to spend part of the winter at Stanford University I urged him to stop off in Boston and speak to us;

I knew that he had performed all kinds of experiments on himself, such as testing mustard gas in the war, so I suggested the subject, "On Being One's Own Rabbit."

The meeting was to be held at the Boylston Beals' on Beacon Street in their long handsome library overlooking the Esplanade. But when the temperature dropped below zero Mrs. Beal ordered a roaring fire in the manorial fireplace at the end of the room, before which Haldane was to speak, and the radiance was almost overpowering. When the time came, the butler, with gloves, had done his best to quiet the fire before I made the introduction. Then I sat facing the listeners, most of whom had retreated to the gilt chairs to the rear. Haldane, an outsize Englishman, in heavy broadcloth, perspired from the start, and it should not have surprised me when in the course of his talk he described — or invented on the spot — an experiment on the effect of heat on the blood-stream. Said he in his elegant accent, "A biffsteak, a spanel, and myself in the buff, were hermetically sealed within a chamber; the heat was turned on and when it had reached the climax, the door was opened, the biffsteak was frizzling, the dog was dead, and I was half-conscious — which only goes to show that I can even stand the temperature of a Boston drawing room." The laughter at that sally cheered him on and when he had finished, never was champagne more gratefully received.

The other contretemps was still more of my doing. I had been convulsed when I first heard Robert Benchley do his "Treasurer's Report" as an entr'acte in *The Music Box Revue*. His impersonation of a man, not very sure of his figures, trying to cover up the annual deficit at a church supper, was — given Bob's delivery — one of the funniest monologues ever written, and I persuaded the committee to offer him $1,000 to put it on for our November meeting. Benchley, in accepting, wrote that the report only ran to fourteen minutes; he'd begin with another short skit, a parody of a lecture entitled "The Love Life of a Polyp," and then after a brief intermission do "The Treasurer's Report" He would like to use four slides with the lecture and so would need a screen.

That meeting took place at Mrs. Frank Crowninshield's, one of the jolliest and best-liked of our hostesses, and again I made the introduction. This first meeting in the autumn was always the best attended but as I spoke it was not clear how many knew that we had a famous humorist present and my doubt deepened with Benchley's opening. "At our last meeting, as you will remember," he said, "we studied the Sponge, and at the conclusion I promised that when we resumed I would discuss with you 'The Love Life of the Polyp' . . ." At least a third of the members had been South or abroad in April and they looked askance: "Love Life" had an ugly sound to it, and if this young man had made such a promise what in the world was Abigail thinking of? Benchley went gravely ahead depicting the Polyp Courtship which began "at twenty Polyp paces. First slide please." (The room darkened. On the screen within a circle, two small specks, the Polyps.) After the advance and repulse, "Suppose we now substitute a crumb of cake or a small button for the female. Second slide . . ." Spoofing never reads as well as it sounds; so much depends on the gravity of the presentation which, with Benchley, was perfection. In the semi-dark I looked across at my nearest neighbor, Miss Marian Vaillant, who was shaking with laughter. But beyond I could see a number of straight faces, and when it soon developed that the polyp if frustrated could change its sex, they did not relax.

As the lights went on, not everyone applauded, and after I announced that there would be a brief intermission before Mr. Benchley concluded his performance, a number of the members rose, thanked Mrs. Crownin-shield and made for their wraps. Her protest, "Oh, but the best is still to come!" did not avail. In the stir Benchley, who was sitting beside me, remarked in a low voice, "Mrs. Benchley would not be proud of her boy tonight." Perhaps dismay added to his feigned embarrassment as he gave "The Treasurer's Report," and when in a nervous tug he dissolved his black bow tie and sought to do something with the dangling end, the Contemporary Club broke down. The applause at the end made up for those who had bolted and he and I had the gratification of seeing the hostess wipe away her tears of laughter. Again, the champagne was consoling.

2

To publish twenty-five new books a year, which was my aim, three times that number must be seeded and in various stages of development. The ideal was to find a writer who was about to bud and who would produce not one but a succession of acceptable books. For this I had three sources of supply. The first were the writers who came "over the transom," unknown and uninvited, to the *Atlantic*. As I still wrote the biographical notes about them for the Contributors' Column I could easily spot the promising newcomers. For example, from Canton, China, we received a little descriptive sketch, typed on thin Oriental paper. Mr. Sedgwick printed it, and in answer to my questioning, the author, Nora Waln, proved to be a Philadelphia Quaker who had become the adopted daughter of a wealthy Chinese family. She had been commissioned by a Swedish publisher to write the life story of a Bible salesman named Larson, who had swapped Bibles for ponies with such success that he became known as "Larson, Duke of Mongolia." I secured the American rights on that bizarre book but what I really wanted was her own story of an American girl living in that ancient Cantonese compound — she referred to it as "The House of Exile." I estimated it would be at least three years in the writing, and my letter commissioning it reached her only a few days before she was approached by a come-on from Charles Scribner.

Second example: Mr. Sedgwick received from an English publisher page proofs of a short piece of fiction, charged with sentiment, about an English schoolmaster in a boys' school. The impecunious author, James Hilton, had been offered fifty pounds to do the centerpiece in a Christmas supplement and, casting about desperately for a subject, had memorialized his father in a story entitled "Good-bye, Mr. Chips." The *Atlantic* printed it, and five months later the Press brought it out as a small book in a cautious edition of twenty-five hundred copies. Rhapsodies of praise poured out of critics as different as Bishop Lawrence of Massachusetts and Alexander Woollcott; *Chips* was reprinted fifteen times in the first six months, in ever larger editions, and we never could keep it in stock. Hilton went on to write six more novels for us.

The prize contests were my second source. The awards in nonfiction — we were trying to forget "the Lincoln Letters" — were conferred on authentic Americana, books like *Grandmother Brown's Hundred Years,* the biography of a great humanitarian who had lived through the opening of the Middle West; *The Forty-Niners* by Archer Butler Hurlbert, a vivid documentary of the diaries, the letters, songs and drawings of the men and women who sailed on the prairie schooners and of the heartbreak of those who broke down or perished on the way. And this was followed by *Old Jules,* in which Mari Sandoz wrote of that fastidious, angry man, her Swiss father, as he pioneered in the sandhills of Nebraska.

Jalna by Mazo de la Roche was to be the most far-reaching of our prize novels, American and foreign sales of over a million copies, but we turned up a second talented woman when the next prize was awarded to Ann Bridge for *Peking Picnic,* and I have always felt that a later award should have been made to Owen Wister's nephew, William Wister Haines. Bill's family was hard hit early in the Depression and he worked his way through the University of Pennsylvania as one of the high-paid crew who were electrifying the Pennsylvania Railroad on the New York–to–Washington run. It was dangerous, some of the time over "hot wire," always in short spurts between trains and always at the peril of being blown off the elevated platform by the blast from a stray shunting engine passing beneath. There were life belts, but hell, who used them? Bill himself was blown into the Passaic River and I always figured the convalescence gave him time to plot his fine novel *Slim.* It scored a success under our imprint and later on film. As a minority of one I always thought it deserved our prize.

A most difficult man to cope with was one of Mr. Sedgwick's highest paid contributors, the historian James Truslow Adams. On his graduation from Yale he had confided to his favorite professor that he wanted to write, and would it help if he took a Ph.D.? No, said that astute man, go down to Wall Street, promise yourself to save as much as you can, and after ten or twelve years, if you still wish to write, you'll have the independence to do so. Adams followed that advice and when he withdrew from the market, long before the Crash, he had an income sufficient for a bachelor and could write as he pleased. His subject was colonial America. The Atlantic Monthly Press published his first books, *The Founding of New England* and *Revolutionary New England,* which soundly established his reputation without adding much to his bank balance. Adams, who spent a part of each year in London, was of a fiery disposition; he preferred the quietude of England to the noise and turbulence of New York; his discontent smoldered like coals in a grate and when Sedgwick blew on them he would burst into flame in *Atlantic* articles.

But Adams was dissatisfied both with his fees from the magazine and the earning from his books. He needed a popular success, and to get it Sedgwick and Mark Howe proposed two projects: the first, a book about the Adams family, a series of portraits beginning with John and Abigail, and coming down to the then Secretary of the Navy, Charles Francis Adams. The clan, wrote the historian, had lost none of their capability; why then were they no longer elected to public office? Had they lost touch with the country or had the country grown away from them? *The Adams Family* was a Literary Guild selection and for the first time Adams, who incidentally came from the Virginia branch of the tribe, saw himself on the list of national best sellers. Mr. Sedgwick's second project was for a one-volume, affirmative history of the American people, to be called *The Epic of America.* Adams carried it out admirably and when it rose to be Number One on the list of best sellers, with royalties already upwards of $70,000, Adams calmly announced that he was leaving us to take his future work to Scribner's. I felt that he had been disloyal at the height of his success and I blazed away at him in a long angry letter. What neither Sedgwick nor I had heeded was that in mid-life Adams, no longer in robust health, had fallen in love; he would need a larger income when he married and at that precise moment Scribner's offered him a big rewrite job at a retainer that promised security for years, and he jumped at it. It did not occur to me that Ellery and I were remiss.

That was my first lesson in the motives that prompt an author to leave his original publisher. We had lost a prominent writer, primarily because we had not bothered to work out with him the long-time security he wanted. As it happened, two other spectacular separations were taking place in New York. When Arthur Harcourt formed his firm, one of his initial authors was Sinclair Lewis, whose early books were failures but who felt so confident of this fresh connection that he wished to invest some of his meager capital in the enterprise. The sweeping success of *Main Street,* followed by *Babbitt, Arrowsmith, Elmer Gantry,* and *Dodsworth* put both Harcourt, Brace and the author on Easy Street. Then Lewis felt aggrieved about advertising and promotion, his remonstrance led to coldness, and he eventually shifted his books and allegiance to Bennett Cerf. Had Harcourt been too complacent about his once-struggling author?

Harder for me to comprehend was the shock that came later to Maxwell Perkins, the editor of Scribner's book department, who was, so many of us thought, the best in the business. Thomas Wolfe had been eager to accept the cutting and editing which Max suggested for his first novel, *Look Homeward, Angel,* but he no longer welcomed such firm attention when, after a triumph, he had finished his second and even more formless novel, *Of Time and the River.* Cuts were made, episodes moved from one part to another, but in the end Wolfe wanted it his way and despite friendly protestations he took his future books to another house. Since Max had not changed, Tom Wolfe must have: evidently there was always the danger that too much attention is as bad as too little. I was begining to learn that what is true of friendship is equally true of editing: the understanding between the two parties must be continually refreshed, never taken for granted.

I shopped this out with Bill Whitman at luncheon, and he consoled me by saying that I took it all too personally; authors were like streetcars, another would be along in a minute. We were in the habit of checking our positions with each other: I had the feeling that Ellery was delegating to me more freedom of action than Ferris was giving Bill at Houghton Mifflin. I knew there was a power struggle among the younger executives in that big firm and I was not sure how Bill was making out. I was sure that at heart he still thought of himself as a writer. He and Marjorie with their growing family had moved out to what he called "Dog Corner" in Needham, and his first book, *Dog Corner Papers,* was a collection of amiable short essays, literary and quizzical. Now he was working on a book for young readers which drew on his love of fantasy, but Pargie, so eager for his success, kept saying he should write a murder mystery.

I showed Bill proofs of an anonymous article, "Halfway," which I had written for the *Atlantic*. It was signed "Thirty," and in accepting it Mr. Sedgwick had said that by my yardstick he would soon be underground. Bill grinned at my discussion of economy, the paragraph reading:

> I should put $4000 as the minimum that a college graduate of thirty and his wife can live on in a city; $5000 if they have a child. The average earnings of men eight years out of college and five years out of their professional schools, in law, architecture, engineering, and teaching, are less than $4000. Children later in life or not at all is the easiest answer. Nor has the professional man much redress against his employer; as the colleges increase their output the professions have more and cheaper men to draw on.

That was published in June 1931, and the estimate was considerably higher than many young graduates were then earning — or would be two years hence.

There was another passage we talked about in which I argued that young couples are apt to drink more than is good for them, and that their drinking had been aggravated by the increased use of hard liquor under Prohibition. "It is begun," I wrote, "when the first wonder of marriage has faded, and when couples feel the need for a little stimulating illusion. The trouble is, the illusion is apt to make the other fellow's wife the more attractive, sometimes with unhappy consequences for all members concerned. Most of us outgrow this middle-distance recklessness . . ."

Bill told Pargie about this, and when next the four of us dined together, she asked whom I had in mind. I alluded to the summer entanglements of a generation older than ourselves on the North Shore, and pouring ourselves another cocktail, we felt virtuous. As a foursome we were utterly at ease: in our criticism, our picnics, our rather casual golf on the nine holes in Dover. Late one June afternoon when we reached the short water hole, the course was deserted. Pargie drove first and topped it in close to the near bank. "That's a new ball," she said. "Damned if I don't get it!" Shoes and stockings off, skirts and plus-fours rolled up, we four waded in to retrieve a total of forty-two balls, the oldest of which Pargie promised to repaint. Economy.

Mr. L. C. Page, who operated his own small but prosperous publishing company, invited me to lunch with him at his home in Brookline and after a delicious lobster with Rhine wine proposed that I take over the operation of his firm. He said he was getting ready to retire, the house had solid assets — he showed me the financial statement — and he believed I would do well with it; he named a salary a third more than I was receiving. Over the coffee he expanded about the rules on which he based his success:

1. Never pay an author a royalty; buy the book and all rights for a flat sum.
2. Never give a discount larger than 33⅓ percent.
3. Serve only those booksellers who will order at least one copy of every new title in the Page catalogue.

"But, Mr. Page," I said, "you mean you got *Pollyanna* that way? For a lump sum?"

"Yes, indeed" — and he named it — "and most of the other good properties on our list, too."

"Well," I said, inwardly amazed, "I'm sure I couldn't approach the authors I'm interested in on those terms."

We talked a little further, and then, "You go home and think about it," he said as we shook hands. This was good for my self-esteem, but I knew I must decline; I could not follow in those footprints.

The publisher whom I most admired and with whom I was in constant touch was Alfred McIntyre. Alfred, who graduated from Harvard in 1907, succeeded to the presidency of Little, Brown and Company following the sudden death of his father in 1926. He was diffident, painfully so, and I can imagine what an ordeal it was to walk out of his shyness and be his forthright self in handling a nervous author or in facing a sales conference.

He was slender, remarkably erect and wiry, and he had the wide smile of a strong jaw, a jaw which could set with a Scotch tenacity that was not stubbornness. His gaze was level and his integrity a byword in the profession. "You always know where to find him" was the way his competitor, Ferris Greenslet, put it.

The eyes, the smile, and the jaw — and as I came to know him, I watched his hands. They were thin-fingered and at times could be more expressive than his words. His hands would rise instinctively from the desk, as his eyes lit up to a new possibility. I remember the sweep of his right hand, as if to wipe the slate clean, when with the words, "Forget it. You can't always be right," he would dismiss a problem that had been worrying us. And there was another gesture, when he would raise both hands chest high and suddenly drop them to the desk in honest doubt — he did not know the answer, we had made our investment in the book, and only time would tell if the public would like it.

Tenacity is a rare quality in publishing. I mean the quality of holding on to an author and continuing to believe in him (and to pay him his advance royalties) when year after year the public ignores his new books. Such was Alfred's belief in Evelyn Waugh. Twice a year our traveling salesmen would gather in Boston to get the word — and their expected quotas — about our new books. It took tenacity on Alfred's part to make his men believe that this Englishman was far better than the American public yet realized, especially after *Decline and Fall* had achieved a sale of 1,546 copies in the first year, and *A Handful of Dust*, 2,170 copies. But Alfred persisted, the salesmen took hope, and after the success of *Brideshead Revisited*, Waugh's early books, reprinted, sprang to life.

Alfred did the same thing with C. S. Forester, publishing four failures in succession before *Captain Horatio Hornblower* at last captured half a million readers. Alfred's acumen as a publisher was to give John Marquand the backing John so desperately needed at the turning point in his career. When Marquand began the writing of a satire on the life and letters of a Bostonian, his New York agent was skeptical; before *The Late George Apley* was half done, the advice from Brandt and Brandt was "desist." Then Alfred read the manuscript and he said, "John, I think it is swell. I can't tell you whether it will sell more than two thousand copies — it may be too highly specialized. But by all means, go ahead with it!"

A light sleeper, he took manuscripts home, reading late or between four and seven in the morning. I was with him the day when he had finished the manuscript of a new novel by Walter D. Edmonds about some colonists who were vulnerable to attack in the Mohawk Valley at the time of the Revolution. *A Starving Wilderness* was the tentative title and Alfred did not think it inviting. He began to ruminate.

"These people lived in the Mohawk Valley . . . Mohawk is a good word . . . How did the news of the Revolution first reach them?"

"Why," I said, "I guess it was when they first heard the drums of the Continentals."

"Drums . . . drums on the Mohawk. No, more movement . . . *Drums Along the Mohawk*."

Alfred believed in the dignity of the book and he sought to preserve it. He believed, as all good publishers do, that on rare occasions he would have the opportunity of publishing literature. He had respect for the complete book and it hurt him to see a book he believed in cut down and printed as a one- or two-part serial. He believed in the discriminating reader and that the books under our imprint were not

Alfred McIntyre

merely merchandise to be peddled to magazines and movie studios. He liked my eagerness and he profoundly admired what the *Atlantic* stood for.

It was providential that in the autumn of 1929 the leading spirits in the National Association of Book Publishers, of whom Mr. McIntyre was one, agreed to sponsor an economic survey of the book industry in 1930 and 1931. It was directed by O. H. Cheney, who was given access to the records of every major firm, and when the Cheney Report was published, it revealed the entire book industry — the author, the agent, the publisher, the bookseller, and the reader — giving an honest accounting of the good intentions and the bad practices, of profits and losses, and of subsidies. Such information had never been assembled before. Many of these hard truths had been suspected; now we had to live with them in the open.

I was surprised to learn how general was the practice of paying prominent authors advances, beginning at $10,000 and zooming up, for books which never earned out that amount. These gambles, when added up, showed annual losses of close to $800,000. I was disturbed by the section entitled "Book Murder," which began with these words:

The acceptance of a manuscript by a publisher, under present conditions, means that in the majority of cases a book will receive a christening celebration, a short — and frequently ignoble — life and an early death, without peace. The manuscripts which escape this fate are few and far between and the books we hear about are usually those which escape.

It went on to say that the active life of a poor seller, fiction or nonfiction, was at best three months, and that only in extremely rare cases did the life of a best seller go beyond eighteen months. I was troubled by the section describing "Author Stealing," and by the realization of how much the publisher pays for what he steals. And I was shocked by the blunt warning in these words: "*A subsidized industry* would seem to be the ultimate end toward which trade book publishing is tending, if present trends continue to develop" — in short, that magazines through their serials subsidize the popular authors and, incidentally, the book industry, as do the movies. The report estimated that there might be as many as sixty "subsidized" authors in a given year, sixty out of twelve thousand writers being published! In the case of the older houses like Macmillan and Houghton Mifflin, the college textbook, the schoolbook, and the religious book departments were earning six dollars to every dollar earned from the sale of fiction and nonfiction. These were painful facts for an editor intent on publishing new writers.

Joan and Bill Wetmore

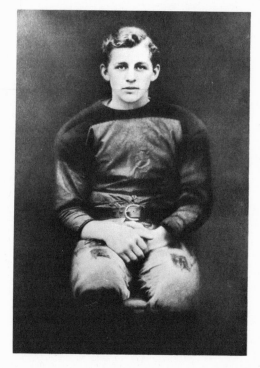

While the Depression deepened, Fritzy and I went up to Long Point for my vacation. The great oaks towering over the chalet with its gaily striped awning, the emerald turf, and the beauty of the lake with its slowly trolling fishermen were as they should be. But now we were the benedicts and Fritzy's brother, Bill Wetmore and his lovely bride Joan, were the young lovers. Bill had handsomely fulfilled his youthful promise; there are some youngsters who reach their peak in college and he was one of them. Short and well proportioned, with strong legs, he was fast and a born competitor. He had been football captain at St. Mark's, and a year later, captain of the Harvard Freshman, he scored two touchdowns in defeating Yale. A quarterback of 145 pounds is light for the varsity, but Bill as a sophomore was the leading contender until an injured cartilage in his knee ruined his chance. He went on to win his *H* at hockey and a year later, in football, was elected to the Porcellian (where the drinking did not agree with him), and fell in love with Joan on the boat taking them on their first trip to Europe. Bill with his blond good looks and Joan with her dark Celtic beauty were a delight to the eye. Books were always the least part of Bill's education and following their sudden marriage he wanted to leave college and work with his hands — raise horses, perhaps. Mr. Wetmore, who had more ambitious ideas for him, talked him out of that dream, and the problem of a career — which Bill was never to solve — had been temporarily shelved in the dulcet summer.

I was struggling with my first book and arrived for my fortnight's holiday in August intending to write in the privacy of the little boathouse, but this didn't agree with the family regime and I was lucky to get ninety minutes by myself in the early morning. Then there was tennis and a swim before lunch and golf in the afternoon on the lakeside links at Chautauqua, with Bill and myself pitted against Unkie and the Club professional. I had become more aggressive at that time-consuming, infuriating game: I had learned to control my temper and as a result of Charlie Wetmore's taunts had improved my swing, practicing through the winter, hitting balls into a fishnet under the coaching of a good pro. I didn't tell Charlie about this, and on our opening match in the summer, after I had scored two pars in succession, he shouted across the green, "What in hell has happened to you!" So I got back a little of my own until he raised his handicap.

After the drive home and the ferry ride across the lake we would sip gin fizzes or French 75's on the porch as the sun set and then take our hot baths and dress for cocktails and one of Bollard's delectable dinners. Later we danced to the new Gershwin record ("'S wonderful, 's marvelous") or played family cards until the moonlight made bed desir-

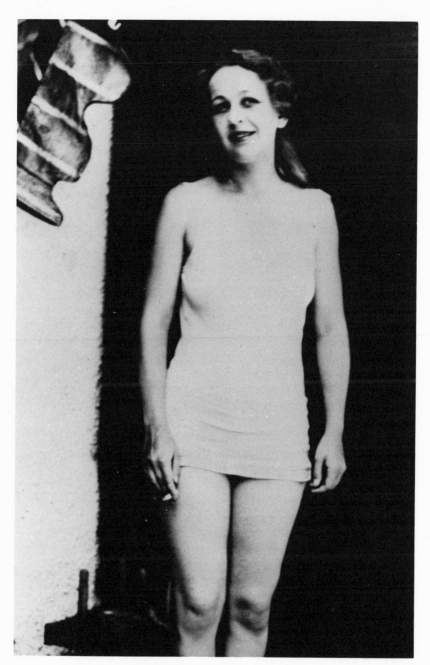

Fritzy, ready for the canoe

able. This was luxury in a loving atmosphere, as even Sara, aged five, was beginning to appreciate; she was a delight to her grandmother, who gave us the daily chronicle of what she said and did. If Mrs. Wetmore, dear "Go-Go," was worried about her own health, she did not show it.

Is there an apperception which warns us that this may be the last time? I think so. Fritzy and I paddled across the lake to the pine grove where nine years earlier we had buried the heart-shaped lichen with the initials "E.A.W.III" on it — only it had turned out to be Sara. We strolled down to the tip of the point in the moonlight, careful to avoid the poison oak, and at sunrise one morning we walked up to the now rickety summer house, the Crow's Nest, where we had first embraced. "Are you sorry?" I asked. She looked at me and shook her head and we ambled back for breakfast, holding hands.

3

When Ivar Kreuger committed suicide on March 12, 1932, the extensiveness of his deficits hurt Boston only a little less severely than it did Stockholm. Lee, Higginson and Company, so long the standard bearer of financial trust, was the victim, and although the partners rallied honorably, the damage was done and some of their clients emerged angrily disillusioned or depressed. More than any other event this told us that we were in deep trouble. Storm signals were going up across the nation. At the peak of the boom the New York *Times* had devoted a full page to the photographs of the fourscore bankers and industrialists who, in a manner of speaking, owned the United States; I had cut it out, wondering if it were so; now one could check off those like Samuel Insull and the Van Sweringen brothers, whose empires were crumbling. That page was an historic document. Only the rare mavericks like Clarence Dillon and Frederick H. Prince of Hamilton, Massachusetts, consistently sold short and were now reaping the benefit.

One begins to measure a national calamity by its effect on one's personal fortunes and those of one's friends. I had borrowed money to buy my *Atlantic* stock in 1929, and I was stuck with that loan. But my best friend in finance, Jim White, had advised Fritzy and me, a month before the crash, to convert our little nest egg into cash, which we had done, so we were only partly singed. Jim was proving himself a rock of Gibraltar: he had moved up from salesman to a partner of Scudder, Stevens and Clark in six years.

On January 1, 1929, the Atlantic Monthly Company was publishing four magazines; then it began to sell, first, the *Youth's Companion,* to its rival, the *American Boy,* for $80,000; then the *Scholastic;* then *House Beautiful,* which we lacked the capital to sustain till good times returned. By the end of 1934 there was one left, the *Atlantic,* and that one was floating just above water. "Magazines," as my friend Stewart Beach once remarked, "don't die. They are simply replaced by a more up-to-date model." There is a good deal of truth in that, and as a rule of thumb one could apply it to what happened throughout the 1930's. Once the *New Yorker* had turned the corner it cut the ground out from under those old-fashioned comics *Life* and *Judge.* The breadth of interest and the more personal touch which De Witt and Lila Wallace brought to the editing of the *Reader's Digest,* would have made the *Literary Digest* obsolete — even if the latter had not come out for Landon in 1936. Frank Crowninshield's *Vanity Fair* was feeling the pinch before Henry Luce's new *Life,* with aggressive, more inquisitive photography, replaced it.

In the so-called "Quality Group" there were too many competitors for hard times and those periodicals which clung to their aging editors succumbed early: the *Century,* once the leader in the field, died, then the *Forum;* in the mid-thirties Henry Mencken gave up his struggle with the *American Mercury,* which had never been self-supporting; and in 1939, *Scribner's Magazine,* which had sagged under an outworn editor, one who could tolerate neither of those Scribner authors Hemingway or Thomas Wolfe, suspended publication — and I was saddened to see it go. When the smoke cleared there were two survivors in the field of literary monthlies: *Harper's* and the *Atlantic.*

An even more drastic record of deaths or consolidation was occurring in the newspaper world — one third of the dailies published in 1929 were now in the process of being liquidated — and if this was symptomatic of what was happening in heavy industry, as it clearly was in automobiles, it did not take a soothsayer to tell that Franklin Delano Roosevelt would swamp the inept Hoover in the 1932 election. Although both Mr. Sedgwick and I were Democrats, this prospect gave me more confidence than it did him: he had been for Governor Al Smith and at the 1932 Convention he was a Newton D. Baker man. Roosevelt he had known at Groton and did not like. This was the first of the political differences that were to crop up between us.

When the company was in clover, Ellery had turned deaf ears on my request that I be paid a commission on the successful new books I was bringing to the Press; now that we were struggling, I knew that the money was not available and that I should have to earn it on the outside. Dear Mark Howe had seen this coming and in his kindly, stuttering way he said that when he was a young editor and married, he had found it necessary "to supplement his salary" and he thought I might like to join him in writing editorials for the *Harvard Alumni Bulletin*. They didn't pay much — $10 an editorial — but it kept one in closer touch with the university and the weekly meetings were a delight. The board lunched together at the Faculty Club each Friday through the academic year and present would be John Merrill, the *Bulletin* editor, a wise old wheel horse from the Boston *Globe;* Joseph Hamlin, president of the paper, passionately loyal to Harvard, Maine, and the Republican Party; Ralph Barton Perry, the philosopher; William Dean Munro, the rugged, clear-minded head of the Department of Government, whose college texts were widely used — $90,000 royalties in fourteen years he once told me; idealistic Harry Holmes, dean of the Graduate School of Education; Mark and myself. I was there to supply the response of the younger alumni, and I was industrious, writing fifty-one editorials, sometimes two an issue, my first year.

These were "insiders," knowledgeable and discriminating, and I listened far more than I spoke. "Tom" Perry, whose *Thought and Character of William James* I would soon be editing (it would win a Pulitzer Prize under our imprint) I liked immensely. In Eliot's day he had been the youngest member of the faculty, a body then small enough to meet in University Hall, and as the kid he sat on the floor facing the presidential throne. On a controversial issue Eliot would state the question and then sit back with restraint as speaker after speaker rose. "I could see his knuckles grow white with anger, as he grasped the knobs of the chair," Tom said. When the last had been heard, Eliot would rise and sum up the action to be taken, precisely what he had decided in advance, but in such a way that everyone who had spoken felt he had contributed to the solution. Autocratic leadership, Tom called it. There was, of course, lively speculation about who would be nominated to succeed President Lowell.

On one occasion when we had an elderly New York alumnus named Pell in our midst, Joe Hamlin began inveighing against F.D.R. — "a traitor to his class," and so on, at which our guest interrupted. "You know, Joe," said Mr. Pell, "I could close my eyes and believe I was back in Boston twenty-five years ago when exactly the same things were being said about T.R." Those luncheons gave me a keener perspective on Harvard and I had the wise afterthought of Mark Howe as I drove him home.

Out of the blue came an invitation from Ellen Bullard to do a series of parlor readings for her friends on the North Shore during the coming summer. (This paid for our summer cottage.) I found I could entertain them for ninety minutes a sitting, by combining and contrasting the contemporary and the past — Keats and his letters with comments by

Amy Lowell; Japan, the novels of Lady Murasaki and Lafcadio Hearn; James Boswell and *Portrait of Zélide* by Geoffrey Scott were three programs — and the circle widened when Mrs. Henry F. du Pont came as a guest of Mrs. Crowninshield and asked if I would be willing to do an autumn series in her apartment in New York. Mrs. Harold Coolidge, Jr., formed a third circle. Knitters were no problem but when one lady brought a tambour frame and began popping her needle through the stiff-fibered tapestry, she was as much of a distraction to the group as to me and was asked to desist.

Finally, the bread I had cast on the water as "the dirty-book man" came back in the form of a contract with the Handley Agency to lecture at New England preparatory schools and women's clubs — not, of course, exclusively on the subject of censorship. I made my debut at Deerfield Academy. They wanted me in formal dress, so I put on my dinner jacket in early afternoon and was driven up through the October foliage by Mr. Handley's secretary who had been sent along to scout the performance. We arrived at the headmaster's house a little before the hour and she accompanied me to the door which was opened by Frank Boyden.

"The artist is here," said the secretary.

"Come in," said the headmaster, and to me. "We'll begin at once, if you're ready."

I was, and he led me into a very large room, crowded with boys, all sitting on the floor, and the faculty on leather settees at the back. "My, you've got a big turnout," I exclaimed, feeling a wave of nervousness.

"Yes," he said dryly — I think he was still resisting that word "artist" — "it's compulsory."

My subject that first evening was "In the Editor's Chair"; I used no notes, just a white card with a few transitions, and it went well: the boys were responsive and crowded around with questions afterwards. There is an underground circuit in such matters, and I soon had as many requests as I had time for. At Phillips Andover, the headmaster, Al Stearns, took exception to my castigation of the Watch and Ward Society in the question period and observed that they had helped to root out pornography in shops pandering to students. Dr. Peabody, the Rector, invited me to Groton to address a conference of English teachers on the subject "New Reading for Older Boys," and I deliberately weeded out of the old "required" list such chestnuts as *The Rise of Silas Lapham*, substituting in their stead novels like *The Great Gatsby, All Quiet on the Western Front*, and for the authentic coloring of the Civil War, *Marching On* by James Boyd. I spoke in the chapel, and after a brief introduction Dr. Peabody took his seat alone in the front pew. In his letter he had asked that I confine my remarks to twenty-three minutes, which was no problem, as I seldom was allotted as much as that in my talks on censorship. But he must have suffered from those who over-stayed their time, for precisely as I approached the twenty-minute mark, out came his large gold turnip of a watch, which he studied and then looked up at me. I went placidly on as if I had all the morning and not until my watch said twenty-three did I come to an abrupt, effective close. The teasing was good for that great disciplinarian.

I worked hard at my lecturing, determined to be good at it, better certainly than the British authors and aristocrats who, with the rare exception of a Winston Churchill or a Haldane, came to this country ill-prepared and unaware of what was expected of them. The British excel at informal, graceful, after-dinner remarks and at political debate; the American audiences come to a lecture expecting sixty minutes of talk that will be entertaining, at times moving, and always substantial. This they got, pressed down and running over from Dickens. They got it less emotionally from Thackeray; each of those celebrities had given thought to his performance in advance and deserved the ovation he received. But they were the exception.

The worst English lecture I ever tried to hear was by H. G. Wells. Shortly after the publication of the *Outline of History,* he came to America to deliver ten talks at $2,500 apiece. Symphony Hall in Boston was packed when he stepped to the podium, bearing with him a packet of notes three inches thick. No one had lowered the amplifiers which are hung high for the orchestra; no one had realized what a thin, squeaky voice that short, stocky man possessed. His efforts to pitch his voice aloft while finding his way through his notes produced an in-audible confusion which I who was sitting close could only get snatches of. The audience, meekly protesting, "Louder, please!" or "Can't hear," stood it for thirty minutes and left.

The next worst was by a couple who should have known better, Harold Nicolson and V. Sackville-West. They sat at opposite ends of the platform and lamented in a condescending dialogue the difficulty of running a house as vast as Knole with so little domestic help.

I worked up four topics freshly after Labor Day, 1934, spoke spontaneously, without notes, and had the advantage of facing my audience. A question period I welcomed, for like all eager speakers — and I enjoyed lecturing — I was learning from the questions how to make my next presentation better. I had my reward when W. Colston Leigh, the most professional of the New York agents, asked me to join his stable. Bill Leigh, who had the shoulders of a football player, a nose broken in combat, and a generous smile, maintained one rule: he would never go to hear any of his speakers; he sent his staff and his sales force. He made his money on block booking, had a flair for publicity — and retained at the outset 55 percent of the lecturer's fee. He tripled my price, arranged and paid for my transportation, and if I allowed him a fortnight in the autumn and another in the spring would book me for thirty engagements, one a day or more, depending on the distance between. I became too expensive for most forums in New England, and I was called and sometimes recalled to localities as different as Midland, Michigan, and Corpus Christi, Texas, and in the journeys came to know and appreciate the country as I never would have otherwise.

I was lecturing in Des Moines, Iowa, on the publication date of my book *This Trade of Writing;* on a table at the back of the hall was a pile of fresh copies which I autographed for enthusiasts. For ten years I had been encouraging or rejecting manuscripts. Now out of my sympathy for young writers and prompted by the Cheney Report I tried to tell beginners what to expect and what to avoid in the bedeviled, fascinating struggle for recognition. I had accumulated the testimony of those who had gone through the mill and their true stories set an example. The reviews were helpful, especially an appreciative one by Stephen Vincent Benét, and *This Trade of Writing* continued to be read through five printings. From my lectures, my readings, and the income from my writing, in two years I had doubled my *Atlantic* salary.

Mother came in to hear my series of book talks at the Town Hall in New York, where I was taking the place on the program vacated by William Lyon Phelps of Yale, and after a complimentary luncheon with George Denny, the director, and his staff, she and I would return to Elizabeth for the weekend. I enjoyed the kudos and the chance to catch up with the kids — Rufus was now my father's best salesman, Frederika had married my classmate Curtis Fisher, Eliza, a newlywed, was living in Montclair, Jack was with Standard Oil and Hendryk was getting ready for college. Best of all I came to a frank and affectionate understanding with my father. Dad was a member of the Baltesrol Golf Club, one of the last extravagances he could afford; he played with a baseball grip and profanity Mark Twain would have admired, but the committee gave him a big handicap and on days when he put his shots together he might figure in the Sweepstakes. For my visits he would arrange a foursome with my cousin Nick Brewster, and the charming Robert Cade Wilson, a very active director of *McCall's* and *Popular Science*. Bob Wilson hit his wood shots a country mile; the "Young Bloods" played the "Old Dogs," and usually paid for it; then after the nineteenth hole, Dad and I would get down to fundamentals as I drove us back to Clinton Place.

He was proud of the way I was going, eager to hear of the Press earnings and the contribution they were making to the solvency of the Atlantic Monthly Company. He had cut out clippings about my book and my talks. But if my star was rising his was going down: the new synthetics and the merging of the big department stores into a single purchasing unit were forcing him to the wall. He continued to battle against hopeless odds (during the war he hefted bolts of khaki in and out of army warehouses until someone discovered a better way of using his brains), and it saddened me to see the humbling of his spirit. The loneliness, the sense of ebbing power, the lack of money suffered by so many in the Depression, hit my father hard. I was more fortunate because I was not hitched to one plow. He no longer took a lead in community affairs, seldom saw his old friends, and confided in me that he and Mother were drifting apart, and that it was his fault. I told him I would help finance Hendryk, my youngest brother, through Princeton, and he knew I would look out for Mother if the time came when they lived apart.

X

For my first lecture tour in Texas I had to pack enough shirts for eight one-night stands. I traveled every foot of the way by train, living in a compartment on the long runs, sitting in the day coaches on short ones, and tugging along my heavy leather suitcase. My first engagement was in Dallas and there to meet me as I stepped off the Pullman was Colston Leigh's representative, a large woman heavily coated with make-up, perfume and costume jewelry. We taxied to the hotel, where she suggested that we breakfast together while she went over my schedule. Hardly had we been served when in came two Bostonians; they were seated three tables away, took one look, and then studiously averted their gaze. When I glanced again in their direction, Sewall Barrell grinned at me and lifted his eyes. Oh, what the hell, I thought, there's no explaining, and turned back to my itinerary.

From Dallas, where I spoke to a large, expensive-looking audience, I headed east to Tyler, "the rose capital of the world." At Hershey, Pennsylvania, where Mr. Hershey came to hear me, the air was saturated with the sweet odor of chocolate; at Tyler one lives with the redolence of roses, which was pleasanter. Like a gigantic vineyard, the rows of bushes in bloom stretched out for miles; long-stemmed American Beauties sold on the street for a quarter a dozen, and my hostess took me to see the loading of a fleet of cold-storage trucks filled with buds destined for northern florists. Her daughter, she told me, was to be Queen of the Rose Festival in the autumn, and she described her costume, her attendants — one princess always came from Mexico — the pageantry — and what it cost. Wow!

From Tyler I went south to Corpus Christi on the Gulf, a town then booming in oil and natural gas. There were vents of gas with a steady flame coming out of the ground, but no one seemed to care; the place had the stir and anticipation of a gold rush — which it was. Two Texans in high-heeled boots and five-gallon hats met my train. "Are you a Moose?" they asked. "Well, no matter. There's a luncheon meeting to hear Judge Coburn, and we'd be obliged if you would speak for two minutes. But no more." They carried my bag and briefcase to the hotel lobby, whose walls were vibrating to the blasts of a WPA band, and as soon as I signed the register I was escorted to the place that had been saved for me on the dais. When my turn came I said I was glad to be there, and that I was sure this was the first time a Damyankee had ever been welcomed to Corpus Christi by a band playing "Dixie" and sat down. Then the judge who pictured the town's origin and came to the point: "You'all know how fast Corpus Christi has shot up," he said, "and you'all know how concerned some of us have been about our water supply. Well, I'm here to give you my word of honor that we now have in wells or reservoir water enough for a population of two hundred and fifty thousand, if the good Lord wants us to grow that big." Cheers and we all stood as the band played "The Eyes of Texas Are Upon You."

Along the way I was meeting unusual people: at Dallas Miss Ima Hogg, whose famous brother Will had prevented the Texas Legislature from reclaiming the oil lands with which they had endowed the University of Texas — before the oil was discovered. Will was dead, but the parkways and gardens which were one of his endowments to Dallas, and the great stories about him made me wish I could have known him. At Houston I stayed with John Lomax, who had completed the recording of the Songs of the Plains and with the help of his son Alan was now collecting the songs of the chain gangs. Leadbelly, the most talented of the prisoners he brought to light, had been paroled in John's care to sing and record. Over a delicious supper cooked by Mrs. Lomax, whom he always addressed as "Miss Bess," John spoke of his happiness at Harvard and of what he owed to Professor Kittredge. (In my bread-and-butter letter I signed him up to do an article on Will Hogg.) At Fort Worth, where I had a free Sunday, the program chairman, Mrs. Robert Hardwicke, moved me out of the hotel into their guest room: she and her lawyer husband Bob were ardent naturalists, and they fed me the good writing about their beloved state: Roy Bedichek on the whooping cranes; J. Frank Dobie, the storyteller of the cow country, and that glowing short novel about the great ranches, *The Sea of Grass*, by Conrad Richter.

There were usually interviews with the press or on the air, and in their course I questioned the reporters about local problems — and sometimes alluded to them in my talks. The immense flocks of wild fowl feeding on the cornlands of the Dakotas in the autumn made me appreciate the necessity of protecting their flyways, and in a state as dry as Arizona I realized the value of water — "Here we're mining for it!" the president of the state university told me.

I returned from such expeditions with an enlarged concept of the country and impelled to talk about it, but my wife and friends were not quite so eager to listen as the strangers on the road, and the afflatus that comes from applause gradually subsided. Block booking meant hard traveling: I did not have to carry my blankets as Emerson did on his night journeys, but my engagements were sometimes a thousand miles apart; and the reception following the talk and, after that, drinks with the chairman left less than six hours for sleep before making the next connection. I was keyed up while in motion but frayed and dog-tired at the end. A lecturer earns his money when he covers the United States. "When I remember what a skinny hypochondriac you were on your arrival in Boston," said my doctor, Roy Wheeler, after an examination, "and what a rugged bastard you've become . . ."

I was determined to prove that I could get ahead despite Ellery's niggardliness. As men do, I was enjoying competitive golf for the winning I had seldom tasted in boyhood, and I was so caught up in my work that I took Fritzy and our love, that mutual, delicately balanced satisfaction, without question. I knew she was attractive to other men and when, with astonishing honesty, she told me that one of her beaux had asked her to go off with him for a weekend and would I mind, I was brought up short. Now that she mentioned it, I minded like hell, and I told her so. But with bruised feelings I knew I had been neglecting her. "Lover, Come Back to Me" was a popular tune that year — and I still wince when I hear it.

We were members of a small, friendly circle, calling ourselves the Boston Parlor Club. We put on skits for each other's amusement either in Kay Lane's ballroom or at Pauline Fenno's luxurious country place high above the Rowley marsh. We thought well enough of ourselves to stage a Revue in Boston during the winter of 1931 for the benefit of the North Bennett Street Settlement; it netted a couple of thousands at our first two performances and, in my time of trouble, we were preparing fresh numbers for a second revue in Mrs. Fenno's ballroom. Modesty aside, we were entertaining: Edward Ballantine, with his variations on "Mary Had a Little Lamb" as ten classic composers would have written it; Katherine Lane in an amusing take-off of Irene Bordoni; David McCord and Jim White in their harmonizing of Hasty Pudding and French-Canadian songs; and Dick Mallaby with his own version of Tin Pan Alley. I did monologues: the first, a Recital by a Modern Poet; the second, a parody of a big-game hunter lecturing on the tsetse fly. I also danced a solo with a broom which, when reversed, became a Boston deb at a coming-out party — with her face suggested by black court-plaster eyelashes and a pert red mouth. By altering her height and my style I became her various partners: the usher, the New York beau, the little freshman, Mr. A. D. Porc — no dancer but well liquored, and her Uncle Henry. And — more symbolic than anyone knew — Fritzy and I danced a flirtatious duet to "She Didn't Say 'Yes' (She Didn't Say 'No')."

Seeing each other as others saw us, in make-up at a fancy dress ball, may have added to our rediscovery that summer. You were supposed to go as Your Favorite Sport. I went as Miss Eleanora Sears, who could walk longer and faster than any undergraduate and was national champion at squash rackets. After I had shaved and browned my legs, "Eleo" dressed me in her white linen riding jacket, cloth skirt, and small gray cloche hat, and I was such a horrid resemblance that a picture of me found its way into *Vanity Fair*. Fritzy went as Mme Piccard, the wife of the Swiss balloonist, who almost set an altitude record before his gas gave out. Across her bosom was a broad ribbon, reading "Stratosphere Or Bust" and she was one mass of toy balloons of all shades which she cleverly attached to the skimpiest of slips. I could hardly squeeze her into the car. But when the dancing began her partners started exploding her balloons with their cigarettes, and she was more like Annette Keller-man, the diver, when the time came for "Good Night, Ladies."

It was grief that brought us finally back. Death had never come close to either of us, but now Fritzy's mother, Sara's dear "Go-Go," was suffering a protracted, agonizing siege of cancer that repeatedly called both daughters to 8 West Fifty-third Street, Fritzy from Boston and Martha from Montreal. Unkie, red-eyed, was inconsolable, for there was no hope and no alleviation. We were a stricken small group at her funeral and when we departed Unkie's loneliness was pathetic. In a matter of months Long Point was shut and sold, Bollard forlornly packing up for storage the laces, the chintzes, the jade — all the shimmering lovely reminders of Sara Wetmore's presence.

Fritzy and I were intent on having Mr. Wetmore with us for a month that summer, and we went shopping for a cottage that would be big enough. We found it in Ipswich, on Labor-in-Vain Road, at a figure we could afford. The bedrooms were high and cool; there was a piano in the living room and a screened porch for cocktails looking out toward Plum Island. Stout, good-natured Agnes was the best cook we ever had, and to cheer us we had just acquired Mickey, a black, curly cocker spaniel. We were sure that we could offer Unkie comfort and distraction and urged him to come.

Unkie was designing the interiors of the new Matson liners, then on the ways at the Quincy shipyards—it was one of his last commissions. I drove him to Quincy and on weekends he found distraction at the Myopia Hunt Club, of which I was an associate member, where he met old friends and enjoyed sunning on the porch, glass in hand, watching the tennis. The Myopia links he could take for nine holes, after that the hills were too much. What he most relished was a supper of Essex lobster, with a bottle of Liebfraumilch, followed by a victorious bout with me at the backgammon table. To help with the dishes we had hired the blond daughter of a nearby farmer, a very pretty sixteen-year-old, and the first time she passed him the platter of lobsters, Unkie reached down and gave her a pinch. She had never been pinched there or so firmly before. She gasped, jumped, and turned as red as the lobsters, which she dumped in Unkie's lap.

But it was the puppy and the house that provided the natural comedy. The first time I struck a chord on the keyboard a small, emaciated mouse crept out between the foot pedals of the piano and died. We had given Charlie the big double bed in the west room — luckily, for the other beds proved treacherous. Agnes's iron bedstead would support her weight for a week and then let her down, feet first, with a bang that aroused us all. The coal stove was so filled with rust we could get no proper heat in the oven. "Lucky it didn't blow your roof off!" said the plumber who tried to fix it. Our water was pumped to the house by an electric motor, set in a greasy pit, deep in a blackberry patch. "There's no water. The belt must be off," Agnes would remark as I came down to breakfast, freshly starched and spic for the city. Cursing I would wade through the wet blackberries, remove the covering of the pit, wrestle the bloody, greasy belt back on the revolving drum, glance at my stained cuffs, and go in for quick repairs. Not once but twenty mornings. All this was the reason our rent was low, but laughter even at one's expense is a distraction from sorrow.

At the end of the judging of the prize novel contest in 1934 my eyes were twitching and the oculist insisted I give them a rest. In May Fritzy accompanied me on an editorial trip which would end at Hot Springs, Virginia. We stopped off first at Paoli for an overnight stay with A. Edward Newton, the Philadelphia book collector who was finishing a new book. On Sunday afternoon we were part of an audience that filled his famous library, come to hear him read aloud his chapter on Charles Lamb and then be refreshed by delicacies and drinks — I remember tiny fishballs so hot that they burned as they melted on the tongue.

On to Washington for a visit with Mrs. Winthrop Chanler, whose love for Europe matched that of her friend Edith Wharton. She was also finishing a book for us, her first, to be called *Roman Spring*, depicting her girlhood in Rome where she had made her debut under the wing of her older brother, the novelist F. Marion Crawford. Her zest for life was impervious to time: her late husband had adored her and so had her intimates in England: Gaillard Lapsley, my old tutor, and Logan Pearsall Smith. Watching her preside at her dinner table, listening to her appraisal of the pictures in the Phillips Gallery was a treat.

Then, to be to ourselves, we went to the Homestead at Hot Springs, Virginia. It was my first time, but for Fritzy it was nostalgia, close to tears, for she had come here spring and autumn for years with Bill and her mother. We took the carriage drives through the mountains they had taken, she introduced me to the old golf pro who had taught her her swing, and over our drinks the first evening we agreed that the time had come for us to have another child — and would she please try hard to produce a son! We ate huge breakfasts, topped off with waffles, we golfed, and didn't care if we were held up, we napped and waking, read aloud; we sipped our drinks, strolled at sunset, sampled the exotic dishes on the long menu, had a different wine each night, and looked forward to making love.

We stopped off at New York on the way back and while she went shopping with Martha, I buttoned up a book which Dr. Josephine Kenyon, a famous baby doctor, and I had been working on for months, and for which we had finally found a good title: *Healthy Babies Are Happy Babies*. It was certainly propitious: the book, published that fall, has been reprinted and revised, revised and reprinted, again and again, and young Ted, our son, formally Edward Francis, named for my grandfather, was born within the year.

While Fritzy was convalescing in the hospital after young Ted's birth, I went househunting. We could not yet afford to buy, but I found on my favorite street on Beacon Hill an old brick dwelling with a long living room, hardwood floors and open fires, and ample room for bookshelves. Fritzy liked the sound of it so I signed a five-year lease and began the packing. While this was going on, Sara, on her return from school, went out for a dutiful walk with her nurse, and it was an act of kindness for Mrs. Gordon Abbott to take her for an afternoon drive in her limousine. The two sat side by side in the back of the big Pierce Arrow and the conversation opened with Mrs. Abbott asking about my health.

Ted, Jr., in the snow on Chestnut Street

"I don't see him very much," replied my daughter, "he's out every night." And the baby brother? "He's a very plain baby," said the nine-year-old. "Takes after Pa and he's no thing of beauty!"

That autumn, early in the symphony season, I proposed to Fritzy that we have a housewarming on an evening when Serge and Nathalie Koussevitzky could be with us. My friendship with Serge was a here-today-and-gone-tomorrow affair and always rewarding. I saw him at a distance every Saturday night at the concerts, and when closer to I enjoyed the quickness of his mind, his Russian sense of humor, and his sentiment, all of which ingratiated him to his men. Of the many I have heard conduct that magnificent orchestra, whether as guests or regulars, "K" was the best: more exciting than "Papa" Monteux, more versatile than Munch, who except for Berlioz, always seemed in a hurry to get the damn thing over, more inspiring than Leinsdorf. At a Pension Fund concert with an all-Tchaikovsky program I drew a house seat next to Paul Whiteman and George Gershwin, and their rapture as they listened spoke for the professionals. The rapport between "K" and the orchestra produced, at its best, a magic, whether they were playing Brahms, Prokofiev or Debussy, and the Beethoven Ninth sent me home treading on air. The Harvard Glee Club and the Radcliffe Choral Society, whose voices were so triumphant in the last movement, must have experienced the same uplift. The orchestra had the incentive of knowing that they were being heard nationwide over the airways and that their only rival was the NBC orchestra under Toscanini.

Our regular seats were in the row directly behind John Burk, who wrote the program notes, a full and illuminating blend of biography and interpretation, and I came early to read them. (I kicked myself for not signing up his biographies of Beethoven, Mozart, and Clara Schumann, which he wrote for Bennett Cerf later.) John, his wife, and daughter lived for music, they attended rehearsals, and from them we got a familiar glimpse of each concert while the instruments were tuning up. Afterwards, accompanied by Fritzy or Sara, I often went backstage to the Green Room to congratulate the maestro when he reappeared in freshly starched shirt and white tie, his face flushed, and the big vein in his forehead still throbbing.

I wanted him to write for us, short pieces I hoped might pave the way to a memoir, and I urged him to do it in Russian and then work out the translation with Olga, his niece. This led to a luncheon at their home in Brookline, the promise of an essay on the essence of Brahms, and a second on Debussy. I kept the heat on when, as sometimes happened, our trails crossed in our journeying. One afternoon, outward bound for an evening lecture in New York, I found myself in the orchestra's Pullman. Koussevitzky beckoned me to the seat beside him and I learned they were to play at Carnegie Hall that same night.

"K," I asked as we skirted the Connecticut shore, "what do you eat before a concert?"

"Ah," he said, "toujours le gaz. I try teeny bits of chicken with rice. No good. Toujours le gaz. Then a Greek, he tells me, 'Porridge, honey and butter. No gaz.' He is right!"

Our next chance encounter was at the old Schenley Hotel in Pittsburgh. I was free for the Saturday afternoon concert and "K" gave me an aisle seat. The lights were lowered as he walked to the podium and at that moment a figure whom I recognized as Frank Sinatra and a state trooper sidled by me to the seats at my left. Sinatra was singing at a theater downtown for some fabulous fee, had made it to the auditorium just in time, and darted backstage where he shook Koussevitzky's hand, saying, "I am Sinatra." "K" beamed at him and went onstage, but at the intermission asked, "Who is Sinatra?"

One summer the Koussevitzkys invited Fritzy and me to Tanglewood, where he wished me to address the orchestra. I was supposed to entertain them about another art, and I believe I did. This was why we wanted the Koussevitzkys at the housewarming for our neighbors on Beacon Hill. "Let's keep it small," said Fritzy. Beside the Koussevitzkys we had the Zinssers, the Samuel Eliot Morisons, the Charlie Curtises — and a case of champagne. Still in a courting mood I engaged a one-man orchestra, Herbie and his accordion, to play for us after dinner. I have said that Sara was beguiling. She came down in her wrapper to say good night and when she approached Hans Zinsser, she paused.

"Dr. Zinsser, do you know why cream is more expensive than milk?"

"No, Sara. Why is cream more expensive?"

"Because it's harder for the cows to sit on the little bottles."

Some parties catch fire and this one did. We danced, "K" waltzed to the accordion, we drank and talked and danced again until the last cork had popped.

2

Alfred McIntyre had set our sights on "fewer and better books." In fiction, thanks to our prizes, a bit of luck, and a bit of hunting, the Atlantic Press was doing well. The list of best sellers in the mid-thirties, in which we twice placed two of the top ten, gave indisputable evidence that readers wanted to be distracted from contemporary problems they could not solve. The historical novel was one answer, as *Anthony Adverse* and *Gone With the Wind* would testify.

Our luck was the result of Ellery's gamble on the boys in the South

Pacific: his faith in Nordhoff and Hall was repaid abundantly. Confident of their new-found power in collaboration, they began to write the story of the mutiny on the *Bounty*, the most spectacular and human adventure in the annals of the British navy. It took place on a small armed transport, H.M.S. *Bounty* of two hundred tons, while on the peaceful mission of transporting breadfruit trees from Tahiti to islands in the West Indies, and it was provoked by the brutal discipline of Captain Bligh. Bloodshed was narrowly averted on the voyage out, and after a brief sweet sojourn ashore, in which the crew found their sweethearts, mutiny swept through the overcrowded ship shortly after they sailed away. Through the forbearance of Fletcher Christian, the second officer, Bligh was not killed. He and the nineteen men loyal to him were set adrift with provisions in an open boat; the mutineers, under the command of Christian, returned to Papeete, where a few elected to hide; the majority, with their girls and some friendly natives, disappeared under the horizon, not to be heard from for eighteen years. So much is history. The story must have been known to Robert Louis Stevenson when he was in Samoa, but he was ailing and did not possess the knowledge of Polynesia which Nordhoff had acquired.

Nordhoff and Hall had to assimilate the books we sent them about the British navy under Nelson (Bligh served as one of his captains) until the flavor and vernacular became so familiar that they could write in one style. They had the log of the 3,618-mile voyage in the longboat which brought Bligh and his men to safety and the confession of those mutineers who were captured and court-martialed. And a retired British naval officer sent them the deck plan and, in time, a perfect model of the *Bounty*.

Next, they made a thematic division of the story. Nordhoff, the hard-driving narrator, would write the outward voyage, draw the contrasting portraits of the brutal Bligh and of Christian who interceded for the crew, and give the impressions of the seamen as they entered the almost untouched beauty of Tahiti. Hall, compassionate and poetic, would describe the outbreak; the return of the mutineers; their quarrel about where to hide; the arrival of the *Pandora*, the ship sent from London to capture the mutineers that could be found; and their trial and execution. They read aloud the chapters to each other in their old workroom at the Aina Paré, Hall interrupting for more description, Nordhoff, impatient lest the narrative drag. It was soon impossible to tell where one began and the other ended. I once asked them to initial their individual passages but they gave up after the first chapter.

When the manuscript of *Mutiny on the Bounty* reached Boston in the early spring of 1932, it did not take us long to realize that we had

James Norman Hall and Charles Nordhoff at Papeete, Tahiti

a book of exceptional beauty. It was a big novel, and our confidence in it was sustained when it was selected for the Book-of-the-Month Club; and when this was announced, the bidding began in Hollywood. Paramount seemed keenly interested but backed away when they estimated the production costs if the shooting were to be done in the South Seas as the authors insisted. At the very bottom of the Depression, the film rights were sold for a down payment of $1,000 against a final price of $12,500. What a figure for a film in which Charles Laughton as Captain Bligh was so superbly supported by Clark Gable as Mr. Christian and Franchot Tone as Midshipman Byam!

With hardly a day's pause the authors began work on the sequel, the novel about what had happened to the mutineers after they had set Bligh adrift. In 1789, under Mr. Christian's command and with native wives aboard, the *Bounty*, hundreds of miles from Tahiti, sighted a shark's tooth, a small, peaked island with a fertile plateau on top, and here the men demolished their ship, saving everything that could be put to use in their hidden community. It might have been idyllic had there been enough women for all; what happened was a fierce race riot in which every male was slain except one sailor. Badly wounded, he was rolled up in matting and hidden by the women. Time passed, and in February 1808, American sealers in need of water sent a boat ashore to the uncharted island, now known as Pitcairn, where they discovered a colony of many women and English-speaking children, presided over by Alexander Smith, a white-bearded patriarch, once a crewman on the *Bounty*.

But with every killing accounted for, the story was simply too bloody for enjoyment: they had written the narrative in the third person, by omniscience, as murder followed murder. The boys were dismayed. "You'll receive the first thirteen chapters of *Pitcairn's Island*, by this mail," Nordhoff wrote me. "Hall and I agree that it is no good, though we differ strongly as to why. If you could tell us precisely what is wrong with the story, and why, one or the other of our opinions would be confirmed and we should be able to go on with it immediately having agreed to abide by your word. Please go into all the detail you have time for, as this is damned important to us."

When I read the beginning, I had to agree. It was much too full of bloodshed for either interest or sympathy. Walking to the office one morning soon after, I had a clue. I had been thinking of the American ship *Topaz*, and of what a surprise it must have been to the boatswain when with his crew he toiled up the path to the plateau, there to be greeted by that incredible colony. There must have been a feast, and while they were eating, Alex Smith would surely have told the American sailors how the islanders got there and of the fighting which almost wiped them out. He would recall only as much of the final tragedy as he could have seen before he was wounded, and his telling of it would have been softened by time and by loyalty. If the boys related the story through his eyes, it would hold the warmth and pathos it lacked. They responded to my outline gratefully, and in six months we had their second big novel in our hands.

I have gone into such detail because the success of the three novels about the *Bounty* — *Mutiny on the Bounty, Men Against the Sea* (the story of Bligh's anguish in the open boat), and *Pitcairn's Island* — and in 1934 of *Hurricane*, which was dedicated to me, was our silver lining in bleak years.

With Nordhoff and Hall, the novels by Mazo de la Roche and James Hilton, and *Drums Along the Mohawk* by Walter D. Edmonds, we did uncommonly well in fiction. In nonfiction Nora Waln had written about her "House of Exile" in Canton, and from Moscow came the sober-sided, illuminating books *Russia's Iron Age* and *Russia's Five Year Plan* from William Henry Chamberlin, who had recently been admitted to the Soviet Union — in all a harvest that saw us through the closing of the banks and that made up for what the magazine was losing. "William Henry," as he was known, was the foreign correspondent for the *Christian Science Monitor*. He neither smoked nor drank, but he did eat his weight each year in sweet chocolate. The Soviets like chocolate, too, and how to get that much to him in Moscow was a problem. We sent more than he asked for hoping the censors would let enough through.

My love for autobiography frequently led me to men at the peak of their careers. In 1932 Dr. Harvey Cushing knew that he was entering his last year before mandatory retirement: he had lost most of his savings in the wiping out of Kreuger and Toll; he had installed Dr. Elliott Cutler as his successor at the Peter Bent Brigham Hospital, but he was still operating on a full-time schedule and privately hoping that the Harvard Corporation might prolong his usefulness at the Medical School. But down in New Haven one of his former pupils, Dr. John F. Fulton, had different ideas and Harvey had accepted the Sterling Chair of Neurology at Yale, which, in effect, transferred his genius (and his valuable library) to his Alma Mater before President Lowell realized what was happening.

This meant his leaving Boston after twenty-five years. If I was ever to have access to those war journals, it would have to be the summer before Dr. Cushing cleared out for good. The books, I understood, had been transported from his office to his home in Brookline, and there in

June I went to see him. The Doctor greeted me in his shirt sleeves. "We've been uprooting," he said, and the house showed it, for the rooms had already been half dismantled. "The family has gone up to Boar's Head for the summer, but I think I'll stay on here. I've got twenty years of records to sort out."

"Let me get a man to help you," I said. "Listen, I'll get a Ph.D. from Yale. You can stow him in one of the empty rooms upstairs, and together he and I will go through those journals of yours, marking the passages which we think are of general interest and which ought to be published. We'll pay for him; it won't commit you to a thing if you don't like the final result. Besides, his companionship may compensate a little for your not being at Old Boar's Head."

"Boar's Head," he said, correcting me, and then he saw I was teasing. "Well, if you want to take the risk, it's all right with me."

Yale willingly supplied me with the Ph.D.: Ralph E. Collins, a quiet-spoken, agreeable individual who could type like the wind, and together we took our way slowly through those eight huge volumes, marking with white slips the passages to be copied. Cushing had served as an operating surgeon with the French in the first winter of the war, and in the spring of 1915 he visited the Royal Medical Corps in Flanders. In 1916, sure that we would be involved, he was intent on organizing a medical unit in America. With Base Hospital No. 5 he went back to the Front early in 1917 and was attached to the British army through the campaigns of Messines Ridge and during the dreadful slaughter on the Somme and at Passchendaele that autumn. In 1918 he was attached to the AEF and with his operating teams he took care of most of the head wounds resulting from the fighting at Château-Thierry, the Argonne and St.-Mihiel.

The diary was graphic and sparky, forthright, crackling with anger or humor, full of denunciation of all that was unsanitary and incompetent, charged with compassion for those who bore the brunt of the fighting. He began operating at 8:30 A.M., and on record days he would be called on for as many as *twelve* head cases. No operation was of less than an hour's duration; many took twice that amount of time. There he would stand hour after hour on the little stool which gave him the elevation he needed as he worked over the unconscious soldier. By midnight or after he would be too excited, his nerves too taut for sleep, and so, on old temperature charts, scraps of yellow paper, anything that was handy, he would write down the details, humor and exasperation of that exhausting day, and so the piano wires of his mind were relaxed. For example:

Harvey Cushing

Operating from 8:30 A.M. one day till 2:00 A.M. the next; standing in a pair of rubber boots, and periodically full of tea as a stimulant . . . It's an awful business, probably the worst possible training in surgery for a young man, and ruinous for the carefully acquired technique of an oldster. Something over 2000 wounded have passed, so far, through this one Casualty Clearing Station.

Some of the journal was indeed too personal and some of it too technical; but the great passages were a spirited, magnificent chronicle of a doctor at war, his resentment and his humor:

This sergeant of the Machine Gunners had almost the whole of his right frontal lobe blown out, with a lodged piece of shell almost an inch square, and extensive radiating fractures, which meant taking off most of his frontal bone, including the frontal sinuses — an enormous operation done under local anaesthesia. We crawled home for some eggs in the mess and to bed at 2:30 A.M. — six hours for these two cases.

This man "Chave" — queer name — when roused from his semi-conscious made it known that he had some precious false teeth. They were removed, somewhat more easily than was his broken frontal bone. They must have been on his mind, for I remember when rongeuring out fragments of his skull he kept muttering that I was breaking his teeth. . . . He seems to be all right today, and is wearing his teeth.

There was a fierce, driving dedication in Dr. Cushing which showed in his features: the long dominating nose, the blue eyes that could turn so swiftly cold or angry, the tight lips with the lines of sorrow. Harvey could steel himself against death on the operating table, but the death of friends was a different matter, as witness this account of Jack McCrae, the Canadian poet and physician:

January 28, 1918
Boulogne

I saw poor Jack McCrae with Elder at No. 14 General last night — the last time. A bright flame rapidly burning out. He died early this morning. Just made Consulting Physician to the 1st Army — the only Canadian so far to be thus honored. Never strong, he gave his all with the Canadian Artillery during the prolonged second battle of Ypres and after, at which time he wrote his imperishable verses. Since those frightful days he has never been his old gay and companionable self, but has rather sought solitude. A soldier from top to toe — how he would have hated to die in a bed.

At the summer's end, and before the family had returned from Boar's Head, Collins had typed up approximately forty-five thousand words, enough for four full-length articles in the *Atlantic*. The master copy was given to the Doctor, I kept the carbon; and we shook hands all around and then went our separate ways. But I had left a number of slips in the big books just in case someday I might be asked back.

Two years went by without a word from him although I heard indirectly that his legs were giving him trouble. Then I had a call from New Haven. "Ted," Harvey said, "I've been rereading those passages you marked in my Journal. They seem to me safe enough if you and Sedgwick really want to print them in the magazine." At last! We sent out announcements that the series was coming and we featured the articles in the *Atlantic,* and in response letters poured in from all over the world, one of the first a note of thanksgiving from a veteran in Texas whose life he had saved. Old friends at Johns Hopkins, doctors in England, urged him to continue. Other publishers, of course, wrote to him asking for the book rights, and to protect our priority, Ellery intervened:

2 January, 1935

Dear Harvey:

I really hope very much you will see Weeks. His confidence in the proposed book is complete, and he is not by profession a chaser of rainbows. To me, there is interest in the fact that during a period of five weeks, while your articles have been running, a count was made of the new subscriptions received from physicians and surgeons. They amounted to almost 1900. But even if I had no statistics at my disposal, I should be sure in a realistic meaning of the word that your war diaries would not only sell widely, but that they would take a permanent place.

Please don't let this chance go, but whatever is your final decision this letter is simply to ask you to give an hour to Weeks.

On January 20 I made my initial visit to the big house on Whitney Avenue, where I was installed with the journal in a little sun porch off the living room. I got in the habit of stopping off for the night on my way to New York and while there we both relived the war. Fourteen months later, after eleven visits and the exchange of 113 letters, *From a Surgeon's Journal* came off the press. The manuscript had grown from 4,000 to 190,000 words. Not a sentence was rewritten; my editorial touch was needed in the cutting and in the preparation of an introduction and an afterword — and here Harvey edited me.

Caring for Cushing as an author was a full-time occupation. As the book grew, so did the royalty terms he demanded — the contract was renegotiated three times; he never would accept the libel clause, and midway in the manufacture he obliged us to discard all the galley proofs, five hundred of them, and reset the entire text in a format more closely resembling a diary — which we did at a cost of $2,100. But he was right.

We assumed the risk of libel, which the British publisher and the author were usually responsible for. All went well on this side, but on the day when Constable published the English edition, there was an instant explosion in London. In one passage Harvey had remarked inadvertently that it had been raining pitchforks and his Burberry had leaked like a sieve. We had spelled it with a lower-case *b*, but even so the manufacturers of the famous British waterproof were not to be mollified. A "burberry" was a "Burberry" and no Burberry ever leaked! They sued for damages, demanded that we apologize and that the offending page be corrected and reprinted — all of which was done at our expense.

Our work together was not as fractious as it must sound. The visits to New Haven were often gay. Barbara, the Doctor's daughter, was a debutante and a perfectly lovely one, and girl friends of hers from Brookline and Dedham were usually in attendance, with Yale undergraduates swarming in and out; doctors from England dropped by occasionally to take tea and to tell Harvey what it was like to practice socialized medicine, and when the weather was fair Thornton Wilder and John Fulton might spend the afternoon with us, taking part in the croquet game which was now the Doctor's way of exercising. He was in a wheelchair: the circulation in his legs was beginning to give him serious trouble (the price of having operated so long standing on that little stool). I saved up stories about Boston and Harvard and the Tavern to tell him, and I never ceased to tease him. He who had once been so fierce, so unsparing in his attitude toward the interns and nurses, seemed to relish my ribbing. Perhaps it was a favor granted to me in recognition of my nine-year courtship.

From a Surgeon's Journal ran into several editions and eventually attracted letters from Warner Brothers, saying that they were considering the film rights, in which he was not the least interested. Before one of our last meetings, Harvey had been sorting through the records of his more difficult cases and he spoke with humbleness of his operation on Leonard Wood. The Colonel had come to him straight from the Philippines in the early 1900's, lopsided, unable to disengage his left hand from his trouser pocket, the victim of a brain tumor and a big one, which Harvey removed. He had not been too sure of the operation at the time, Harvey told me. "If I'd known then what I know now, I could have gone deeper," he said, "and there would have been no need for the second operation at the height of his career in 1922." He was remorseful and I sought to divert him.

It was very fortunate that our new home on Chestnut Street was directly opposite the residence of Dr. Hans Zinsser, for we became friends at a time when my stock was rising at the *Atlantic* and when I needed the advice of an older man who was equally fond of Ellery. Hans's library, with bookshelves up to the ceiling and mounds of books stacked on the floor, was in the front of the house. He did most of his writing at night and when his light was on I might saunter across for a beer at ten, and if he didn't want to be interrupted he would throw me out. On Sunday evenings my wife and I were often invited for supper with the hint that we bring with us any tasty leftovers from our icebox to add to the buffet, as there was no telling how many might turn up. The Bernard De Votos would come in from Cambridge, Charlie and Frances Curtis down from Joy Street, and likely as not, ex-Chancellor Bruening of Germany, now teaching at Harvard, or Lawrence Henderson, and former students from India or China or Paris, with the talk ranging from T. S. Eliot to Pareto, to Hitler and the Black Death.

Hans and I had been drawn closer by the editing of his book *Rats, Lice and History*. He had accepted my suggestions, indeed he had written to Ellery, although I did not know it at the time: "Ted Weeks is perhaps the most skillful pruner I have ever known. I think he could get a larger yield of applejack from a barrel of hard cider than anybody I know." As for myself, I was enormously taken with his style, his far-ranging mind, and the skepticism which he brought to this book. The text is written in the vein of one of his favorite authors, Laurence Sterne, and it indulges in the discursions, the sudden pauses for reflections and satire, which one finds in *Tristram Shandy*. *Rats, Lice and History* purports to be the biography of a disease, typhus, and in passages of fascinating analysis he shows how that enemy of man, by ravaging the armies of the Crusaders and those which Napoleon had led to Moscow, had changed the fate of Europe. Hans's statistics were appalling, and they came right down to our own time. I remember one in particular: "between 1917 and 1923 there were 30,000,000 cases of typhus with 3,000,000 deaths in European Russia alone."

For thirty years Dr. Zinsser had campaigned against infectious diseases. He carried the fight to the vulnerable front in the Balkans in the First World War, and thereafter to those points of outbreak where his foreign students were most in need of his aid. The finest portrayal of Hans's spirit was written by his good friend Dr. John F. Enders, when he said: "Always loving and even often seeking out a struggle where benevolent causes were at stake, this lifelong conflict with the agents of syphilis, tuberculosis, typhus, and the rest — which he regarded perhaps only half humorously as sentient malignities — satisfied in large

305

Hans Zinsser

part his need for dangerous experience in the pursuit of generous ends. Those who surrounded him were set alight and newly energized by this flaming idealism." In his exposure he had contracted typhus fever and it was characteristic of Hans that in his most personal book he employed the incident as an opening for his tribute to the nursing profession and, in particular, the nurse who prevented him from jumping out of a fourth-story window.

The grandson of one of the German revolutionaries of 1848, Hans was a cultivated blend of the liberal European tradition and American audacity. He had within him the resources of four men, and it was part of his greatness that he kept all four actively employed. Poetry was an early love, and he published his first volume of verse while still an undergraduate at Columbia. He wrote in the traditional forms, taking infinite pains in revision; he knew precisely what he wanted to say and if he had trouble it was in making his lines scan. When in doubt, he let the sense override the meter.

He was grounded in the classics, and since his family made annual sojourns on the Continent he came to speak French and German fluently. With this background and his love for poetry it would have been quite natural had he devoted himself to letters. But he went straight from college to enlist in the cavalry and saw service in the Spanish-American War. He was shocked at the "unbelievable, miserable sanitary condition of the camps." It was after this time, I believe at the urging of his father, that his thoughts turned to medicine, and the relatively new field of immunology. "I had luck with me," he once told me, "when I began studying the infections of the blood. It was like stepping into a new hotel on the coast: I could have any room for the asking and they all looked out to sea."

Then there was his love for music. He played the violin and the piano with considerable skill, and they were as necessary to him as his versification. On Hans' appointment to Harvard, Dr. Harvey Cushing made a visit of welcome to the College of Physicians and Surgeons, then in the old building on Forty-ninth Street. It was after five on a wintry afternoon and Harvey was told by those homeward bound that he would find Dr. Zinsser two flights up, at the end of the corridor. As he approached, Cushing thought he heard the sounds of music, and there was no doubt about it as he opened the door. Before him were two men in their stained lab coats: the Professor of Bacteriology playing intently on his violin, and his laboratory assistant playing just as intently on his flute. Cushing was motioned to a seat until the piece was finished. With all this went Zinsser's passion for horses and for riding (which, of course, was why he was in the cavalry).

The reception accorded *Rats, Lice and History* was gratifying and the demand for the book continues to this day: it is now in the thirty-fourth printing. Hans was always happy writing, and he next began some preliminary sketches about his parents and about travel in Europe in the manner of the *Sentimental Journey.* "I stub my toe against the first person singular," he wrote me in January 1937, "and know that I could write faster and better if, in some way, I could write more impersonally." What he was aiming for was, in his own words, "as much as possible, an optimistic *Education of Henry Adams* somewhat disconnected, dealing with the educational career, medical development in America, episodes and occurrences in epidemic regions, war and hospital and university life, etc. . . . Of course, it sounds ambitious when I mention Henry Adams because I think he was a great artist." This is what we would talk about when I saw his light burning.

3

I never knew where the next lead might come from. Esther Forbes, the novelist, invited me to speak before the Woman's College Club of Worcester and promised me a treat afterwards. When I had performed, we walked across lawns to the home of Francis Henry Taylor, the new director of the Worcester Art Museum. Taylor with his Renaissance features, the strong nose and sparkling dark eyes, sat there stirring our martinis in a tall glass tube while he told stories about the art dealers of Florence who lay in wait for the annual visitation of J. P. Morgan. I had never heard such museum talk, and as he went on to tell of Duveen and Berenson, whom he called "B.B.," I decided, fortified by my third cocktail, that it was time for a proposition. "How would you like to write for us a history of collecting in America? It's never been done." He sounded eager, and on my return I was able to convince Ellery and Alfred that we had a good prospect. It took only a little research for Francis to ascertain that there was no readable history of collecting in Europe, so the contract came to be written for three books, the first beginning with the conquests of Gustavus Adolphus, showing how the art treasures followed the flight of gold, from Charles I of England to the Netherlands, thence to the Sun King and on to Catherine the Great; the second would carry through Napoleon's plundering; and the third would tell how the treasures came to the New World. *The Taste of Angels,* was, alas, the first and only one that Francis had time and strength for when he was called to New York to become director of the Metropolitan Museum of Art. It stands today as one of the handsomest of our books.

At Dayton, Ohio, in 1938, when I had a free afternoon before my lecture, the program chairman asked: "Mr. Weeks, what would you like to do, visit the Art Museum, or pay a call on Mr. Orville Wright?" When I plumped for Mr. Wright she drove me to an inconspicuous garage. The main entrance was shut; we entered through the small side door and there in a tiny office surrounded by dust-covered silver trophies was the solid, pink-cheeked pioneer, who after our introduction sat uneasily on a cushion of sponge rubber. I felt in the presence of History and said I hoped that my visit was not causing him discomfort.

"Oh, that," he said, rubbing his hips, "I've had to put up with it a long time." He went on to describe the crucial trial flight before representatives of the War Department at Fort Myer in 1908, with himself at the controls and Lieutenant Selfridge of the Army Signal Corps in the front seat. They made their take-off on the parade ground, and at an altitude of 125 feet began a circular course that took them over a gully filled with small trees, where Orville felt the plane vibrate and begin to nose down. When he looked back, he saw that one of the propellers had severed the wires leading to the tail. "We got out of there fast," he said, "and headed back but in the landing poor Selfridge was killed. I broke both femurs."

"Were you in pain?" I asked.

"I don't think so," he replied. "It was sunny but things seemed to have turned gray and I remember someone leaning over me, saying, 'Orville, what the hell happened?'

"We had to wait a long time for an ambulance," he mused. "Trouble is now the vibration prohibits the long flights I'd like to take."

He was so clear-minded and spoke so graphically that I came away eager to find someone who might collaborate with him in the writing of his autobiography. If Mr. Wright were willing, the perfect choice would be Charles Lindbergh and the opportunity to sound this out came a little later, at the time when I was publishing a number of Anne Lindbergh poems in the *Atlantic*. I knew then that the Colonel, apprehensive that war was coming, had been instrumental in having the original Wright plane recalled from London, where it had been on loan, and set up with a proper attribution in the Smithsonian Institution. At a happy luncheon Fritzy and I had with the Lindberghs in New York the talk turned to the restoration of the plane, and I raised the possibility of his doing the book with Orville but he was not hopeful. He understood that a number of well-known authors had made the attempt, unsuccessfully, and as he wrote me later, "It seems to be impossible for anyone to write with accuracy and shading satisfactory to Orville Wright." But as things turned out, Fred C. Kelly did what I had hoped for in his authorized biography five years later — only I did not get the book!

It was coincidence that brought me to our first black author. Roland Hayes and I had the same insurance agent, Herbert Sargent, who had tried for a career in music only to discover that his tenor was too light. He sang duets informally with Mr. Hayes and he told me he was sure there was a good story there. I asked for a meeting and was invited to Roland's home in Brookline at three-thirty in the afternoon; surprisingly, we sat down to a full-course chicken dinner since he had a concert in Springfield that evening. He had just returned from a European tour and in Berlin, he told me, he had faced a large and very hostile audience. It was after the Olympics, in which Hitler's hopes had been dashed by American athletes, notably by that great Negro, Jesse Owens, and when Roland came onstage the hissing was so loud that he could not begin. He had intended to open with some spirituals but as the derision continued he walked over to his accompanist and switched to the group of German lieder, and as the words of "Du bist wie eine Blume" soared above the hissing, the hall stilled. When he had finished they were applauding and then he resumed his program.

My eyes had been drawn to a portrait hanging over the mantel in the living room, the painting of an elderly Negress with a gentle smile, her hair in a turban. "That's my mother, Angel Mo'," he said, "the most important person in my life; she accompanied me on all my early tours. Any book I write will have to begin with her."

Yes, he thought he would like to do a book and do it himself. It could be a good story. His mother, he said, wanted him to be a lawyer or a preacher; she did not trust his singing. But she accompanied him on his first tours where his fees were as little as $35, and she was with him when a white critic made him wonder about his work. "His questions made me ask myself whether I had been trying to turn myself into a white artist, instead of making the most of what I was born with."

"I am glad you are finding yourself out, son," said his mother when Roland told her. "Now go ahead and work hard and be your own man."

With his savings he went to London to perfect his accent in French and in German, and to approach Brahms and Bach from the inside. On his return, his mother heard him sing with the Boston Symphony. "I think she was at last convinced," he said.

For the present he was busy with his concerts and with the summer school he was setting up for young singers — and before anything else he wanted to write a black opera. I wonder if he had felt the spur of Gershwin's poignant *Porgy and Bess* but I did not ask; what I did ask was that when he wrote this autobiography I should have the book, and he agreed. (Like the Cushing journal, this would be deferred: not till Roland's white friend and neighbor, McKinley Helm, sat with him during two summers, drawing out the story of Roland's struggle, did *Angel Mo' and Her Son* become a reality.)

For my evening lectures at Columbia I went to some pains to prepare reading lists. First, a list of American best sellers since 1875, the year when the new copyright law began to cut off pirating. This required my writing to all the publishers in business as I wanted their final estimate of the copies sold, and it cost me a fortune. I had innocently subscribed to a clipping service and when the New York *Times* printed my list in full, it seemed as if every other paper in the country picked it up. My next venture was more serious. I wanted to list the twenty-five most influential books published since 1885, not necessarily books of artistic merit, but books which over the years had influenced human thought and action. In this I needed collaborators and I found them in the educator John Dewey and in the historian Charles A. Beard, who warned me that no one in his right mind would undertake such an impossible job! But they both made their selections and the three lists, mine included, were so striking in their divergence that I had no trouble shaping an effective lecture. In it I referred to the books as "Telegrams to Mankind," warnings which at first we often did not heed.

We were all agreed on four titles: *Das Kapital* by Karl Marx, *Looking Backward* by Edward Bellamy, *The Golden Bough* by Sir James George Frazer, and *The Decline of the West* by Oswald Spengler. After that we separated. Two of us voted for Freud's *Interpretation of Dreams* (but not Charles Beard); two voted for Remarque's *All Quiet on the Western Front* (but not Dewey); two for Lenin's *Imperialism: The State and Revolution;* and another two for *Economic Consequences of the Peace* by John Maynard Keynes. Charles Beard was the only one not to list Einstein on relativity, and the only one who did spot *My Battle* by Adolf Hitler. This English version of *Mein Kampf* by E. T. S. Dugdale contained less than half the original text; it was published in 1933, and was the single translation to circulate in America prior to 1938.

I think the explanation is that we were looking the other way: we were in the worst of our troubles at home, and to the few who did read *Mein Kampf,* it seemed a mad mixture of German grievance and anti-Semitism. This was a "telegram" not many of us opened; that it threatened to change the world we did not comprehend. When the Germans marched into the Rhineland, it seemed to me an inevitable amendment to a bad peace. My emotions at that time were more involved in the Civil War in Spain, and when the fighting worsened as Hitler and Mussolini went to Franco's aid, I was one of a group that brought André Malraux to Cambridge to raise money for the Loyalists. He spoke in French, passionately, then stood silent as the translation was read; he had been to the Front and his sniffing, a nervous tic, revealed his strain, and added to his appeal.

Of our *Atlantic* contributors, the first to see that war was inevitable was Walter Lippmann. After watching the League of Nations' attempt to deal with the Japanese seizure of Manchuria, and fail, and after attending the London Economic Conference of 1933, which F.D.R. scuttled, Lippmann returned to New York, full of forebodings and in a mood to write a book, "a post-war book" about a war that had not yet taken place. To do so he had to detach himself from journalism and in this he had Ellery's intelligent and persistent encouragement. I followed their correspondence with great respect for both parties as *The Good Society* began to take shape in 1936. The book, in the author's words,

is stamped with the realization that the dominant fact in the contemporary world is the return of the European and Asiatic great powers to the conception of total war; that Germany, renascent under Nazi leadership, would . . . seek to annihilate all rival powers in Europe, and that in Russia the form of the political state, the plan of the economy, the determining policies of the regime, are what they are because Russia has been preparing for war on her European and on her Asiatic frontiers.

Those were prophetic words. The first eight chapters were a critical analysis of the falsities, beginning in 1870, which doomed our generation to pass through the terrible ordeal of total wars and of revolutionary dictatorship; the author explained why fascism, communism, socialism, and nineteenth-century laissez-faire were "incapable of reconciling the modern economy with our cultural heritage" and then affirmed the principles of "the Good Society" which he hoped would evolve when the fighting subsided in peace. The book went through six printings after its publication in the autumn of 1937; after Pearl Harbor it was revised, the ending strengthened, and the reprintings of this second run were proof of its importance. I thought it profound in its criticism and forethought and was proud to have a subordinate part in its preparation. From first to last it was Ellery's reassurance that counted and when Lippmann wrote, "I am more grateful to you than you will ever know for having bullied me into the writing of this book," the tribute was deserved.

4

I had a more personal warning from Ray Atherton, our Ambassador to Romania, home on leave the summer of 1937. "Your lovely North Shore," he said as we sat together after a dinner party, "it's an island of oblivion. They don't understand, they don't want to hear what Hitler is up to." But, of course, it wasn't just New England; it was the Midwest and the Pacific Coast too, who would neither listen nor prepare. The Neutrality Act was our shield if trouble began. By the time of the Czech crisis, American foreign correspondents were writing with indignation, notably Dorothy Thompson. Three times, she told me, as conditions worsened, she had been asked by Henry Luce to write for *Life* an article about "the uprooted"; each time she had done so at an enhanced fee, and each time her paper had been pulled out for something more "timely."

At home the ax continued to fall. *Collier's* was beginning to go down under the competition of *Time* and *Newsweek*. The Boston *Evening Transcript* was shorn of advertising, salaries had been cut one-third and cut again. But before the end I was relieved to hear that my old boss, Henry Claus, now the editor, had been bidden away by the du Pont paper in Wilmington, Delaware.

"Do you suppose your editor would consider an offer of $35,000?" asked the Wilmington correspondent of the *Transcript* reporter in Washington, who well knew the score.

"He might, why don't you try him?"

When the offer came through, and Henry, after the momentary stun, had considered it, he went home, to find the two scoured milk bottles which he was in the habit of returning to the grocer for the five-cent refund. Instead, he took each one by the neck and flung it at the brick wall behind the kitchen. "Henry, you fool!" called his wife. "What do you mean by breaking those bottles." And he went in to tell her.

Our next-door neighbors on Arlington Street, Christian Herter and Richard E. Danielson, after an auspicious start, had run into doldrums. Their first venture, the *Independent*, the old weekly they bought for $25,000 and enlivened for a little, was given up in 1928. But the *Sportsman*, which was Danielson's baby, a handsome monthly on coated stock with lively text and action-photographs, made money in its first year; with gusto it celebrated the thoroughbred and the hunt, the steeplechase and the America's Cup races, tennis, golf, and the world of the amateur, as it had never been so colorfully shown before — and when that world had to economize, the revenue dwindled. Herter withdrew to enter the Massachusetts Legislature, and Dick carried on the fight single-handed. He was an able editor and writer with impeccable standards and his vigorous appetite for sport might have sustained the paper through a short slump, but after seven years of red ink he had to give it up and the effort had been crushing. In the privacy of the *Atlantic* office we, too, had our anxiety: Ellery had trimmed the size of the *Atlantic*'s page, which saved us many tons of paper; he had cut back the fees to the contributors, and instead of being hand-stitched, the magazine was stapled together at a saving of $2,000 a month — and still the books would not balance. For four of the five years 1934–1938, the earnings of the Atlantic Monthly Press books paid the deficits of the magazine, and on the strength of this I thought I should be a member of the Board. But no call came and I nursed a grievance.

Then Mrs. Sedgwick, that shy, dark, gracious lady, became seriously ill and as her life began to fade, "E.S.," as I had come to call him, was inconsolable. He rarely came to the office and in his absence asked that I act as his deputy. My own staff had been strengthened by the addition of Archibald Ogden, a boy I had known in Elizabeth, who had built up the Everyman's Library for E. P. Dutton: he was my assistant, and I had an efficient managerial secretary in Jeannette Cloud, a terrier for work. With them to mind the Press, I took up the reins of the magazine and this did admit me to the Board of Directors which E.S. attended in dolor. His big head with the crisp sideburns would sink forward, his hand half covering his eyes, and he would be gone, no rearing back as he used to do when a new idea caught his imagination. Reginald Washburn, the saltiest member of the Board, a Yankee from Worcester, and Ellery's closest friend, would try to rouse him from his apathy. On one occasion when we were reviewing the dismal response to a form letter soliciting new subscribers, Reg said with a smile, "Wouldn't it be simpler to send these people a dollar bill clipped to a postcard, saying: 'Return this dollar to us and you will receive the next five issues of the *Atlantic?*'" Ellery saw the humor but pushed it away with a groan.

On a day in the midst of this overcast, E.S. called me down to his desk. "Can you think of any of your contemporaries who would make a good editor of the *Atlantic?*" he asked when I was seated. I looked away from him, out to the Public Garden, to collect myself and to wonder. Ever since I had been with him he had abided by his three-year rule: Theodore Morrison had been replaced by Edward C. Aswell, and Ed by Joseph Barber, who I knew was leaving. And now, apparently, he had passed me over, too.

"Yes," I said, "I can think of one, if we can get him — Thornton Wilder."

"Do you know him well enough to sound him out?"

"Yes," I said. "I do."

Thornton was then teaching for a year at the University of Chicago and through the help of a friend I was given the use of Mrs. Richard McCormick's beautiful apartment overlooking the lake where Thornton and I could lunch together in private. When I led up to my proposal Thornton gave me an appraising look and then began to ruminate aloud: "Ted, there are several Thornton Wilders," he said. "There's the Wilder who loves to teach and who feels starved if he doesn't occasionally have the chance to do so. There's the Wilder who must write novels and plays. There's the Wilder who enjoys Hollywood and the torment of having his stories manhandled by Sam Goldwyn. And there is Wilder, the scholar, who hopes someday to complete the bibliography of Lope de Vega, the most fertile playwright in the Spanish world. Now you're asking for Wilder to edit, and even if he could do it, well, I think he'd begrudge the time." We went on to talk about the *Atlantic* and what could be done to make it the best literary review in the English reading world; he asked how soon a change was contemplated, and continued firm in his refusal, adding affectionately, "Why don't you speak for yourself, John?"

When this conversation — without the John Alden postscript — was reported to Mr. Sedgwick, he and the directors went into a huddle to which I was not privy. What I had working for me was the record of the Press and, I am sure, the backing of Reggy Washburn and Teresa Fitzpatrick. I was there, I knew the ropes, and I was on friendly terms with our dependable contributors. Whatever misgivings E.S. had in his grief, they were cleared away before our next talk when he asked me to be his successor. It was good to hear and, impulsively, I said it had been my luck to work for the two men I most admired, Dean Briggs and himself. This seemed to embarrass him; he said, "I think you are the most highly personalized young man I know." I wasn't sure what he meant but I took it for a compliment. Then he went on to say that I would take charge unofficially on January 1, 1938, and the announcement would be made that June, when he would have rounded out his thirty years. He hoped I wouldn't mind the wait.

I suppose it is natural for any executive, when he moves to the top, to try to do everything himself. I know I did, and for a time almost succeeded. The responsibility went to my head and I was unwilling to delegate — except to our publisher, Don Snyder, who was struggling to keep the costs down and our sales up. Don was a Quaker and forthright; we trusted each other without a trace of jealousy and he knew better than I how acute our financial position was. There were three thermometers we lived by: the newsstand sale which had been slipping for months; the advertising, which rarely grossed more than $350,000 a year (what we now take in two good issues); and the rise or decline of our renewals and new-reader subscriptions, which came to a head in the three fall months (for more summers than I care to remember Don and I signed notes at our bank to finance the operation through the long drought).

In this first period of trial I had to build bricks without straw. I intended to find better short stories, keener controversy, more vital poetry, knowing full well I could not pay more for them until our sales went up. On my frequent lecture trips to New York I stayed with my elderly cousin, Mrs. Harriet Cheney. Books were her world. She was an old friend of Rudyard Kipling and intervened when the great man would not reply to my requests for permission to reprint his letters to William James.

"Dear Rud," I watched her write. "My cousin, Edward Weeks, has twice requested . . . Now, Rud, don't be a fool; tell him to go ahead . . ." Which he promptly did. Cousin Harriet and her daughter Barbara drove me to my lectures at the Town Hall and Columbia, and stayed to listen, and between talks I scouted my favorite literary agents, Bernice Baumgarten, Harold Ober, and Diarmuid Russell. Bernice handled the fiction for Brandt and Brandt, whose office was close by Grand Central Station. I stopped by one afternoon and asked her for a good story to read on the train to Boston. "Here's a long one," she said, "by an English writer with the improbable name of Geoffrey Household. I haven't read it yet, but London says it's exceptional." London was right and I wrote her the next day accepting Geoffrey's offering and asking for a first option on whatever else he might write for a year. (The only other time I made such a gamble was for Peter Ustinov.)

Maxwell Perkins of Scribner's was the book editor we younger men most revered, and I never went to see him without paging through their catalogue of new books, checking in my mind those titles which sounded as if they might contain *Atlantic* material. Max occupied a small office hanging out over the southwest corner of Fifth Avenue and Forty-eighth Street; he sat at a naked desk, not a paper on it, and often had his hat on (to suggest to the visitor that he was in a hurry?), but his classical features broke into a smile as I began poking about his new books, asking for "Skin and Bleed."

"What's that, 'Skin and what?'"

The phrase was an invention of Reggie Washburn's: "Ted," he'd say, stopping by my desk with the new issue in his hand, "what's the Skin and Bleed in this number?" — meaning, the adventure story, the odd

Donald B. Snyder, the new publisher of the *Atlantic*

confession, the startling slice of autobiography. It is a good phrase for the unexpected feature that will attract readers, and it never failed to arouse Max.

I had to "personalize" — in Ellery's word — a magazine that had grown dreary, too scholarly, too habitual in the Depression, and I had to use every form of inexpensive advertisement. If my December lectures went well in St. Louis and Kansas City, as they did, why not send a Christmas issue to every non-subscriber in those two large audiences? A gentle hint and one that worked. Above all I wanted young blood: George Lott, the Davis Cup player, who wrote "Inside Tennis"; John Steinbeck, and William Saroyan, who came to their power in hard times; and young William P. Bundy, who wrote "The Rift Between the Generations."

I would leave the office sometime after 6:00 P.M., groggy, and after this had continued for three months, I came down on my fortieth birthday with an attack of shingles, most excruciating. My doctor was not too sympathetic: "It's taken you a long time to get as nervously exhausted as this and it will take you nearly as long to recuperate. Don't be surprised if you have spells of melancholy for a while."

In the doldrums of recuperation I was troubled about E.S. Not long after Mrs. Sedgwick's death he had received an invitation to visit Spain and witness, as Franco's guest, the Civil War which was nearing a climax. It perked him up and for a time he thought it might be possible to cover both sides, but this proved impracticable. He departed in the winter of 1938, was wined and dined and impressed by the heroism. He saw the Communists as the devil in the struggle, and the articles he wrote for the New York *Times* on his return, reporting that "the liberal spirit is clearly in the ascendant" in Franco Spain, brought down on his head — and on ours — angry protests from those who like myself supported the Loyalists. I knew that he had been working on an article for the *Atlantic,* and while I hated to hurt his feelings I felt that I must oppose its publication. In a memo to Don Snyder I wrote my protest:

I have mulled over this article of Mr. Sedgwick's for thirty-six hours. . . . The article concerns the capture of Seville — a Robin Hood exploit accredited to the hero on Franco's staff. The exploit has by now assumed the proportions of a legend, and it is this legend which Mr. Sedgwick describes — partly in realistic terms, partly in paragraphs which are obscure. Naturally it is written with the bias of a partisan, and that bias has evoked an undertone of propaganda which I suspect is seldom absent from anything written about Spain today.

It is because of this bias and propaganda that I oppose the publication of the paper in the *Atlantic.* Mr. Sedgwick has been in seclusion for the year past, and has not had as much opportunity to feel the pulse of the American people as in other years, and, in consequence, I think he has missed what Walter Lippmann has so accurately reported — the growing sense of moral indignation against Hitler and his works. We are beginning to feel against Hitler as the English once felt against Napoleon, and if the Nazis go into Czechoslovakia this indignation will rise still higher. To publish a military exploit from the camp which at this moment is enjoying the support of Hitler would be, in my opinion, to bring down upon the magazine the indignation of those who consider themselves of Liberal temper in this country.

It is not true to assume that those who sympathize with the present Spanish government are necessarily Communists. . . .

Snyder with characteristic common sense reminded me that "as long as Mr. Sedgwick is editor-in-chief, you must recognize his right to insist that the paper be published. In this respect you and I are bound by the same code." (Don was right. "The Patron Saint of Andalusia" appeared in the last issue for which E.S. was responsible, and although I winced at the sight of it the ceiling did not fall in.)

In June, *Time* published Mr. Sedgwick's picture and, explaining the change of pilots, stated that "wiry, effervescent 'Ted' Weeks got the title but not the magazine. . . . 66-year-old Ellery Sedgwick, still spry and still owner of the *Atlantic,* will continue to be its dominant voice." This mixture of denigration and fact was half true: at no time after his retirement did E.S. interfere with, much less "dominate," my editing. But he did own the magazine, a fact of which I grew increasingly conscious. Ellery had assured me that he intended to keep the magazine in Boston, that it must never lose its identity with New England. But it was assumed that he would sell, and bids began to come in from New York, one of the most persistent from William Randolph Hearst; a rumor kept appearing in the Hearst papers that the *Atlantic* was about to join the *Cosmopolitan* in the Hearst group of periodicals. How soon could we stop the magazine's losses? Where could I find the capital to keep it in Boston? I had no family capital to draw on and I knew that Charlie Wetmore's fortune had drained away as building after building in which he had invested passed into bankruptcy. Such misgivings were perhaps in the mind of Raymond Everitt, the aggressive vice-president of Little, Brown, who was lunching with me the day my appointment was announced. "I suppose I ought to congratulate you," he said. "But, brother, I wouldn't be in your shoes for a million!"

I confided my worries to Bill Whitman when he congratulated me. He was sure things would work out. "You damn well deserve it; you've worked fourteen years without a letup, and you've grown," he said with that wide sunny smile I had not seen for too long. Bill and I had been separated by distance. He had pulled out of publishing, spent a year on the island of Jersey, struggling with a stubborn book, and then, much I believe to Marjorie's relief, had decided to make a fresh start in anthropology. His brother was studying medicine in New York, and Bill moved in with him to work for his doctorate at Columbia. He chose for his thesis "The Pueblo Indians of San Ildefonso," and with Pargie and the children made his first visit to their pueblo outside of Santa Fe in the summer of 1936. The Indians asked him back and he returned for the following winter with the family in a trailer. He told me his children were a great help: they played in the dust with the Indian kids, exchanged sniffles and fleas, and, incidentally, opened the way for his inquiry.

"Any more poetry, Bill?" I asked.

"Haven't time for it now," he said. "I'll be going back to Santa Fe for one more look."

I threw my arm about him as we parted; it is sad when men who love each other drift apart.

While Ellery had been in Spain, Hans Zinsser was in China, helping pupils of his stave off an epidemic of typhus which came raging on the heels of the Japanese invasion. He returned to Boston feeling poorly and went for a physical checkup to his physician and personal friend, Bill Breed. He could not have been prepared for the finding, but was stoic when it came: he was incurably ill with lymphatic leukemia. He let me know in July, saying he thought he had twelve months in which to revise and finish that book about another doctor he knew so well, and he needed my help. I had never seen anyone face death so calmly.

He carried on his work at the Harvard Medical School and in the laboratory, he submitted himself as a guinea pig for the most exhausting X-ray treatment for leukemia, and in the evenings he devoted himself to the big manuscript. He was determined to finish it and, "Damn you, don't you ever refer to it as an autobiography," he said jokingly, "for it isn't." I crossed Chestnut Street many times in those early summer evenings, for I needed his help, too. Under his relentless concentration the book began to come into the clear, a work in biography whose irony and laughter, whose tenderness, whose understanding of men and of medicine make it unique. Of self-pity there is none in *As I Remember Him.* "Ted," he said to me one morning when the book was nearly done, "if I could only find a raft to step onto from this old hulk — there is so much more writing I would like to do."

5

One of my innovations was to set up a new department entitled "Under Thirty," and the young writers who appeared there in its first year included C. L. Sulzberger, Joseph P. Kennedy, Jr., David Riesman, Jr., Maurice Heckscher, and Kenneth Chappell. Now that I was my own man I relied — unknown to them — on a cabinet of contributors: in Washington, Walter Lippmann, a friend of whom I stood in awe, and Archibald MacLeish, whose feeling for the country and whose exhortation stirred me; in criticism, Edmund Wilson, whose essay on Hemingway was the first of eight; in economics, Sumner Slichter of Harvard, and Herbert B. Elliston, the economics editor of the *Christian Science Monitor,* who was shortly to take over the editorship of the Washington *Post;* in San Francisco, Joseph Henry Jackson, the best bookman on the coast; and, for whatever aroused him, that indignant, lovable Southerner David L. Cohn. These at the outset were my dependables: I turned to them for advice and trusted them to turn to me with what they wanted to see in the *Atlantic.* Soon I added the witty, penetrating Raoul de Roussy de Sales, the American correspondent for *Paris-Soir* and *Havas,* a Frenchman who knew this country almost as well as he knew his own; the satire in his article "Love in America" was the gayest I printed in my first year.

In poetry, I made overtures to T. S. Eliot, for whom Ellery had no use (though he never gave us a poem, eventually we did publish his essays), and I stopped by for late evening talks with Robert Frost, who had moved from Amherst to Beacon Hill after his wife's death. He was lonely and needed cheering. I published two lovely ballads by Stephen Vincent Benét; and Robert Hillyer and I were happily together again. For his *Collected Poems* Bob had been awarded the Pulitzer Prize in 1934, and now I pressed him to write a series of letters, in heroic couplets, one to his son Stanley, one to Robert Frost, a third to a friend killed in action in 1918 — they were scornful of folly, cleverly rhymed and more full of his loves and his prejudices than anything he had written before. I published them all and was particularly touched by these lines to Dean Briggs, written after the Dean's death:

> *As dusk comes on, I almost hope to meet*
> *Dean Briggs once more in the familiar street.*
> *His head thrown back, his amiable walk*
> *Timed equally to progress or to talk.*
> *I, whom life changes with its every whim*

Remember now his steadfastness. In him
Was a perfection, an unworldly grace,
Life could not mar and death can not efface.
I know the wrinkled smile, the kindly eyes,
Keen with a wit both humorous and wise, —
These I remember, and remembering, see
The Dean walk home toward Immortality.
The Dean walks home, his cheerful task complete;
He walks at dusk down the familiar street,
Stopping to share some story with a friend,
Or murmur words of counsel. At the end
He pauses for a moment, and with shy
Farewell looks back, looks back and says Goodbye;
Then rounds the corner of his shining days,
His smile at parting bright through April haze.

In his office above mine Don Snyder was redesigning the magazine. He planned to enlarge the page (which Ellery had shortened) to a size that would accommodate the advertising plates used in *Time* and *Newsweek* — should the agencies be persuaded to turn our way. We were agreed that the cover had to be changed and were planning to test three midwestern cities with photographic covers to see what effect they had on the newsstand. Together we drove out to the studio of W. A. Dwiggins in Hingham, that artist with type, to see his designs for a more readable page. (All these changes, of course, were predicated on our finding or earning the money.) On the drawing board next to ours Dwiggins showed us the layout for a new magazine, to be called *Measure,* with which Henry Luce was threatening to invade our field. (Perhaps he did not have the right editor in Willi Schlamm, perhaps the picking seemed too thin, but it never materialized.)

The St. Botolph Club in the spring of 1939 gave a dinner in my honor, a crowded, hazy affair to the nervous recipient. As I entered I heard above the din Bliss Perry's voice saying, "Here comes the next victim!" He sat on my right, Ellery on my left, and over the soup Bliss gave me two bits of advice: "Whatever your fee is," he said, "pay it on the day of acceptance. It will never seem larger"; and "Remember how vulnerable we all are to insomnia and indigestion. When you feel bilious, try to postpone your difficult decisions to the next day." Ellery said he was pleased that our newsstand sales were running several thousand copies ahead of last year's, and was not disturbed by our idea for a new format.

The dishes come at you fast and you don't swallow much but wine

322

when you're planning how to respond. The Chief Justice of the Massachusetts Supreme Court conveyed the greetings of the Commonwealth; Alfred McIntyre and Walt Edmonds gave their smiling tributes; and Dave McCord read some verses of blandishment. When Robert Frost was called on, he announced, "I have here a new poem," and produced a long, sealed envelope. "But I shan't read it unless Ted agrees to publish it, sight unseen." Naturally I promised, and he read "A Considerable Speck," the manuscript of which he passed to me. He was pulling Ellery's leg, as I learned later. Back in 1915 Sedgwick had asked Frost for some poems, promising to print them. Robert submitted a group, including "Birches" and "The Road Not Taken" and E.S. accepted them —but with such hesitation that the poet still remembered. Then Ferris Greenslet, who had written a biography of James Russell Lowell, the first *Atlantic* editor, and who had known personally the last seven, made a Plutarchian comparison of us all, "as Editors and as Fellows"; and the room roared at his felicities. To which the ninth editor replied as best he could.

The big boost we got at this critical time came from Arthur Kudner, who had become a minority stockholder in the *Atlantic*. Tall and broad-shouldered, brimming with confidence, Art was founder and president of the advertising agency that bore his name and that he had built into a powerhouse. He loved words and used them well, was perhaps the best copywriter on Madison Avenue, and owed part of his success to the charm he exerted in Detroit, his home country. Self-educated, he had taken Irvin Cobb's place on the Detroit *Free Press* when he was only nineteen and had scored one of his first scoops on Henry Ford's fiftieth birthday. The lobby in the Dearborn office was full of reporters when Art arrived and the great man would see none of them. Art sat down and wrote a note: "Dear Mr. Ford, My new car is giving me trouble. I wish I could talk to you about it for a minute," signed it, and handed it in at the Complaint Window. Shortly, a messenger was paging Mr. Kudner and led the way to Mr. Ford's office. After he had confessed, Art said, "Sir, there is one question I'd like to ask you. What do you miss the most now that you're fifty, with the world at your feet?" Ford crossed to the window and gazed out, then said over his shoulder, "Ma's cooking." This was the kind of thing that delighted the men in motors and when Art came back in his prime to solicit the big accounts, he spoke their language and knew the right approach. He acquired the Fisher Body account on his honeymoon, and Buick and Goodyear followed soon after.

He bought into the *Atlantic* out of respect for what it stood for and partly, I think, because he hoped to write for it some day, as he did. His exuberance was contagious: he found for us an experienced advertising manager, and in a few months we had new accounts in cigarettes and motors. When I told Art that NBC had just invited me to do a thirty-minute radio program on Tuesday nights, following "Information, Please," he was elated. "On both networks?" he asked. "Great! That's just what we need, better even than the lectures. I want you to be recognized. People have got to know that you're the new *Atlantic!*"

That summer we moved down to the Red Cottage at Prides Crossing. The old part of it, the small rooms with low ceilings and open hearth, went back to the eighteenth century, but larger bedrooms and a screened porch had been added and its easy access to the beach made it ideal for young couples with children. One of our early guests was the tall, blond, affable Theodore Spencer. Ted had gone through a hellish year: he and his wife had separated and Harvard had failed to grant him the tenure he deserved. He was a popular teacher, badly needed in the depleted English Department and President Conant would soon make amends, but the reprieve was in the future. At the moment Ted wanted friendliness, martinis and advice as he tried to decide whether to cross the ocean and accept a lectureship at Cambridge University.

We must have been thinking of each other as we drove over to Myopia for a round of golf as he remarked, a shade wistfully, "You've certainly got yourself happily fixed." His words surprised me; I did not think of myself that way. Things falling apart in Elizabeth, the house on the market, Mother and Dad about to separate, and here in Boston the rug liable to be pulled out from under me if Ellery got a tempting offer. I guess I appeared more secure than I was. At a recent dinner party my friend, Gilbert Steward, had remarked to Fritzy, "Your husband is the only man present who isn't living on his wife's money." Well, there was that. But what neither Ted nor Gil could know was that I had the title but not the capital to keep it. Those words in *Time* still rankled.

Outwardly the North Shore was still cleaning up after the hurricane of 1938, the power saws chewing to bits the old elms, lindens, and beeches that had been uprooted; the cathedral pines which once crowned the moraine almost to Gloucester lay in windrows, pushed down as by a giant thumb. I shall always associate the angry note of those saws with disaster. We lived with the feeling of entrapment as the evening news from London, in the voice of Edward R. Murrow, became ever more ominous. On the first of September, Hitler's dive bombers and armor invaded Poland. On the third, England and France declared war on Germany, and I felt sure we would join them. The evening following, Fritzy and I were invited to dine with Dick and Barbara Danielson at their summer house overlooking Manchester Harbor. The tide was in and the harbor filled with yachts, some with their riding lights on, and as we drove past I remembered Ray Ather-ton's warning, "an isle of oblivion." But no longer: over cocktails the war was the sole topic of conversation. Would the Maginot Line hold? Was the French air force as obsolete — well, as our own? Would Paris be bombed? I was glad to hear Dick, one of the most patriotic of men, declare that we would have to give the English everything we could spare while we ourselves were rearming. As we went in to dinner, I found my place to the right of the hostess with Adelaide Whitman, Bill's aunt by marriage, on my other side. She turned to me:

"Isn't it terrible about Bill Whitman," she said.

"Bill? What about him?"

"He died this morning of his burns."

"Oh, no! No!" Tears started to my eyes. Bill at our last meeting so confident that now he had found what he wanted, so hoping that his thesis on the Pueblo could be turned into a decent book . . . The gen-erosity with which he spoke of my work. That great guy.

"How did it happen?"

"I thought you had heard," said Adelaide, and went on to tell as I stared at my plate. "The incinerator in their cellar blew up . . . he was emptying the ashes." The words sent me groping for that remembrance of another man's grief:

> *. . . they told me you were dead*
> *They brought me bitter news to hear and bitter tears to shed.*
> *I wept as I remembered how often you and I*
> *Had tired the sun with talking and sent him down the sky.*
>
> *· ·*
>
> *A handful of grey ashes . . .*

The talk shifted and, struggling for composure, I faced Barbara, dark-haired, cool and patrician, in my hazy sight.

"What am I going to do about my Dick?" she said in her low, firm voice.

It took time for the full implication to sink in. I cleared my throat.

"I wish he would come with me," I said.

"Can you make a go of it?" she asked. "Dick couldn't stand another failure."

"I can," I said. "I know I can."

That evening, which began with foreboding and personal grief, was unforeseeably to resolve my future. Within ninety days Dick and Barbara had purchased the *Atlantic* at seven times what Ellery paid for it; Dick was installed as the new president at 8 Arlington Street, and I as vice-president and editor.

I had found where I belonged, and only later was I to appreciate the chain of circumstances, the accidents, that shaped my career: how, from being so long a runt, I had learned to compensate by using my voice and my wits; how my friendships in the war led me from a failure in engineering, to Harvard, Dean Briggs, and on to Cambridge, and how the rejecting of my war letters had started me thinking about the *Atlantic*. My turning away from Manhattan to the greater congeniality of Boston was in fact a switch from the high pressure of Horace Liveright (who had no editorial opening anyway), to Ellery Sedgwick, who was the most creative editor of his day. I learned from his fervor and discrimination; even what I considered his niggardliness had impelled me to lecture and so gradually to comprehend the breadth and greatness of this country. My happiest accident was that summer of 1921 when, tutoring for money, I found Fritzy. I had never expected a pot of gold in Boston but I had my resources; I was rich in friendships, and as the ninth editor of a great literary monthly — which I intended to make the best in the English-speaking world — I was to be given by the Danielsons, for twenty-eight years, a latitude and a backing such as my predecessors would have envied. With their trust I entered a new world. I put aside the thought of going into uniform and, at forty-one, devoted myself to recording the courage, the rallying power, the wry humor, and the compassion with which we rose to the crisis. My Green Age was behind me.

INDEX

329